THE POSTAL SERVICE GUIDE TO U.S. STAMPS

STAMP VALUES

UNITED STATES
POSTAL SERVICE
WASHINGTON, D.C.
20260-6757
ITEM NO. 8891

Library of Congress Catalogue Card Number 87-656545
ISBN: 1-877707-01-5
Printed in the United States of America

Editorial and Design: Mobium Corporation for Design and Communication, Chicago, IL
Printing: R. R. Donnelley & Sons Co., Crawfordsville, IN
Cover Photography: The Image Bank/Hans Wendler
Electronic Art: Ralph Greenhow
Inside Photography: Allsport USA/Tim Daggett; Pamela Bernstein; The Bettmann Archive; Big Brothers/Big Sisters of America; Historical Pictures Service; Sharon Hoogstraten Photography; The Image Bank; NASA; National Park Service/Helen Longest-Slaughter; The North American Bluebird Society; Penfield Gallery, Albuquerque/Doris Patricio; Princeton University; Frederic Remington Museum; Winterthur Museum

Table of Contents

Celebrating America's Winners

- U.S. commemorative stamps issued during the year
- Large-format, informative booklet for displaying stamps
- Clear acetate mounts to protect stamps

A Tribute to America's Best
Whether it's people, places, ideals or events, you'll meet America's winners through U.S. commemorative stamps.

Fun, Informative and Valuable
Commemorative Mint Sets gather the year's honorees in one convenient, collectible and colorful package. The current Set contains all 1991 commemoratives, including the 10 Space Exploration booklet designs, the World War II souvenir sheetlet of 10 stamps, the five Summer Olympics issues and the five Fishing Flies and five Comedians booklet designs.

The 1991 Set also features the new additions to the Black Heritage Series (Jan Matzeliger), the Performing Arts Series (Cole Porter) and the Literary Arts Series (William Saroyan). And you'll find commemorated such popular subjects as Basketball, Numismatics (coin collecting), Love and Christmas.

The 1991 Commemorative Mint Set is available for $19.95.

To Obtain a Commemorative Mint Set

The 1991 Set and several earlier sets are available at your local post office or Philatelic Center. You can also fill out the postage-paid request card in this book or write directly to:

USPS GUIDE
COMMEMORATIVE MINT SETS
PHILATELIC SALES DIVISION
UNITED STATES POSTAL SERVICE
BOX 449997
KANSAS CITY, MO 64144-9997

Past Sets Include:

1990 Commemorative Mint Set
Includes the five Olympians issues, five Lighthouses and five Indian Headdresses booklet pane designs, the Classic Films and Creatures of the Sea blocks of four and the Ida B. Wells and Marianne Moore issues. ($16.50)

1989 Commemorative Mint Set
Includes the Prehistoric Animals quartet; Steamboats booklet pane of five stamps; five Statehood stamps; House of Representatives, Senate and Executive Branch stamps; and Lou Gehrig, Ernest Hemingway, Arturo Toscanini and A. Philip Randolph issues. ($14.50)

Expanding the Edges of Your World

You can experience legendary events in history; meet famous and accomplished people; visit beautiful and exotic places. How? Through stamp collecting. This thrilling pastime lets you expand the edges of your world—it brings America's happenings right to your home in dazzling color. Every time you open a stamp album, the world you live in becomes a little larger.

You'll experience the scope and splendor of our country's history, celebrate our heroes and heroines and chronicle the achievements and achievers, inventions and inventors and arts and artists. Stamp collecting lets you discover new and exciting corners of the universe—from faraway planets to your own backyard.

What is Philately? Philately (fi-lat-el-lee) is the collecting and study of postage stamps and other postal materials. The name is derived from the Greek words *philos,* which means "loving," and *atelos,* which means "free of tax." In their most basic form, stamps are signs that the postal fees have been prepaid.

Stamp collectors are called philatelists. Collecting stamps is easy. The key to enjoying philately is to save the types of stamps you like best.

General collecting—saving as many stamps as possible—is a good way to start.

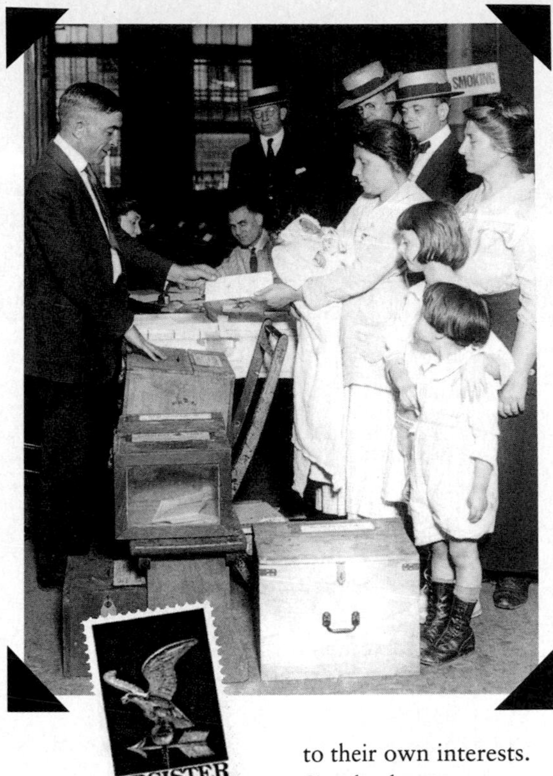

To help build your collection, check your mailbox daily for letters, postcards and packages with used stamps on them. Have your friends and family save envelopes they receive in the mail. Ask people who write you to use interesting stamps. Neighborhood businesses that get a lot of mail—banks, stores, travel agencies—may be sources of stamps for you as well.

Topical collecting is another popular way to collect stamps because it lets people tailor their collections to their own interests. Simply choose one or two specific themes that really interest you. Art and history, science and technology, sports and transportation are just a few of the possibilities.

If, for example, you are interested in sports, you can start a topical collection using U.S. stamps commemorating sports figures. You could begin with the American Sports Series issues of 1981, depicting golfing greats Babe Zaharias and Bobby Jones, then gather the other six issues through the Lou Gehrig stamp issued in 1989. And you can create a special sports category—the Olympics—with the addition of the

Definitive

Commemorative

Special

Olympians strip of five, issued in 1990. This year's strip of five Olympics stamps will help you build up the category.

Whatever stamps you choose to collect, there are additional sources where you can obtain them. Some stamp clubs meet at schools, YMCAs and community centers. If you are fortunate enough to have one of these in your area, it may be a great place for stamps and philatelic advice. If you do not know of a stamp club in your area, the people at

LINN'S CLUB CENTER
PO BOX 29
SIDNEY OH
45365-0029

can help you locate clubs near you. Just write to them.

For information on the Postal Service's popular Benjamin Franklin Stamp Club program for elementary school students, read the special article elsewhere in this book.

Another good source of stamps is the classified ads in philatelic newspapers and magazines available at your library. Also, elsewhere in this book is a listing of philatelic publishers who are willing to send you a free copy of their publications. After reviewing these publications, you may wish to subscribe.

Stamps are classified into several major categories:

Definitive stamps are found on most mail in denominations ranging from 1¢ to $13.95. Their subjects frequently are former presidents, statesmen, other prominent persons and national shrines. Printed in unlimited quantities for specific postal rates, definitives usually are available for several years.

Commemoratives honor important people, events or special subjects of national appeal and significance. They usually are larger and more colorful than definitives. Printed in limited quantities, commemoratives are available for only two or three months at most post offices and for about one year by mail order from the Postal Service's Philatelic Sales Division.

Special stamps include issues that supplement the regular stamps, such as Christmas and Love stamps.

Airmail stamps are used primarily for sending mail overseas.

Booklet stamps are issued in small folders containing one or more panes of 3 to 20 stamps each. Each stamp has one, two or three straight edges.

Coil stamps are issued in rolls. Each coil stamp has two

Airmail

Booklet

Coil

straight and two perforated edges.

Caring For Your Collection

Your stamps are just that—*your* stamps. You can do whatever you want with them. You can save entire envelopes and store them anywhere, from shoe boxes to special albums. Or you can try to peel the stamps off the envelopes. The proper way to remove stamps from envelopes is to soak them.

Stamps are delicate little pieces of paper, so be careful. Tear or cut off the upper right-hand corner of the envelope or cover. Place the stamp face down in a small pan of warm water. After a few minutes, the stamp will float off the paper and sink to the bottom. Allow a few more minutes for any remaining gum to dislodge from the stamp, then lift it out using tongs—a metal grasping device with flat ends, similar to tweezers—if you have a pair. (Although many collectors touch stamps with their fingers, it is better to handle them with tongs. Even if your hands are clean, oil from your skin can damage stamps.)

To keep a stamp from curling while it dries, put it between two paper towels and apply pressure with a heavy object, such as a book. Leave the stamp there overnight and it will be flat the next day. Stamps with new, "invisible" gum are trickier to dry because they tend to retain gum after soaking and stick fast to paper when drying.

Dry these stamps face down with nothing touching the back side, and flatten them later if they curl. To learn more about soaking stamps, look for a detailed handbook on stamp collecting at your local library.

Organizing Your Collection

You will want to protect your stamps so they do not get damaged or lost. As they accumulate, it is a good idea to put them in some kind of order. You can attach your

stamps to loose-leaf paper organized in a simple three-ring binder. Or arrange them in a more formal album available in stores.

Some stamp albums feature specific categories with pictures of the stamps that are supposed to appear on each page. It is usually best to select an album with loose-leaf pages so you can add pages easily as your collection grows.

A stock book is an album with plastic or paper pockets on each page; there are no pictures of stamps, so you can organize it *your* way.

It is best to use a small strip of thin plastic, gummed on one side, to put stamps in your album. Called a hinge, this strip is available either folded or unfolded. If you use a folded hinge, lightly moisten the short end and press it to the back of the stamp with the fold about 1/8" from the top of the stamp.

Then hold the stamp (with your tongs) and lightly moisten the long end of the hinge. Place the stamp where you want it in the album and secure it by pressing down. Using your tongs, gently lift the stamp's corners to make sure none have stuck to the page. By using a hinge—instead of tape or glue—you can peel the stamp from the page, if you wish, without damaging it. Collectors may use mounts instead of hinges to prevent air and dirt from damaging their stamps and to keep excess moisture from disturbing the gum.

A mount is a small, clear (usually plastic) sleeve into which an entire stamp is inserted. Mounts are more expensive than hinges, but many collectors believe the extra protection is well worth the price.

With used stamps and a few inexpensive accessories, such as a small album and a package of hinges, even collectors with a limited budget can have a great time. Remember to mention stamps, stamp albums and hinges to your friends and relatives before Christmas and your birthday!

TOOLS OF THE TRADE

In addition to the tongs, hinges and mounts previously described, other equipment that can aid stamp collectors includes:

Glassine (glass-een) envelopes are used to store and keep stamps that you have yet to add to your album. Glassine is a special thin paper that keeps grease and air from damaging stamps.

A *stamp catalog* is a handy reference with many illustrations that can help identify stamps; it also provides information such as values for used and unused stamps.

A *magnifying glass* helps examine stamps.

A *perforation gauge* measures the jagged cuts or little holes, called *perforations,* along the edges of stamps. Size and number of perforations are sometimes needed to identify stamps. "Perfs" make stamps easy to tear apart.

Superb

Light Cancel–Very Fine

Very Fine

Medium Cancel–Fine

Fine

Heavy Cancel

Good

A *watermark tray* and *watermark fluid* are used to make more visible the designs or patterns (called *watermarks*) that are pressed into some stamp paper during its manufacture.

STAMP CONDITION

Like an old book, the value of a stamp depends largely on two factors: How rare it is and what condition it is in. You can get an idea of how rare a stamp is by the price listed for it in a catalog. Depending on its condition, however, a stamp may sell for more or less than the catalog price. A very rare stamp may be quite expensive even though it is in poor condition. At first, you'll probably be collecting stamps that are not very expensive, but you still should try to get them in the best condition you can find. Here are some things to look for when judging stamp condition:

Examine the front of the stamp. Are the colors bright or faded? Is the stamp dirty, stained or clean? Is the stamp torn? Torn stamps are not considered "collectible." Is the design in the center of the paper, or is it a little crooked or off to the side? Are the edges in good condition, or are some of the perforations missing? A stamp with a light cancellation mark is in better condition than one with heavy marks across it. Now look at the back of the stamp. Is there a thin spot in the paper? It may have been caused by careless removal from an envelope or a hinge.

Stamp dealers put stamps into categories according to their condition. Look at the examples to see the differences in these categories. A stamp listed as mint is in the same condition as when purchased from the post office. An unused stamp has not been canceled but may not have any gum on it. Stamps in mint condition usually are more valuable than unused stamps.

Catalog prices listed in *The Postal Service Guide to U.S. Stamps* are for used and unused stamps in Fine condition that have been hinged. A stamp that has not been hinged and has excellent centering and color may cost more; a stamp in less than Fine condition that has been heavily canceled may be worth less than the catalog listing.

Choosing Subjects For Stamps

Who decides what subjects will be honored on stamps? The USPS's Citizens' Stamp Advisory Committee receives hundreds of suggestions every week. But just a few can be recommended because of the limited number of stamps issued each year.

Established more than 30 years ago, the Committee meets six times a year. It consists of historians, artists, business people, philatelists and others interested in American history and culture. Keeping all postal customers in mind, they use a set of eligibility guidelines to aid in their difficult task. Once a recommended subject receives the "stamp of approval," a Committee design coordinator assists in selecting a professional artist to design the stamp. The Committee reviews preliminary artwork and may request changes before a final version is approved.

If you think a story should be told on a stamp, submit your idea at least 36 months before its logical date of issuance. Send suggestions, along with helpful background information—but with no artwork—to:

United States Postal Service
Citizens' Stamp Advisory Committee
Room 5800
475 L'Enfant Plaza West SW
Washington DC 20260-6352

Other Postal Collectibles

Stamp designs are also printed or embossed (made with a raised design) directly on envelopes, postal cards and aerogrammes. Available at post offices, these postal stationery products are particularly popular among some serious collectors.

Stamped Envelopes were first issued in 1853. More than

600 million stamped envelopes are now printed every year.

Postal Cards were first issued in 1873, and the first U.S. multicolored commemorative postal card came out in 1956. Several different postal cards usually are issued during a year and approximately 800 million are printed annually.

Aerogrammes (air letters) are letters and envelopes all in one. They are specially stamped, marked for folding and already gummed.

Other philatelic items for collecting include:

Plate Blocks of Four, usually four stamps from a corner of a pane with the printing plate number in the margin, or selvage, of the pane.

Copyright Blocks, which feature the copyright symbol © followed by "United States Postal Service" or "USPS" and the year in the margin of each pane of stamps. The USPS began copyrighting new stamp designs in 1978.

Booklet Panes are panes with three or more of the same stamps. One or more panes of stamps are affixed inside a thin folder to form a booklet. Booklet pane collectors usually save entire panes.

First Day Covers (*FDCs*) are envelopes with new stamps that have been postmarked on the first day of sale at a city designated by the USPS. Collecting of First Day Covers is now honored by the USPS and the American First Day Cover Society with an annual First Day Cover Collecting Week.

Souvenir Cards are issued as keepsakes of stamp exhibitions. Although they cannot be used for postage,

some souvenir cards are available cancelled. Of special interest is the annual souvenir card for National Stamp Collecting Month each October, first issued in 1981.

Souvenir Programs from first day ceremonies are given to people who attend those events. Souvenir programs contain a list of participants and biographical or background information on the stamp subject and have the actual stamp(s) affixed and postmarked with the first day of issue cancellation.

Many stamp collectors also enjoy the variety of postmarks available. Some collect cancellations from every city or town in their respective counties or even states.

Remember, a stamp collection is whatever you, personally, want to make it. Nearly 1 in 10 Americans collects stamps for the fun of it—join them as they expand the edges of their worlds!

Ordering First Day Covers

For each new postal issue, the USPS selects one town or city, usually related to the stamp's subject, as the site for the first day dedication ceremony. First day covers (FDCs) are envelopes with new stamps affixed and canceled with the "First Day of Issue" date and city.

The fastest way to receive a first day cover is to buy the stamp yourself (new stamps usually go on sale the day after the first day of issue), attach it to your own cover and send it to the first day post office for cancellation. You may submit up to 50 envelopes. Write your address in the lower right-hand corner of each first day envelope, at least 5/8" from the bottom; use a peel-off label if you prefer. Leave plenty of room for the stamp(s) and the cancellation. Fill each envelope with cardboard about the thickness of a postal card. You can tuck in the flap or seal it.

Put your first day envelope(s) inside another, larger envelope and mail it to "Customer-Affixed Envelopes" in care of the postmaster of the first day city. Your envelope(s) will be canceled and returned. First day envelopes may be mailed up to 30 days after the stamp's issue date.

Or, you can send an envelope addressed to yourself, but without a stamp attached. Put the self-addressed envelope(s) into another, larger envelope. Address this outside envelope to the name of the stamp, in care of the postmaster of the first day city. Send a check, bank draft or U.S. Postal money order (made out to the United States Postal Service) to pay for the stamp(s) that are to be put on your envelope(s). Do not send cash.

If a new stamp has a denomination less than the First-Class rate, add postage or payment to bring each first day envelope up to the First-Class rate. Do not send requests more than 60 days prior to the issue date.

Benjamin Franklin Stamp Clubs

A stamp collection is a gallery of Americana. The people, places and events of our country's history are framed in each colorful stamp issue. Stamp collecting at any age creates awareness of United States culture and heritage; for children, it means learning about our country in a way that's easy and fun.

In 1974, the United States Postal Service created Benjamin Franklin Stamp Clubs to introduce stamp collecting to grade-school students. The clubs help children appreciate the recreational and educational values of stamp collecting. In addition, they serve as teaching tools that encourage learning about important topics. Since their establishment, Benjamin Franklin Stamp Clubs (BFSCs) have introduced more than 8 million students and teachers to the hobby—and the number grows each year.

The Postal Service currently supports about 42,000 BFSCs in public and private elementary schools and libraries through-

Children at Spring Garden Elementary School display their prized possessions at a Benjamin Franklin Stamp Club meeting.

Spring Garden teacher Ulana Strutz smiles in appreciation as teacher Kim Bogues and Shelley DeVinny examine stamps.

Walter Mentzer, right, and classmates at Spring Garden Elementary School in Bedford, Texas, prepare to sign a BFSC membership poster.

out the nation. Through the BFSCs, students in the fourth through seventh grades can experience the wonders of stamp collecting while developing important skills for everyday life—such as organization, attention to detail and money management.

BFSC Activities

In Bedford, Texas, more than 60 children at Spring Garden Elementary School have discovered the stamp collecting hobby through the Benjamin Franklin Stamp Club. By participating in activities administered by their teachers, Ulana Strutz and Kim Bogues, club members become proficient in stamp collecting skills as they learn about the subjects depicted on each stamp. They especially enjoy trading stamps among themselves. And, according to Mrs. Strutz, "The children have grown to appreciate the value of the stamps" by examining them for minute details.

BFSC members' enthusiasm is demonstrated by the "Draw Your Own Stamp" contest held each October to celebrate National Stamp Collecting Month. Entries from the club members at Spring Garden in Bedford—a town of only 43,000 people—dominated recent competitions for the entire Dallas-Fort Worth area. Ryan Peters' design was awarded first place in 1989 and designs by Sean Sweat, Stephen Latham and Shelley DeVinny captured first, second and third place, respectively, in 1990.

The members of the Spring Garden Elementary School BFSC meet every two weeks, either after school or during lunch hour. Meetings are conducted by club president Jessica Ellis, secretary Chaney King and reporter Jody Mancuso. The club receives a great deal of support from Char Page, the area's Benjamin Franklin Project Leader, and Bedford Postmaster Tony Reichert. Children enjoy visiting the Bedford Post Office each October, when employees decorate its lobby with the theme for the National Stamp Collecting Month celebration.

At the beginning of each school year, clubs receive copies of "Introduction to Stamp Collecting," a reprint of selected sections of *The Postal Service Guide to U.S. Stamps*. Two BFSC newsletters, *Stamp Fun* (for club members) and *Leader Feature* (for teachers), are sent several times during the school year; they suggest a broad range of enjoyable and educational activities such as games, puzzles and class projects.

In addition, each club member receives a *Treasury of Stamps Album*. This album,

Spring Garden BFSC President Jessica Ellis, left, studies a collection of plate blocks with Club Secretary Chaney King.

which is distributed to the clubs in January, enables the children to collect the year's stamps as they are issued. It contains spaces to mount the stamps scheduled to be issued that year, along with a brief essay on the significance of each. A typical club activity might be for children to soak stamps off of envelopes at home and affix them in their albums. Also, club members and leaders can take advantage of free stamp activity guides and free films available on loan from the Postal Service.

STARTING A BFSC
Teachers or administrators interested in starting clubs may call their local postmasters; or for more information on the BFSC program, they may write to:

BENJAMIN FRANKLIN
STAMP CLUB
REGISTRATION OFFICE
UNITED STATES
POSTAL SERVICE
PO BOX 449994
KANSAS CITY MO
64144-9994

OLYMPIC PEN PALS MAKE NEW FRIENDS
The U.S. Postal Service Olympic Pen Pal Club offers a unique opportunity for children between 6 and 18 years of age to make new friends while learning more about stamps. The Club matches each participant with a pen pal of the same age in a faraway place. By corresponding with pen pals, young people may learn about life "down under" in Australia, in Korea or in one of many other participating nations. Pen pals also may exchange Olympic theme-related postage stamps.

For just $5.95, children may join the Olympic Pen Pal Club. This fee covers the cost of obtaining the name of a pen pal and receiving an official Club membership kit. Each kit includes stationery, envelopes and note pad (all featuring Stamper™, the pen pal mascot), calendar, membership card, badge, door sign, photo holder, a coloring book that helps children write to their new pen pals and, every three months, a Club newsletter.

The USPS Olympic Pen Pal Club is an activity related to USPS sponsorship of the 1992 Summer and Winter Games. The U.S. Postal Service is one of several sponsors.

To join the club, children should send name, address (including city, state and zip code), gender and date of birth, along with a check or money order for $5.95, to: USPS Olympic Pen Pal Club, PO Box 9419, Gaithersburg, MD 20898-9419.

For Convenience and Completeness

- Automatic shipment of the new stamps, stationery and/ or philatelic products *you* want via mail order
- Quality guaranteed

Automatic and Convenient

Armchair collectors need never leave the comfort of home to use the U.S. Postal Service's Standing Order Service subscription program. Sign up once, make an advance deposit, and all postal items you desire will be shipped to you automatically on a quarterly basis.

Exceptional Quality Guaranteed

Subscribers to the Standing Order Service receive mint-condition postal items of exceptional quality—the best available centering, color and printing registration. If you are not completely satisfied, return the item within 30 days for a full refund or replacement.

All products are sold at face value—there are no markups, extra fees or shipping and handling charges. Just make an advance deposit based on the items and quantities you plan to select. You will be notified when you need to replenish your deposit account.

For Information

Send in the postage-paid request card in this book or write to:

USPS GUIDE
STANDING ORDER
SUBSCRIPTION SERVICE
PHILATELIC SALES DIVISION
UNITED STATES POSTAL SERVICE
BOX 449980
KANSAS CITY MO 64144-9980

Stamp Collecting Words and Phrases

Accessories The tools used by stamp collectors, such as tongs, hinges, etc.

Adhesive A gummed stamp made to be attached to mail.

Album A book designed to hold stamps and covers.

Approvals Stamps sent by a dealer to a collector for examination. Approvals must either be bought or returned to the dealer within a specified time.

Auction A sale at which philatelic material is sold to the highest bidder.

Block An unseparated group of stamps, at least two stamps high and two stamps wide.

Booklet Pane A small sheet of stamps specially cut to be sold in booklets.

Bourse A marketplace, such as a stamp exhibition, where stamps are bought, sold or exchanged.

Bluish Paper Used to print portions of several issues in 1909; the paper was made with 35 percent rag stock instead of all wood pulp. The color goes through the paper, showing clearly on back and face.

Cachet (ka-shay') A design on an envelope describing an event. Cachets appear on first day of issue, first flight and stamp exhibition covers, etc.

Cancellation A mark placed on a stamp by a postal authority to show that it has been used.

Centering The position of the design on a postage stamp. On perfectly centered stamps the design is exactly in the middle.

Coils Stamps issued in rolls (one stamp wide) for use in dispensers or vending machines.

Commemoratives Stamps that honor anniversaries, important people or special events.

Condition The state of a stamp in regard to such details as centering, color and gum.

Cover An envelope that has been sent through the mail.

Cracked Plate A term used to describe stamps which show evidence that the plate from which they were printed was cracked.

Definitives Regular issues of postage stamps, usually sold over long periods of time.

Denomination The postage value appearing on a stamp, such as 5 cents.

Double Transfer The condition on a printing plate that shows evidence of a duplication of all or part of the design.

Dry Printing Begun as an experiment in 1953, this type of printing results in a whiter paper, a higher sheen on the surface, a thicker and stiffer feel and designs that stand out more clearly than on more standard "wet" printings.

Duplicates Extra copies of stamps that can be sold or traded. Duplicates should be examined carefully for color and perforation variations.

Error A stamp with something incorrect in its design or manufacture.

Face Value The monetary value or denomination of a stamp.

First Day Cover (FDC) An envelope with a new stamp and cancellation showing the date the stamp was issued.

Grill A pattern of small, square pyramids in parallel rows impressed or embossed on the stamp to break paper fibers, allowing cancellation ink to soak in and preventing washing and reuse.

Gum The coating of glue on the back of an unused stamp.

Hinges Small strips of gummed material used by collectors to affix stamps to album pages.

Imperforate Indicates stamps without perforations or separating holes. They usually are separated by scissors and collected in pairs.

Label Any stamp-like adhesive that is not a postage stamp.

Laid Paper When held to the light, the paper shows alternate light and dark crossed lines.

Line Pairs (LPs) Most coil stamp rolls prior to #1891 feature a line of ink printed between two stamps at varying intervals.

Miniature Sheet A single stamp or block of stamps with a margin on all sides bearing some special wording or design.

Mint Indicates a stamp in the same condition as when it was issued.

Overprint Additional printing on a stamp that was not part of the original design.

Pane A full "sheet" of stamps as sold by a Post Office. Four panes make up the original sheet of stamps as printed.

Perforations Lines of small holes or cuts between rows of stamps that make them easy to separate.

Philately The collection and study of postage stamps and other postal materials.

Plate Block (or **Plate Number Block**) (**PB**) A block of stamps with the margin attached that bears the plate number used in printing that sheet.

Plate Number Coils (PNC) For most coil stamp rolls beginning with #1891, a small plate number appears at varying intervals in the roll in the design of the stamp.

Postage Due A stamp issued to collect unpaid postage.

Postal Stationery Envelopes, postal cards and aerogrammes with stamp designs printed or embossed on them.

Postmark A mark put on envelopes or other mailing pieces showing the date and location of the post office where it was mailed.

Precancels Cancellations applied to stamps before the stamps were affixed to mail.

Reissue An official reprinting of a stamp that was no longer being printed.

Revenue Stamps Stamps not valid for postal use but issued for collecting taxes.

Ribbed Paper Paper which shows fine parallel ridges on one or both sides of a stamp.

Selvage The unprinted paper around panes of stamps, sometimes called the margin.

Se-tenant An attached pair, strip or block of stamps that differ in design, value or surcharge.

Surcharge An overprint that changes the denomination of a stamp from its original face value.

Tagging Chemical marking applied to stamps so they can be "read" by mail-sorting machines.

Tied On Indicates a stamp whose postmark touches the envelope.

Tongs A tool, used to handle stamps, that resembles a tweezers with rounded or flattened tips.

Topicals Indicates a group of stamps with the same theme–space travel, for example.

Unused The condition of a stamp that has no cancellation or other sign of use.

Used The condition of a stamp that has been canceled.

Want List A list of philatelic material needed by a collector.

Watermark A design pressed into stamp paper during its manufacture.

Wet Printing Has a moisture content of 15-35 percent, compared to 5-10 percent for "dry" printings, and has a duller look than "dry" printings.

Wove Paper A uniform paper which, when held to the light, shows no light or dark figures.

Coils

Overprint

Precancel

Perforate

Imperforate

Se-tenant

Surcharge

Organizations, Publications and Resources

For Your Information ...

Here's a list of philatelic resources that can increase your knowledge of stamps as well as your collecting enjoyment.

Organizations

Please enclose a stamped, self-addressed envelope when writing to these organizations.

American Air Mail Society
Stephen Reinhard
P.O. Box 110
Mineola, NY 11501
Specializes in all phases of aerophilately. Membership services include Advance Bulletin Service, Auction Service, free want ads, Sales Department, monthly journal, discounts on Society publications, translation service.

American First Day Cover Society
Mrs. Monte Eiserman
Dept. USG
14359 Chadbourne
Houston, TX 77079-8811
A full-service, not-for-profit, noncommercial society devoted exclusively to First Day Covers and First Day Cover collecting. Offers information on 300 current cachet producers, expertizing, foreign covers, translation service, color slide programs and archives covering First Day Covers.

American Philatelic Society
Keith A. Wagner, Exec. Dir.
P.O. Box 8000, Dept. PG
State College, PA 16803-8000
A full complement of services and resources for stamp collectors. Annual membership offers: library services, educational seminars and correspondence courses, expertizing service, estate advisory service, translation service, a stamp theft committee that functions as a clearing house for philatelic crime information, intramember sales service and a monthly journal, *The American Philatelist*, sent to all members. Membership 57,000 worldwide.

American Society for Philatelic Pages and Panels
Gerald Blankenship
P.O. Box 475
Crosby, TX 77532
Focuses on souvenir pages and commemorative panels, with reports on news, varieties, errors, oddities and discoveries; free ads.

American Stamp Dealers' Association
Joseph B. Savarese
3 School Street
Glen Cove, NY 11542
Association of dealers engaged in every facet of philately, with 11 regional chapters nationwide. Sponsors national and local shows. Will send you a complete listing of dealers in your area or collecting specialty. A #10 SASE must accompany your request.

American Topical Association
Donald W. Smith
P.O. Box 630
Johnstown, PA 15907-0630
A service organization concentrating on the specialty of topical stamp collecting. Offers handbooks and checklists on specific topics; exhibition awards; *Topical Time*, a bimonthly publication dealing with topical interest areas; a slide loan service; information, translation, biography and sales services; and an heirs' estate service.

Booklet Collectors Club
Larry Rosenblum
1016 E. El Camino Real, #107-U
Sunnyvale, CA 94087-3759
Devoted to the study of worldwide booklets and booklet collecting, with special emphasis on U.S. booklets. Publishes *The Interleaf*, a quarterly journal.

Bureau Issues Association
P.O. Box 1047
Belleville, IL 62223-1047
Devoted to the study of all U.S. stamps, principally those produced by the Bureau of Engraving and Printing.

Council of Philatelic Organizations
P.O. Box COPO
State College, PA 16803-8340
A nonprofit marketing and public relations organization comprised of more than 400 national, regional and local stamp clubs, organizations, societies and philatelic business firms. Membership is open only to organizations. COPO uses a variety of methods to promote stamp collecting, including an ongoing publicity campaign, a quarterly newsletter and joint sponsorship (with the USPS) of National Stamp Collecting Month.

Errors, Freaks and Oddities Collectors Club
CWO James E. McDevitt
1903 Village Road West
Norwood, MA 02062-2516
Studies stamp production mistakes.

Junior Philatelists of America
Central Office
P.O. Box 557
Boalsburg, PA 16827-0557
Publishes a bimonthly newsletter, *The Philatelic Observer*, and offers auction, exchange, penpal and other services to young stamp collectors. Adult supporting membership and gift memberships are available. The Society also publishes various brochures on stamp collecting.

Linn's Stamp Club Center
P.O. Box 29
Sidney, OH 45365-0029
Write for the address of a stamp club near your ZIP Code.

Mailer's Postmark Permit Club
Florence M. Sugarberg
P.O. Box 5793
Akron, OH 44372-5793
Publishes bimonthly newsletter, *Permit Patter*, which covers all aspects of mailer's precancel postmarks, as well as a catalog and two checklists.

Modern Postal History Society
Terence Hines
P.O. Box 629
Chappaqua, NY 10514-0629
Emphasizes the collection and study of postal history, procedures and rates beginning with the early 20th century and including rates as shown by use of definitive stamps on commercial covers, modern markings such as bar codes and ink-jet postmarks, and auxiliary markings such as "Return to Sender," etc. Publishes the quarterly *Modern Postal History Journal*.

National Association of Precancel Collectors
Glenn W. Dye
5121 Park Blvd.
Wildwood, NJ 08260-0121
Publishes *Precancel Stamp Collector*, a monthly newsletter that contains information on precanceled stamps. Operates Bert Hoover Arboretum and Chester Davis Memorial Library. Dues $10 per year.

Perfins Club
Ralph W. Smith, Secretary
RR 1, Box 5645
Dryden, ME 04225
Send SASE for information.

Philatelic Foundation
21 E. 40th Street
New York, NY 10016
Telephone: (212) 889-6483
Fax: (212) 447-5258
A nonprofit organization known for its excellent expertization service. The Foundation's broad resources, including extensive reference collections, 5,000-volume library and Expert Committee, provide collectors with comprehensive consumer protection. Slide and cassette programs are available on such subjects as the Pony Express, classic U.S. stamps, Confederate Postal History and collecting basics for beginners. Book series include expertizing case histories in *Opinions*, Foundation seminar subjects in "textbooks" and specialized U.S. subjects in monographs.

Pictorial Cancellation Society
Nicholas Shestople
HHD, USMCA
Neu-Ulm, Box 182
APO NY 09035-0509
Studies and catalogues USPS pictorial cancellations.

Plate Number Society
9600 Colesville Road
Silver Spring, MD 20901-3144

Postal History Society
Diane Boehret, President
P.O. Box 61774
Virginia Beach, VA 23462-9129
Devoted to the study of various aspects of the development of the mails and local, national and international postal systems; UPU treaties, and means of transporting mail.

Post Mark Collectors Club
Lawrence Boing
2351 Grandview Road
Crest Hill, IL 60435-1951
Collects and preserves postmarks on U.S. and foreign letters.

Souvenir Card Collectors Society
Dana M. Marr
P.O. Box 4155
Tulsa, OK 74159-4155
Provides member auctions, a quarterly journal and access to limited-edition souvenir cards.

United Postal Stationery Society
Mrs. Joann Thomas
Box 48
Redlands, CA 92373-0601

Universal Ship Cancellation Society
David Kent
P.O. Box 127
New Britain, CT 06050-0127
Specializes in naval ship postmarks.

Free Periodicals

The following publications will send you a free copy of their magazine or newspaper upon request:

Linn's Stamp News
P.O. Box 29
Sidney, OH 45365-0029
The largest weekly stamp newspaper.

Mekeel's Weekly Stamp News
P.O. Box 5050-f
White Plains, NY 10602

Philatelic Sales Catalog
United States Postal Service
Kansas City, MO 64144-9975
Published bimonthly; includes every philatelic item offered by the USPS.

Stamp Collector
Box 10
Albany, OR 97321-0006
For beginning and advanced collectors of all ages.

Stamps Magazine
85 Canisteo St.
Hornell, NY 14843-1544
The weekly magazine of philately.

Stamps Auction News
85 Canisteo Street
Hornell, NY 14843-1544
The monthly financial journal of the stamp market.

Stamp Collecting Made Easy
P.O. Box 29
Sidney, OH 45365-0029
An illustrated, easy-to-read, 96-page booklet for beginning collectors.

Museums, Libraries and Displays

There is *no charge* to visit any of the following institutions. Please contact them before visiting because their hours may vary.

American Philatelic Research Library
P.O. Box 8338
State College, PA 16803-8338
Founded in 1968; now the largest philatelic library in the U.S. Currently receives more than 400 worldwide periodical titles and houses extensive collections of bound journals, books, auction catalogs and dealer pricelists. Directly serves members of the APS and APRL (library members also receive the quarterly *Philatelic Literature Review*). The public may purchase photocopies directly or borrow materials through the national interlibrary loan system.

Cardinal Spellman Philatelic Museum
235 Wellesley St.
Weston, MA 02193-1538
America's only fully accredited museum devoted to the display, collection and preservation of stamps and postal history. It has three galleries of rare stamps, a philatelic library and a post office/philatelic counter.
Telephone: (617) 894-6735.

The Collectors Club
22 East 35th St.
New York, NY 10016-3806
Bimonthly journal, publication of various reference works, one of the most extensive reference libraries in the world, reading and study rooms. Regular meetings on the first and third Wednesdays of each month at 7:30 p.m., except July, August.
Telephone: (212) 683-0559.

Hall of Stamps
United States Postal Service
475 L'Enfant Plaza
Washington, DC 20260-0001
Located at USPS headquarters, this exhibit features more than $500,000 worth of rare U.S. stamps, a moon rock and letter canceled on the moon, original stamp design art, etc.

National Philatelic Collection
National Museum
of American History
Fourth Floor
Smithsonian Institution
Washington, DC 20560
Houses more than 16 million items for exhibition and study purposes. Research may be conducted by appointment only on materials in the collection and library. Exhibit hall closed until the opening of the new National Postal Museum in the old Washington, D.C. Post Office next to Union Station in the spring of 1993.
Telephone: (202) 357-1796.

The Postal History Foundation
Box 40725
Tucson, AZ 85717-0725
Regular services include a library, philatelic sales, archives, artifacts and collections and a Youth Department. Membership includes subscription to a quarterly journal, *The Heliograph.* Telephone: (602) 623-6652.

San Diego County Philatelic Library
4133 Poplar St.
San Diego, CA 92105-4541

Western Philatelic Library
Sunnyvale Public Library
665 West Olive Ave.
Sunnyvale, CA 94087

Wineburgh Philatelic Research Library
University of Texas at Dallas
P.O. Box 830643
Richardson, TX 75083-0643
Open Monday-Thursday, 9 a.m.– 6 p.m.; Friday, 9 a.m.–5 p.m.; first Saturday each month (except May and June), 1 p.m.– 5 p.m.

Literature

Basic Philately
Stamp Collector
Box 10
Albany, OR 97321-0006

Brookman Disney Stamp Price Guide
Arlene Dunn
Brookman Stamp Company
10 Chestnut Drive
Bedford, NH 03102-5457
Illustrated, 128-page, perfect-bound book.

Brookman Price Guide of United States Stamps
Arlene Dunn
Brookman Stamp Company
10 Chestnut Drive
Bedford, NH 03102-5457
Illustrated, 160-page, perfect-bound catalog.

Brookman Price Guide of U.S., U.N. & Canada Stamps
Arlene Dunn
Brookman Stamp Company
10 Chestnut Drive
Bedford, NH 03102-5457
Illustrated, 256-page, spiral-bound catalog.

Brookman Price Guide of U.S. First Day Covers, Souvenir Cards, USPS Panels & Pages
Arlene Dunn
Brookman Stamp Company
10 Chestnut Drive
Bedford, NH 03102-5457
Illustrated, 176-page, spiral-bound catalog.

Catalogue of United States Souvenir Cards
Washington Press
2 Vreeland Road
Florham Park, NJ 07932-1587

1989 Commemorative Cancellation Catalog
General Image, Inc.
P.O. Box 335
Maplewood, NJ 07040
Catalogs covering all pictorial cancellations used in the U.S. during 1988 and 1989 are available. Please send self-addressed, stamped envelope for prices and description.

Compilation of U.S. Souvenir Cards
P.O. Box 4155
Tulsa, OK 74159-4155

First Day Cover Catalogue (U.S.-U.N.)
Washington Press
2 Vreeland Road
Florham Park, NJ 07932-1587
Includes Presidential Inaugural covers.

Fleetwood's Standard First Day Cover Catalog
Fleetwood
Cheyenne, WY 82008-0001

The Fun Of Stamp Collecting
Arlene Dunn
Brookman Stamp Company
10 Chestnut Drive
Bedford, NH 03102-5457
Illustrated, 96-page, perfect-bound book.

The Hammarskjold Invert
Washington Press
2 Vreeland Road
Florham Park, NJ 07932-1587
Tells the story of the Dag Hammarskjold error/invert. FREE for #10 SASE.

Linn's U.S. Stamp Yearbook
P.O. Box 29
Sidney, OH 45365-0029
A series of books providing facts and figures on every collectible variety of U.S. stamps, postal stationery and souvenir cards issued since 1983.

Linn's World Stamp Almanac
P.O. Box 29
Sidney, OH 45365-0029
The most useful single reference source for stamp collectors. Contains detailed information on U.S. stamps.

19th Century Envelopes Catalog
Box 48
Redlands, CA 92373-0601

Postage Stamp Identifier & Dictionary of Philatelic Terms
Washington Press
2 Vreeland Road
Florham Park, NJ 07932-1587

Scott Stamp Monthly
P.O. Box 828
Sidney, OH 45365-0828

Scott Standard Postage Stamp Catalogue
Box 828
Sidney, OH 45365-8959

Scott Specialized Catalogue of United States Stamps
Box 828
Sidney, OH 45365-8959

Souvenir Pages Price List
Charles D. Simmons
P.O. Box 6238
Buena Park, CA 90622-6238
Please send self-addressed, stamped envelope to receive current listings.

20th Century Envelopes Catalog
Box 48
Redlands, CA 92373-0601

The 24¢ 1918 Air Mail Invert
Washington Press
2 Vreeland Road
Florham Park, NJ 07932-1587
Tells all there is to know about this famous stamp. FREE for #10 SASE.

U.S. Postal Card Catalog
Box 48
Redlands, CA 92373-0601

The United States Transportation Coils
Washington Press
2 Vreeland Road
Florham Park, NJ 07932-1587
FREE for #10 SASE.

Exchange Service

Stamp Master
Box 17
Putnam Hall, FL 32685
An "electronic connection" for philatelists via modem and computer to display/review members' stamp inventories for trading purposes, etc.

PHILATELIC CENTERS

In addition to the more than 20,000 postal facilities authorized to sell philatelic products, the U.S. Postal Service also maintains more than 460 Philatelic Centers located in major population centers.

These Philatelic Centers have been established to serve stamp collectors and make it convenient for them to acquire an extensive range of all current postage stamps, postal stationery and philatelic products issued by the Postal Service.

Centers are located at Main Post Offices unless otherwise indicated.

Alabama
351 North 24th Street
Birmingham, AL 35203

Philatelic Center
Space 102
2000 Riverchase Galleria
Birmingham, AL 35244

615 Clinton Street
Huntsville, AL 35801

250 St. Joseph
Mobile, AL 36601

Downtown Station
135 Catoma Street
Montgomery, AL 36104

Alaska
Downtown Station
3rd & C Streets
Anchorage, AK 99510

Downtown Station
315 Barnette Street
Fairbanks, AK 99707

Arizona
2400 N. Postal Blvd.
Flagstaff, AZ 86004

Osborn Station
3905 North 7th Avenue
Phoenix, AZ 85013

General Mail Facility
4949 East Van Buren
Phoenix, AZ 85026

1501 South Cherrybell
Tucson, AZ 85726

Arkansas
30 South 6th Street
Fort Smith, AR 72901

600 West Capitol
Little Rock, AR 72201

California
Holiday Station
1180 West Ball Road
Anaheim, CA 92802

Cerritos Branch
18122 Carmencita
Artesia, CA 90701

General Mail Facility
3400 Pegasus Drive
Bakersfield, CA 93380

2000 Allston Way
Berkeley, CA 94704

135 East Olive Street
Burbank, CA 91502

6330 Fountains Square Dr.
Citrus Heights, CA 95621

2121 Meridian Park Blvd.
Concord, CA 94520

2020 Fifth Street
Davis, CA 95616

8111 East Firestone
Downey, CA 90241

401 W. Lexington Ave.
El Cajon, CA 92020

Cotten Station
3901 Walnut Drive
Eureka, CA 95501

1900 E Street
Fresno, CA 93706

313 East Broadway
Glendale, CA 91209

Hillcrest Station
303 East Hillcrest
Inglewood, CA 90311

5200 Clark Avenue
Lakewood, CA 90712

300 Long Beach Blvd.
Long Beach, CA 90801

Terminal Annex
900 North Alameda
Los Angeles, CA 90052

Village Station
11000 Wilshire Blvd.
Los Angeles, CA 90024

Worldway Postal Center
5800 W. Century Blvd.
Los Angeles, CA 90009

407 C Street
Marysville, CA 95901

2334 M Street
Merced, CA 95340

El Viejo Station
1125 "I" Street
Modesto, CA 95354

565 Hartnell Street
Monterey, CA 93940

Civic Center Annex
201 13th Street
Oakland, CA 94612

211 Brooks
Oceansido, CA 92054

1075 North Tustin
Orange, CA 92667

281 E. Colorado Blvd.
Pasadena, CA 91109

1647 Yuba Street
Redding, CA 96001

General Mail Facility
1900 W. Redlands Blvd.
Redlands, CA 92373

1201 North Catalina
Redondo Beach, CA
90277

Downtown Station
3890 Orange Street
Riverside, CA 92501

330 Vernon Street
Roseville, CA 95678

2000 Royal Oaks Drive
Sacramento, CA 95813

Base Line Station
1164 North E Street
San Bernardino, CA
92410

2535 Midway Drive
San Diego, CA 92199

Rincon Finance Station
180 Stewart Street
San Francisco, CA 94119

1750 Meridian Drive
San Jose, CA 95125

St. Matthews Station
210 South Ellsworth
San Mateo, CA 94401

Simms Station
41 Simms Street
San Rafael, CA 94901

Spurgeon Station
615 North Bush
Santa Ana, CA 92701

836 Anacapa Street
Santa Barbara, CA
93102

120 W. Cypress Street
Santa Maria, CA 93454

730 Second Street
Santa Rosa, CA 95404

Hammer Ranch Station
7554 Pacific Avenue
Stockton, CA 95210

4245 West Lane
Stockton, CA 95208

200 Prairie Court
Vacaville, CA 95687

15701 Sherman Way
Van Nuys, CA 91408

Channel Islands Station
675 E. Santa Clara St.
Ventura, CA 93001

396 South California St.
West Covina, CA 91790

Area Mail Processing
Center
3775 Industrial Blvd.
West Sacramento, CA
95647

Colorado
1905 15th Street
Boulder, CO 80302

201 East Pikes Peak
Colorado Springs, CO
80901

1823 Stout Street
Denver, CO 80202

222 West Eighth Street
Durango, CO 81301

241 North 4th Street
Grand Junction, CO
81501

5733 South Prince Street
Littleton, CO 80120

421 North Main Street
Pueblo, CO 81003

Connecticut
141 Weston Street
Hartford, CT 06101

Meridian & Waterbury Tpk.
Marion, CT 06444

11 Silver Street
Middletown, CT 06457

50 Brewery Street
New Haven, CT 06511

27 Masonic Street
New London, CT 06320

469 Main Street
Ridgefield, CT 06877

421 Atlantic Street
Stamford, CT 06904

Stratford Branch
3100 Main Street
Stratford, CT 06497

135 Grand Street
Waterbury, CT 06701

Delaware
55 The Plaza
Dover, DE 19901

Federal Station
110 East Main Street
Newark, DE 19711

General Mail Facility
147 Quigley Blvd.
Airport Industrial Park
New Castle, DE 19720

Rodney Square Station
1101 North King St.
Wilmington, DE 19801

District of Columbia
Headsville Postal Station
National Museum
of American History
12th & Constitution NW
Washington, DC 20560

National Capitol Station
North Capitol Street &
Massachusetts Avenue
Washington, DC 20002

Pavilion Post Office
Old Post Office Bldg.
1100 Pennsylvania NW
Washington, DC 20265

USPS Headquarters
475 L'Enfant Plaza SW
Washington, DC 20260

Florida
824 Manatee Ave. West
Bradenton, FL 33506

100 South Belcher Road
Clearwater, FL 33515

Downtown Station
220 North Beach Street
Daytona Beach, FL 32015

1900 West Oakland Park
Fort Lauderdale, FL 33310

2655 North Airport Road
Fort Myers, FL 33906

1717 Orange Avenue
Fort Pierce, FL 34950

401 SE 1st Avenue
Gainesville, FL 32601

1801 Polk Street
Hollywood, FL 33022

1110 Kings Road
Jacksonville, FL 32203

210 North Missouri Ave.
Lakeland, FL 33802

50 8th Avenue SW
Largo, FL 33640

Suntree Branch
6105 N. Wickham Road
Melbourne, FL 32940

2200 NW 72nd Avenue
Miami, FL 33101

1200 Goodlette
Naples, FL 33940

1111 E. Nebraska Avenue
New Port Ritchey, FL 34653

400 SW First Avenue
Ocala, FL 32678

1335 Kingsley Avenue
Orange Park, FL 32073

46 East Robinson Street
Orlando, FL 32801

1400 West Jordan St.
Pensacola, FL 32501

99 King Street
St. Augustine, FL 32084

3135 First Avenue North
St. Petersburg, FL 33730

Open Air Postique
76 4th Street North
St. Petersburg, FL 33701

1661 Ringland Blvd.
Sarasota, FL 33578

2800 South Adams Street
Tallahassee, FL 32301

5201 W. Spruce Street
Tampa, FL 33630

850 East Lime Street
Tarpon Springs, FL 34689

3200 Summit Blvd.
West Palm Beach, FL 33406

Georgia
115 Hancock Avenue
Athens, GA 30601

Downtown Station
101 Marietta Street
Atlanta, GA 30301

Perimeter Branch
4400 Ashford-
Dunwoody Road
Atlanta, GA 30346

Downtown Station
120-12th Street
Columbus, GA 31908

3470 McClure Bridge Road
Duluth, GA 30136

364 Green Street
Gainesville, GA 30501

451 College Street
Macon, GA 31201

257 Lawrence Street
Marietta, GA 30060

5600 Spaulding Drive
Norcross, GA 30092

2 North Fahm Street
Savannah, GA 31401

904 Russell Parkway
Warner Robins, GA 31088

Hawaii
3600 Aolele Street
Honolulu, HI 96819

Idaho
770 South 13th Street
Boise, ID 83708

220 East 5th Street
Moscow, ID 83843

730 East Clark Street
Pocatello, ID 83201

Illinois
909 West Euclid Ave.
Arlington Heights, IL
60004

Moraine Valley Station
7401 100th Place
Bridgeview, IL 60455

1301 East Main Street
Carbondale, IL 62901

Loop Station
211 South Clark Street
Chicago, IL 60604

433 West Van Buren St.
Chicago, IL 60607

1000 East Oakton
Des Plaines, IL 60018

1101 Davis Street
Evanston, IL 60204

2359 Madison Avenue
Granite City, IL 62040

2000 McDonough St.
Joliet, IL 60436

1750 W. Ogden Avenue
Naperville, IL 60566

901 Lake Street
Oak Park, IL 60301

123 Indianwood
Park Forest, IL 60466

North University Station
6310 North University
Peoria, IL 61614

5225 Harrison Avenue
Rockford, IL 61125

211-19th Street
Rock Island, IL 61201

Schaumburg Station
450 W. Schaumburg
Roselle, IL 60194

2105 E. Cook Street
Springfield, IL 62703

Edison Square Station
1520 Washington
Waukegan, IL 60085

1241 Central Avenue
Wilmette, IL 60091

Indiana
North Park Branch
4492-B 1st Avenue
Evansville, IN 47710

Fort Wayne
Postal Facility
1501 S. Clinton Street
Fort Wayne, IN 46802

5530 Sohl Street
Hammond, IN 46320

125 West South Street
Indianapolis, IN 46206

2719 South Webster
Kokomo, IN 46901

3450 State Road 26 E.
Lafayette, IN 47901

424 South Michigan
South Bend, IN 46624

Cross Roads Station
70 Rose Avenue
Terre Haute, IN 47803

Iowa
615 6th Avenue SE
Cedar Rapids, IA 52401

1165 Second Avenue
Des Moines, IA 50318

24 Johnson Street
Sioux City, IA 51100

Kansas
Indian Springs Station
4953 State Avenue
Kansas City, KS 66102

6029 Broadmoor
Shawnee Mission, KS
66202

43415 Kansas Avenue
Topeka, KS 66603

Downtown Station
330 West 2nd Street
Wichita, KS 67202

Kentucky
1140 Carter Avenue
Ashland, KY 41101

1088 Nadino Blvd.
Lexington, KY 40511

Okolona Branch
7400 Jefferson Blvd.
Louisville, KY 40219

St. Mathews Station
4600 Shelbyville Road
Louisville, KY 40207

Louisiana
1715 Odom Street
Alexandria, LA 71301

750 Florida Street
Baton Rouge, LA 70821

General Mail Facility
1105 Moss Street
Lafayette, LA 70501

3301 17th Street
Metairie, LA 70002

501 Sterlington Road
Monroe, LA 71201

701 Loyola Avenue
New Orleans, LA 70113

Vieux Carre Station
1022 Iberville Street
New Orleans, LA 70112

2400 Texas Avenue
Shreveport, LA 71102

Maine
40 Western Avenue
Augusta, ME 04330

202 Harlow Street
Bangor, ME 04401

125 Forest Avenue
Portland, ME 04101

Maryland
1 Church Circle
Annapolis, MD 21401

900 E. Fayette Street
Baltimore, MD 21233

Chevy Chase
Financial Unit
5910 Connecticut Ave.
Bethesda, MD 20815

215 Park Street
Cumberland, MD 21502

201 East Patrick Street
Frederick, MD 21701

6411 Baltimore Avenue
Riverdale, MD 20840

500 N. Washington St.
Rockville, MD 20850

U.S. Route 50
& Naylor Road
Salisbury, MD 21801

Silver Spring Centre
Finance Station
8455 Colesville Road
Silver Spring, MD 20911

Massachusetts
McCormick Station
Post Office &
Courthouse Bldg.
Boston, MA 02109

120 Commercial Street
Brockton, MA 02401

7 Bedford Street
Burlington, MA 01803

Center Station
100 Center Street
Chicopee, MA 01014

2 Government Center
Fall River, MA 02722

881 Main Street
Fitchburg, MA 01420

330 Cocituate Road
Framingham, MA 01701

385 Main Street
Hyannis, MA 02601

431 Common Street
Lawrence, MA 01842

Post Office Square
Lowell, MA 01853

695 Pleasant Street
New Bedford, MA 02741

212 Fenn Street
Pittsfield, MA 01201

2 Margin Street
Salem, MA 01970

Main Street Station
1883 Main Street
Springfield, MA 01101

462 Washington Street
Woburn, MA 01888

4 East Central Street
Worcester, MA 01603

Michigan
2075 W. Stadium Blvd.
Ann Arbor, MI 48106

90 South McCamly
Battle Creek, MI 49106

26200 Ford Road
Dearborn Heights, MI 48127

1401 West Fort Street
Detroit, MI 48233

250 East Boulevard Dr.
Flint, MI 48502

225 Michigan Avenue
Grand Rapids, MI 49501

200 South Otsego
Jackson, MI 49201

1121 Miller Road
Kalamazoo, MI 49001

General Mail Facility
4800 Collins Road
Lansing, MI 48924

735 West Huron Street
Pontiac, MI 48056

1300 Military Street
Port Huron, MI 48060

30550 Gratiot Street
Roseville, MI 48066

200 West 2nd Street
Royal Oak, MI 48068

1233 South Washington
Saginaw, MI 48605

6300 North Wayne Road
Westland, MI 48185

Minnesota
2800 West Michigan
Duluth, MN 55806

100 South First Street
Minneapolis, MN 55401

Downtown Station
102 South Broadway
Rochester, MN 55904

The Pioneer
Postal Emporium
133 Endicott Arcade
St. Paul, MN 55101

Burnsville Branch
12212 12th Avenue South
Savage, MN 55378

Mississippi
2421-13th Street
Gulfport, MS 39501

La Fleur Station
1501 Jacksonian Plaza
Jackson, MS 39211

401 E. South Street
Jackson, MS 39201

500 West Miln Street
Tupelo, MS 38801

Missouri
920 Washington
Chillicothe, MO 64601

Columbia Mall Station
Columbia, MO 65203

315 Pershing Road
Kansas City, MO 64108

Northwest Plaza Station
500 Northwest Plaza
St. Ann, MO 63074

Pony Express Station
8th & Edmond
St. Joseph, MO 64503

Clayton Branch
7750 Maryland
St. Louis, MO 63105

Trading Post
1720 Market Street
St. Louis, MO 63155

500 W. Chestnut Expwy.
Springfield, MO 65801

Montana
841 South 26th
Billings, MO 59101

215 First Ave. North
Great Falls, MT 59401

1100 West Kent
Missoula, MT 59801

Nebraska
204 W. South Front St.
Grand Island, NE 68801

700 R Street
Lincoln, NE 68501

300 East Third Street
North Platte, NE 69101

1124 Pacific
Omaha, NE 68108

Nevada
1001 Circus Circus Dr.
Las Vegas, NV 89114

200 Vassar Street
Reno, NV 89510

New Hampshire
55 Pleasant Street
Concord, NH 03301

50 South Main Street
Hanover, NH 03755

955 Goffs Falls Road
Manchester, NH 03103

80 Daniel Street
Portsmouth, NH 03801

New Jersey
1701 Pacific Avenue
Atlantic City, NJ 08401

Veterans Plaza
Bergenfield, NJ 07621

3 Miln Street
Cranford, NJ 07016

229 Main Street
Fort Lee, NJ 07024

Bellmawr Branch
Haag Ave. & Benigno
Gloucester, NJ 08031

Route 35 & Hazlet Ave.
Hazlet, NJ 07730

Borough Complex
East End & Van Sant Ave.
Island Heights, NJ 08732

69 Montgomery Street
Jersey City, NJ 07305

160 Maplewood Avenue
Maplewood, NJ 07040

150 Ridgedale
Morristown, NJ 07960

Federal Square
Newark, NJ 07102

86 Bayard Street
New Brunswick, NJ 08906

Nutley Branch
372 Franklin Avenue
Nutley, NJ 07110

194 Ward Street
Paterson, NJ 07510

171 Broad Street
Red Bank, NJ 07701

757 Broad Avenue
Ridgefield, NJ 07657

76 Huyler Street
South Hackensack, NJ
07606

680 Highway 130
Trenton, NJ 08650

155 Clinton Road
West Caldwell, NJ
07006

41 Greenwood Ave.
Wykoff, NJ 07481

New Mexico
1135 Broadway NE
Albuquerque, NM 87101

200 E. Las Cruces Ave.
Las Cruces, NM 88001

415 N. Pennsylvania Ave.
Roswell, NM 88201

New York
Empire State
Plaza Station
Rockefeller Plaza N.E.
Albany, NY 12220

General Mail Facility
30 Old Karner Road
Albany, NY 12212

115 Henry Street
Binghamton, NY 13902

Bronx General P.O.
149th Street &
Grand Concourse
Bronx, NY 10451

Parkchester Station
1449 West Avenue
Bronx, NY 10462

Riverdale Station
5951 Riverdale Avenue
Bronx, NY 10471

Throggs Neck Station
3630 East Tremont Ave.
Bronx, NY 10465

Wakefield Station
4165 White Plains Rd.
Bronx, NY 10466

Bayridge Station
5501 7th Avenue
Brooklyn, NY 11220

Brooklyn General P.O.
271 Cadman Plaza East
Brooklyn, NY 11201

Greenpoint Station
66 Meserole Avenue
Brooklyn, NY 11222

Homecrest Station
2002 Avenue U
Brooklyn, NY 11229

Kensington Station
421 McDonald Avenue
Brooklyn, NY 11218

1200 William Street
Buffalo, NY 14240

1764 Route 9
Clifton Park, NY 12065

40 Main Street
Cooperstown, NY 13326

Baron deHirsch Road
Crempond, NY 10517

Downtown Station
255 Clemens Center Pkwy.
Elmira, NY 14901

1836 Mott Avenue
Far Rockaway, NY 11691

41-65 Main Street
Flushing, NY 11351

Ridgewood Station
869 Cypress Avenue
Flushing, NY 11385

Broadway & Maple St.
Glenham, NY 12527

16 Hudson Avenue
Glens Falls, NY 12801

185 West John Street
Hicksville, NY 11802

88-40 164th Street
Jamaica, NY 11431

300 East 3rd Street
Jamestown, NY 14701

324 Broadway
Monticello, NY 12701

Ansonia Station
1980 Broadway
New York, NY 10023

Bowling Green Station
25 Broadway
New York, NY 10004

Church Street Station
90 Church Street
New York, NY 10007

Empire State Station
350 Fifth Avenue
New York, NY 10001

F.D.R. Station
909 Third Avenue
New York, NY 10022

Grand Central Station
45th St. & Lexington Ave.
New York, NY 10017

Madison Square Station
149 East 23rd Street
New York, NY 10010

New York General P.O.
33rd St. and 8th Ave.
New York, NY 10001

Rockefeller Center
610 Fifth Avenue
New York, NY 10020

Times Square Station
340 West 42nd Street
New York, NY 10036

Main & Hunt Streets
Oneonta, NY 13820

Franklin & S. Main Sts.
Pearl River, NY 10965

10 Miller Street
Plattsburg, NY 12901

Branch Office
407 East Main Street
Port Jefferson, NY 11777

55 Mansion Street
Poughkeepsie, NY 12601

1335 Jefferson Road
Rochester, NY 14692

Ridgemont Branch
2899 Ridge Road West
Rochester, NY 14626

250 Merrick Road
Rockville Centre, NY 11570

29 Jay Street
Schenectady, NY 12305

25 Route 11
Smithtown, NY 11787

550 Manor Road
Staten Island, NY 10314

New Springville Station
2843 Richmond Avenue
Staten Island, NY 10314

5640 East Taft Road
Syracuse, NY 13220

10 Broad Street
Utica, NY 13503

108 Main Street
Warwick, NY 10990

100 Fisher Avenue
White Plains, NY 10602

78-81 Main Street
Yonkers, NY 10701

North Carolina
West Asheville Station
1300 Patton Avenue
Asheville, NC 28806

Eastway Station
3065 Eastway Drive
Charlotte, NC 28205

301 Green Street
Fayetteville, NC 28302

Four Seasons Station
Four Seasons Town Centre
High Point Road
Greensboro, NC 27427

310 New Bern Avenue
Raleigh, NC 27611

North Dakota
220 East Rosser Ave.
Bismarck, ND 58501

675 2nd Avenue North
Fargo, ND 58102

Ohio
675 Wolf Ledges Pkwy.
Akron, OH 44309

2650 Cleveland Street
Canton, OH 44701

Fountain Square Station
5th & Walnut Street
Cincinnati, OH 45202

301 W. Prospect Ave.
Cleveland, OH 44101

850 Twin Rivers Drive
Columbus, OH 43216

1111 East 5th Street
Dayton, OH 45401

345 East Bridge Street
Elyria, OH 44035

105 Court Street
Hamilton, OH 45011

200 North Diamond St.
Mansfield, OH 44901

200 North 4th Street
Steubenville, OH 43952

435 S. St. Clair Street
Toledo, OH 43601

99 South Walnut Street
Youngstown, OH 44503

Oklahoma
208 First Street SW
Ardmore, OK 73401

101 East First
Edmond, OK 73034

115 West Broadway
Enid, OK 73701

102 South 5th
Lawton, OK 73501

525 West Okmulgee
Muskogee, OK 74401

129 West Gray
Norman, OK 73069

320 SW 5th Street
Oklahoma, City, OK 73125

116 East 9th Street
Shawnee, OK 74801

333 West 4th
Tulsa, OK 74101

12 South 5th
Yukon, OK 73099

Oregon
311 SW 2nd Street
Corvallis, OR 97333

520 Willamette Street
Eugene, OR 97401

751 NW Hoyt
Portland, OR 97208

1050 25th Street SW
Salem, OR 97301

Pennsylvania
442-456 Hamilton St.
Allentown, PA 18101

535 Wood Street
Bethlehem, PA 18016

115 Boylston Street
Bradford, PA 16701

229 Beaver Drive
Du Bois, PA 15801

Griswold Plaza
Erie, PA 16501

115 Buford Avenue
Gettysburg, PA 17325

238 S. Pennsylvania
Greensburg, PA 15601

10th and Markets Sts.
Harrisburg, PA 17105

Downtown Station
48-50 W. Chestnut St.
Lancaster, PA 17603

980 Wheeler Way
Langhorne, PA 19047

Lehigh Valley Branch
Airport Rd. & Route 22
Lehigh Valley, PA 18001

Monroeville Mall Branch
348 Mall Circle Drive
Monroeville, PA 15146

1 W. Washington Street
Kennedy Square
New Castle, PA 16101

501 11th Street
New Kensington, PA 15068

28 East Airy Street
Norristown, PA 19401

B. Free Franklin Station
316 Market Street
Philadelphia, PA 19106

30th & Market Streets
Philadelphia, PA 19104

William Penn Annex
9th & Chestnut Streets
Philadelphia, PA 19107

Castle Shannon Branch
307 Castle Shannon Blvd.
Pittsburgh, PA 15234

General Mail Facility
1001 California Avenue
Pittsburgh, PA 15290

Seventh Avenue
& Grant Street
Pittsburgh, PA 15219

McKnight Branch
McKnight & Seibert Rds.
Pittsburgh, PA 15237

59 North 5th Street
Reading, PA 19603

North Washington Ave.
& Linden St.
Scranton, PA 18503

237 South Frazer Street
State College, PA 16801

7th & Ann Streets
Stroudsburg, PA 18360

300 South Main Street
Wilkes Barre, PA 18701

Center City Finance Station
240 West Third Street
Williamsport, PA 17703

200 S. George Street
York, PA 17405

Puerto Rico
General Post Office
18 Roosevelt Avenue
Hate Rey
San Juan, PR 00918

Plaza Las Americas Sta.
San Juan, PR 00938

Rhode Island
320 Thames Street
Newport, RI 02840

40 Montgomery Street
Pawtucket, RI 02860

24 Corliss Street
Providence, RI 02904

South Carolina
4290 Daley Avenue
Charleston, SC 29402

1601 Assembly Street
Columbia, SC 29201

600 West Washington
Greenville, SC 29602

South Dakota
500 East Boulevard
Rapid City, SD 57701

320 S. 2nd Avenue
Sioux Falls, SD 57101

Tennessee
General Mail Facility
6050 Shallowford Road
Chattanooga, TN 37401

Tom Murray Station
133 Tucker Street
Jackson, TN 38301

50 East Main Street
Johnson City, TN 37601

501 West Main Avenue
Knoxville, TN 37901

Colonial Finance Unit
4695 Southern Avenue
Memphis, TN 38124

Crosstown Finance Unit
1520 Union Avenue
Memphis, TN 38174

901 Broadway
Nashville, TN 37202

Texas
341 Pine Street
Abilene, TX 79604

2300 South Ross
Amarillo, TX 79105

300 East South Street
Arlington, TX 76010

Downtown Station
300 East 9th
Austin, TX 78701

General Mail Facility
8225 Cross Park Drive
Austin, TX 78710

300 Willow
Beaumont, TX 77704

1535 Los Ebanos
Brownsville, TX 78520

2201 Hilltop Drive
College Station, TX 77840

809 Nueces Bay
Corpus Christi, TX 78408

400 North Ervay Street
Dallas, TX 75221

Olla Podrida
Finance Station
12215 Coit Road
Dallas, TX 75251

5300 East Paisano Dr.
El Paso, TX 79910

251 West Lancaster
Fort Worth, TX 76101

401 Franklin Avenue
Houston, TX 77201

300 North 10th
Killeen, TX 76541

411 "L" Avenue
Lubbock, TX 79408

601 East Pecan
McAllen, TX 78501

100 East Wall
Midland, TX 79702

1 North Bryant
San Angelo, TX 76902

Downtown Station
615 East Houston
San Antonio, TX 78205

10410 Perrin Beitel Road
San Antonio, TX 78284

1411 Wunsche Loop
Spring, TX 77373

2211 North Robinson
Texarkana, TX 75501

221 West Ferguson
Tyler, TX 75702

800 Franklin
Waco, TX 76701

1000 Lamar Street
Wichita Falls, TX 76307

Utah
3680 Pacific Avenue
Ogden, UT 84401

95 West 100 South
Provo, UT 84601

1760 West 2100 South
Salt Lake City, UT 84119

Vermont
204 Main Street
Brattleboro, VT 05301

1 Elmwood Avenue
Burlington, VT 05401

151 West Street
Rutland, VT 05701

Sykes Avenue
White River Junction, VT
05001

Virginia
111 Sixth Street
Bristol, VA 24201

1155 Seminole Trail
Charlottesville, VA 22906

1425 Battlefield Blvd. N.
Chesapeake, VA 23320

700 Main Street
Danville, VA 24541

Merrifield Branch
8409 Lee Highway
Fairfax, VA 22116

809 Aberdeen Road
Hampton, VA 23670

300 Odd Fellows Road
Lynchburg, VA 24506

Denbigh Station
14104 Warwick Blvd.
Newport News, VA
23602

600 Church Street
Norfolk, VA 23501

Thomas Corner Station
6274 East Virginia
Beach Boulevard
Norfolk, VA 23502

1801 Brook Road
Richmond, VA 23232

419 Rutherford Ave. NE
Roanoke, VA 24022

1430 North Augusta
Staunton, VA 24401

501 Viking Drive
Virginia Beach, VA 23450

Washington
11 3rd Street NW
Auburn, WA 98001

Crossroads Station
15800 NE 8th
Bellevue, WA 98008

315 Prospect Street
Bellingham, WA 98225

3102 Hoyt
Everett, WA 98201

3500 West Court
Pasco, WA 99301

424 East 1st Street
Port Angeles, WA 98362

301 Union Street
Seattle, WA 98101

West 904 Riverside
Spokane, WA 99210

1102 A Street
Tacoma, WA 98402

205 West Washington
Yakima, WA 98903

West Virginia
301 North Street
Bluefield, WV 24701

Lee & Dickinson St.
Charleston, WV 25301

500 West Pike Street
Clarksburg, WV 26301

1000 Virginia Ave. West
Huntington, WV 25704

217 King Street
Martinsburg, WV 25401

Wisconsin
126 N. Barstow Street
Eau Claire, WI 54703

325 East Walnut
Green Bay, WI 54301

3902 Milwaukee Street
Madison, WI 53707

345 West St. Paul Ave.
Milwaukee, WI 53203

235 Forrest Street
Wausau, WI 54401

Wyoming
150 East B Street
Casper, WY 82601

2120 Capitol Avenue
Cheyenne, WY 82001

FOREIGN CENTERS

Australia
Max Stern & Co.
Port Phillip Arcade
234 Flinders Street
Melbourne 3000

France
Theodore Champion
13 Rue Drouot
75009 Paris

Federal Republic of Germany
Hermann W. Sieger
Venusbert 32-34
D-7073
Lorch/Wurttemberg

Great Britain
Harry Allen
Langwood House
Rickmansworth
Herts WD3 1EY

Japan
Japan Philatelic Co., Ltd.
Post Office Box 2
Suginami-Minami
Tokyo 168-91

Netherlands
J.A. Visser
Post Office Box 184
3300 Ad Dordrecht

Sweden
Bo Follin
Frimarkshuset AB
S-793 01 Leksand

Switzerland
De Rosa International S.A.
Av Du Tribunal
Federal 34
Ch-1005 Lausanne

Pressing the Edges of the Unknown

We shall not cease from exploration
And the end of all our exploring
Will be to arrive where we started
And know the place for the first time.
—*T.S. Eliot*

Since the launch of the first artificial satellite in 1957, humans have been trailblazers in a cosmic wilderness—the realms of outer space. In 1969, three U.S. astronauts became the first human beings to set foot on the Moon. In 1981, the first space shuttle rocketed into space with its crew, transforming the possibility of regular manned space flights into reality.

Throughout this "space age," U.S. space efforts have continued to press the edges of the unknown, harvesting new knowledge about the cosmos. Ultimately, scientists hope this knowledge will lead to a greater understanding of life on our own planet Earth.

The U.S. Postal Service recently commemorated this quest for greater wisdom about space with a colorful stamp booklet. Depicting the Moon and the nine planets of our solar system, the Space Exploration Issue also illustrates the spacecraft that have served as our windows to these heavenly bodies. While less publicized than manned space flights, the missions of these U.S. satellites and space probes have yielded breathtaking discoveries about Earth and its celestial neighbors.

Satellites: Manmade moons

An artificial satellite, like our Moon, orbits the Earth. It carries a radio transmitter and other equipment that may include television cameras, infrared detectors and instruments to measure radiation. Satellites circling the Earth are used for meteorological, communications, navigation, scientific and military purposes. They allow us to watch the Earth's weather patterns, predict crop harvests and urban expansion and send television programs around the world.

From 1972 to 1984, five *Landsat* satellites were launched by the U.S. These spacecraft have scrutinized Earth from every angle, every few weeks, returning a wealth of detailed data and images used by scientists and others in more than 100 countries.

Space probes: Planetary pioneers

The "bravest" of spacecraft, space probes are unmanned vehicles that explore planets, moons and the space between them. A probe may fly

Satellite pictures paved the way for man to walk on the Moon.

A *VIKING* SPACE PROBE EXPLORES THE ROCKY SURFACE OF MARS.

past a planet, go into orbit around it, or land. These craft give humankind a glimpse of planets vastly different from our own. Sometimes, space probes never come back. They are sent to plunge into a planet's atmosphere, relaying signals back to Earth until heat or atmospheric pressure destroys them. Early space probes included *Mariner 2*, which in 1962 confirmed the forbiddingly high surface temperature of Venus. *Lunar Orbiter* circled the Moon in 1966, paving the way for human explorers.

In 1973, *Mariner 10* flew within 600 miles of Mercury. It sent back the first-ever photos of the planet, completing three "flybys" during its mission. The probe revealed a lifeless planet with no atmosphere. The closest planet to the sun, Mercury has a daytime surface temperature of 800°F—hot enough to melt lead.

Pioneer 11 flew within 26,000 miles of Jupiter in 1974, providing extensive photographs and data. Called the "giant" of the solar system, Jupiter weighs more than twice as much as all the other planets combined. The planet's red-and-brown swirled surface is marked by a red spot as big as Earth—actually a huge storm ever-brewing on Jupiter's surface.

Two *Viking* probes in 1975 landed on Mars, the Red Planet, and gathered soil samples from this mysterious cousin of Earth. No microbes or traces of life were found in the Martian soil. If life did exist on Mars, it would live in a landscape with reddish, sandy soil and many rocks and boulders—topped by a pinkish sky. NASA plans a new spacecraft launch to observe Mars in 1992.

THE *VOYAGERS:* STELLAR PERFORMANCES

Two *Voyager* space probes launched in 1977 proved brilliantly successful, covering four planets and making several new discoveries. Each carried 10 experimental instruments, a radio transmitter and three kinds of computers with backup systems—making them the most intelligent spacecraft of their time. Like *Pioneer 11*, *Voyager 1* visited Jupiter, taking thousands of photos.

Voyager 2 visited Saturn, one of the most beautiful planets. "Butterscotch" in color with lines of pink, tan and brown, Saturn is well-known for its amazing rings, composed of millions of minuscule icy particles. Although the rings appear to be smooth, *Voyager 2* found strange formations in them, described as "kinks, spokes and braids," that scientists still cannot fully explain.

The next destination on the *Voyager 2* itinerary was Uranus, a distant planet never before visited. The historic Uranus flyby occurred in the same week as the tragic explosion of the space shuttle *Challenger* in 1986, and received less attention than it might have otherwise. Nevertheless, *Voyager 2* made some spectacular discoveries, including the wildly undulating terrain of the Uranian moon Miranda.

Last stop on the *Voyager 2* mission was Neptune, which the craft visited in 1989. So far from Earth that ancient astronomers didn't know it existed, Neptune had never before been closely observed. The probe discovered six Neptunian moons in addition to the two already known to exist, and rings

SATURN'S MYSTERIOUS RINGS WERE EXAMINED BY VOYAGER 2.

SPACE-AGE SAILBOATS

Five hundred years after Columbus sailed to America, scientists and engineers will send "sailboats" to another destination—Mars. Scheduled for October, 1992, the Columbus 500 Space Sail Cup will pit at least three solar sailcraft against each other in a race to the Red Planet.

Solar sailing is a mode of space travel using the pressure of sunlight to propel the craft, much like a terrestrial sailboat uses the wind. Solar sailcraft have enormous sails. One preliminary design features a round sail 550 feet in diameter! They travel quite slowly at first, but gradually build up enough speed to sail at a good clip. About three months after launch, a craft would be traveling fast enough to escape its orbit and could reach Mars 500 days after that.

Scientists are excited about the crafts' ability to adjust their sails to change direction and speed, which means they can maneuver without carrying heavy propellants and fuels. If the crafts succeed in their journey, future astronauts may glide through space on solar "wings"!

GETTING SMARTER THROUGH SPACE EXPLORATION

The technology developed for use on spacecraft pays off daily for all of us. Countless "spinoffs" of space technology have been introduced commercially for use by earthbound humans. Computer-generated artwork, for example, was first developed for use in space research and exploration.

Here's a short list of other space-age spinoffs:

- *robotics*
- *heat-resistant paint*
- *cooling sportswear for athletes*
- *scratch-resistant sunglasses*
- *fireproof building materials*
- *improved solar cell collectors and superinsulation materials*
- *home "dish" antennae*
- *sensors for smoke alarms and security devices*
- *ultrasound equipment and other medical imaging devices*
- *talking wheelchairs*
- *advanced shock absorbers for highway crash barriers*

around the planet as well. It also provided the first closeup pictures of the planet's surface, including the Great Dark Spot, which is actually violently swirling masses of gas.

Today's space probes continue to make new and fascinating discoveries about our universe. *Galileo* recently took time-lapse photos of the Earth's rotation and provided some views of the Moon never seen before. The probe is actually on its way to a "suicide mission" investigating Jupiter's highly pressurized atmosphere. *Magellan,* a probe that uses radar imagery instead of photography, recently relayed back to Earth the most detailed views of Venus ever seen. *Ulysses,* launched in late 1990, will expand our knowledge about the Sun when it reaches the big star in 1994.

The Hubble Space Telescope, despite some initial disappointments in picture quality, has provided photographs far superior to those from ground-based telescopes. It has shown us the clearest pictures ever of Pluto, the most distant

JUPITER'S GREAT RED SPOT IS ACTUALLY A GIGANTIC, SWIRLING STORM.

planet and the only one not yet visited with a flyby spacecraft. Launched by the space shuttle *Discovery* in 1990, the telescope also revealed a giant storm on Saturn that has so far mystified scientists.

The Future: Benefiting Earth

What's in the future? NASA intends to begin building a U.S. space station in 1995. This orbiting space laboratory could be permanently staffed by the year 2000. Completing the station would be the first step in sending a manned mission to Mars, which the U.S. and the U.S.S.R. hope to do cooperatively in the next 25 years.

Exploring the mysteries of the "final frontier" can only increase our appreciation for our own planet, described by one astronaut as "the jewel of the solar system." Aviation pioneer Charles Lindbergh put it in perspective:

"Whether we travel in a jet transport or in a spacecraft, we still look down...to life on the crowded surface of the Earth as both our source and our destination."

Celebrating space achievements

The U.S. Postal Service has paid tribute to the pioneering spirit of American space exploration with several stamp issues. They provide a colorful record of U.S. space efforts and hint at future hopes as well.

Scott #	Description	Issue Date
976	*3¢ Fort Bliss*	*1948*
1173	*4¢* Echo I—*Communications in Space*	*1960*
1193	*4¢* Project Mercury	*1962*
C69	*8¢ Robert H. Goddard*	*1964*
1331	*5¢ Space-Walking Astronaut*	*1967*
1332	*5¢* Gemini 4 *(#1331-32): Accomplishments in Space Issue—se-tenant pair)*	*1967*
1371	*6¢* Apollo 8	*1969*
C76	*10¢ Moon Landing*	*1969*
1434	*8¢ Earth, Sun, Moon*	*1971*
1435	*8¢ Lunar Rover and Astronauts (#1434-35: Space Achievement Decade Issue—se-tenant pair)*	*1971*
1529	*10¢* Skylab	*1974*
1556	*10¢* Pioneer/*Jupiter*	*1975*
1557	*10¢* Mariner 10	*1975*
1569	*10¢* Apollo Soyuz	*1975*
1570	*10¢ Spacecraft (#1569-70:* Apollo Soyuz *Space Issue—se-tenant pair)*	*1975*
1759	*15¢* Viking *Missions to Mars*	*1978*
1912-19a	*18¢ Space Achievement Issue (se-tenant block of eight)*	*1981*
2419	*$2.40 20th Anniversary of Moon Landing*	*1989*
C122-125a	*45¢ Future Mail Transportation (se-tenant block of four)*	*1989*
2568-77a	*29¢ Space Exploration (se-tenant block of 10)*	*1991*

Join the Club and Begin the Adventure

- A Commemorative Stamp Club Album
- Custom-printed album pages featuring illustrations and mounting areas for individual issues
- Stamps and mounts mailed conveniently to your home

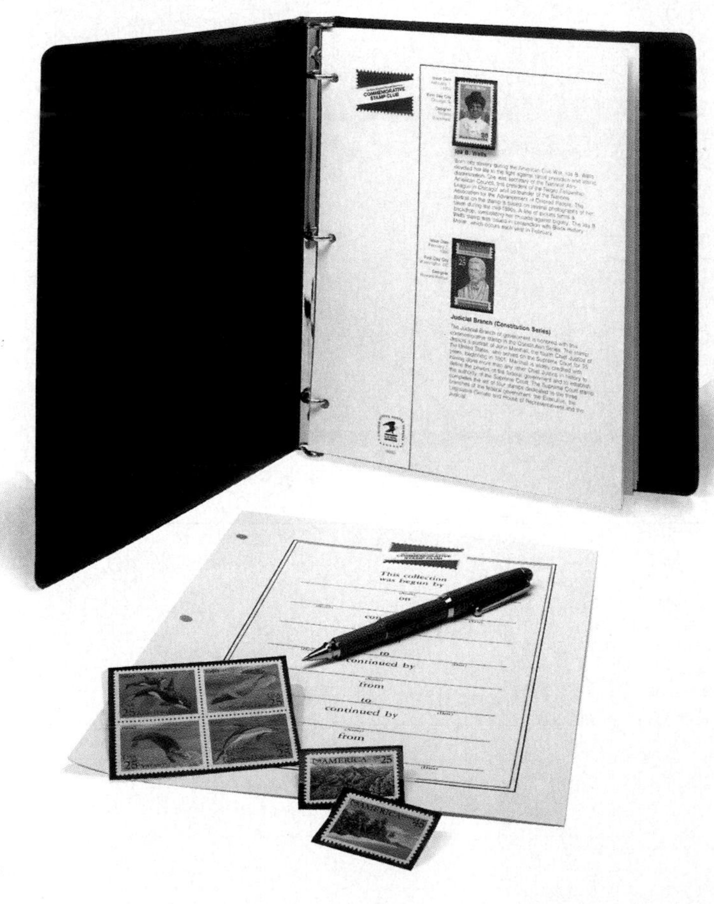

A Visit With America's Best

The Commemorative Stamp Club provides a convenient, comprehensive and attractive method for collecting and saving U.S. stamps.. Your membership means the start of an exciting adventure, one that will introduce you to America's best–the places, people, events and ideals honored through commemorative stamps.

And if you're looking for further excitement, you can expand your horizons by choosing to receive definitive stamps and album pages offered at the end of each year.

Other Membership Benefits

You'll receive clear acetate mounts to hold and protect your stamps and a *free* one-year subscription to the *Philatelic Catalog,* a bimonthly publication with full-color illustrations of all stamps, postal cards, aerogrammes, stamped envelopes and other collectibles available through mail order.

Get Your Ticket to Collecting Adventure

A no-risk, money-back guarantee assures your satisfaction. If you discontinue your membership within 30 days, simply return the album pages and stamps with a label from one of your shipments, and we'll send you a complete refund; the album is yours to keep. Annual membership in the Commemorative Stamp Club for 1991 costs just $25.95.

To Join

For more detailed information, use the postage-paid request card in this book or write to:

USPS GUIDE
COMMEMORATIVE STAMP CLUB
PHILATELIC SALES DIVISION
UNITED STATES POSTAL SERVICE
BOX 449980
KANSAS CITY MO 64144-9980

The Brave, the Best and the Beautiful

- Comprehensive stamp collections devoted to special subjects
- Interesting, informative text in colorfully illustrated books
- Artistic display arrangements complete with protective stamp mounts

Topical Mint Sets Have Wide Appeal

Whether it's the pure visual appeal of some of America's best stamp designs, the psychological appeal of subjects that evoke fond memories or stir emotions, or the educational appeal of interesting background material on intriguing topics, Topical Mint Sets contain something for everyone.

Topical Mint Sets still available include:

World War II

Designed for all those whose lives have been affected by the war, this 44-page deluxe, hardbound book, first of five annual editions, focuses on the year 1941 and features two of the striking World War II sheetlets of 10 stamps–one to grace the front of the book, the other to be broken up and mounted in sections devoted to such subjects as the Burma Road, the Lend-Lease Act, the Atlantic Charter, Liberty ships and the bombing of Pearl Harbor. ($15.95)

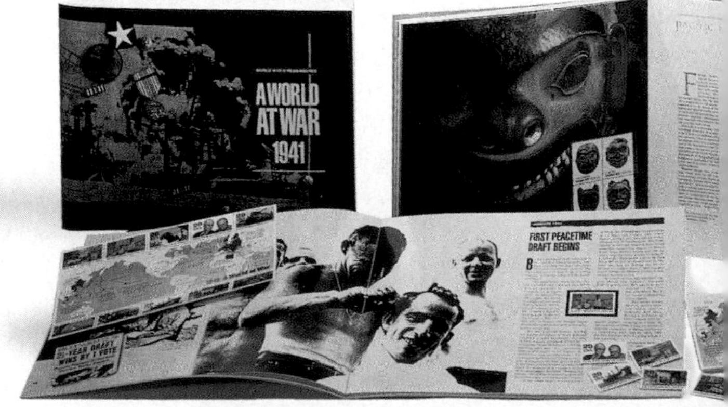

Best of the Decade

Featuring the most popular stamps of the 1980s as voted by readers of *Linn's Stamp News* and *Stamp Collector*, this 52-page book is full of fascinating details about the creation of those issues, along with 51 stamps themselves, including such dazzling issues as Coral Reefs; the Space Achievement block of eight; Birds & Flowers; American Dogs, Horses and Cats, and American Wildlife. ($18.95)

Folk Art & Crafts: An American Collection

A beautiful 44-page book that focuses on the techniques and traditions behind the objects on 32 stamps in the Folk Art Series. Includes the Carousel Animals, Lacemaking, Indian Masks, Quilts, Duck Decoys and Navajo Blankets issues. ($9.95 softbound, $16.50 hardbound)

To Obtain Topical Mint Sets

Topical Mint Sets are available at many local post offices and Philatelic Centers. You can also fill out the postage-paid request card in this book or write to:

USPS GUIDE
TOPICAL MINT SETS
PHILATELIC SALES DIVISION
UNITED STATES POSTAL SERVICE
BOX 449997
KANSAS CITY MO 64144-9997

1¢ Franklin Types I-V of 1851-57

5

Bust of **5**

Detail of **5, 18, 40** Type I
Has curved, unbroken lines outside labels.
Scrollwork is substantially complete at top, forms little balls at bottom.

Detail of **5A** Type Ib
Lower scrollwork is incomplete, the little balls are not so clear.

Bust of **5**

Detail of **6, 19** Type Ia
Same as Type I at bottom but top ornaments and outer line partly cut away.
Lower scrollwork is complete.

Bust of **5**

Detail of **7, 20** Type II
Lower scrollwork incomplete (lacks little balls and lower plume ornaments).
Side ornaments are complete.

Bust of **5**

Detail of **8, 21** Type III
Outer lines broken in the middle.
Side ornaments are substantially complete.

Detail of **8A, 22** Type IIIa
Outer lines broken top or bottom but not both.

Bust of **5**

Detail of **9, 23** Type IV
Similar to Type II, but outer lines recut top, bottom, or both.

Bust of **5**

Detail of **24** Type V
Similar to Type III of 1851-57 but with side ornaments partly cut away.

3¢ Washington Types I-IIa of 1851-57

10

Bust of **10**

Detail of **10, 11, 25, 41** Type I
There is an outer frame line at top and bottom.

Bust of **10**

Detail of **26** Type II
The outer frame line has been removed at top and bottom.
The side frame lines were recut so as to be continuous from the top to the bottom of the plate.

Bust of **10**

Detail of **26a** Type IIa
The side frame lines extend only to the bottom of the stamp design.

5¢ Jefferson Types I-II of 1851-57

12

Bust of **12**

Detail of **12, 27-29** Type I
There are projections on all four sides.

Bust of **12**

Detail of **30-30A** Type II
The projections at top and bottom are partly cut away.

10¢ Washington Types I-V of 1851-57

15

Bust of **15**

Detail of **13, 31, 43** Type I
The "shells" at the lower corners are practically complete. The outer line below the label is very nearly complete. The outer lines are broken above the middle of the top label and the "X" in each upper corner.

Bust of **15**

Detail of **14, 32** Type II
The design is complete at the top. The outer line at the bottom is broken in the middle. The shells are partly cut away.

Bust of **15**

Detail of **15, 33** Type III
The outer lines are broken above the top label and the "X" numerals. The outer line at the bottom and the shells are partly cut away, as in Type II.

Bust of **15**

Detail of **16, 34** Type IV
The outer lines have been recut at top or bottom or both. Types I, II, III and IV have complete ornaments at the sides of the stamps and three pearls at each outer edge of the bottom panel.

Bust of **15**

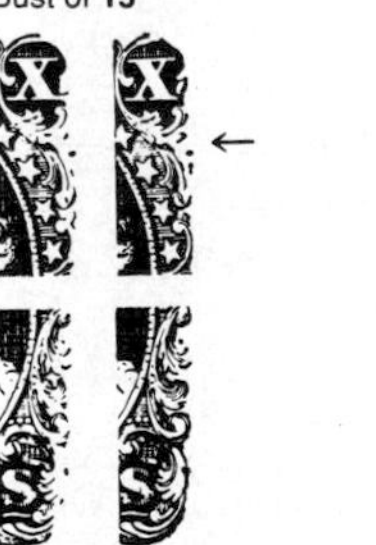

Detail of **35** Type V
(Two typical examples). Side ornaments slightly cut away. Outer lines complete at top except over right "X". Outer lines complete at bottom and shells nearly so.

1¢ Franklin of 1861-75

55

Detail of **55**

Detail of **63, 86, 92**
In **63, 86** and **92**, a dash has been added under the tip of the ornament at right of the numeral in upper left corner.

3¢ Washington of 1861-75

56

Detail of **56**

Detail of **64-66, 74, 79, 82-83, 85, 85C, 88, 94**
In **64-66, 74, 79, 82-83, 85, 85C, 88** and **94**, ornaments at corners have been enlarged and end in a small ball.

5¢ Jefferson of 1861-75

57

Detail of **57**

Detail of **67, 75, 80, 95**
In **67, 75, 80** and **95**, a leaf has been added to the foliated ornaments at each corner.

10¢ Washington of 1861-75

58

Detail of **58, 62B**

Detail of **68, 85D, 89, 96**
In **68, 85D, 89** and **96**, a heavy, curved line has been cut below the stars and an outer line added to the ornaments above them.

12¢ Washington of 1861-75

59

Detail of **59**

Detail of **69, 85E, 90, 97**
In **69, 85E, 90** and **97**, ovals and scrolls have been added at the corners.

90¢ Washington of 1861-75

62

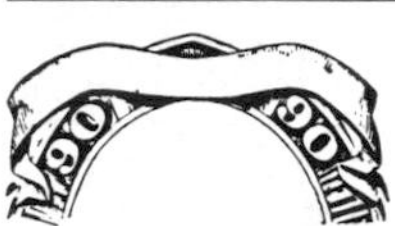

Detail of **62**

Detail of **72, 101**
In **72** and **101,** parallel lines form an angle above the ribbon containing "U.S. Postage"; between these lines a row of dashes has been added, along with a point of color to the apex of the lower line.

15¢ Columbus Landing Types I-III of 1869-75

118

Vignette of **118**

Detail of **118** Type I
Picture unframed.

Vignette of **118**

Detail of **119** Type II
Picture framed.

Vignette of **118**

129 Type III. Same as Type I but without fringe of brown shading lines around central vignette.

Comparison of Issue of 1870-71: Printed by National Bank Note Company. Issued without secret marks (134-141, 145-152, 187) and **Issues of 1873-80: Printed by Continental and American Bank Note Companies.** Issued with secret marks (156-163, 167-174, 178, 180, 182-184, 186, 188-190, 192-199).

134 **135** **136** **137** **138**

Detail of **134, 145**

Detail of **156, 167, 182, 192**
1¢. In the pearl at the left of the numeral "1" there is a small crescent.

Detail of **135, 146**

Detail of **157, 168, 178, 180, 183, 193**
2¢. Under the scroll at the left of "U.S." there is small diagonal line. This mark seldom shows clearly.

Detail of **136, 147**

Detail of **158, 169, 184, 194**
3¢. The under part of the upper tail of the left ribbon is heavily shaded.

Detail of **137, 148**

Detail of **159, 170, 186, 195**
6¢. The first four vertical lines of the shading in the lower part of the left ribbon have been strengthened.

Detail of **138, 149**

Detail of **160, 171, 196**
7¢. Two small semicircles are drawn around the ends of the lines that outline the ball in the lower righthand corner.

139

140

141

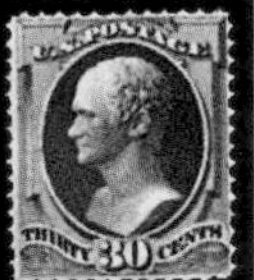
143

206

207

Detail of **139, 150, 187**

Detail of **161, 172, 188, 197**
10¢. There is a small semicircle in the scroll at the right end of the upper label.

Detail of **140, 151**

Detail of **162, 173, 198**
12¢. The balls of the figure "2" are crescent-shaped.

Detail of **141, 152**

Detail of **163, 174, 189, 199**
15¢. In the lower part of the triangle in the upper left corner two lines have been made heavier, forming a "V". This mark can be found on some of the Continental and American (1879) printings, but not all stamps show it.

Detail of **143, 154, 165, 176**

Detail of **190,** 30¢. In the "S" of "CENTS," the vertical spike across the middle section of the letter has been broadened.

Detail of **206**
1¢. Upper vertical lines have been deepened, creating a solid effect in parts of background. Upper arabesques shaded.

Detail of **207**
3¢. Shading at sides of central oval is half its previous width. A short horizontal dash has been cut below the "TS" of "CENTS."

208 **209**

Detail of **208**
6¢. Has three vertical lines instead of four between the edge of the panel and the outside of the stamp.

Detail of **209**
10¢. Has four vertical lines instead of five between left side of oval and edge of the shield. Horizontal lines in lower part of background strengthened.

2¢Washington
Types of I-III of 1894-1898

248

Triangle of **248-250, 265**
Type I
Horizontal lines of uniform thickness run across the triangle.

Triangle of **251, 266** Type II
Horizontal lines cross the triangle, but are thinner within than without.

Triangle of **252, 267, 279B-279Be** Type III
The horizontal lines do not cross the double frame lines of the triangle.

$1 Perry Types I-II of 1894

261

Detail of **261, 276** Type I
The circles enclosing $1 are broken.

Detail of **261A, 276A** Type II
The circles enclosing $1 are complete.

10¢ Webster
Types I-II of 1898

282C

Detail of **282C** Type I
The tips of the foliate ornaments do not impinge on the white curved line below "TEN CENTS."

Detail of **283** Type II
The lips of the ornaments break the curved line below the "E" of "TEN" and the "T" of "CENTS."

2¢ Washington
of 1903

319

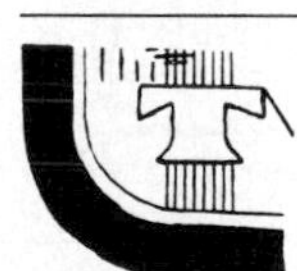

Detail of **319a, 319b, 319g** Die I

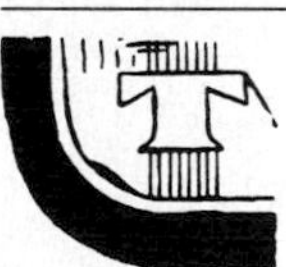

Detail of **319c, 319f, 319h, 319i** Die II

3¢ Washington Types I-IV
of 1908-19

333

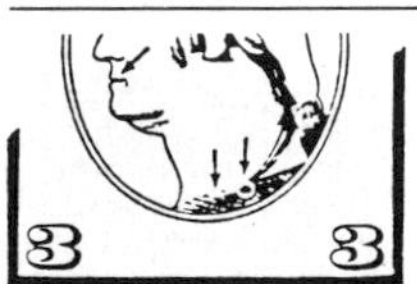

Detail of **333, 345, 359, 376, 389, 394, 426, 445, 456, 464, 483, 493, 501-01b** Type I
Top line of toga rope is weak and rope shading lines are thin. Fifth line from left is missing. Line between lips is thin.

Detail of **484, 494, 502, 541** Type II
Top line of toga rope is strong and rope shading lines are heavy and complete. Line between lips is heavy.

Detail of **529** Type III
Top row of toga rope is strong but fifth shading line is missing as in Type I. Toga button center shading line consists of two dashes, central dot. "P," "O" of "POSTAGE" are separated by line of color.

Detail of **530, 535** Type IV
Toga rope shading lines are complete. Second, fourth toga button shading lines are broken in middle; third line is continuous with dot in center. "P," "O" of "POSTAGE" are joined.

2¢ Washington Types I-VII of 1912-21

406

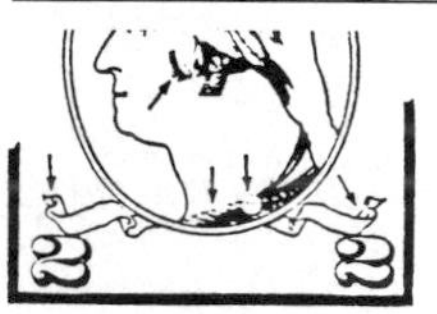

Detail of **406-406a, 411, 413, 425-25e, 442, 444, 449, 453, 461, 463-63a, 482, 499-99f** Type I
One shading line in first curve of ribbon above left "2" and one in second curve of ribbon above right "2". Toga button has only a faint outline. Top line of toga rope, from button to front of the throat, is very faint. Shading lines of face end in front of ear, with little or no joining, to form lock of hair.

Detail of **482a, 500** Type Ia
Similar to Type I but all lines are stronger.

Detail of **454, 487, 491, 539** Type II
Shading lines in ribbons as in Type I. Toga button, rope and rope shading lines are heavy. Shading lines of face at lock of hair end in strong vertical curved line.

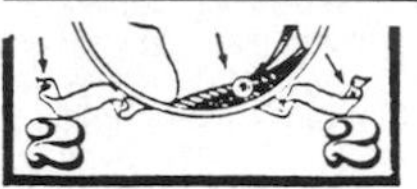

Detail of **450, 455, 488, 492, 540, 546** Type III
Two lines of shading in curves of ribbons.

Detail of **526, 532** Type IV
Top line of toga rope is broken. Toga button shading lines form "DID". Line of color in left "2" is very thin and usually broken.

Detail of **527, 533** Type V
Top line of toga is complete. Toga button has five vertical shading lines. Line of color in left "2" is very thin and usually broken. Nose shading dots are as shown.

Detail of **528, 534** Type Va
Same as Type V except third row from bottom of nose shading dots has four dots instead of six. Overall height of design is 1/3 mm shorter than Type V.

Detail of **528A, 534A** Type VI
Generally same as Type V except line of color in left "2" is very heavy.

Detail of **528B, 534B** Type VII
Line of color in left "2" is continuous, clearly defined and heavier than in Type V or Va but not as heavy as Type VI. An additional vertical row of dots has been added to upper lip. Numerous additional dots appear in hair at top of head.

2¢ Washington Types I-II of 1923-29

599

Detail of **599, 634** Type I
No heavy hair lines at top center of head.

Detail of **599A, 634A** Type II
Three heavy hair lines at top center of head.

Explanation of Catalog Prices

The United States Postal Service sells only the commemoratives released during the past few years and current regular and special stamps and postal stationery.

Prices in this book are called "catalog prices" by stamp collectors. Collectors use catalog prices as guidelines when buying or trading stamps. It is important to remember the prices are simply guidelines to the stamp values. Stamp condition (see pp 12-13) is very important in determining the actual value of a stamp.

The catalog prices are given for unused (mint) stamps and used (cancelled) stamps, which have been hinged and are in Fine condition. Stamps in Superb condition that have never been hinged may cost more than the listed price. Stamps in less than Fine condition may cost less.

The prices for used stamps are based on a light cancellation; a heavy cancellation lessens a stamp's value. Cancelled stamps may be worth more than uncancelled stamps. This happens if the cancellation is of a special type or for a significant date. Therefore, it is important to study an envelope before removing a stamp and discarding its "cover."

Listed prices are estimates of how much you can expect to pay for a stamp from a dealer. **In this edition, a new 15-cent minimum valuation has been established which represents a fair-market price to have a dealer locate and provide a single stamp to a customer. Dealers may charge less per stamp to provide a group of such stamps, and may charge less for such a single stamp.** If you sell a stamp to a dealer, he may offer you much less than the catalog price. Dealers pay based on their interest in owning that stamp. If they already have a full supply, they may only buy additional stamps at a low price.

Prices in regular type for single unused and used stamps are taken from the *Scott 1992 Standard Postage Stamp Catalogue, Volume 1* © 1991, whose editors have based these prices on **actual retail values** as they found them in the marketplace. Prices quoted for unused and used stamps are for "Fine" condition, except where Fine is not available. Stamp values in *italics* generally refer to items difficult to value accurately. A dash in a value column means the item is known to exist but information is insufficient for establishing a value.

Prices for Plate Blocks and First Day Covers are taken from *Scott's Specialized Catalogue of U.S. Stamps*, 1991 Edition, © 1990. The Scott numbering system for stamps is used in this book. Prices for American Commemorative Panels and Souvenir Pages are from the American Society of Philatelic Pages and Panels.

			Un	U	PB/LP/PNC	#	FDC	Q
2538	29¢	William Saroyan, May 22	.00	.00	0.00	( )	0.00	000,000,000

Scott Catalog Number
Denomination
Description
First Day of Issue
Unused Catalog Price
Used Catalog Price
Plate Block Price, Line Pair Price or Plate Number Coil Price
# of stamps in Plate Block, Line Pair or Plate Number Coil
First Day Cover Price
Quantity Issued (Where Known)

2538

1

2

3

4

5

11

12

14

17

30

37

38

39

		Issues of 1847, Imperf., July 1, Unwmkd.		
			Un	U
1		5¢ Benjamin Franklin	3,500.00	425.00
	b	5¢ orange brown	4,000.00	525.00
	c	5¢ red orange	*10,000.00*	*1,850.00*
		Double transfer of top, or top and bottom, or bottom and lower left frame lines		500.00
		Double transfer of top, bottom and left frame lines and numerals		850.00
2		10¢ George Washington	*15,000.00*	1,100.00
		Vertical line through second "F" of "OFFICE," or with "stick pin" in tie, or with "harelip," or double transfer in lower right "X," or in "POST OFFICE," or of left and bottom frame lines	—	1,250.00

The stamp listings contain a number of "a," "b," "c," etc. additions which include recognized varieties and errors. These listings are as complete as space permits.

	Issues of 1875, Reproductions of 1 and 2		
		Un	U
3	5¢ Franklin	850.00	—
4	10¢ Washington	1,000.00	—

5¢. On the original, the left side of the white shirt frill touches the oval on a level with the top of the "F" of "Five." On the reproduction, it touches the oval about on a level with the top of the figure "5."

10¢. On the reproduction, line of coat at left points to right of "X" and line of coat at right points to center of "S" of CENTS. On the original, line of coat points to "T" of TEN and between "T" and "S" of CENTS.

On the reproduction, the eyes have a sleepy look, the line of the mouth is straighter and in the curl of hair near the left cheek is a strong black dot, while the original has only a faint one.

	Issues of 1851-57, Imperf.	Un	U
5	1¢ Franklin, type I	*200,000.00*	*17,500.00*
5A	1¢ blue, type Ib	*8,000.00*	*2,500.00*
	#6-9: Franklin (5), 1851		
6	1¢ dark blue, type Ia	*22,500.00*	*6,500.00*
7	1¢ blue, type II	500.00	90.00
	Cracked plate	700.00	200.00
8	1¢ blue, type III	*6,500.00*	1,500.00
8A	1¢ pale blue, type IIIA	2,500.00	600.00
9	1¢ blue, type IV	350.00	80.00
	Triple transfer, one inverted	800.00	225.00
	#10-11, #25-26a all had plates on which at least four outer frame lines were recut, and usually much more, adding to their value.		
10	3¢ orange brown Washington, type I (11)	950.00	40.00
	3¢ copper brown	1,100.00	
	On part-India paper		250.00
11	3¢ Washington, type I	130.00	7.00
	3¢ deep claret	185.00	13.50
	Double transfer, "GENTS" for "CENTS"	200.00	25.00
12	5¢ Jefferson, type I	*8,500.00*	950.00
13	10¢ green Washington, type I (14)	9,000.00	600.00
14	10¢ green, type II	2,000.00	225.00
15	10¢ Washington, type III	2,000.00	225.00
16	10¢ green, type IV (14)	*11,500.00*	1,100.00
17	12¢ Washington	2,500.00	250.00
	Issues of 1857-61, Perf. 15 (Issued in 1857 except #18, 27, 28A, 29, 30, 30A, 35, 36b, 37, 38, 39)		
	#18-24: Franklin (5)		
18	1¢ blue, type I, 1861	750.00	350.00
19	1¢ blue, type Ia, July 26	*11,500.00*	*2,500.00*
20	1¢ blue, type II, July 25	450.00	125.00
21	1¢ blue, type III, July 26	5,000.00	1.400.00
22	1¢ blue, type IIIa, July 26	750.00	250.00
23	1¢ blue, type IV, July 25	2,000.00	325.00
24	1¢ blue, type V	110.00	22.50
	"Curl" on shoulder	150.00	37.50
	"Earring" below ear	200.00	52.50
	Long double "curl" in hair	185.00	42.50
b	Laid paper	—	—
	#25-26a: Washington (11)		
25	3¢ rose, type I, Feb. 28	675.00	27.50
	Cracked plate	900.00	100.00
26	3¢ dull red, type II	45.00	2.75
	3¢ brownish carmine	50.00	3.00
	3¢ claret	60.00	3.50
	Left or right frame line double	65.00	8.75
	Cracked plate	*425.00*	125.00
26a	3¢ dull red, type IIa	110.00	20.00
	Double transfer	175.00	30.00
	Left frame line double	—	45.00

		Un	U
	#27-29: Jefferson (12)		
27	5¢ brick red, type I, 1858	*8,000.00*	750.00
28	5¢ red brown, type I	1,350.00	250.00
b	5¢ brt. red brn., type I	1,850.00	400.00
28A	5¢ Indian red, type I	*10,000.00*	2,000.00
29	5¢ brown, type I, 1859	850.00	200.00
30	5¢ Jefferson, type II, 1861	750.00	750.00
30A	5¢ orange brown Jefferson, type II (30)	450.00	175.00
b	Printed on both sides	*3,750.00*	*3,000.00*
	#31-35: Washington (15)		
31	10¢ grn., type I, July 27	5,750.00	525.00
32	10¢ grn., type II, July 27	2,000.00	165.00
33	10¢ grn., type III, July 27	2,000.00	165.00
	"Curl" in forehead or in left "X"		235.00
34	10¢ grn., type IV, July 27	*17,500.00*	1,600.00
35	10¢ green, type V, 1859	200.00	50.00
	"Curl" in "E" or "T" of "CENTS"	250.00	70.00
	Small "curl" in forehead	235.00	60.00
36	12¢ blk. Washington (17), plate I, July 30	375.00	85.00
	Triple transfer	500.00	—
36b	12¢ black, plate III, 1859	350.00	110.00
	Plate I-Outer frame lines complete.		
37	24¢ Washington, 1860	600.00	235.00
a	24¢ gray	600.00	235.00
b	24¢ red lilac	1,000.00	
38	30¢ Franklin, Aug. 8, 1860	675.00	300.00
	Recut at bottom	825.00	400.00
39	90¢ Washington, 1860	1,000.00	*3,500.00*
	Double transfer at top or bottom	1,150.00	—
	90¢ Same, with pen cancel		1,000.00
	Note: Beware of forged cancellations of #39. Genuine cancellations are rare.		
	Issues of 1875, Government Reprints, White Paper, Without Gum, Perf. 12		
40	1¢ bright blue Franklin (5)	*500.00*	
41	3¢ scrlt. Washington (11)	*2,250.00*	
42	5¢ orange brown Jefferson (30)	*1,000.00*	
43	10¢ blue green Washington (14)	*2,000.00*	
44	12¢ greenish black Washington (17)	*2,250.00*	
45	24¢ blackish violet Washington (37)	*2,250.00*	
46	30¢ yellow orange Franklin (38)	*2,250.00*	
47	90¢ deep blue Washington (39)	*3,500.00*	
48-54	not assigned		

	Issues of 1861, Thin, Semi-Transparent Paper, Perf.12	Un	U
55	1¢ Franklin	*20,000.00*	
56	3¢ Washington	500.00	
57	5¢ Jefferson	*14,000.00*	
58	10¢ Washington	*6,000.00*	
59	12¢ Washington	*40,000.00*	
60	24¢ Washington	*6,500.00*	
61	30¢ Franklin	*17,500.00*	
62	90¢ Washington	*22,500.00*	
62B	10¢ dark green Washington (58), Sept. 17	*6,000.00*	450.00
	Issues of 1861-62		
63	1¢ blue Franklin (55)	140.00	15.00
a	1¢ ultramarine	250.00	40.00
b	1¢ dark blue	190.00	25.00
	Double transfer	—	22.50
	Dot in "U"	150.00	17.50
c	Laid paper	—	—
e	Printed on both sides	—	*2,500.00*
64	3¢ pink Washington (56)	4,500.00	300.00
a	3¢ pigeon blood pink	—	*1,350.00*
b	3¢ rose pink	300.00	45.00
65	3¢ rose Washington (56)	70.00	1.00
b	Laid paper	—	—
	Double impression		*1,200.00*
	Cracked plate	—	—
f	Double impression		*1,200.00*
66	3¢ lake Washington (56)	1,650.00	
	Double transfer	*2,000.00*	
67	5¢ buff Jefferson (57)	5,750.00	400.00
68	10¢ yellow green Washington (58)	275.00	30.00
	10¢ deep yellow green on thin paper	350.00	40.00
a	10¢ dark green	290.00	31.00
	Double transfer	325.00	40.00
69	12¢ blk. Washington (59)	550.00	67.50
	12¢ intense black	575.00	60.00
	Double transfer of top or bottom frame line	575.00	60.00
	Double transfer of top and bottom frame lines	600.00	70.00
70	24¢ red lilac Washington (60)	650.00	80.00
a	24¢ brown lilac	550.00	67.50
b	24¢ steel blue	4,000.00	275.00
c	24¢ violet	4,500.00	550.00
d	24¢ grayish lilac	1,400.00	275.00
	Scratch under "A" of "POSTAGE"		*95.00*
71	30¢ orange Franklin (61)	525.00	70.00
72	90¢ bl. Washington (62)	1,450.00	250.00
b	90¢ dark blue	1,600.00	275.00

	Issues of 1861-66	Un	U
73	2¢ Andrew Jackson	120.00	22.50
	2¢ intense black	130.00	27.50
	Double transfer	135.00	25.00
	Major double transfer of top left corner and "POSTAGE"		*6,000.00*
	Cracked plate	—	—
74	3¢ scarlet Washington (56)	*5,500.00*	
75	5¢ red brown Jefferson (57)	1,450.00	225.00
76	5¢ brown Jefferson (57)	375.00	57.50
a	5¢ dark brown	425.00	70.00
	Double transfer of top or bottom frame line	425.00	70.00
77	15¢ Abraham Lincoln	575.00	67.50
	Double transfer	600.00	75.00
78	24¢ lilac Washington (60)	300.00	50.00
c	24¢ blackish violet	*10,000.00*	*600.00*
	Scratch under "A" of "POSTAGE"	*500.00*	*100.00*
	#74 was not regularly issued.		

Grills on U.S. Stamps

Between 1867 and 1870, postage stamps were embossed with pyramid-shaped grills that absorbed cancellation ink to prevent re-use of canceled stamps.

	Issues of 1867, With Grills	Un	U
	Grills A, B, C: Points Up		
	A. Grill Covers Entire Stamp		
79	3¢ rose Washington (56)	2,000.00	400.00
	Printed on both sides		—
80	5¢ brown Jefferson (57)	*40,000.00*	—
a	5¢ dark brown		*37,500.00*
81	30¢ orange Franklin (61)		*32,500.00*
	B. Grill about 18 x 15mm		
82	3¢ rose Washington (56)		*45,000.00*
	C. Grill about 13 x 16mm		
83	3¢ rose Washington (56)	2,000.00	400.00
	Double grill	*3,750.00*	1,500.00
	Grills, D, Z, E, F: Points Down		
	D. Grill about 12 x 14mm		
84	2¢ black Jackson (73)	4,500.00	1,100.00
85	3¢ rose Washington (56)	1,750.00	450.00
	Split grill		500.00
	Z. Grill about 11 x 14mm		
85A	1¢ blue Franklin (55)		*450,000.00*
85B	2¢ black Jackson (73)	1,500.00	350.00
	Double transfer	1,600.00	375.00
85C	3¢ rose Washington (56)	4,500.00	950.00
	Double grill	*5,500.00*	
85D	10¢ grn. Washington (58)	—	*25,000.00*
85E	12¢ blk. Washington (59)	2,000.00	575.00
	Double transfer of top frame line		625.00
85F	15¢ black Lincoln (77)		—

55

56

57

58

59

60

61

62

73

77

	1867 continued, Perf. 12	Un	U
	Grill about 11 x 13mm		
8	¢ blue Franklin (55)	900.00	250.00
	Double grill	—	375.00
	Split grill	450.00	80.00
87	2¢ black Jackson (73)	400.00	70.00
	2¢ intense black	425.00	75.00
	Double grill	—	—
	Double transfer	425.00	75.00
88	3¢ rose Washington (56)	300.00	10.00
a	3¢ lake red	350.00	12.50
	Double grill	—	—
	Very thin paper	325.00	11.00
89	10¢ grn. Washington (68)	1,650.00	175.00
	Double grill	2,000.00	300.00
90	12¢ blk. Washington (69)	1,900.00	190.00
	Double transfer of top or bottom frame line	1,850.00	210.00
91	15¢ black Lincoln (77)	3,750.00	450.00
	Double grill	—	700.00
	Grill about 9 x 13mm		
92	1¢ blue Franklin (55)	450.00	100.00
	Double transfer	425.00	120.00
	Double grill	—	200.00
93	2¢ black Jackson (73)	150.00	25.00
	Double grill	—	100.00
	Very thin paper	160.00	30.00
94	3¢ red Washington (56)	110.00	2.50
b	Imperf. pair	*650.00*	
c	Vertical pair, imperf. horizontally	*1,000.00*	
d	Printed on both sides	*950.00*	
	Double grill	—	—
	End roller grill		200.00
	Quadruple split grill	250.00	75.00

		Un	U
95	5¢ brown Jefferson (57)	1,050.00	225.00
a	5¢ dark brown	1,100.00	250.00
95a	Double transfer of top frame line	—	—
	Double grill	—	—
96	10¢ yellow green Washington (58)	800.00	110.00
	Double transfer	—	—
	Quadruple split grill		350.00
97	12¢ blk. Washington (59)	800.00	20.00
	Double transfer of top or bottom frame line	850.00	130.00
	Triple grill		—
98	15¢ black Lincoln (77)	800.00	35.00
	Double transfer of upper right corner	—	—
	Double grill	—	250.00
	Quadruple split grill	1,600.00	350.00
99	24¢ gray lilac Washington (60)	1,650.00	400.00
100	30¢ orange Franklin (61)	1,900.00	350.00
	Double grill	2,250.00	700.00
101	90¢ bl. Washington (62)	4,750.00	750.00
	Double grill	*7,000*	
	Issues of 1875, Reissue of 1861-66 Issue, Without Grill		
102	1¢ blue Franklin (55)	*500.00*	*800.00*
103	2¢ black Jackson (73)	*2,500.00*	*,000.00*
104	3¢ brown red Washington (56)	*3,250.00*	*4,250.00*
105	5¢ brown Jefferson (57)	*1,800.00*	*2,250.00*
106	10¢ grn. Washington (58)	*2,100.00*	*3,750.00*
107	12¢ blk. Washington (59)	*3,000.00*	*,500.00*
108	15¢ black Lincoln (77)	*3,000.00*	*,750.00*
109	24¢ deep violet Washington (60)	*4,000.00*	*6,000.00*
110	30¢ brownish orange Franklin (61)	*4,500.00*	*6,000.00*
111	90¢ bl. Washington (62)	*5,500.00*	*20,000.00*

1869-1880

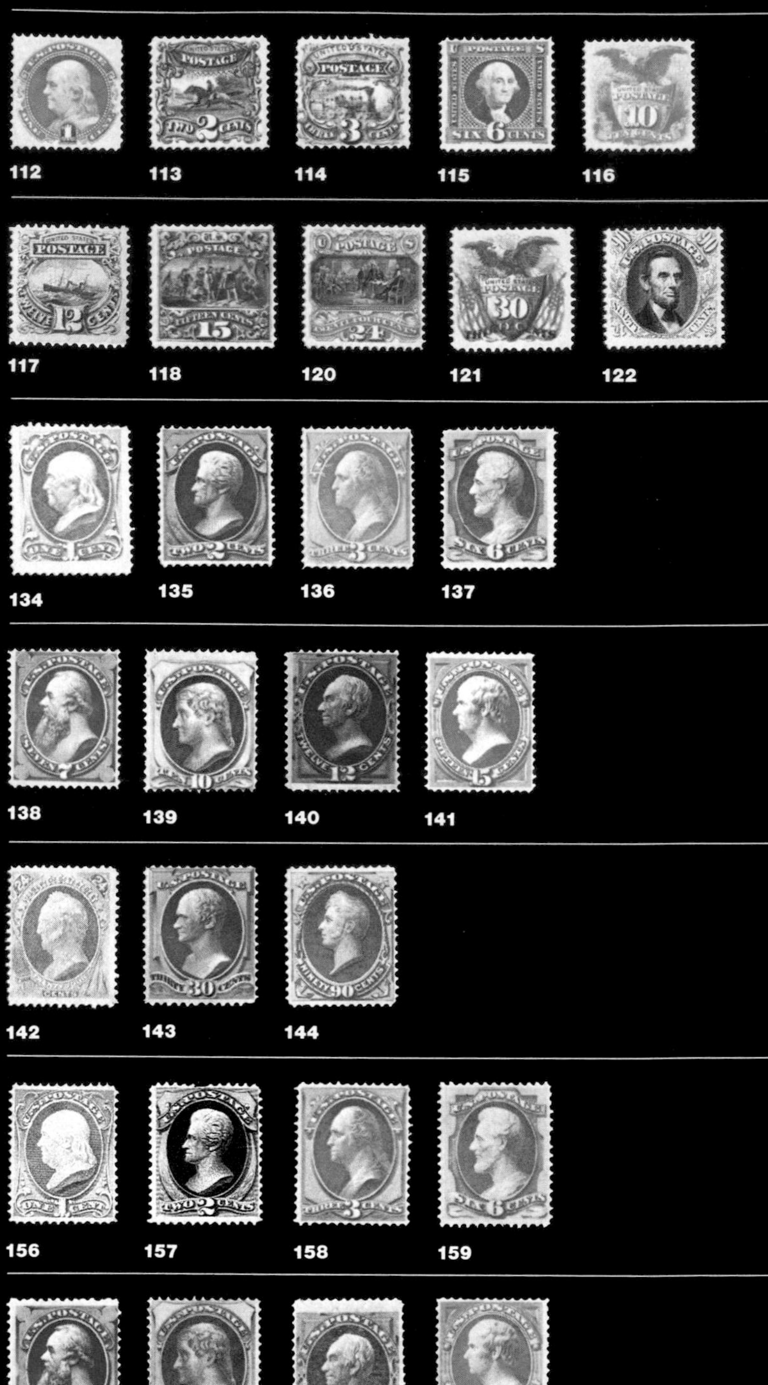

112 113 114 115 116

117 118 120 121 122

134 135 136 137

138 139 140 141

142 143 144

156 157 158 159

160 161 162 163

Issues of 1869, With Grill Measuring 9½ x 9mm, Perf. 12

		Un	U
112	1¢ Franklin, Mar. 27	225.00	60.00
b	Without grill, original gum	*600.00*	
	Double grill	450.00	150.00
113	2¢ Post Rider, Mar. 27	190.00	25.00
	Split grill	210.00	35.00
	Double transfer		30.00
114	3¢ Locomotive, Mar. 27	150.00	5.50
a	Without grill, original gum	*600.00*	
d	Double impression		—
	Triple grill	—	—
	Sextuple grill	*2,000.00*	
	Gray paper	—	—
115	6¢ Washington	775.00	100.00
	Quadruple split grill	—	400.00
116	10¢ Shield and Eagle	850.00	95.00
	End roller grill	—	—
117	12¢ S.S. Adriatic, Apr. 5	750.00	90.00
	Split grill	800.00	100.00
118	15¢ Columbus Landing, type I, Apr. 2	1,900.00	300.00
119	15¢ type II (118)	950.00	150.00
b	Center inverted	*145,000.00*	*17,500.00*
	Center double, one inverted	—	
120	24¢ Declaration of Independence, Apr. 7	2,000.00	450.00
b	Center inverted	*125,000.00*	*16,500.00*
121	30¢ Shield, Eagle and Flags, May 15	2,250.00	225.00
	Double grill	—	500.00
b	Flags inverted	*120,000.00*	*45,000.00*
122	90¢ Lincoln	6,000.00	1,000.00
	Split grill	—	—

Issues of 1875, Reissue of 1869 Issue, Without Grill, Hard, White Paper

		Un	U
123	1¢ buff (112)	325.00	225.00
124	2¢ brown (113)	375.00	325.00
125	3¢ blue (114)	3,000.00	*10,000.00*
126	6¢ blue (115)	850.00	550.00
127	10¢ yellow (116)	1,400.00	1,200.00
128	12¢ green (117)	1,500.00	1,200.00
129	15¢ brown and blue, type III (118)	1,300.00	550.00
a	Imperf. horizontally	1,600.00	—
130	24¢ grn. & violet (120)	1,250.00	550.00
131	30¢ bl. & carmine (121)	1,750.00	1,000.00
132	90¢ car. & black (122)	5,500.00	*6,000.00*

Issues of 1880, Reissue of 1869 Issue, Soft, Porous Paper

		Un	U
133	1¢ buff (112)	200.00	135.00
a	1¢ brown orange, issued without gum	175.00	120.00

Issues of 1870-71, With Grill, White Wove Paper, No Secret Marks

		Un	U
134	1¢ Franklin, April 1870	575.00	60.00
	End roller grill		300.00
135	2¢ Jackson, April 1870	425.00	37.50
136	3¢ Washington	325.00	10.00
b	Imperf. pair	*1,200.00*	
137	6¢ Lincoln, April 1870	1,850.00	250.00
	Double grill	—	450.00
138	7¢ Edwin M. Stanton	1,250.00	225.00
139	10¢ Jefferson	1,600.00	400.00
140	12¢ Henry Clay	*13,000.00*	1,500.00
141	15¢ Daniel Webster	2,100.00	700.00
142	24¢ Gen. Winfield Scott	—	*9,500.00*
143	30¢ Alexander Hamilton	5,000.00	825.00
144	90¢ Commodore Perry	6,750.00	750.00
	Split grill		800.00

Without Grill, White Wove Paper, No Secret Marks

		Un	U
145	1¢ ultra. Franklin (134)	190.00	7.00
146	2¢ red brn. Jackson (135)	70.00	5.00
147	3¢ grn. Washington (136)	140.00	.50
148	6¢ carmine Lincoln (137)	250.00	12.00
	6¢ violet carmine	265.00	15.00
149	7¢ verm. Stanton (138)	365.00	50.00
150	10¢ brown Jefferson (139)	250.00	12.00
151	12¢ dull violet Clay (140)	575.00	62.50
152	15¢ brt. or. Webster (141)	550.00	60.00
153	24¢ purple Scott (142)	675.00	80.00
154	30¢ black Hamilton (143)	1,150.00	95.00
155	90¢ carmine Perry (144)	1,500.00	175.00

Issues of 1873, Without Grill, White Wove Paper, Thin to Thick, Secret Marks

		Un	U
156	1¢ Franklin	62.50	1.75
	Paper with silk fibers	—	15.00
f	Imperf. pair	—	*500.00*
157	2¢ Jackson	170.00	7.00
	Double paper	250.00	20.00
c	With grill	*850.00*	*600.00*
158	3¢ Washington	52.50	.15
	3¢ olive green	67.50	2.50
	Cracked plate	—	27.50
159	6¢ Lincoln	225.00	9.50
b	With grill	*650.00*	
160	7¢ Stanton	450.00	55.00
	Ribbed paper	—	70.00
161	10¢ Jefferson	250.00	10.00
162	12¢ Clay	675.00	65.00
163	15¢ Webster	650.00	60.00
a	With grill	*3,000.00*	
164	not assigned		
165	30¢ Hamilton	725.00	60.00
166	90¢ Perry	1,500.00	185.00

	Issues of 1875, Special Printing, Hard, White Wove Paper, Without Gum, Secret Marks, Perf. 12	Un	U
	Although perforated, these stamps were usually cut apart with scissors. As a result, the perforations are often much mutilated and the design is frequently damaged.		
167	1¢ ultra. Franklin (156)	*8,000.00*	—
168	2¢ dark brown Jackson (157)	*3,500.00*	—
169	3¢ blue green Washington (158)	*9,500.00*	—
170	6¢ dull rose Lincoln (159)	*8,500.00*	—
171	7¢ reddish vermilion Stanton (160)	*2,250.00*	—
172	10¢ pale brown Jefferson (161)	*8,250.00*	—
173	12¢ dark vio. Clay (162)	*3,000.00*	—
174	15¢ bright orange Webster (163)	*8,250.00*	—
175	24¢ dull pur. Scott (142)	*1,850.00*	—
176	30¢ greenish black Hamilton (143)	*7,500.00*	—
177	90¢ vio. car. Perry (144)	*7,500.00*	—
	Yellowish Wove Paper		
178	2¢ verm. Jackson (157)	180.00	5.00
c	With grill	*300.00*	
179	5¢ Zachary Taylor, June	200.00	9.00
	Cracked plate	—	*100.00*
	Double paper	*235.00*	
c	With grill	350.00	
	Paper with silk fibers	—	15.00
	Special Printing, Hard, White Wove Paper, Without Gum		
180	2¢ carmine vermilion Jackson (157)	*17,500.00*	—
181	5¢ br. bl. Taylor (179)	*32,500.00*	—
	Issues of 1879, Soft, Porous Paper, Thin to Thick		
182	1¢ dark ultramarine Franklin (156)	140.00	1.25
183	2¢ verm. Jackson (157)	65.00	1.25
a	Double impression	—	*500.00*
184	3¢ grn. Washington (158)	50.00	.15
	Double transfer	—	4.00
	Short transfer	—	5.00
185	5¢ blue Taylor (179)	260.00	7.50
186	6¢ pink Lincoln (159)	500.00	12.00
187	10¢ brown Jefferson (139) (no secret mark)	850.00	14.00
188	10¢ brown Jefferson (161) (with secret mark)	525.00	15.00
	10¢ black brown	575.00	22.50
	Double transfer		30.00
189	15¢ red or. Webster (163)	190.00	14.00
190	30¢ full blk. Hamilton (143)	525.00	32.50
191	90¢ carmine Perry (144)	1,150.00	150.00

	Issues of 1880, Special Printing, Soft, Porous Paper, Without Gum	Un	U
192	1¢ dark ultramarine Franklin (156)	*10,000.00*	—
193	2¢ black brown Jackson (157)	*6,500.00*	—
194	3¢ blue green Washington (158)	*15,000.00*	—
195	6¢ dull rose Lincoln (159)	*11,000.00*	—
196	7¢ scarlet vermilion Stanton (160)	*2,250.00*	—
197	10¢ deep brown Jefferson (161)	*10,000.00*	—
198	12¢ blackish purple Clay (162)	*4,500.00*	—
199	15¢ or. Webster (163)	*9,750.00*	—
200	24¢ dk. vio. Scott (142)	*3,500.00*	—
201	30¢ greenish black Hamilton (143)	*8,500.00*	—
202	90¢ dull carmine Perry (144)	*9,000.00*	—
203	2¢ scarlet vermilion Jackson (157)	*18,000.00*	—
204	5¢ dp. bl. Taylor (179)	*30,000.00*	—
	Issues of 1882		
205	5¢ Garfield, Apr. 10	120.00	4.00
	Special Printing, Soft, Porous Paper, Without Gum		
205C	5¢ gray brown Garfield (205)	*20,000.00*	—
	Issues of 1881-82, Designs of 1873 Re-engraved		
206	1¢ Franklin, Aug. 1881	37.50	.40
	Double transfer	52.50	4.00
207	3¢ Washington, July 16, 1881	45.00	.15
	Double transfer	—	7.50
	Cracked plate	—	
208	6¢ Lincoln, June 1882	250.00	45.00
a	6¢ brown red	225.00	55.00
209	10¢ Jefferson, Apr. 1882	85.00	2.50
	10¢ pur. or olive brown	95.00	2.75
b	10¢ black brown	110.00	6.75
	Issues of 1883		
210	2¢ Washington, Oct. 1	35.00	.15
	Double transfer	37.50	1.25
211	4¢ Jackson, Oct. 1	155.00	7.50
	Cracked plate	—	
	Special Printing, Soft, Porous Paper		
211B	2¢ pale red brown Washington (210)	600.00	—
c	Horizontal pair, imperf. between	*2,750.00*	
211D	4¢ deep blue green Jackson (211) no gum	*15,000.00*	—

179  205  206 207 208

209  210  211 212

219  220  221  222 223 224

225  226  227 228 229

	Issues of 1887, Perf. 12	Un	U
212	1¢ Franklin, June	65.00	.65
	Double transfer		—
213	2¢ green Washington (210), Sept. 10	25.00	.15
b	Printed on both sides		—
	Double transfer	—	3.00
214	3¢ vermilion Washington (207), Oct. 3	50.00	37.50
	Issues of 1888		
215	4¢ carmine Jackson (211), Nov.	160.00	11.00
216	5¢ indigo Garfield (205), Feb.	160.00	6.50
217	30¢ orange brown Hamilton (165), Jan.	360.00	75.00
218	90¢ pur. Perry (166), Feb.	700.00	130.00
	Issues of 1890-93		
219	1¢ Franklin, Feb. 22, 1890	18.50	.15
	Double transfer	—	—
219D	2¢ lake Washington (220), Feb. 22, 1890	150.00	.45
	Double transfer	—	—

		Un	U
220	2¢ Washington, 1890	15.00	.15
a	Cap on left "2"	35.00	1.00
c	Cap on both "2's"	110.00	8.00
	Double transfer	—	3.00
221	3¢ Jackson, Feb. 22, 1890	50.00	4.50
222	4¢ Lincoln, June 2, 1890	50.00	1.50
	Double transfer	65.00	—
223	5¢ Grant, June 2, 1890	50.00	1.50
	Double transfer	65.00	1.75
224	6¢ Garfield, Feb. 22, 1890	55.00	15.00
225	8¢ Sherman, Mar. 21, 1893	40.00	8.50
226	10¢ Webster, Feb. 22, 1890	95.00	1.75
	Double transfer	—	—
227	15¢ Clay, Feb. 22, 1890	135.00	15.00
	Double transfer	—	—
	Triple transfer		—
228	30¢ Jefferson, Feb. 22, 1890	225.00	20.00
	Double transfer	—	—
229	90¢ Perry, Feb. 22, 1890	325.00	95.00
	Short transfer at bottom	—	—

1893

230

231

232

233

234

235

236

237

238

239

240

241

242

243

244

245

	1893 continued	Un	U	PB	#	FDC	Q
	Columbian Exposition Issue, Printed by the American Bank Note Co., Jan. 2 (8¢ March), Perf. 12						
230	1¢ Columbus Sights Land	18.50	.25	275.00	(6)	*3,500.00*	449,195,550
	Double transfer	24.00	.50				
	Cracked plate	80.00					
231	2¢ Landing of Columbus	17.00	.15	225.00	(6)	*2,600.00*	1,464,588,750
	Double transfer	22.50	.25				
	Triple transfer	57.50	—				
	Quadruple transfer	85.00					
	Broken hat on third figure left of Columbus	50.00	.20				
	Broken frame line	19.00	.15				
	Recut frame lines	19.00	—				
	Cracked plate	80.00	—				
232	3¢ The Santa Maria	42.50	12.50	500.00	(6)	*6,000.00*	11,501,250
	Double transfer	57.50	—				
233	4¢ ultramarine Fleet of Columbus	62.50	5.50	750.00	(6)	*6000.00*	19,181,550
a	4¢ blue (error)	*8,500.00*	*3,250.00*	*42,500.00*	(4)		
	Double transfer	87.50	—				
234	5¢ Columbus Seeking Aid	67.50	6.50	1,350.00	(6)	*6,250.00*	35,248,250
	Double transfer	120.00	—				
235	6¢ Columbus at Barcelona	62.50	18.00	825.00	(6)	*6,750.00*	4,707,550
a	6¢ red violet	62.50	18.00				
	Double transfer	80.00	25.00				
236	8¢ Columbus Restored to Favor	50.00	8.00	510.00	(6)		10,656,550
	Double transfer	58.50	—				
237	10¢ Columbus Presenting Indians	100.00	5.50	2,250.00	(6)	*7,500.00*	16,516,950
	Double transfer	135.00	10.00				
	Triple transfer	—					
238	15¢ Columbus Announcing His Discovery	170.00	50.00	*3,600.00*	(6)		1,576,950
	Double transfer	—	—				
239	30¢ Columbus at La Rabida	225.00	70.00	*5,400.00*	(6)		617,250
240	50¢ Recall of Columbus	350.00	120.00	*8,500.00*	(6)		243,750
	Double transfer	—	—				
	Triple transfer	—	—				
241	$1 Isabella Pledging Her Jewels	1,150.00	525.00	*20,000.00*	(6)		55,050
	Double transfer	—	—				
242	$2 Columbus in Chains	1,250.00	450.00	*20,000.00*	(6)	*18,000.00*	45,550
243	$3 Columbus Describing His Third Voyage	2,100.00	800.00	*34,000.00*	(6)		27,650
a	$3 olive green	2,100.00	800.00				
244	$4 Isabella and Columbus	2,500.00	1,000.00	*72,500.00*	(6)		26,350
a	$4 rose carmine	2,500.00	1,000.00				
245	$5 Portrait of Columbus	2,850.00	1,200.00	*82,500.00*	(6)		27,350

Bureau Issues Starting in 1894, the Bureau of Engraving and Printing in Washington has produced all U.S. postage stamps except #909-921, 1335, 1355, 1410-1418, 1789, 1804, 1825, 1833, 2023, 2038, 2065-66, 2073, 2080, 2087, 2091, 2093, 2102, 2110, 2137-41, 2153, 2159-64, 2167, 2203-04, 2210-11, 2220-23, 2240-43, 2250, 2283, 2337-39, 2343-44, 2347, 2369, 2371-75, 2377, 2386-89, 2395-98, 2403-04, 2411, 2416-18, 2420, 2426, 2439-41, 2445-49, 2496-2500, 2506-7, 2512-13, 2515, C121 and C127.

Issues of 1894, Perf. 12, Unwmkd.

		Un	U	PB	#
246	1¢ Franklin, Oct.	15.00	2.00	200.00	(6)
	Double transfer	20.00	3.00		
247	1¢ blue Franklin (246)	37.50	.85	400.00	(6)
	Double transfer	—	2.50		
248	2¢ pink Washington, type I, Oct.	12.50	1.50	145.00	(6)
	Double transfer	—	—		
249	2¢ carmine lake, type I (248)	75.00	.95	850.00	(6)
	Double transfer	—	1.50		
250	2¢ carmine, type I (248)	14.00	.25	200.00	(6)
a	Vertical pair, imperf. horizontally	*1,500.00*			
b	Horizontal pair, imperf. between	*1,500.00*			
	Double transfer	—	1.10		
251	2¢ carmine, type II (248)	125.00	1.50	1,450.00	(6)
252	2¢ carmine, type III (248)	70.00	2.00	950.00	(6)
b	Horizontal pair, imperf. between	*1,500.00*			
253	3¢ Jackson, Sept.	50.00	4.25	700.00	(6)
254	4¢ Lincoln, Sept.	60.00	1.75	850.00	(6)
255	5¢ Grant, Sept.	47.50	2.50	575.00	(6)
c	Vertical pair, imperf. vertically	*1,000.00*			
	Worn plate, diagonal lines missing in oval background	57.00	3.00		
256	6¢ Garfield, July	90.00	12.00	1,500.00	(6)
a	Vertical pair, imperf. horizontally	*850.00*			
257	8¢ Sherman, Mar.	80.00	8.00	800.00	(6)
258	10¢ Webster, Sept.	115.00	5.00	1,600.00	(6)
	Double transfer	150.00	6.00		
259	15¢ Clay, Oct.	185.00	30.00	2,750.00	(6)
260	50¢ Jefferson, Nov.	225.00	50.00	4,250.00	(6)
261	$1 Perry, type I, Nov.	500.00	160.00	*11,000.00*	(6)
261A	$1 black Perry, type II (261), Nov.	1,200.00	325.00	*18,500.00*	(6)
262	$2 James Madison, Dec.	1,500.00	400.00	*26,000.00*	(6)
263	$5 John Marshall, Dec.	2,000.00	650.00	*10,000.00*	(3)
	Issues of 1895, Wmkd. (191)				
264	1¢ blue Franklin (246), Apr.	3.50	.15	130.00	(6)
265	2¢ carmine Washington, type I (248), May 1	18.00	.40	225.00	(6)
	Double transfer	25.00	3.00		
266	2¢ carmine, type II (248)	15.00	1.75	200.00	(6)
267	2¢ carmine, type III (248)	3.00	.15	90.00	(6)
	Triple transfer	—			
	Triangle at right without shading	17.50	5.00		

246

248

253

254

255

256

257

258

259

260

261

262

263

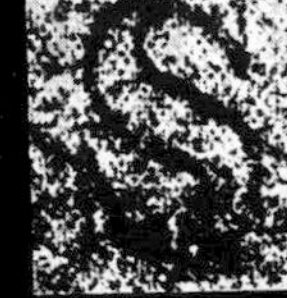
Watermark 191

	1895 continued, Perf. 12	Un	U	PB	#
268	3¢ purple Jackson (253), Oct.	22.50	.65	375.00	(6)
	Double transfer	32.50	2.25		
269	4¢ dark brown Lincoln (254), June	24.00	.75	400.00	(6)
270	5¢ chocolate Grant (255), June 11	22.50	1.20	400.00	(6)
	Worn plate, diagonal lines missing in oval background	25.00	1.60		
271	6¢ dull brown Garfield (256), Aug.	42.50	2.50	1,100.00	(6)
a	Wmkd. USIR	*2,250.00*	350.00		
272	8¢ violet brown Sherman (257), July	30.00	.65	475.00	(6)
a	Wmkd. USIR	1,100.00	110.00		
	Double transfer	45.00	2.00		
273	10¢ dark green Webster (258), June	40.00	.80	800.00	(6)
274	15¢ dark blue Clay (259), Sept.	110.00	5.50	2,100.00	(6)
275	50¢ orange Jefferson (260), Nov.	160.00	14.00	4,000.00	(6)
a	50¢ red orange	170.00	16.00		
276	$1 black Perry, type I (261), Aug.	375.00	45.00	*7,500.00*	(6)
276A	$1 black Perry, type II (261)	825.00	92.50	*15,000.00*	(6)
277	$2 bright blue Madison (262), Aug.	600.00	200.00	*14,000.00*	(6)
a	$2 dark blue	650.00	210.00		
278	$5 dark green Marshall (263), Aug.	1,350.00	275.00	*50,000.00*	(6)

1898-1901

285

286

287

288

289

290

291

292

293

294

295

296

297

298

299

	Issues of 1898-1900, Perf. 12, Wmkd. (191) (279Be issued in 1900, rest in 1898)	Un	U	PB	#	FDC	Q
279	1¢ dp. grn. Franklin (246), Jan.	6.00	.15	110.00	(6)		
	Double transfer	9.00	.75				
279B	2¢ red Washington, type III (248)	5.50	.15	120.00	(6)		
c	2¢ rose carmine, type III	120.00	20.00	1,500.00	(6)		
d	2¢ orange red, type III	6.50	.15	120.00	(6)		
e	Booklet pane of 6, Apr. 16, 1900	350.00	*200.00*				
f	2¢ deep red, type III	12.50	.75				
280	4¢ rose brn. Lincoln (254), Oct.	20.00	.45	400.00	(6)		
a	4¢ lilac brown	20.00	.45				
b	4¢ orange brown	20.00	.45				
	Extra frame line at top	32.50	3.50				
281	5¢ dark blue Grant (255), Mar.	22.50	.40	425.00	(6)		
	Double transfer	32.50	1.75				
	Worn plate, diagonal lines missing in oval background	26.00	.55				
282	6¢ lake Garfield (256), Dec.	32.50	1.40	650.00	(6)		
	Double transfer	42.50	2.50				
a	6¢ purplish lake	35.00	1.65	750.00	(6)		
282C	10¢ brown Webster (258), type I, Nov.	100.00	1.20	1,600.00	(6)		
	Double transfer	125.00	3.00				
283	10¢ orange brown Webster (258), type II	60.00	1.00	950.00	(6)		
284	15¢ olive grn. Clay (259), Nov.	85.00	4.50	1,600.00	(6)		
	Issues of 1898, Trans-Mississippi Exposition Issue, June 17						
285	1¢ Marquette on the Mississippi	20.00	3.75	250.00	(6)	*4,500.00*	70,993,400
	Double transfer	30.00	5.25				
286	2¢ Farming in the West	17.50	1.00	210.00	(6)	*4,000.00*	159,720,800
	Double transfer	27.50	1.75				
	Worn plate	20.00	1.25				
287	4¢ Indian Hunting Buffalo	110.00	16.00	1,150.00	(6)		4,924,500
288	5¢ John Charles Fremont on the Rocky Mountains	80.00	14.00	1,000.00	(6)	*5,000.00*	7,694,180
289	8¢ Troops Guarding Wagon Train	120.00	30.00	1,900.00	(6)	*7,500.00*	2,927,200
a	Vertical pair, imperf. horizontally	*13,500.00*					
290	10¢ Hardships of Emigration	125.00	17.50	2,500.00	(6)		4,629,760
291	50¢ Western Mining Prospector	400.00	150.00	*13,000.00*	(6)	*9,000.00*	530,400
292	$1 Western Cattle in Storm	1,150.00	400.00	*37,500.00*	(6)	*12,500.00*	56,900
293	$2 Mississippi River Bridge, St. Louis	1,800.00	700.00	*75,000.00*	(6)		56,200
	Issues of 1901, Pan-American Exposition Issue, May 1						
294	1¢ Great Lakes Steamer	13.50	2.50	210.00	(6)	*3,750.00*	91,401,500
a	Center inverted	*9,000.00*	*4,500.00*	*39,000.00*	(3)		
295	2¢ An Early Locomotive	13.50	.75	210.00	(6)	*3,250.00*	209,759,700
a	Center inverted	*35,000.00*	*13,500.00*				
296	4¢ Closed Coach Automobile	70.00	12.50	1,900.00	(6)	*4,250.00*	5,737,100
a	Center inverted	*10,000.00*		*52,500.00*	(4)		
297	5¢ Bridge at Niagara Falls	82.50	11.00	2,250.00	(6)	*4,500.00*	7,201,300
298	8¢ Sault Ste. Marie Canal Locks	95.00	45.00	3,700.00	(6)		4,921,700
299	10¢ American Line Steamship	150.00	20.00	5,750.00	(6)		5,043,700

	Issues of 1902-07, Perf. 12, Wmkd. (191) (all issued 1903 except #300b, 306, 308)					
		Un	U	PB/LP	#	FDC
300	1¢ Franklin, Feb.	6.50	.15	125.00	(6)	
b	Booklet pane of 6, Mar. 6, 1907	*400.00*	*250.00*			
	Double transfer	10.00	1.00			
	Worn plate	7.00	.25			
301	2¢ Washington, Jan. 17	7.50	.15	125.00	(6)	*2,750.00*
c	Booklet pane of 6, Jan. 24	*400.00*	*250.00*			
	Double transfer	12.50	.90			
	Cracked plate	—				
302	3¢ Jackson, Feb.	30.00	2.00	535.00	(6)	
	Cracked plate	—				
303	4¢ Grant, Feb.	30.00	.60	535.00	(6)	
	Double transfer	47.50	2.00			
304	5¢ Lincoln, Jan.	35.00	.65	600.00	(6)	
305	6¢ Garfield, Feb.	37.50	1.50	625.00	(6)	
	6¢ brownish lake	45.00	1.50			
	Double transfer	57.50	2.00			
306	8¢ M. Washington, Dec. 1902	25.00	1.25	450.00	(6)	
	8¢ lavender	32.50	1.50			
307	10¢ Webster, Feb.	30.00	.70	700.00	(6)	
308	13¢ B. Harrison, Nov. 18, 1902	25.00	5.00	425.00	(6)	
309	15¢ Clay, May 27	87.50	3.75	2,000.00	(6)	
	Double transfer	135.00	7.50			
310	50¢ Jefferson, Mar. 23	285.00	17.50	4,750.00	(6)	
311	$1 David G. Farragut, June 5	450.00	35.00	*10,000.00*	(6)	
312	$2 Madison, June 5	600.00	125.00	*17,500.00*	(6)	
313	$5 Marshall, June 5	1,500.00	450.00	*45,000.00*	(6)	
	For listings of #312 and 313 with Perf. 10, see #479 and 480.					
	Issues of 1906-08, Imperf. (All issued 1908 except #314)					
314	1¢ blue green Franklin (300), Oct. 2, 1906	16.00	13.00	150.00	(6)	
314A	4¢ brown Grant (303), Apr.	*18,500.00*	*10,000.00*	—		
315	5¢ blue Lincoln (304), May 12	375.00	*250.00*	3,250.00	(6)	
	#314A was issued imperforate, but all copies were privately perforated at the sides.					
	Coil Stamps, Perf. 12 Horizontally					
316	1¢ blue green pair Franklin (300), Feb. 18	*50,000.00*	—	*100,000.00*	(2)	
317	5¢ blue pair Lincoln (304), Feb. 24	*5,000.00*	—	*8,000.00*	(2)	
	Coil Stamps, Perf. 12 Vertically					
318	1¢ blue green pair Franklin (300), July 31	*4,750.00*	—	*6,750.00*	(2)	
	Issue of 1903, Perf. 12					
319	2¢ Washington, Nov. 12	4.00	.15	67.50	(6)	
a	2¢ lake, die I	—	—			
b	2¢ carmine rose, die I	6.00	.20	125.00	(6)	
c	2¢ scarlet, die I	4.00	.15	60.00	(6)	
d	Vertical pair, imperf. horizontally	*1,750.00*				
f	2¢ lake, die II	4.50	.15			
g	Booklet pane of 6, carm. (I)	90.00	*30.00*			
h	Booklet pane of 6, carm. (II)	125.00				
i	2¢ carmine, die II	17.50	—			
q	Booklet pane of 6, lake (II)	125.00				

300

301

302

303

304

305

306

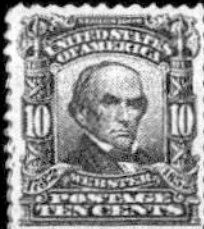
307

308

309

310

311

312

313

319

323

324

325

326

327

		Un	U	PB/LP	#	FDC	Q
	Issues of 1906, Washington (319), Imperf.						
320	2¢ carmine, Oct. 2	17.50	11.00	200.00	(6)		
a	2¢ lake, die II	50.00	35.00	625.00	(6)		
b	2¢ scarlet	16.00	12.00				
	Double transfer	24.00	15.00				
	Issues of 1908, Coil Stamps (319), Perf. 12 Horizontally						
321	2¢ carmine pair, Feb. 18	—	—	—			
	Coil Stamp, Perf. 12 Vertically						
322	2¢ carmine pair, July 31	*6,000.00*	—	*8,000.00*	(2)		
	Issues of 1904, Louisiana Purchase Exposition Issue, Apr. 30, Perf. 12						
323	1¢ Robert R. Livingston	17.50	2.75	200.00	(6)	*3,500.00*	79,779,200
	Diagonal line through left "1"	35.00	10.00				
324	2¢ Thomas Jefferson	15.00	.90	200.00	(6)	*3,250.00*	192,732,400
325	3¢ James Monroe	60.00	22.50	750.00	(6)	*[illegible],250.00*	4,542,600
326	5¢ William McKinley	65.00	14.50	800.00	(6)	*[illegible],000.00*	6,926,700
327	10¢ Map of Louisiana Purchase	115.00	20.00	1,600.00	(6)	*[illegible],500.00*	4,011,200

328

329

330

331

332

333

334

335

336

337

338

339

340

341

342

	Issues of 1907, Perf. 12	Un	U	PB/LP	#	FDC	Q
	Jamestown Exposition Issue, Apr. 26						
328	1¢ Captain John Smith	11.50	1.90	175.00	(6)	*3,750.00*	77,728,794
	Double transfer	15.00	3.00				
329	2¢ Founding of Jamestown	15.00	1.65	250.00	(6)	*5,500.00*	149,497,994
330	5¢ Pocahontas	67.50	15.00	1,600.00	(6)		7,980,594
	Issues of 1908-09, Wmkd. (191)						
331	1¢ Franklin, Dec. 1908	4.50	.15	45.00	(6)		
a	Booklet pane of 6, Dec. 2, 1908	165.00	*35.00*				
	Double transfer	6.75	.60				
332	2¢ Washington, Nov. 1908	4.25	.15	42.50	(6)		
a	Booklet pane of 6, Nov. 16, 1908	100.00	*35.00*				
	Double transfer	9.00	—				
	Cracked plate	—	—				
333	3¢ Washington, type I, Dec. 1908	20.00	1.75	200.00	(6)		
334	4¢ Washington, Dec. 1908	23.50	.55	250.00	(6)		
	Double transfer	40.00	—				
335	5¢ Washington, Dec. 1908	30.00	1.50	345.00	(6)		
336	6¢ Washington, Jan. 1909	32.50	3.50	550.00	(6)		
337	8¢ Washington, Dec. 1908	26.00	1.75	300.00	(6)		
	Double transfer	40.00	—				

	1908-09 continued, Perf. 12	Un	U	PB/LP	#
338	10¢ Washington, Jan. 1909	42.50	1.00	650.00	(6)
a	"China Clay" paper	—			
	Very thin paper	—			
339	13¢ Washington, Jan. 1909	25.00	14.00	300.00	(6)
	Line through "TAG" of "POSTAGE"	47.50	—		
340	15¢ Washington, Jan. 1909	40.00	3.75	400.00	(6)
a	"China Clay" paper	—			
341	50¢ Washington, Jan. 13, 1909	175.00	10.00	*6,000.00*	(6)
342	$1 Washington, Jan. 29, 1909	335.00	50.00	*10,000.00*	(6)
	Imperf.				
343	1¢ green Franklin (331), Dec. 1908	4.50	2.75	45.00	(6)
	Double transfer	11.00	5.50		
344	2¢ carmine Washington (332), Dec. 10, 1908	6.50	2.00	85.00	(6)
	Double transfer	12.00	3.50		
	Double transfer, design of 1¢	*1,250.00*			
	#345-347: Washington (333-335)				
345	3¢ deep violet, type I, Mar. 3, 1909	12.00	10.00	180.00	(6)
	Double transfer	21.00	—		
346	4¢ orange brown, Feb. 25, 1909	21.00	12.00	210.00	(6)
	Double transfer	40.00	—		
347	5¢ blue, Feb. 25, 1909	37.50	27.50	350.00	(6)
	Cracked plate	—			
	Issues of 1908-10, Coil Stamps, Perf. 12 Horizontally				
	#350-351, 354-356: Washington (334-335, 338)				
348	1¢ green Franklin (331), Dec. 29, 1908	21.00	10.00	150.00	(2)
349	2¢ carmine Washington (332), Jan. 1909	37.50	6.00	240.00	(2)
	Double transfer, design of 1¢	—	*1,750.00*		
350	4¢ orange brown, Aug. 15, 1910	80.00	60.00	575.00	(2)
351	5¢ blue, Jan. 1909	90.00	90.00	575.00	(2)
	Issues of 1909, Coil Stamps, Perf. 12 Vertically				
352	1¢ green Franklin (331), Jan.	40.00	25.00	225.00	(2)
	Double transfer	—	—		
353	2¢ carmine Washington (332), Jan. 12	40.00	6.00	225.00	(2)
354	4¢ orange brown, Feb. 23	110.00	45.00	700.00	(2)
355	5¢ blue, Feb. 23	110.00	65.00	725.00	(2)
356	10¢ yellow, Jan. 7	1,500.00	600.00	8,000.00	(2)
	Issues of 1909, Bluish Paper, Perf. 12, Wmkd. (191) #359-366: Washington (333-340)				
357	1¢ green Franklin (331), Feb. 16	75.00	65.00	875.00	(6)
358	2¢ carmine Washington (332), Feb. 16	70.00	55.00	850.00	(6)
	Double transfer	—			
359	3¢ deep violet, type I	1,500.00	*1,400.00*	*15,000.00*	(6)
360	4¢ orange brown	*15.000.00*		*75,000.00*	(3)
361	5¢ blue	2,900.00	*3,500.00*	*30,000.00*	(6)
362	6¢ red orange	1,150.00	850.00	*13,000.00*	(6)
363	8¢ olive green	*15.000.00*		*75,000.00*	(3)
364	10¢ yellow	1,200.00	900.00	*13,500.00*	(6)
365	13¢ blue green	2,000.00	*1,250.00*	*18,500.00*	(6)
366	15¢ pale ultramarine	900.00	700.00	*10,000.00*	(6)

	1909 continued, Perf. 12	Un	U	PB/LP	#	FDC	Q
	Lincoln Memorial Issue, Feb. 12						
367	2¢ Bust of Abraham Lincoln	4.25	1.40	100.00	(6)	*350.00*	148,387,191
	Double transfer	6.75	2.50				
	Imperf.						
368	2¢ carmine (367)	19.50	15.00	190.00	(6)	*7,000.00*	1,273,900
	Double transfer	37.50	24.00				
	Bluish Paper, Perf. 12						
369	2¢ carmine (367)	170.00	165.00	*2,750.00*	(6)		637,000
	Alaska-Yukon-Pacific Exposition Issue, June 1						
370	2¢ Willam H. Seward	7.00	1.10	175.00	(6)	*1,800.00*	152,887,311
	Double transfer	10.00	4.00				
	Imperf.						
371	2¢ carmine (370)	27.50	19.00	225.00	(6)		525,400
	Double transfer	40.00	25.00				
	Hudson-Fulton Celebration Issue, Sept. 25, Perf. 12						
372	2¢ Half Moon & Clermont	10.00	3.25	250.00	(6)	*700.00*	72,634,631
	Double transfer	14.00	4.25				
	Imperf.						
373	2¢ carmine (372)	30.00	21.00	250.00	(6)	*2,000.00*	216,480
	Double transfer	42.50	25.00				
	Issues of 1910-11, Perf. 12, Wmkd. (190) #376-382: Washington (333-338, 340)						
374	1¢ green Franklin (331), Nov. 23, 1910	5.00	.15	65.00	(6)		
a	Bklt. pane of 6, Oct. 7, 1910	110.00	*30.00*				
	Double transfer	12.50	—				
	Cracked plate	—	—				
375	2¢ carmine Washington (332), Nov. 23, 1910	5.00	.15	70.00	(6)		
	2¢ lake	100.00					
a	Bklt. pane of 6, Nov. 30, 1910	95.00	*25.00*				
	Cracked plate	—	—				
	Double transfer	10.00	—				
	Double transfer, design of 1¢	—	*1,000.00*				
376	3¢ dp. vio., type I, Jan. 16, 1911	11.50	1.00	100.00	(6)		
377	4¢ brown, Jan. 20, 1911	17.50	.30	130.00	(6)		
	Double transfer	—	—				
378	5¢ blue, Jan. 25, 1911	17.50	.30	160.00	(6)		
	Double transfer	—	—				
379	6¢ red orange, Jan. 25, 1911	24.00	.40	325.00	(6)		
380	8¢ olive green, Feb. 8, 1911	70.00	8.50	775.00	(6)		
381	10¢ yellow, Jan. 24, 1911	65.00	2.50	775.00	(6)		
382	15¢ pale ultramarine, Mar. 1, 1911	175.00	11.50	1,750.00	(6)		
	Issues of 1911, Jan. 3, Imperf.						
383	1¢ green Franklin (331)	2.25	2.00	37.50	(6)		
	Double transfer	5.75	—				
384	2¢ carmine Washington (332)	3.50	1.75	115.00	(6)		
	Double transfer, design of 1¢	*1,250.00*					
	Double transfer	7.00	—				
	Cracked plate	17.50	—				
	Issues of 1910, Nov.1, Coil Stamps, Perf. 12 Horizontally						
385	1¢ green Franklin (331)	18.00	8.00	200.00	(2)		
386	2¢ carmine Washington (332)	32.50	12.50	375.00	(2)		

367

370

372

Watermark 190

397

398

399

400

		Un	U	PB/LP	#	FDC	Q
	Issues of 1910-11, Coil Stamps, Perf. 12 Vertically						
387	1¢ green Franklin (331), Nov. 1, 1910	47.50	20.00	235.00	(2)		
388	2¢ carmine Washington (332), Nov. 1, 1910	450.00	150.00	3,000.00	(2)		
389	3¢ deep violet Washington, type I (333), Jan. 24, 1911	*15,000.00*	*6,000.00*				
	Issues of 1910-13, Perf. 8½ Horizontally, Wmkd. (190)						
390	1¢ green Franklin (331), Dec. 12, 1910	3.00	4.00	20.00	(2)		
	Double transfer	—	—				
391	2¢ carmine Washington (332), Dec. 23, 1910	20.00	5.75	115.00	(2)		
	Perf. 8½ Vertically #394-396: Washington (333-335)						
392	1¢ green Franklin (331), Dec.12, 1910	12.00	14.00	85.00	(2)		
	Double transfer	—	—				
393	2¢ carmine Washington (332), Dec. 16, 1910	24.00	5.50	140.00	(2)		
394	3¢ deep violet, type I, Sept. 18, 1911	32.50	40.00	210.00	(2)		
395	4¢ brown, Apr. 15, 1912	32.50	30.00	210.00	(2)		
396	5¢ blue, Mar. 1913	32.50	30.00	210.00	(2)		
	Issues of 1913, Panama Pacific Exposition Issue, Perf. 12						
397	1¢ Vasco Nunez de Balboa, Jan. 1	11.00	.85	110.00	(6)	*3,500.00*	167,398,463
	Double transfer	17.50	2.00				
398	2¢ Pedro Miguel Locks, Panama Canal, Jan.	12.50	.28	210.00	(6)		251,856,543
	2¢ lake	200.00					
	Double transfer	35.00	2.00				
399	5¢ Golden Gate, Jan. 1	47.50	6.50	1,500.00	(6)	*4,000.00*	14,544,363
400	10¢ Discovery of San Francisco Bay, Jan. 1	90.00	14.00	2,000.00	(6)	—	8,484,182
400A	10¢ orange (400), Aug.	160.00	10.50	*7,750.00*	(6)		
	Issues of 1914-15, Perf. 10						
401	1¢ green (397), Dec. 1914	16.00	4.00	225.00	(6)		167,398,463
402	2¢ carmine (398), Jan. 1915	52.50	1.00	1,150.00	(6)		251,856,543
403	5¢ blue (399), Feb. 1915	115.00	11.00	3,250.00	(6)		14,544,363
404	10¢ orange (400), July 1915	775.00	42.50	*10,000.00*	(6)		8,484,182

405

406

407

414

415

416

417

418

419

420

421

423

434

	Issues of 1912-14, Perf. 12 Wmkd. (190)				
		Un	U	PB/LP	#
405	1¢ green, Feb. 1912	3.50	.15	67.50	(6)
a	Vertical pair, imperf. horizontally	*650.00*	—		
b	Booklet pane of 6, Feb. 8, 1912	50.00	*7.50*		
	Cracked plate	12.00	—		
	Double transfer	5.75	—		
406	2¢ carmine, type I, Feb. 1912	3.25	.15	85.00	(6)
	2¢ lake	*150.00*			
a	Booklet pane of 6, Feb. 8, 1912	60.00	*17.50*		
b	Double impression	—			
	Double transfer	6.50	—		
407	7¢ black, Apr. 1914	60.00	8.00	900.00	(6)
	Imperf. #408-13: Washington (#405-6)				
408	1¢ green, Mar. 1912	.90	.50	15.00	(6)
	Double transfer	2.50	1.00		
	Cracked plate	—	—		
409	2¢ carmine, type I, Feb. 1912	1.00	.50	30.00	(6)
	Cracked plate	15.00	—		
	Coil Stamps, Perf. 8½ Horizontally				
410	1¢ green, Mar. 1912	4.50	3.00	25.00	(2)
	Double transfer	—	—		
411	2¢ carmine, type I, Mar. 1912	6.00	2.50	30.00	(2)
	Double transfer	9.00	—		
	Coil Stamps, Perf. 8½ Vertically				
412	1¢ green, Mar. 18, 1912	15.00	3.75	65.00	(2)
413	2¢ carmine, type I, Mar. 1912	24.00	.75	130.00	(2)
	Double transfer	40.00	—		

	1912-14 continued, Perf. 12	Un	U	PB/LP	#
414	8¢ Franklin, Feb. 1912	25.00	.85	325.00	(6)
415	9¢ Franklin, Apr. 1914	32.50	9.50	500.00	(6)
416	10¢ Franklin, Jan. 1912	26.00	.25	365.00	(6)
417	12¢ Franklin, Apr. 1914	28.50	3.00	350.00	(6)
	Double transfer	37.50	—		
	Triple transfer	52.50	—		
418	15¢ Franklin, Feb. 1912	47.50	2.00	475.00	(6)
	Double transfer	—	—		
419	20¢ Franklin, Apr. 1914	110.00	9.00	1,300.00	(6)
420	30¢ Franklin, Apr. 1914	80.00	10.00	1,150.00	(6)
421	50¢ Franklin, Aug. 1914	300.00	10.00	5,750.00	(6)
	Wmkd. (191)				
422	50¢ Franklin (421), Feb. 12, 1912	160.00	9.50	3,750.00	(6)
423	$1 Franklin, Feb. 12, 1912	360.00	40.00	*8,000.00*	(6)
	Double transfer	400.00	—		
	Issues of 1914-15, Perf.10 Wmkd. (190) #424-430: Washington (333-336, 407)				
424	1¢ green, Sept. 5, 1914	1.60	.15	35.00	(6)
	Cracked plate	—	—		
	Double transfer	4.25	—		
	Experimental precancel, New Orleans		—		
a	Perf. 12 x 10	*600.00*	*500.00*		
b	Perf. 10 x 12		250.00		
c	Vertical pair, imperf. horizontally	*425.00*	*250.00*		
d	Booklet pane of 6	3.50	*.75*		
e	Vertical pair, imperf. between	—			
425	2¢ rose red, type I, Sept. 5, 1914	1.50	.15	22.50	(6)
	Cracked plate	9.00	—		
	Double transfer	—	—		
c	Perf. 10 x 12		—		
d	Perf. 12 x 10	—	*600.00*		
e	Booklet pane of 6, Jan. 6, 1914	12.50	*3.00*		
426	3¢ deep violet, type I, Sept. 18, 1914	8.50	.90	125.00	(6)
427	4¢ brown, Sept. 7, 1914	22.00	.28	400.00	(6)
	Double transfer	37.50	—		
428	5¢ blue, Sept. 14, 1914	18.50	.28	275.00	(6)
a	Perf. 12 x 10		*1,000.00*		
429	6¢ red orange, Sept. 28, 1914	29.00	.90	425.00	(6)
430	7¢ black, Sept. 10, 1914	55.00	2.50	750.00	(6)
	#431-433, 435, 437-440: Franklin (414-421, 423)				
431	8¢ pale olive green, Sept. 26, 1914	24.00	1.10	425.00	(6)
	Double impression	—			
432	9¢ salmon red, Oct. 6, 1914	32.50	5.00	550.00	(6)
433	10¢ orange yellow, Sept. 9, 1914	30.00	.18	550.00	(6)
434	11¢ dark green, Aug. 11, 1915	13.50	5.50	190.00	(6)
435	12¢ claret brown, Sept. 10, 1914	15.00	2.75	225.00	(6)
a	12¢ copper red	16.00	2.75		
	Double transfer	22.50	—		
	Triple transfer	27.50	—		
436	not assigned				
437	15¢ gray, Sept. 16, 1914	72.50	4.50	700.00	(6)
438	20¢ ultramarine, Sept. 19, 1914	140.00	2.50	2,250.00	(6)
439	30¢ orange red, Sept. 19, 1914	190.00	10.00	3,500.00	(6)
440	50¢ violet, Dec. 10, 1915	500.00	10.00	12,500.00	(6)

	Issues of 1914, Coil Stamps, Perf. 10 Horizontally #441-459: Washington (405-406, 333-335)				
		Un	U	PB/LP	#
441	1¢ green, Nov. 14	.55	.80	4.25	(2)
442	2¢ carmine, type I, July 22	6.00	4.50	35.00	(2)
	Coil Stamps, Perf. 10 Vertically				
443	1¢ green, May 29	14.00	4.00	72.50	(2)
444	2¢ carmine, type I, Apr. 25	19.00	1.00	110.00	(2)
445	3¢ violet, type I, Dec. 18	160.00	100.00	800.00	(2)
446	4¢ brown, Oct. 2	82.50	21.00	410.00	(2)
447	5¢ blue, July 30	27.50	17.50	150.00	(2)
	Issues of 1915-16, Coil Stamps, Perf. 10 Horizontally				
	(Rotary Press, Designs 18 1/2–19 x 22 1/2mm.)				
448	1¢ green, Dec. 12, 1915	4.25	2.25	25.00	(2)
449	2¢ red, type I, Dec. 5, 1915	1,750.00	225.00	8,500.00	(2)
450	2¢ carmine, type III, Feb. 1916	7.00	2.25	35.00	(2)
451	not assigned				
	Issues of 1914-16, Coil Stamps, Perf. 10 Vertically (Rotary Press, Designs 191/2–20 x 22mm.)				
452	1¢ green, Nov. 11, 1914	7.00	1.40	47.50	(2)
453	2¢ red, type I, July 3, 1914	72.50	3.25	375.00	(2)
	Cracked plate	—	—		
454	2¢ carmine, type II, June 1915	70.00	7.50	350.00	(2)
455	2¢ carmine, type III, Dec. 1915	6.50	.75	37.50	(2)
456	3¢ violet, type I, Feb. 2, 1916	190.00	75.00	825.00	(2)
457	4¢ brown, Feb. 18, 1916	18.00	15.00	100.00	(2)
	Cracked plate	35.00	—		
458	5¢ blue, Mar. 9, 1916	22.50	15.00	125.00	(2)
	Issue of 1914, Horizontal Coil Stamp, Imperf.				
459	2¢ carmine, type I, June 30	375.00	*600.00*	1,250.00	(2)
	Issue of 1915, Perf. 10, Wmkd. (191)				
460	$1 violet black Franklin (423), Feb. 8	600.00	55.00	*10,000.00*	(6)
	Double transfer	650.00	—		
	Perf. 11				
461	2¢ pale carmine red Washington (333), type I, June 17	75.00	*110.00*	1,000.00	(6)
	Privately perforated copies of #409 have been made to resemble #461.				
	From 1916 to date, all postage stamps except #519 and #832b are on unwatermarked paper.				
	Issues of 1916-17, Perf. 10, Unwmkd. #462-469: Washington (333-336, 407)				
462	1¢ green, Sept. 27, 1916	5.00	.15	125.00	(6)
	Experimental precancel, Springfield, MA, or New Orleans, LA		10.00		
a	Booklet pane of 6, Oct. 15, 1916	7.50	*1.00*		
463	2¢ carmine, type I, Sept. 25, 1916	3.25	.15	115.00	(6)
	Experimental precancel, Springfield, MA		20.00		
a	Booklet pane of 6, Oct. 8, 1916	70.00	*20.00*		
	Double transfer	5.75	—		
464	3¢ violet, type I, Nov. 11, 1916	52.50	8.00	1,100.00	(6)
	Double transfer in "CENTS"	*70.00*	—		
465	4¢ orange brown, Oct. 7, 1916	30.00	1.00	550.00	(6)
466	5¢ blue, Oct. 17, 1916	52.50	1.00	750.00	(6)
	Experimental precancel, Springfield, MA		150.00		
467	5¢ carmine (error in plate of 2¢)	475.00	500.00		
468	6¢ red orange, Oct. 10, 1916	65.00	5.00	1,000.00	(6)
	Experimental precancel, Springfield, MA		175.00		
469	7¢ black, Oct. 10, 1916	85.00	7.50	1,200.00	(6)
	Experimental precancel, Springfield, MA		175.00		

	1916-17 continued, Perf. 10	Un	U	PB	#	
	#470-478: Franklin (414-419, 421, 423, 434)					
470	8¢ olive green, Nov. 13, 1916	40.00	3.75	450.00	(6)	
	Experimental precancel, Springfield, MA		*165.00*			
471	9¢ salmon red, Nov. 16, 1916	41.00	9.50	600.00	(6)	
472	10¢ orange yellow, Oct. 17, 1916	77.50	.75	1,100.00	(6)	
473	11¢ dark green, Nov. 16, 1916	22.50	11.00	275.00	(6)	
	Experimental precancel, Springfield, MA	*650.00*				
474	12¢ claret brown, Oct. 10, 1916	36.00	3.50	525.00	(6)	
	Double transfer	45.00	5.25			
	Triple transfer	57.50	8.50			
475	15¢ gray, Nov. 16, 1916	120.00	7.00	2,250.00	(6)	
476	20¢ light ultramarine, Dec. 5, 1916	175.00	7.50	3,000.00	(6)	
476A	30¢ orange red	*3,000.00*				
477	50¢ light violet, Mar. 2, 1917	1,000.00	40.00	*40,000.00*	(6)	
478	$1 violet black, Dec. 22, 1916	675.00	11.00	*13,000.00*	(6)	
	Double transfer	750.00	15.00			
479	$2 dark blue Madison (312), Mar. 22, 1917	325.00	30.00	4,250.00	(6)	
480	$5 light green Marshall (313), Mar. 22, 1917	250.00	32.50	3,000.00	(6)	
	Issues of 1916-17, Imperf.					
	#481-496: Washington (333-35)					
481	1¢ green, Nov. 1916	.65	.45	9.75	(6)	
	Double transfer	2.50	1.25			
482	2¢ carmine, type I, Dec. 8, 1916	1.00	1.00	20.00	(6)	
482A	2¢ deep rose, type Ia		*7,000.00*			
483	3¢ violet, type I, Oct. 13, 1917	9.50	6.50	110.00	(6)	
	Double transfer	16.00	—			
484	3¢ violet, type II	7.00	3.00	87.50	(6)	
	Double transfer	12.50	—			
485	5¢ carmine (error in plate of 2¢), Mar. 1917	*9,000.00*				
	Issues of 1916-22, Coil Stamps, Perf. 10 Horizontally					
486	1¢ green, Jan. 1918	.60	.20	3.00	(2)	
	Double transfer	2.25	—			
487	2¢ carmine, type II, Nov. 15, 1916	10.00	2.50	80.00	(2)	
488	2¢ carmine, type III, 1919	1.75	1.35	12.00	(2)	
	Cracked plate	12.00	7.50			
489	3¢ violet, type I, Oct. 10, 1917	3.75	1.00	22.50	(2)	
	Coil Stamps, Perf. 10 Vertically					
490	1¢ green, Nov. 17, 1916	.40	.15	2.50	(2)	
	Cracked plate	7.50	—			
	Cracked plate (vertical) retouched	9.00	—			
	Rosette crack	*35.00*	—			
491	2¢ carmine, type II, Nov. 17, 1916	1,450.00	450.00	7,000.00	(2)	
492	2¢ carmine, type III	5.75	.15	35.00	(2)	
493	3¢ violet, type I, July 23, 1917	13.50	1.75	90.00	(2)	
494	3¢ violet, type II, Feb. 4, 1918	7.50	.90	50.00	(2)	
495	4¢ orange brown, Apr. 15, 1917	8.00	3.00	55.00	(2)	
	Cracked plate	25.00	—			
496	5¢ blue, Jan. 15, 1919	2.75	.90	20.00	(2)	
497	10¢ orange yellow Franklin (416), Jan. 31, 1922	16.00	7.00	100.00	(2)	*2,000.00*

	Issues of 1917-19, Perf. 11 (#405-06, 333-36, 407)	Un	U	PB	#
498	1¢ green, Mar. 1917	.30	.15	13.00	(6)
a	Vertical pair, imperf. horizontally	175.00			
b	Horizontal pair, imperf. between	75.00			
d	Double impression	150.00			
e	Booklet pane of 6, Apr. 6, 1917	3.50	*.35*		
f	Booklet pane of 30, Sept. 1917	*600.00*			
g	Perf. 10 top or bottom	*500.00*			
	Cracked plate	7.50	—		
499	2¢ rose, type I, Mar. 1917	.35	.15	14.00	(6)
a	Vertical pair, imperf. horizontally	150.00			
b	Horizontal pair, imperf. vertically	200.00	*100.00*		
e	Booklet pane of 6, Mar. 31, 1917	3.50	*.50*		
f	Booklet pane of 30, Sept. 1917	*10,000.00*			
g	Double impression	200.00	—		
	Double transfer	6.00	—		
500	2¢ deep rose, type Ia	200.00	110.00	1,650.00	(6)
	Pair, types I and Ia	*1,000.00*			
501	3¢ light violet, type I, Mar. 1917	8.00	.15	80.00	(6)
b	Booklet pane of 6, Oct. 17, 1917	65.00	*15.00*		
d	Double impression	200.00			
502	3¢ dark violet, type II	11.00	.15	120.00	(6)
b	Booklet pane of 6	50.00	*10.00*		
c	Vertical pair, imperf. horizontally	250.00	125.00		
e	Perf. 10, top or bottom	*425.00*	—		
503	4¢ brown, Mar. 1917	7.50	.15	110.00	(6)
504	5¢ blue, Mar. 1917	6.50	.15	110.00	(6)
	Double transfer	10.00	—		
505	5¢ rose (error in plate of 2¢)	350.00	400.00		
506	6¢ red orange, Mar. 1917	9.50	.20	135.00	(6)
507	7¢ black, Mar. 1917	20.00	.85	200.00	(6)
	#508-512, 514-18: Franklin (414-17, 434, 418-21, 423)				
508	8¢ olive bistre, Mar. 1917	8.50	.40	130.00	(6)
c	Perf. 10 top or bottom		*500.00*		
509	9¢ salmon red, Mar. 1917	11.00	1.40	125.00	(6)
510	10¢ orange yellow, Mar. 1917	12.50	.15	160.00	(6)
511	11¢ light green, May 1917	6.75	2.00	115.00	(6)
	Double transfer	12.50	3.00		
512	12¢ claret brown, May 1917	6.50	.30	105.00	(6)
a	12¢ brown carmine	7.00	.35		
b	Perf. 10, top or bottom	—	*300.00*		
513	13¢ apple green, Jan. 10, 1919	8.00	4.75	115.00	(6)
	13¢ deep apple green	9.75	5.25		
514	15¢ gray, May 1917	30.00	.80	425.00	(6)
515	20¢ light ultramarine, May 1917	37.50	.16	475.00	(6)
	20¢ deep ultramarine	39.00	.16		
b	Vertical pair, imperf. between	*325.00*			
516	30¢ orange red, May 1917	30.00	.55	475.00	(6)
a	Perf. 10 top or bottom	*850.00*	—		
517	50¢ red violet, May 1917	60.00	.40	1,500.00	(6)
c	Perf. 10, top or bottom		*700.00*		
518	$1 violet brown, May 1917	45.00	1.10	1,200.00	(6)
b	$1 deep brown	*750.00*	*350.00*		

513

523

524

537

	Issue of 1917, Wmkd. (191)	Un	U
519	2¢ carm. Washington (332), Oct. 10	200.00	*400.00*
	Privately perforated copies of #344 have been made to resemble #519.		
520-2	not assigned		
	Issues of 1918, Aug., Unwmkd.		
523	$2 Franklin	675.00	250.00
524	$5 Franklin	275.00	20.00
	Issues of 1918-20, Perf. 11 #525-535: Washington (405-406, 333)		
525	1¢ gray green, Dec. 1918	1.35	.35
a	1¢ dark green	1.50	.75
	Double impression	15.00	15.00
526	2¢ carmine, type IV, Mar. 15, 1920	19.00	2.75
	Gash on forhead	26.00	—
	Malformed left "2"	26.00	5.25
527	2¢ carmine, type V	10.00	.60
a	Double impression	55.00	10.00
	Line through "2," "EN"	18.50	—
528	2¢ carmine, type Va	5.25	.15
	Double impression	32.50	
528A	2¢ carmine, type VI	32.50	1.00
d	Double impression	150.00	—
528B	2¢ carmine, type VII	12.50	.15
e	Double impression	55.00	
	Retouched on check	—	—
529	3¢ violet, type III, Mar. 1918	2.00	.15
	Double impression	30.00	—
	Printed on both sides	*350.00*	
530	3¢ purple, type IV	.75	.15
a	Double impression	17.50	6.00
b	Printed on both sides	250.00	
	"Blister" under "U.S."	2.00	—
	Recut under "U.S."	2.00	—
	Imperf.		
531	1¢ green, Jan. 1919	6.00	7.00
532	2¢ carmine rose, type IV	30.00	22.50
533	2¢ carmine, type V	150.00	55.00
534	2¢ carmine, type Va	8.50	6.00
534A	2¢ carmine, type VI	27.50	17.50
534B	2¢ carmine, type VII	1,250.00	425.00
535	3¢ violet, type IV, 1918	6.00	4.50
a	Double impression	100.00	—

	Issues of 1919, Perf. 12½	Un	U
536	1¢ gray green Washington (405), Aug.	9.00	11.00
	Horizontal pair, imperf. vertically	*500.00*	
537	3¢ Allied Victory, Mar. 3	6.50	2.75
a	deep red violet	250.00	30.00
c	red violet	30.00	7.50
	Double transfer	—	—
	#538-546: Washington (405-06, 333)		
	Perf. 11 x 10 (Designs 19½–20 x 22-22¼mm)		
538	1¢ green, June	6.50	6.00
a	Vertical pair, imperf. hor.	50.00	*100.00*
539	2¢ carmine rose, type II	2,750.00	750.00
540	2¢ carmine rose, type III, June 14	7.00	6.00
	Double transfer	20.00	—
541	3¢ violet, type II, June	22.50	20.00
	Issue of 1920, Perf. 10 x 11 (Design 19 x 22½–22¾mm)		
542	1¢ green, May 26	6.50	.65
	Issues of 1921, Perf. 10 (Design 19 x 22½mm)		
543	1¢ green, May	.35	.15
	Double transfer		—
	Triple transfer	—	—
a	Horizontal pair, imperf. between	*550.00*	
	Issue of 1923, Perf. 11 (Design 19 x 22½mm)		
544	1¢ green	*8,500.00*	*2,500.00*
	Issues of 1921 (Designs 19½–20 x 22mm)		
545	1¢ green, May	95.00	110.00
546	2¢ carmine rose, type III, May	60.00	*110.00*
a	Perf. 10 at left	*500.00*	
	Recut in hair	85.00	*150.00*

547 548

549

550

551

552

553

554

555

556

557

558

559

560

561

562

563

564

565

566

567

568

569

570

571

572

573

	Issues of 1920, Perf. 11	Un	U	PB	#	FDC	Q
547	$2 Franklin, Nov. 1	225.00	25.00	4,000.00	(8)		
	Pilgrim Tercentenary Issue, Dec. 21						
548	[illegible]¢ The Mayflower	3.25	1.65	40.00	(6[illegible]	*[illegible]00.00*	37,978,207
	Double transfer	—	—				
549	2¢ Landing of the Pilgrims	5.25	1.25	50.00	(6)	*650.00*	96,037,327
550	5¢ Signing of the Compact	32.50	10.00	400.00	(6)	—	11,321,607

	Issues of 1922-25, Perf. 11	Un	U	PB	#	FDC
	(see also #581-91, 594-95, 597-606, 622-23, 631-42, 658-79, 684-87, 692-701, 723)					
551	1/2¢ Nathan Hale, Apr. 4, 1925	.15	.15	4.25	(6)	15.00
	"Cap" on fraction bar	.45	.15			
552	1¢ Franklin, Jan. 17, 1923	1.10	.15	17.50	(6)	20.00
a	Booklet pane of 6, Aug. 11, 1923	4.50	*.50*			
	Double transfer	3.50	—			
553	1 1/2¢ Harding, Mar. 19, 1925	1.90	.15	25.00	(6)	25.00
554	2¢ Washington, Jan. 15, 1923	1.00	.15	17.50	(6)	35.00
a	Horizontal pair, imperf. vertically	175.00				
b	Vertical pair, imperf. horizontally	*500.00*				
c	Booklet pane of 6, Feb. 10, 1923	6.00	*1.00*			
	Double transfer	2.25	.60			
555	3¢ Lincoln, Feb. 12, 1923	12.50	.85	125.00	(6)	27.50
556	4¢ M. Washington, Jan. 15, 1923	12.50	.20	125.00	(6)	50.00
b	Perf. 10, top or bottom	*425.00*				
557	5¢ T. Roosevelt, Oct. 27, 1922	12.50	.15	150.00	(6)	*125.00*
a	Imperf. pair	*800.00*				
c	Perf. 10, top or bottom	—	375.00			
558	6¢ Garfield, Nov. 20, 1922	24.00	.75	325.00	(6)	200.00
	Double transfer	40.00	2.00			
	Same, recut	40.00	2.00			
559	7¢ McKinley, May 1, 1923	5.75	.45	50.00	(6)	125.00
	Double transfer	—	—			
560	8¢ Grant, May 1, 1923	35.00	.35	400.00	(6)	150.00
	Double transfer	—	—			
561	9¢ Jefferson, Jan. 15, 1923	10.00	.90	115.00	(6)	150.00
	Double transfer	—	—			
562	10¢ Monroe, Jan. 15, 1923	14.00	.15	150.00	(6)	140.00
a	Vertical pair, imperf. horizontally	*600.00*				
b	Imperf. pair	*750.00*				
c	Perf. 10, top or bottom		*600.00*			
563	11¢ Hayes, Oct. 4, 1922	1.10	.25	22.50	(6)	550.00
564	12¢ Cleveland, Mar. 20, 1923	4.50	.15	62.50	(6)	150.00
a	Horizontal pair, imperf. vertically	*1,000.00*				
b	Imperf. pair	—				
565	14¢ American Indian, May 1, 1923	3.25	.65	45.00	(6)	325.00
	Double transfer	—	—			
566	15¢ Statue of Liberty, Nov. 11, 1922	17.50	.15	225.00	(6)	400.00
567	20¢ Golden Gate, May 1, 1923	17.50	.15	165.00	(6)	*400.00*
a	Horizontal pair, imperf. vertically	*750.00*				
568	25¢ Niagara Falls, Nov. 11, 1922	15.00	.38	175.00	(6)	*625.00*
b	Vertical pair, imperf. horizontally	*850.00*				
c	Perf. 10 at one side	—				
569	30¢ Buffalo, Mar. 20, 1923	27.50	.30	235.00	(6)	*750.00*
	Double transfer	37.50	1.50			
570	50¢ Arlington Amphitheater, Nov. 11, 1922	50.00	.15	600.00	(6)	*1,100.00*
571	$1 Lincoln Memorial, Feb. 12, 1923	37.50	.35	425.00	(6)	*5,500.00*
	Double transfer	80.00	1.50			
572	$2 U.S. Capitol, Mar. 20, 1923	85.00	8.00	1,000.00	(6)	*11,000.00*
573	$5 Head of Freedom, Capitol Dome, Mar. 20, 1923	200.00	12.50	3,250.00	(8)	*16,000.00*
574	not assigned					

	Issues of 1923-25, Imperf.	Un	U	PB	#	FDC
575	1¢ green Franklin (552), Mar. 20, 1923	6.00	2.75	70.00	(6)	
576	1 1/2¢ yellow brown Harding (553), Apr. 4, 1925	1.25	1.00	17.00	(6)	45.00
577	2¢ carmine Washington (554)	1.40	1.25	25.00	(6)	
	Issues of 1923, Perf. 11 x 10					
578	1¢ green Franklin (552)	60.00	65.00	600.00	(4)	
579	2¢ carmine Washington (554)	50.00	60.00	450.00	(4)	
	Recut in eye	60.00	75.00			
	Issues of 1923-26, Perf. 10 (see also #551-79, 622-23, 631-42, 658-79, 684-87, 692-701, 723)					
580	not assigned					
581	1¢ green Franklin (552), Apr. 21, 1923	6.00	.55	75.00	(4)	*2,000.00*
582	1 1/2¢ brn. Harding (553), Mar. 19, 1925	3.00	.45	27.50	(4)	40.00
	Pair with full horizontal gutter between	*135.00*				
583	2¢ carm. Washington (554), Apr. 14, 1924	1.40	.15	17.00	(4)	
a	Booklet pane of 6, Aug. 27, 1926	75.00	*25.00*			*1,500.00*
584	3¢ violet Lincoln (555), Aug. 1, 1925	17.50	1.75	160.00	(4)	47.50
585	4¢ yellow brown Martha Washington (556), Mar. 1925	11.00	.30	140.00	(4)	47.50
586	5¢ blue T. Roosevelt (557), Dec. 1924	11.50	.18	135.00	(4)	50.00
587	6¢ red orange Garfield (558), Mar. 1925	4.50	.25	60.00	(4)	60.00
588	7¢ black McKinley (559), May 29, 1926	7.00	4.25	67.50	(4)	62.50
589	8¢ olive grn. Grant (560), May 29, 1926	17.50	2.75	150.00	(4)	65.00
590	9¢ rose Jefferson (561), May 29, 1926	3.25	1.90	30.00	(4)	65.00
591	10¢ orange Monroe (562), June 8, 1925	45.00	.15	350.00	(4)	85.00
592-93	not assigned					
	Perf. 11					
594	1¢ green Franklin (552), design 19 3/4 x 22 1/4mm	*10,000.00*	3,500.00			
595	2¢ carmine Washington (554), design 19 3/4 x 22 1/4mm	190.00	225.00	900.00	(4)	
596	1¢ green Franklin (552), design 19 1/4 x 22 3/4mm		*15,000.00*			
	Issues of 1923-29, Coil Stamps, Perf. 10 Vertically					
597	1¢ green Franklin (552), July 18, 1923	.20	.15	1.65	(2)	*550.00*
	Gripper cracks or double transfer	2.25	1.00			
598	1 1/2¢ brown Harding (553), Mar. 19, 1925	.40	.15	2.85	(2)	50.00
599	2¢ carmine Washington (554), type I, Jan. 1923	.25	.15	1.65	(2)	*600.00*
	Double transfer	1.65	1.00			
	Gripper cracks	2.00	2.00			
599A	2¢ carmine Washington (554), type II, Mar. 1929	100.00	8.50	550.00	(2)	
600	3¢ violet Lincoln (555), May 10, 1924	4.25	.15	18.50	(2)	60.00
601	4¢ yellow brown M. Washington (556), Aug. 5, 1923	2.50	.30	17.50	(2)	
602	5¢ dark blue T. Roosevelt (557), Mar. 5, 1924	1.10	.15	7.25	(2)	82.50
603	10¢ orange Monroe (562), Dec. 1, 1924	2.25	.15	17.50	(2)	100.00
	Coil Stamps, Perf. 10 Horizontally					
604	1¢ yel. grn. Franklin (552), July 19, 1924	.18	.15	2.15	(2)	90.00
605	1 1/2¢ yel. brn. Harding (553), May 9, 1925	.18	.15	1.65	(2)	70.00
606	2¢ carmine Washington (554), Dec. 31, 1923	.18	.15	1.25	(2)	100.00
607-09	not assigned					

610

614

615

616

617

618

619

620

621

622

623

	Issues of 1923	Un	U	PB	#	FDC	Q
	Harding Memorial Issue, Perf. 11						
610	2¢ Harding, Sept. 1	.45	.15	18.00	(6)	30.00	1,459,487,085
a	Horizontal pair, imperf. vertically	*800.00*					
	Double transfer	1.75	.50				
	Imperf.						
611	2¢ blk. Harding (610), Nov. 15	6.50	4.25	85.00	(6)	90.00	770,000
	Perf. 10						
612	2¢ blk. Harding (610), Sept. 12	12.00	1.50	225.00	(4)	100.00	99,950,300
	Perf. 11, design 19¼ x 22¾mm						
613	2¢ black Harding (610),		*15,000.00*				
	Issues of 1924, Huguenot-Walloon Tercentary Issue, May 1						
614	1¢ Ship *Nieu Nederland*	2.50	3.00	30.00	(6)	25.00	51,378,023
615	2¢ Walloons' Landing at Fort Orange (Albany)	5.25	1.90	60.00	(6)	27.50	77,753,423
	Double transfer	12.50	3.50				
616	5¢ Huguenot Monument to Jan Ribault at Mayport, FL	25.00	11.00	300.00	(6)	45.00	5,659,023
	Issues of 1925, Lexington-Concord Issue, Apr. 4						
617	1¢ Washington at Cambridge	2.50	2.25	40.00	(6)	25.00	15,615,000
618	2¢ "The Birth of Liberty," by Henry Sandham	5.00	3.75	67.50	(6)	27.50	26,596,600
619	5¢ "The Minute Man," by Daniel Chester French	24.00	12.50	275.00	(6)	60.00	5,348,800
	Line over head	50.00	18.50				
	Norse-American Issue, May 18						
620	2¢ Sloop *Restaurationen*	3.00	2.75	200.00	(8)	20.00	9,104,983
621	5¢ Viking Ship	13.00	10.50	650.00	(8)	30.00	1,900,983
	Issues of 1925-26 (see also #551-79, 581-91, 594-95, 597-606, 631-42, 658-79, 684-87, 692-701, 723)						
622	13¢ B. Harrison, Jan. 11, 1926	11.00	.40	150.00	(6	20.00	
623	17¢ Wilson, Dec. 28, 1925	13.00	.20	165.00	(6	25.00	
624-26	not assigned						

627

628

629

630

643

644

645

646

647

648

	Issues of 1926, Perf. 11	Un	U	PB	#	FDC	Q
627	2¢ Independence Sesquicentennial Exposition, May 10	2.25	.35	35.00	(6)	10.00	307,731,900
628	5¢ John Ericsson Memorial, May 29	5.00	2.50	75.00	(6)	22.50	20,280,500
629	2¢ Battle of White Plains, Oct. 18	1.50	1.25	35.00	(6)	6.25	40,639,485
a	Vertical pair, imperf. between	*1,250.00*					
	International Philatelic Exhibition Issue, Souvenir Sheet, Oct. 18, Perf. 11						
630	2¢ Battle of White Plains, sheet of 25 with selvage inscription (629)	300.00	300.00			1,400.00	107,398
	Dot over first "S" of "STATES"	375.00	325.00				
	Imperf. (see also #551-79, 581-91, 594A-95, 597-606, 622-23, 658-79, 684-87, 692-701, 723)						
631	1½¢ yellow brown Harding (553), design 18½-19 x 22½mm, Aug. 27	1.75	1.40	42.50	(4)	30.00	

	Issues of 1926-34, Perf. 11 x 10½	Un	U	PB	#	FDC	Q
632	1¢ green Franklin (552), June 10, 1927	.15	.15	1.65	(4)	45.00	
a	Booklet pane of 6, Nov. 2, 1927	4.50	*.25*			*3,000.00*	
b	Pair with full vertical gutter between	200.00	*125.00*				
	Cracked plate	—	—				
633	1½¢ yellow brown Harding (553), May 17, 1927	1.25	.15	50.00	(4)	45.00	
634	2¢ carmine Washington (554), type I, Dec. 10, 1926	.15	.15	1.00	(4)	47.50	
	Pair with full vertical gutter between	200.00					
b	2¢ carmine lake, type I	3.00	1.00	30.00			
c	Horizontal pair, imperf. between	*2,000.00*					
d	Booklet pane of 6, Feb. 25, 1927	1.75	*.15*				
634A	2¢ carmine Washington (554), type II, Dec. 1928	285.00	10.00	1,500.00	(4)		
	Pair with full vertical or horizontal gutter between	1,000.00					
635	3¢ violet Lincoln (555), Feb. 3, 1927	.35	.15	5.00	(4)	47.50	
a	3¢ bright. vio. Lincoln, Feb. 7, 1934	.25	.15	3.25	(4)	25.00	
	Gripper cracks	3.25	2.00				
636	4¢ yel. brown M. Washington (556), May 17, 1927	1.75	.15	60.00	(4)	50.00	
	Pair with full vertical gutter between	*200.00*					
637	5¢ dark blue T. Roosevelt (557), Mar. 24, 1927	1.65	.15	12.00	(4)	50.00	
	Pair with full vertical gutter between	*275.00*					
638	6¢ red orange Garfield (558), July 27, 1927	1.75	.15	12.00	(4)	57.50	
	Pair with full vertical gutter between	*200.00*					
639	7¢ black McKinley (559), Mar. 24, 1927	1.75	.15	12.00	(4)	57.50	
a	Vertical pair, imperf. between	125.00	80.00				
640	8¢ olive green Grant (560), June 10, 1927	1.75	.15	12.00	(4)	62.50	
641	9¢ orange red Jefferson (561), 1931	1.75	.15	12.00	(4)	72.50	
642	10¢ orange Monroe (562), Feb. 3, 1927	2.75	.15	23.50	(4)	90.00	
	Double transfer	—	—				
	Issues of 1927, Perf. 11						
643	2¢ Vermont Sesquicentennial, Aug. 3	1.25	.75	35.00	(6)	5.00	39,974,900
644	2¢ Burgoyne Campaign, Aug. 3	3.00	1.90	35.00	(6)	12.50	25,628,450
	Issues of 1928						
645	2¢ Valley Forge, May 26	.90	.35	22.50	(6)	4.00	101,330,328
	Perf. 11 x 10½						
646	2¢ Battle of Monmouth/ Molly Pitcher, Oct. 20	.80	.80	25.00	(4)	15.00	9,779,896
	Wide spacing, vertical pair	20.00					
	Hawaii Sesquicentennial Issue, Aug. 13						
647	2¢ Washington (554)	3.00	3.25	90.00	(4)	15.00	5,519,897
	Wide spacing, vertical pair	75.00					
648	5¢ T. Roosevelt (557)	10.00	10.00	225.00	(4)	22.50	1,459,897

	1928 continued	Un	U	PB/LP	#	FDC	Q
	Aeronautics Conference Issue, Dec. 12, Perf. 11						
649	2¢ Wright Airplane	.90	.75	11.50	(6)	7.00	51,342,273
650	5¢ Globe and Airplane	4.50	3.00	50.00	(6)	10.00	10,319,700
	Plate flaw, "prairie dog"	27.50	12.50				
	Issues of 1929						
651	2¢ George Rogers Clark, Feb. 25	.45	.35	8.50	(6)	6.00	16,684,674
	Double transfer	4.00	2.00				
652	not assigned						
	Perf. 11 x 10½						
653	½¢ olive brown Nathan Hale (551), May 25	.15	.15	1.00	(4)	25.00	
	Electric Light's Golden Jubilee Issue, June 5, Perf. 11						
654	2¢ Thomas Edison's First Lamp	.50	.50	25.00	(6)	8.00	31,679,200
	Perf. 11 x 10½						
655	2¢ carmine rose (654), June 11	.45	.15	30.00	(4)	80.00	210,119,474
	Coil Stamp, Perf. 10 Vertically						
656	2¢ carmine rose (654), June 11	9.50	1.25	50.00	(2)	90.00	133,530,000
	Perf. 11						
657	2¢ Sullivan Expedition, June 17	.60	.50	24.00	(6)	4.00	51,451,880
	2¢ lake	30.00	—				
	658-668 Overprinted "Kans.," May 1, Perf. 11 x 10½						
658	1¢ Franklin	1.40	1.25	25.00	(4)	30.00	13,390,000
a	Vertical pair, one without overprint	*300.00*					
659	1½¢ brown Harding (553)	1.90	1.75	35.00	(4)	30.00	8,240,000
	Wide spacing, pair	65.00					
660	2¢ carmine Washington (554)	2.50	.70	30.00	(4)	30.00	87,410,000
661	3¢ violet Lincoln (555)	11.00	9.00	115.00	(4)	2.50	2,540,000
662	4¢ yellow brown Martha Washington (556)	11.00	5.50	120.00	(4)	35.00	2,290,000
663	5¢ deep blue T. Roosevelt (557)	8.00	6.00	92.50	(4)	35.00	2,700,000
664	6¢ red orange Garfield (558)	17.50	11.50	275.00	(4)	45.00	1,450,000
665	7¢ black McKinley (559)	16.00	17.00	350.00	(4)	45.00	1,320,000
666	8¢ olive green Grant (560)	55.00	45.00	525.00	(4)	85.00	1,530,000
667	9¢ light rose Jefferson (561)	8.00	7.00	110.00	(4)	80.00	1,130,000
668	10¢ orange yel. Monroe (562)	14.00	7.50	200.00	(4)	90.00	2,860,000
	669-679 Overprinted "Nebr.," May 1						
669	1¢ Franklin	2.00	1.40	30.00	(4)	30.00	8,220,000
a	Vertical pair, one without overprint	*275.00*					
670	1½¢ brown Harding (553)	1.65	1.50	32.50	(4)	30.00	8,990,000
671	2¢ carmine Washington (554)	1.65	.70	25.00	(4)	30.00	73,220,000
672	3¢ violet Lincoln (555)	7.00	6.50	87.50	(4)	35.00	2,110,000
673	4¢ yellow brown Martha Washington (556)	12.50	9.00	140.00	(4)	40.00	1,600,000
	Wide spacing, pair	110.00					
674	5¢ deep blue T. Roosevelt (557)	10.00	9.00	150.00	(4)	40.00	1,860,000
675	6¢ red orange Garfield (558)	24.00	14.00	300.00	(4)	60.00	980,000
676	7¢ black McKinley (559)	13.00	11.00	180.00	(4)	65.00	850,000
677	8¢ olive green Grant (560)	17.00	15.00	275.00	(4)	65.00	1,480,000
678	9¢ light rose Jefferson (561)	22.50	17.00	350.00	(4)	70.00	530,000
679	10¢ orange yel. Monroe (562)	70.00	14.00	750.00	(4)	80.00	1,890,000
	Warning: Excellent forgeries of the Kansas and Nebraska overprints exist.						

649

650

651

654

657

658

669

680

681

682

683

684

685

	1929 continued, Perf. 11	Un	U	PB/LP	#	FDC	Q
680	2¢ Battle of Fallen Timbers, Sept. 14	.60	.65	21.00	(6)	3.50	29,338,274
681	2¢ Ohio River Canalization, Oct. 19	.45	.50	16.00	(6)	3.50	32,680,900
	Issues of 1930						
682	2¢ Massachusetts Bay Colony, Apr. 8	.50	.38	20.00	(6)	3.50	74,000,774
683	2¢ Carolina-Charleston, Apr. 10	.85	.85	35.00	(6)	3.50	25,215,574
684	1 1/2¢ Warren G. Harding, Dec. 1	.18	.15	1.25	(4)	4.50	
	Pair with full horizontal gutter between	*175.00*					
	Pair with full vertical gutter between	—					
685	4¢ William H. Taft, June 4	.65	.15	9.00	(4)	6.00	
	Gouge on right "4"	2.00	.60				
	Recut right "4"	2.00	.65				
	Pair with full horizontal gutter between	—					
	Coil Stamps, Perf. 10 Vertically						
686	1 1/2¢ brn. Harding (684), Dec. 1	1.25	.15	4.50	(2)	5.00	
687	¢ brown Taft (685), Sept. 18	2.25	.38	8.50	(2	20.00	

1930-1932

688  689  690  702  703

704  705  706  707  708  709

710

711

712

713

714

715

	1930 continued, Perf. 11	Un	U	PB	#	FDC	Q
688	2¢ Battle of Braddock's Field, July 9	.65	.65	28.50	(6)	4.00	25,609,470
689	2¢ General von Steuben, Sept. 17	.38	.40	17.00	(6)	4.00	66,487,000
a	Imperf. pair	*2,250.00*		*12,000.00*			
	Issues of 1931						
690	2¢ General Pulaski, Jan. 16	.16	.15	10.00	(6)	4.00	96,559,400
691	not assigned						
	Perf. 11 x 10½						
692	11¢ light bl. Hayes (563), Sept. 4	1.65	.15	10.50	(4)	90.00	
	Retouched forehead	6.50	1.00				
693	12¢ brown violet Cleveland (564), Aug. 25	3.50	.15	17.50	(4)	90.00	
694	13¢ yellow green Harrison (622), Sept. 4	1.40	.15	10.00	(4)	90.00	
695	14¢ dark blue American Indian (565), Sept. 8	2.50	.22	12.50	(4)	90.00	
696	15¢ gray Statue of Liberty (566), Aug. 27	6.25	.15	30.00	(4)	110.00	
	Perf. 10½ x 11						
697	17¢ black Wilson (623), July 25	3.50	.15	16.50	(4)	375.00	
698	20¢ carmine rose Golden Gate (567), Sept. 8	7.50	.15	35.00	(4)	300.00	
	Double transfer	20.00	—				
699	25¢ blue green Niagara Falls (568), July 25	6.75	.15	34.00	(4)	400.00	
700	30¢ brown Buffalo (569), Sept. 8	10.50	.15	57.50	(4)	300.00	
	Cracked plate	22.50	.85				
701	50¢ lilac Arlington Amphitheater (570), Sept. 4	30.00	.15	170.00	(4)	400.00	
	Perf. 11						
702	2¢ Red Cross, May 21	.15	.15	1.60	(4)	3.00	99,074,600
	Red cross omitted	—					
703	2¢ Yorktown, Oct. 19	.24	.20	2.25	(4)	3.50	25,006,400
a	2¢ lake and black	3.50	.50				
b	2¢ dark lake and black	*300.00*		*1,750.00*	(4)		
c	Pair, imperf. vertically	*3,250.00*					
	Issues of 1932, Washington Bicentennial Issue, Jan. 1, Perf. 11 x 10½						
704	½¢ Portrait by Charles W. Peale	.15	.15	3.00	(4)	4.00	87,969,700
	Broken circle	.60	.15				
705	1¢ Bust by Jean Antoine Houdon	.15	.15	4.00	(4)	4.00	1,265,555,100
706	1½¢ Portrait by Charles W. Peale	.32	.15	13.00	(4)	4.00	304,926,800
707	2¢ Portrait by Gilbert Stuart	.15	.15	1.50	(4)	4.00	4,222,198,300
	Gripper cracks	2.50	1.50				
708	3¢ Portrait by Charles W. Peale	.40	.15	10.50	(4)	4.00	456,198,500
709	4¢ Portrait by Charles P. Polk	.22	.15	4.25	(4)	4.00	151,201,300
	Broken bottom frame line	1.50	.50				
710	5¢ Portrait by Charles W. Peale	1.40	.15	14.50	(4)	4.00	170,565,100
	Cracked plate	5.00	1.00				
711	6¢ Portrait by John Trumbull	2.75	.15	50.00	(4)	4.00	111,739,400
712	7¢ Portrait by John Trumbull	.22	.15	4.25	(4)	4.00	83,257,400
713	8¢ Portrait by Charles B.J.F. Saint Memin	2.25	.50	50.00	(4)	4.50	96,506,100
	Pair, gutter between	50.00	—				
714	9¢ Portrait by W. Williams	2.00	.15	30.00	(4)	4.50	75,709,200
715	10¢ Portrait by Gilbert Stuart	8.50	.15	95.00	(4)	4.50	147,216,000

	1932 continued	Un	U	PB/LP	#	FDC	Q
	Olympic Winter Games Issue, Jan. 25, Perf. 11						
716	2¢ Ski Jumper	.35	.16	10.00	(6)	6.00	51,102,800
	Recut	3.50	1.50				
	Colored "snowball"	25.00	5.00				
	Perf. 11 x 10½						
717	2¢ Arbor Day, Apr. 22	.15	.15	6.50	(4)	4.00	100,869,300
	Olympic Summer Games Issue, June 15						
718	3¢ Runner at Starting Mark	1.10	.15	9.50	(4)	6.00	168,885,300
	Gripper cracks	4.00	.75				
719	5¢ Myron's Discobolus	1.90	.20	18.00	(4)	8.00	53,376,100
	Gripper cracks	4.00	1.00				
720	3¢ Washington, June 16	.15	.15	1.20	(4)	7.50	
	Pair with full vertical gutter between	*200.00*					
b	Booklet pane of 6, July 25	22.50	*5.00*			100.00	
c	Vertical pair, imperf. between	250.00					
	Double transfer	1.00	.30				
	Recut lines on nose	2.00	.75				
	Coil Stamps, Perf. 10 Vertically						
721	3¢ deep violet (720), June 24	2.25	.15	8.25	(2)	15.00	
	Recut lines around eyes	—	—				
	Perf. 10 Horizontally						
722	3¢ deep violet (720), Oct. 12	1.00	.30	5.00	(2)	15.00	
	Perf. 10 Vertically						
723	6¢ deep orange Garfield (558), Aug. 18	7.50	.25	42.50	(2)	15.00	
	Perf. 11						
724	3¢ William Penn, Oct. 24	.22	.15	8.00	(6)	3.25	49,949,000
a	Vertical pair, imperf. horizontally	—					
725	3¢ Daniel Webster, Oct. 24	.28	.24	16.50	(6)	3.25	49,538,500
	Issues of 1933						
726	3¢ Georgia Settlement, Feb. 12	.20	.18	10.00	(6)	3.25	61,719,200
	Perf. 10½ x 11						
727	3¢ Peace of 1783, Apr. 19	.15	.15	4.00	(4)	3.50	73,382,400
	Century of Progress Issue, May 25						
728	1¢ Restoration of Fort Dearborn	.15	.15	2.00	(4)	3.00	348,266,800
	Gripper cracks	2.00	—				
729	3¢ Federal Building at Chicago	.15	.15	2.00	(4)	3.00	480,239,300
	American Philatelic Society Issue, Souvenir Sheets, Aug. 25, Without Gum, Imperf.						
730	1¢ sheet of 25 (728)	24.00	24.00			100.00	456,704
a	Single stamp from sheet	.65	.35			3.25	11,417,600
731	3¢ sheet of 25 (729)	22.50	22.50			100.00	441,172
a	Single stamp from sheet	.50	.35			3.25	11,029,300
732	3¢ NRA, Aug. 15	.15	.15	1.50	(4)	3.25	1,978,707,300
	Gripper cracks	1.50	—				
	Recut at right	2.00					
	Perf. 11						
733	3¢ Byrd Antarctic Expedition II, Oct. 9	.40	.48	15.00	(6)	5.00	5,735,944
	Double transfer	2.50	1.00				
734	5¢ Kosciuszko, Oct. 13	.40	.22	27.50	(6)	4.50	45,137,700
a	Horizontal pair, imperf. vertically	*2,000.00*					
	Issues of 1934, National Stamp Exhibition Issue, Souvenir Sheet, Feb. 10, Without Gum, Imperf.						
735	3¢ sheet of 6 (733)	15.00	12.50			40.00	811,404
a	Single stamp from sheet	2.00	2.00			5.00	4,868,424

716

717

718

719

720

724

725

726

727

728

729

730

732

733

734

731

735

1934

736

737

739

740

741

742

743

744

745

746

747

748

749

750

751

	1934 continued, Perf. 11	Un	U	PB	#	FDC	Q
736	3¢ Maryland Tercentary, Mar. 23	.15	.15	7.50	(6)	1.60	46,258,300
	Double transfer	—	—				
	Mothers of America Issue, May 2, Perf. 11 x 10½						
737	3¢ Portrait of his Mother, by James A. McNeill Whistler	.15	.15	1.00	(4)	1.60	193,239,100
	Perf. 11						
738	3¢ deep violet (737)	.15	.15	4.25	(6)	1.60	15,432,200
739	3¢ Wisconsin Tercentary, July 7	.15	.15	3.00	(6)	1.10	64,525,400
a	Vertical pair, imperf. horizontally	250.00					
b	Horizontal pair, imperf. vertically	325.00					
	National Parks Issue						
740	1¢ El Capitan, Yosemite (California), July 16	.15	.15	1.00	(6)	2.25	84,896,350
	Recut	1.50	.50				
a	Vertical pair, imperf. horizontally, with gum	450.00					
741	2¢ Grand Canyon (Arizona), July 24	.15	.15	1.25	(6)	2.25	74,400,200
a	Vertical pair, imperf. horizontally, with gum	300.00					
b	Horizontal pair, imperf. vertically, with gum	300.00					
	Double transfer	1.25	—				
742	3¢ Mirror Lake, Mt. Rainier (Washington), Aug. 3	.15	.15	1.75	(6)	2.50	95,089,000
a	Vertical pair, imperf. horizontally, with gum	350.00					
743	4¢ Cliff Palace, Mesa Verde (Colorado), Sept. 25	.35	.32	7.00	(6)	2.25	19,178,650
a	Vertical pair, imperf. horizontally, with gum	500.00					
744	5¢ Old Faithful, Yellowstone (Wyoming), July 30	.60	.55	8.75	(6)	2.25	30,980,100
a	Horizontal pair, imperf. vertically, with gum	400.00					
745	6¢ Crater Lake (Oregon , Sept. 5	1.00	.75	15.00	(6)	3.00	16,923,350
746	7¢ Great Head, Acadia Park (Maine), Oct. 2	.55	.65	10.00	(6)	3.00	15,988,250
a	Horizontal pair, imperf. vertically, with gum	450.00					
747	8¢ Great White Throne, Zion Park (Utah), Sept. 18	1.40	1.65	15.00	(6)	3.25	15,288,700
748	9¢ Mt. Rockwell and Two Medicine Lake, Glacier National Park (Montana), Aug. 27	1.50	.55	15.00	(6)	3.50	17,472,600
749	10¢ Great Smoky Mountains (North Carolina), Oct. 8	2.75	.90	25.00	(6)	6.00	18,874,300
	American Philatelic Society Issue, Souvenir Sheet, Aug. 28, Imperf.						
750	3¢ sheet of 6 (742)	25.00	22.50			40.00	511,391
a	Single stamp from sheet	3.00	2.75			3.25	3,068,346
	Trans-Mississippi Philatelic Exposition Issue, Oct. 10, Souvenir Sheet						
751	1¢ sheet of 6 (740)	10.00	10.00			35.00	793,551
a	Single stamp from sheet	1.25	1.50			3.25	4,761,306

	Issues of 1935, Special Printing (#752 to 771), March 15, Without Gum, Perf. 10½ x 11	Un	U	PB	#	FDC	Q
752	3¢ violet Peace of 1783 (727)	.15	.15	11.00	(4)	5.00	3,274,556
	Perf. 11						
753	3¢ blue Byrd Expedition II (733)	.40	.40	15.00	(6)	6.00	2,040,760
	Imperf.						
754	3¢ dp. vio. Whistler's Mother (737)	.50	.50	16.50	(6)	6.00	2,389,288
755	3¢ deep violet Wisconsin (739)	.50	.50	16.50	(6)	6.00	2,294,948
756	1¢ green Yosemite (740)	.20	.20	3.65	(6)	6.00	3,217,636
757	2¢ red Grand Canyon (741)	.22	.22	4.50	(6)	6.00	2,746,640
	Double transfer	—					
758	3¢ deep violet Mt. Rainier (742)	.45	.40	12.50	(6)	6.00	2,168,088
759	4¢ brown Mesa Verde (743)	.90	.90	16.50	(6)	6.50	1,822,684
760	5¢ blue Yellowstone (744)	1.40	1.25	18.50	(6)	6.50	1,724,576
	Double transfer	—					
761	6¢ dark blue Crater Lake (745)	2.25	2.00	30.00	(6)	6.50	1,647,696
762	7¢ black Acadia (746)	1.40	1.25	25.00	(6)	6.50	1,682,948
	Double transfer	—					
763	8¢ sage green Zion (747)	1.50	1.40	30.00	(6)	7.50	1,638,644
764	9¢ red orange Glacier (748)	1.75	1.50	32.50	(6)	7.50	1,625,224
765	10¢ gray black Smoky Mts. (749)	3.50	3.00	41.50	(6)	7.50	1,644,900
766	1¢ yellow grn. (728), pane of 25	24.00	24.00			*250.00*	98,712
a	Single stamp from pane	.65	.35			5.50	2,467,800
767	3¢ violet (729), pane of 25	22.50	22.50			*250.00*	85,914
a	Single stamp from pane	.50	.35			5.50	2,147,850
768	3¢ dark blue (733), pane of 6	18.00	12.50			*250.00*	267,200
a	Single stamp from pane	2.50	2.00			6.50	1,603,200
769	1¢ green (740), pane of 6	12.00	9.00			*250.00*	279,960
a	Single stamp from pane	1.75	1.50			4.00	1,679,760
770	3¢ deep violet (742), pane of 6	27.50	22.50			*250.00*	215,920
a	Single stamp from pane	3.00	3.00			5.00	1,295,520
771	16¢ dark blue Great Seal of U.S.	2.00	2.00	43.50	(6)	12.50	1,370,560
	For perforate variety, see #CE2.						

A number of position pieces can be collected from the panes of sheets of the 1935 Special Printing issues, including horizontal and vertical gutter (752, 766-770) or line (753-65, 771) blocks of four (HG/L and VG/L), arrow-and-guideline blocks of four (AGL) and crossed-gutter or centerline blocks of four (CG/L). Pairs sell for half the price of blocks of four.

	HG/L	VG/L	AGL	CG/L
752	9.00	15.00		35.00
753	3.50	37.50	40.00	42.50
754	2.10	2.10	2.25	5.00
755	2.10	2.10	2.25	5.00
756	.90	.90	1.00	2.35
757	.95	.95	1.00	2.75
758	1.95	1.95	2.00	4.00
759	3.75	3.75	4.00	5.50
760	6.50	6.50	7.00	11.00
761	9.25	9.25	9.50	14.50
762	6.00	6.00	6.50	10.00
763	6.50	6.50	7.00	11.00
764	7.50	7.50	8.00	21.00
765	14.50	14.50	15.00	21.50
766	8.50	9.75		11.50
767	7.50	8.75		11.50
768	12.00	13.00		15.00
769	11.00	11.00		12.00
770	20.00	20.00		21.50
771	8.75	8.75	10.00	36.50

Examples of Special Printing Position Blocks

Gutter Block 752

Cross-Gutter Block 768

Line Block 756

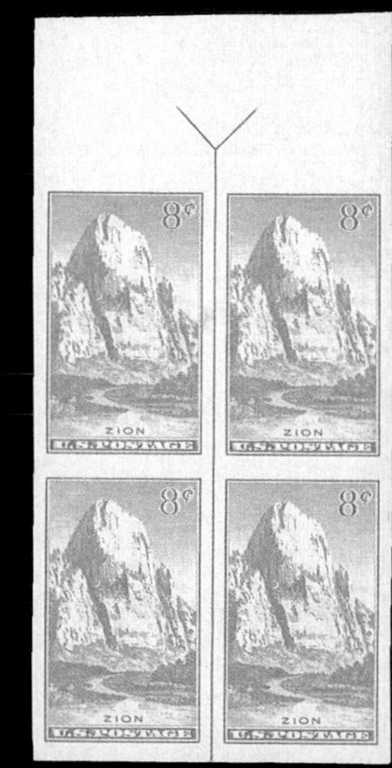

Arrow Block 763

Centerline Block 754

772

773

774

775

776

777

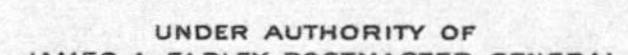

778

782

783

784

	1935 continued, Perf. 11 x 10½	Un	U	PB	#	FDC	Q
772	3¢ Connecticut Settlement, Apr. 26	.15	.15	1.40	(4)	8.00	70,726,800
	Defect in cent design	1.00	.25				
	Beginning with #772, unused values are for never-hinged stamps.						
773	3¢ California Pacific International Exposition, May 29	.15	.15	1.40	(4)	8.00	100,839,600
	Pair with full vertical gutter between	—					
	Perf. 11						
774	3¢ Boulder Dam, Sept. 30	.15	.15	1.85	(6)	10.00	73,610,650
	Perf. 11 x 10½						
775	3¢ Michigan Statehood, Nov. 1	.15	.15	1.40	(4)	8.00	75,823,900
	Issues of 1936						
776	3¢ Republic of Texas Independence, Mar. 2	.15	.15	1.40	(4)	15.00	124,324,500
	Perf. 10½ x 11						
777	3¢ Rhode Island Settlement, May 4	.15	.15	1.40	(4)	8.00	67,127,650
	Pair with full gutter between	*200.00*					
	Third International Philatelic Exhibition Issue, Souvenir Sheet, May 9, Imperf.						
778	Sheet of 4 different stamps (772, 773, 775 and 776)	1.75	1.75			13.00	2,809,039
779-81	not assigned						
	Perf. 11 x 10½						
782	3¢ Arkansas Statehood, June 15	.15	.15	1.40	(4)	8.00	72,992,650
783	3¢ Oregon Territory, July 14	.15	.15	1.40	(4)	8.50	74,407,450
	Double transfer	1.00	.50				
784	3¢ Susan B. Anthony, Aug. 26	.15	.15	.75	(4)	5.00	269,522,200
	Period missing after "B"	.75	.25				

DAM LOOMS LARGE IN COLORADO RIVER'S BLACK CANYON

Located in the Black Canyon of the Colorado River on the Arizona-Nevada border, Hoover Dam is one of the world's highest concrete dams. The huge structure—along with a reservoir and a hydroelectric power plant—is part of the Boulder Canyon Project, authorized by Congress in 1928. Previously referred to as Boulder Dam and Boulder Canyon Dam, the dam was officially designated by Congress as the Hoover Dam in 1947. Twelve years earlier, in 1935, a U.S. postal issue (#774) commemorated Boulder Dam.

	Issues of 1936-37	Un	U	PB	#	FDC	Q
	Army Issue, Perf. 11 x 10½						
785	1¢ George Washington, Nathanael Green and Mount Vernon, Dec. 15, 1936	.15	.15	.85	(4)	5.00	105,196,150
	Pair with full vertical gutter between	—					
786	2¢ Andrew Jackson, Winfield Scott and The Hermitage, Jan. 15, 1937	.15	.15	.85	(4)	5.00	93,848,500
787	3¢ Generals Sherman, Grant and Sheridan, Feb. 18, 1937	.15	.15	1.10	(4)	5.00	87,741,150
788	4¢ Generals Robert E. Lee and "Stonewall" Jackson and Stratford Hall, Mar. 23, 1937	.30	.15	8.00	(4)	5.50	35,794,150
789	5¢ U.S. Military Academy at West Point, May 26, 1937	.60	.15	8.50	(4)	5.50	36,839,250
	Navy Issue						
790	1¢ John Paul Jones, John Barry, *Bon Homme Richard* and *Lexington,* Dec. 15, 1936	.15	.15	.85	(4)	5.00	104,773,450
791	2¢ Stephen Decatur, Thomas Macdonough and *Saratoga,* Jan. 15, 1937	.15	.15	.80	(4)	5.00	92,054,550
792	3¢ David G. Farragut and David D. Porter, *Hartford* and *Powhatan,* Feb. 18, 1937	.15	.15	1.00	(4)	5.00	93,291,650
793	4¢ Admirals William T. Sampson, George Dewey and Winfield S. Schley, Mar. 23, 1937	.30	.15	8.00	(4)	5.50	34,552,950
794	5¢ Seal of U.S. Naval Academy and Naval Cadets, May 26, 1937	.60	.15	8.50	(4)	5.50	36,819,050
	Pair with full vertical gutter between	—					
	Issues of 1937						
795	3¢ Northwest Territory Ordinance, July 13	.15	.15	1.10	(4)	6.00	84,825,250
	Perf. 11						
796	5¢ Virginia Dare, Aug. 18	.20	18	7.00	(6)	7.00	25,040,400
	Society of Philatelic Americans Issue, Souvenir Sheet, Aug. 26, Imperf.						
797	10¢ blue green (749)	.60	.40			6.00	5,277,445
	Perf. 11 x 10½						
798	3¢ Constitution Sesquicentennial, Sept. 17	15	.15	1.00	(4)	6.50	99,882,300
	Territorial Issues, Perf. 10½ x 11						
799	3¢ Hawaii, Oct. 18	.15	.15	1.25	(4)	7.00	78,454,450
	Perf. 11 x 10½						
800	3¢ Alaska, Nov. 12	.15	.15	1.25	(4)	7.00	77,004,200
	Pair with full gutter between	—					
801	3¢ Puerto Rico, Nov. 25	.15	.15	1.25	(4)	7.00	81,292,450
802	3¢ Virgin Islands, Dec. 15	.15	.15	1.25	(4)	7.00	76,474,550
	Pair with full vertical gutter between	*275.00*					

Minimum value listed for a stamp is 15 cents. This minimum represents a fair-market price for having a dealer locate and provide a single stamp from his or her stock. Dealers may charge less per stamp for a group of such stamps, or less for a single stamp.

785

786

787

788

789

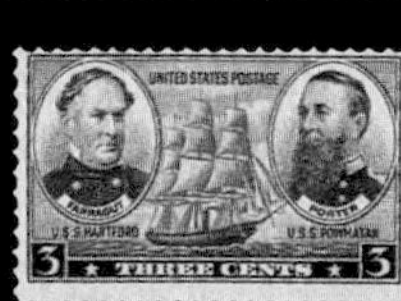

790

791

792

793

794

795

796

798

799

800

801

802

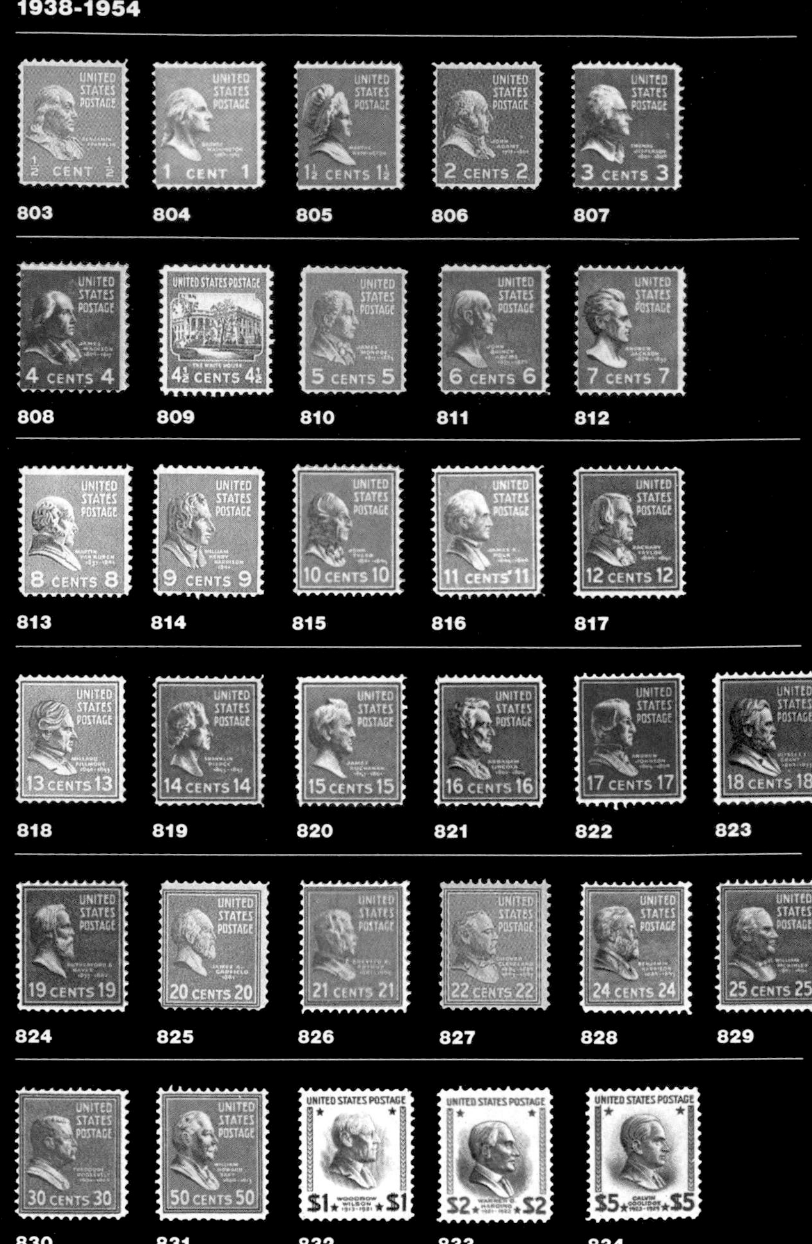

	Issues of 1938-54, Perf. 11 x 10½	Un	U	PB	#	FDC
	Presidential Issue (#804b, 806b, 807a issued in 1939, 832b in 1951, 832c in 1954, rest in 1938; see also #839-851)					
803	½¢ Benjamin Franklin, May 19	.15	.15	.35	(4)	1.75
804	1¢ George Washington, Apr. 25	.15	.15	.35	(4)	2.00
b	Booklet pane of 6, Jan. 27, 1939	1.50	*.20*			15.00
	Pair with full vertical gutter between	*125.00*	—			

	1938-54 continued, Perf. 11 x $10^1/_2$	Un	U	PB	#	FDC
805	$1^1/_2$¢ Martha Washington, May 5	.15	.15	.30	(4)	2.00
b	Horizontal pair, imperf. between	175.00	25.00			
	Pair with full horizontal gutter between	—				
806	2¢ John Adams, June 3	.15	.15	.35	(4)	2.00
b	Booklet pane of 6, Jan. 27, 1939	5.00	*.85*			15.00
	Recut at top of head	3.00	1.50			
807	3¢ Thomas Jefferson, June 16	.15	.15	.35	(4)	2.00
a	Booklet pane of 6, Jan. 27, 1939	10.00	*1.50*			20.00
b	Horizontal pair, imperf. between	*650.00*				
c	Imperf. pair	*2,500.00*				
808	4¢ James Madison, July 1	.80	.15	4.00	(4)	2.00
809	$4^1/_2$¢ The White House, July 11	.15	.15	1.60	(4)	2.00
810	5¢ James Monroe, July 21	.22	.15	1.25	(4)	2.00
811	6¢ John Quincy Adams, July 28	.25	.15	1.75	(4)	2.00
812	7¢ Andrew Jackson, Aug. 4	.28	.15	1.75	(4)	2.00
813	8¢ Martin Van Buren, Aug. 11	.30	.15	1.75	(4)	2.00
814	9¢ William H. Harrison, Aug. 18	.38	.15	1.90	(4)	3.00
	Pair with full vertical gutter between	—				
815	10¢ John Tyler, Sept. 2	.28	.15	1.40	(4)	3.00
816	11¢ James K. Polk, Sept. 8	.65	.15	3.25	(4)	3.00
817	12¢ Zachary Taylor, Sept. 14	1.10	.15	4.50	(4)	3.00
818	13¢ Millard Fillmore, Sept. 22	1.50	.15	6.75	(4)	3.00
819	14¢ Franklin Pierce, Oct. 6	.90	.15	4.50	(4)	3.00
820	15¢ James Buchanan, Oct. 13	.50	.15	2.50	(4)	3.00
821	16¢ Abraham Lincoln, Oct. 20	.90	.25	4.50	(4)	5.00
822	17¢ Andrew Johnson, Oct. 27	.85	.15	4.25	(4)	5.00
823	18¢ Ulysses S. Grant, Nov. 3	1.50	.15	7.50	(4)	5.00
824	19¢ Rutherford B. Hayes, Nov. 10	1.25	.35	6.25	(4)	5.00
825	20¢ James A. Garfield, Nov. 10	.70	.15	3.50	(4)	5.00
826	21¢ Chester A. Arthur, Nov. 22	1.50	.15	7.50	(4)	5.00
827	22¢ Grover Cleveland, Nov. 22	1.25	.40	9.50	(4)	5.00
828	24¢ Benjamin Harrison, Dec. 2	3.50	.18	18.75	(4)	5.00
829	25¢ William McKinley, Dec. 2	.80	.15	4.00	(4)	6.00
830	30¢ Theodore Roosevelt, Dec. 8	4.25	.15	24.00	(4)	7.50
831	50¢ William Howard Taft, Dec. 8	7.00	.15	37.50	(4)	10.00
	Perf. 11					
832	$1 Woodrow Wilson, Aug. 29	8.00	.15	37.50	(4)	45.00
a	Vertical pair, imperf. horizontally	*1,000.00*				
	Wmkd. USIR					
b	$1 purple and black, 1951	300.00	70.00	1,850.00	(4)	
	Unwmkd.					
c	$1 red violet and black, Aug. 31, 1954	6.75	.15	34.00	(4)	25.00
d	As "c," vertical pair, imperf. horizontally	*1,000.00*				
e	Vertical pair, imperf. between	*2,500.00*				
f	As "c," vertical pair, imperf. between	6,000.00				
833	$2 Warren G. Harding, Sept. 29	21.00	3.75	110.00	(4)	90.00
834	$5 Calvin Coolidge, Nov. 17	95.00	3.00	450.00	(4)	125.00
a	$5 red, brown and black	*1,000.00*	*500.00*			

	Issues of 1938, Perf. 11 x 10½	Un	U	PB	#	FDC	Q
835	3¢ Constitution Ratification, June 21	.18	.15	3.50	(4)	6.50	73,043,650
	Perf. 11						
836	3¢ Swedish-Finnish Tercentary,						
	June 27	.15	.15	2.75	(6)	6.00	58,564,368
	Perf. 11 x 10½						
837	3¢ Northwest Territory Sesquicentennial, July 15	.15	.15	8.00	(4)	6.00	65,939,500
838	3¢ Iowa Territorial Centennial, Aug. 24	.15	.15	4.50	(4)	6.00	47,064,300
	Pair with full vertical gutter between	—					
	Issues of 1939, Coil Stamps, Jan. 20, Perf. 10 Vertically						
839	1¢ green Washington (804)	.20	.15	.90	(2)	5.00	
840	1½¢ bistre brown Martha Washington (805)	.24	.15	.95	(2)	5.00	
841	2¢ rose carmine, John Adams (806)	.24	.15	1.25	(2)	5.00	
842	3¢ deep violet Jefferson (807)	.42	.15	1.50	(2)	5.00	
	Gripper cracks	—					
	Thin, translucent paper	2.00	—				
843	4¢ red violet Madison (808)	6.75	.35	22.50	(2)	5.00	
844	4½¢ dark gray White House (809)	.42	.35	3.25	(2)	5.00	
845	5¢ bright blue Monroe (810)	4.50	.30	20.00	(2)	5.00	
846	6¢ red orange John Quincy Adams (811)	1.10	.15	7.00	(2)	7.00	
847	10¢ brown red Tyler (815)	10.00	.40	35.00	(2)	9.00	
	Coil Stamps, Jan. 27, Perf. 10 Horizontally						
848	1¢ green Washington (804)	.55	.15	2.00	(2)	5.00	
849	1½¢ bistre brown Martha Washington (805)	1.10	.30	3.00	(2)	5.00	
850	2¢ rose carmine John Adams (806)	2.00	.40	6.00	(2)	5.00	
851	3¢ deep violet Jefferson (807)	1.90	.35	5.00	(2)	6.00	
	Perf. 10½ x 11						
852	3¢ Golden Gate Exposition, Feb. 18	.15	.15	1.40	(4)	6.00	114,439,600
853	3¢ New York World's Fair, Apr. 1	.15	.15	1.90	(4)	8.00	101,699,550
	Perf. 11						
854	3¢ Washington's Inauguration, Apr. 30	.30	.15	3.00	(6)	6.00	72,764,550
	Perf. 11 x 10½						
855	3¢ Baseball, June 12	.80	.15	3.25	(4)	20.00	81,269,600
	Perf. 11						
856	3¢ Panama Canal, Aug. 15	.18	.15	3.00	(6)	5.00	67,813,350
	Perf. 10½ x 11						
857	3¢ Printing, Sept. 25	.15	.15	1.00	(4)	5.00	71,394,750
	Perf. 11 x 10½						
858	3¢ 50th Anniversary of Statehood (Montana, North Dakota, South Dakota, Washington), Nov. 2	.15	.15	1.25	(4)	5.00	66,835,000

835

836

837

838

852

853

854

855

856

857

858

1940

859 860 861 862 863

864 865 866 867 868

869 870 871 872 873

874 875 876 877 878

879 880 881 882 883

884 885 886 887 888

889 890 891 892 893

	Issues of 1940	Un	U	PB	#	FDC	Q
	Famous Americans Issue, Perf. 10½ x 11						
	Authors						
859	1¢ Washington Irving, Jan. 29	.15	.15	.90	(4)	1.50	56,348,320
860	2¢ James Fenimore Cooper, Jan. 29	.15	.15	.90	(4)	1.50	53,177,110
861	3¢ Ralph Waldo Emerson, Feb. 5	.15	.15	1.25	(4)	1.50	53,260,270
862	5¢ Louisa May Alcott, Feb. 5	.28	.20	8.00	(4)	2.25	22,104,950
863	10¢ Samuel L. Clemens (Mark Twain), Feb. 13	1.60	1.35	35.00	(4)	3.75	13,201,270
	Poets						
864	1¢ Henry W. Longfellow, Feb. 16	.15	.15	2.00	(4)	1.50	51,603,580
865	2¢ John Greenleaf Whittier, Feb. 16	.15	.15	2.00	(4)	1.50	52,100,510
866	3¢ James Russell Lowell, Feb. 20	.15	.15	2.50	(4)	1.50	51,666,580
867	5¢ Walt Whitman, Feb. 20	.32	.18	10.50	(4)	4.00	22,207,780
868	10¢ James Whitcomb Riley, Feb. 24	1.75	1.40	35.00	(4)	6.00	11,835,530
	Educators						
869	1¢ Horace Mann, Mar. 14	.15	.15	2.25	(4)	1.50	52,471,160
870	2¢ Mark Hopkins, Mar. 14	.15	.15	1.00	(4)	1.50	52,366,440
871	3¢ Charles W. Eliot, Mar. 28	.15	.15	2.00	(4)	1.50	51,636,270
872	5¢ Frances E. Willard, Mar. 28	.38	.25	10.00	(4)	4.00	20,729,030
873	10¢ Booker T. Washington, Apr. 7	1.25	1.25	25.00	(4)	6.00	14,125,580
	Scientists						
874	1¢ John James Audubon, Apr. 8	.15	.15	.90	(4)	1.50	59,409,000
875	2¢ Dr. Crawford W. Long, Apr. 8	.15	.15	.75	(4)	1.50	57,888,600
876	3¢ Luther Burbank, Apr. 17	.15	.15	1.00	(4)	2.00	58,273,180
877	5¢ Dr. Walter Reed, Apr. 17	.25	.15	7.00	(4)	2.50	23,779,000
878	10¢ Jane Addams, Apr. 26	1.05	.95	20.00	(4)	5.00	15,112,580
	Composers						
879	1¢ Stephen Collins Foster, May 3	.15	.15	1.00	(4)	1.50	57,322,790
880	2¢ John Philip Sousa, May 3	.15	.15	1.00	(4)	1.50	58,281,580
881	3¢ Victor Herbert, May 13	.15	.15	1.00	(4)	1.50	56,398,790
882	5¢ Edward A. MacDowell, May 13	.40	.22	9.00	(4)	2.50	21,147,000
883	10¢ Ethelbert Nevin, June 10	3.50	1.35	32.50	(4)	5.00	13,328,000
	Artists						
884	1¢ Gilbert Charles Stuart, Sept. 5	.15	.15	1.00	(4)	1.50	54,389,510
885	2¢ James A. McNeill Whistler, Sept. 5	.15	.15	1.00	(4)	1.50	53,636,580
886	3¢ Augustus Saint-Gaudens, Sept. 16	.15	.15	1.00	(4)	1.50	55,313,230
887	5¢ Daniel Chester French, Sept. 16	.48	.22	8.00	(4)	1.75	21,720,580
888	10¢ Frederic Remington, Sept. 30	1.75	1.40	30.00	(4)	5.00	13,600,580
	Inventors						
889	1¢ Eli Whitney, Oct. 7	.15	.15	2.00	(4)	1.50	47,599,580
890	2¢ Samuel F.B. Morse, Oct. 7	.15	.15	1.10	(4)	1.50	53,766,510
891	3¢ Cyrus Hall McCormick, Oct. 14	.25	.15	1.75	(4)	1.50	54,193,580
892	5¢ Elias Howe, Oct. 14	1.00	.32	14.00	(4)	3.00	20,264,580
893	10¢ Alexander Graham Bell, Oct. 28	10.50	2.25	70.00	(4)	7.50	13,726,580

Minimum value listed for a stamp is 15 cents. This minimum represents a fair-market price for having a dealer locate and provide a single stamp from his or her stock. Dealers may charge less per stamp for a group of such stamps, or less for a single stamp.

	1940 continued, Perf. 11 x 10½	Un	U	PB	#	FDC	Q
894	3¢ Pony Express, Apr. 3	.25	.15	3.00	(4)	5.00	46,497,400
	Perf. 10½ x 11						
895	3¢ Pan American Union, Apr. 14	.20	.15	2.75	(4)	4.50	47,700,000
	Perf. 11 x 10½						
896	3¢ Idaho Statehood, July 3	.15	.15	1.75	(4)	4.50	50,618,150
	Perf. 10½ x 11						
897	3¢ Wyoming Statehood, July 10	.15	.15	1.50	(4)	4.50	50,034,400
	Perf. 11 x 10½						
898	3¢ Coronado Expedition, Sept. 7	.15	.15	1.50	(4)	4.50	60,943,700
	National Defense Issue, Oct. 16						
899	1¢ Statue of Liberty	.15	.15	.45	(4)	4.25	
a	Vertical pair, imperf. between	*500.00*	—				
b	Horizontal pair, imperf. between	40.00	—				
	Pair with full vertical gutter between	*200.00*					
	Cracked plate	3.00					
	Gripper cracks	3.00					
900	2¢ 90mm Anti-aircraft Gun	.15	.15	.50	(4)	4.25	
a	Horizontal pair, imperf. between	40.00	—				
	Pair with full vertical gutter between	*275.00*					
901	3¢ Torch of Enlightenment	.15	.15	.70	(4)	4.25	
a	Horizontal pair, imperf. between	30.00	—				
	Pair with full vertical gutter between	—					
	Perf. 10½ x 11						
902	3¢ Thirteenth Amendment, Oct. 20	.16	.15	3.25	(4)	5.00	44,389,550
	Issue of 1941, Perf. 11 x 10½						
903	3¢ Vermont Statehood, Mar. 4	.15	.15	1.75	(4)	6.00	54,574,550
	Issues of 1942						
904	3¢ Kentucky Statehood, June 1	.15	.15	1.10	(4)	4.00	63,558,400
905	3¢ Win the War, July 4	.15	.15	.40	(4)	3.75	
a	3¢ purple	20.00	8.00				
	Pair with full vertical or horizontal gutter between	*175.00*					
906	5¢ Chinese Resistance, July 7	.18	.16	10.00	(4)	6.00	21,272,800
	Issues of 1943						
907	2¢ Allied Nations, Jan. 14	.15	.15	.40	(4)	3.50	1,671,564,200
908	1¢ Four Freedoms, Feb. 12	.15	.15	.50	(4)	3.50	1,227,334,200

894

895

896

897

898

899

900

901

902

903

904

905

906

907

908

909

910

911

912

913

914

915

916

917

918

919

920

921

922

923

924

925

926

	Issues of 1943-44	Un	U	PB	#	FDC	Q
	Overrun Countries Issue, Perf. 12 (#921 issued in 1944, rest in 1943)						
909	5¢ Poland, June 22	.18	.15	6.00*	(4)	5.00	19,999,646
910	5¢ Czechoslovakia, July 12	.18	.15	3.00*	(4)	4.00	19,999,646
911	5¢ Norway, July 27	.15	.15	1.50*	(4)	4.00	19,999,646
912	5¢ Luxembourg, Aug. 10	.15	.15	1.25*	(4)	4.00	19,999,646
913	5¢ Netherlands, Aug. 24	.15	.15	1.25*	(4)	4.00	19,999,646
914	5¢ Belgium, Sept. 14	.15	.15	1.25*	(4)	4.00	19,999,646
915	5¢ France, Sept. 28	.15	.15	1.25*	(4)	4.00	19,999,646
916	5¢ Greece, Oct. 12	.38	.25	13.00*	(4)	4.00	14,999,646
917	5¢ Yugoslavia, Oct. 26	.28	.15	7.00*	(4)	4.00	14,999,646
918	5¢ Albania, Nov. 9	.18	.15	7.50*	(4)	4.00	14,999,646
919	5¢ Austria, Nov. 23	.18	.15	4.00*	(4)	4.00	14,999,646
920	5¢ Denmark, Dec. 7	.18	.15	6.00*	(4)	4.00	14,999,646
921	5¢ Korea, Nov. 2, 1944	.15	.15	5.25*	(4)	4.00	14,999,646
	"KORPA" plate flaw	17.50	12.50				
	*Instead of plate numbers, the selvage is inscribed with the name of the country.						
	Issues of 1944, Perf. 11 x 10½						
922	3¢ Transcontinental Railroad, May 10	.18	.15	1.50	(4)	5.00	61,303,000
923	3¢ Steamship, May 22	.15	.15	1.50	(4)	4.00	61,001,450
924	3¢ Telegraph, May 24	.15	.15	.90	(4)	3.50	60,605,000
925	3¢ Philippines, Sept. 27	.15	.15	1.00	(4)	3.50	50,129,350
926	3¢ Motion Pictures, Oct. 31	.15	.15	.85	(4)	3.50	53,479,400

EAST MEETS WEST AT GOLDEN SPIKE

On May 10, 1869, a golden spike driven into a railroad tie in Promontory, Utah, marked the completion of the Transcontinental Railroad (#922). For the first time, coast-to-coast train travel in the United States was possible. The railroad was built by the Union Pacific, which laid track west from Omaha, and the Central Pacific, which laid track east from Sacramento. For each mile of track, thousands of laborers— primarily Chinese and European immigrants—pounded in 4,000 spikes.

	Issues of 1945, Perf. 11 x 10½	Un	U	PB	#	FDC	Q
927	3¢ Florida Statehood, Mar. 3	.15	.15	.50	(4)	3.50	61,617,350
928	5¢ United Nations Conference, Apr. 25	.15	.15	.45	(4)	3.50	75,500,000
	Perf. 10½ x 11						
929	3¢ Iwo Jima (Marines), July 11	.15	.15	.40	(4)	6.00	137,321,000
	Issues of 1945-46, Franklin D. Roosevelt Issue, Perf. 11 x 10½						
930	1¢ Roosevelt and Hyde Park Residence, July 26, 1945	.15	.15	.25	(4)	2.50	128,140,000
931	2¢ Roosevelt and "The Little White House" at Warm Springs, Ga., Aug. 24, 1945	.15	.15	.30	(4)	2.50	67,255,000
932	3¢ Roosevelt and White House, June 27, 1945	.15	.15	.30	(4)	2.50	133,870,000
933	5¢ Roosevelt, Map of Western Hemisphere and Four Freedoms, Jan. 30, 1946	.15	.15	.45	(4)	3.00	76,455,400
934	3¢ Army, Sept. 28	.15	.15	.30	(4)	4.00	128,357,750
935	3¢ Navy, Oct. 27	.15	.15	.30	(4)	4.00	135,863,000
936	3¢ Coast Guard, Nov. 10	.15	.15	.30	(4)	4.00	111,616,700
937	3¢ Alfred E. Smith, Nov. 26	.15	.15	.30	(4)	2.50	308,587,700
	Pair with full vertical gutter between	—	—				
938	3¢ Texas Statehood, Dec. 29	.15	.15	.30	(4)	4.00	170,640,000
	Issues of 1946						
939	3¢ Merchant Marine, Feb. 26	.15	.15	.30	(4)	4.00	135,927,000
940	3¢ Veterans of World War II, May 9	.15	.15	.30	(4)	1.50	260,339,100
941	3¢ Tennessee Statehood, June 1	.15	.15	.30	(4)	1.50	132,274,500
942	3¢ Iowa Statehood, Aug. 3	.15	.15	.30	(4)	1.50	132,430,000
943	3¢ Smithsonian Institution, Aug. 10	.15	.15	.30	(4)	1.50	139,209,500
944	3¢ Kearny Expedition, Oct. 16	.15	.15	.30	(4)	1.50	114,684,450
	Issues of 1947, Perf. 10½ x 11						
945	3¢ Thomas A. Edison, Feb. 11	.15	.15	.30	(4)	2.00	156,540,510
	Perf. 11 x 10½						
946	3¢ Joseph Pulitzer, Apr. 10	.15	.15	.30	(4)	1.50	120,452,600
947	3¢ Postage Stamps Centenary, May 17	.15	.15	.30	(4)	1.50	127,104,300

Kearny Claimed New Mexico

Ownership of the territory of New Mexico was one of the main issues of the Mexican War, fought between Mexico and the United States. In August, 1846, U.S. troops commanded by General Stephen Watts Kearny entered Santa Fe and successfully took control of New Mexico. To symbolize their success, they flew the American flag—as shown on a 1946 U.S. stamp issue (#944) commemorating the centennial of the Kearny Expedition. At the war's end, Mexico ceded New Mexico to the United States.

927

"TOWARD
UNITED NATIONS
APRIL 25, 1945"
FRANKLIN D. ROOSEVELT
5¢ UNITED STATES POSTAGE

928

929

930

931

932

933

934

935

UNITED STATES POSTAGE
3
1790
U.S. COAST GUARD
1945

936

937

938

939

940

941

942

943

944

945

946

947

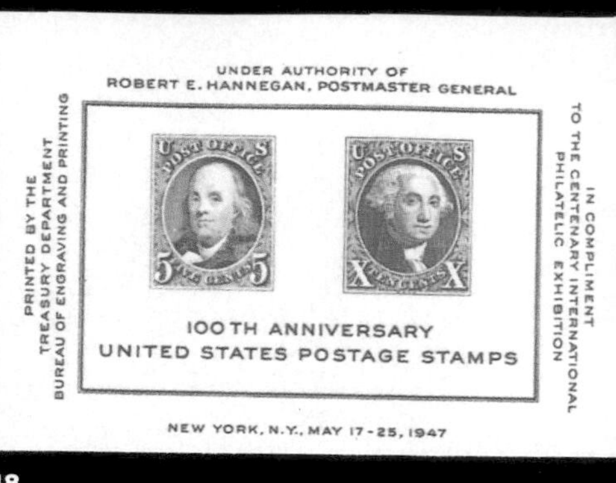

948

949

950

951

952

953

954

955

956

957

958

959

960

961

962

963

964

965

966

967

	1947 continued	Un	U	PB	#	FDC	Q
	Centenary International Philatelic Exhibition Issue, Souvenir Sheet, May 19, Imperf.						
948	Souvenir sheet of 2 stamps (#1-2)	.55	.45			2.00	10,299,600
a	5¢ single stamp from sheet	.25	.20				
b	10¢ single stamp from sheet	.30	.25				
	Perf. 11 x 10½						
949	3¢ Doctors, June 9	.15	.15	.30	(4)	1.00	132,902,000
950	3¢ Utah Settlement, July 24	.15	.15	.30	(4)	1.00	131,968,000
951	3¢ U.S. Frigate Constitution, Oct. 21	.15	.15	.30	(4)	1.00	131,488,000
	Perf. 10½ x 11						
952	3¢ Everglades National Park, Dec. 5	.15	.15	.30	(4)	1.00	122,362,000
	Issues of 1948, Perf. 10½ x 11						
953	3¢ Dr. George Washington Carver, Jan. 5	.15	.15	.30	(4)	1.00	121,548,000
	Perf. 11 x 10½						
954	3¢ California Gold, Jan. 24	.15	.15	.30	(4)	1.00	131,109,500
955	3¢ Mississippi Territory, Apr. 7	.15	.15	.30	(4)	1.00	122,650,500
956	3¢ Four Chaplains, May 28	.15	.15	.30	(4)	1.00	121,953,500
957	3¢ Wisconsin Statehood, May 29	.15	.15	.30	(4)	1.00	115,250,000
958	5¢ Swedish Pioneer, June 4	.15	.15	.45	(4)	1.00	64,198,500
959	3¢ Progress of Women, July 19	.15	.15	.30	(4)	1.00	117,642,500
	Perf. 10½ x 11						
960	3¢ William Allen White, July 31	.15	.15	.30	(4)	1.00	77,649,600
	Perf. 11 x 10½						
961	3¢ U.S.-Canada Friendship, Aug. 2	.15	.15	.30	(4)	1.00	113,474,500
962	3¢ Francis Scott Key, Aug. 9	.15	.15	.30	(4)	1.00	120,868,500
963	3¢ Salute to Youth, Aug. 11	.15	.15	.30	(4)	1.00	77,800,500
964	3¢ Oregon Territory, Aug. 14	.15	.15	.30	(4)	1.00	52,214,000
	Perf. 10½ x 11						
965	3¢ Harlan F. Stone, Aug. 25	.15	.15	.60	(4)	1.00	53,958,100
966	3¢ Palomar Mountain Observatory, Aug. 30	.15	.15	1.10	(4)	1.00	61,120,010
a	Vertical pair, imperf. between	*550.00*					
	Perf. 11 x 10½						
967	3¢ Clara Barton, Sept. 7	.15	.15	.30	(4)	.90	57,823,000

Everglades Enjoys Park Status

Located in southern Florida, the Everglades is a fragile, marshy ecosystem encompassing a diversity of animal and plant life. In 1947, a portion of the Everglades—along with the Big Cypress Swamp—became the Everglades National Park (#952). The park also includes Ten Thousand Islands along the Gulf of Mexico. The Anhinga Trail—named for the bird shown here—offers visitors an opportunity to closely observe birds, alligators, turtles and many other forms of Everglades' wildlife.

	1948 continued, Perf. 11 x 10½	Un	U	PB	#	FDC	Q
968	3¢ Poultry Industry, Sept. 9	.15	.15	.35	(4)	.90	52,975,000
	Perf. 10½ x 11						
969	3¢ Gold Star Mothers, Sept. 21	.15	.15	.35	(4)	1.00	77,149,000
	Perf. 11 x 10½						
970	3¢ Fort Kearny, Sept. 22	15	.15	.35	(4)	1.00	58,332,000
971	3¢ Volunteer Firemen, Oct. 4	.15	.15	.35	(4)	1.00	56,228,000
972	3¢ Indian Centennial, Oct. 15	.15	.15	.35	(4)	.90	57,832,000
973	3¢ Rough Riders, Oct. 27	.15	.15	.35	(4)	.90	53,875,000
974	3¢ Juliette Gordon Low, Oct. 29	.15	.15	.35	(4)	.90	63,834,000
	Perf. 10½ x 11						
975	3¢ Will Rogers, Nov. 4	.15	.15	.40	(4)	.90	67,162,200
976	3¢ Fort Bliss, Nov. 5	.15	.15	1.25	(4)	.90	64,561,000
	Perf. 11 x 10½						
977	3¢ Moina Michael, Nov. 9	.15	.15	.35	(4)	.90	64,079,500
978	3¢ Gettysburg Address, Nov. 19	.15	.15	.35	(4)	.90	63,388,000
	Perf. 10½ x 11						
979	3¢ American Turners, Nov. 20	.15	.15	.35	(4)	.90	62,285,000
980	3¢ Joel Chandler Harris, Dec. 9	.15	.15	.50	(4)	.90	57,492,610
	Issues of 1949, Perf. 11 x 10½						
981	3¢ Minnesota Territory, Mar. 3	.15	.15	.30	(4)	.90	99,190,000
982	3¢ Washington and Lee University, Apr. 12	.15	.15	.30	(4)	.90	104,790,000
983	3¢ Puerto Rico Election, Apr. 27	.15	.15	.30	(4)	.90	108,805,000
984	3¢ Annapolis Tercentary, May 23	.15	.15	.30	(4)	.90	107,340,000
985	3¢ Grand Army of the Republic, Aug. 29	.15	.15	.30	(4)	.90	117,020,000
	Perf. 10½ x 11						
986	3¢ Edgar Allan Poe, Oct. 7	.15	.15	.45	(4)	.90	122,633,000
	Thin outer frame line at top, inner frame line missing	6.00					
	Issues of 1950, Perf. 11 x 10½						
987	3¢ American Bankers Association, Jan. 3	.15	.15	.30	(4)	1.00	130,960,000
	Perf. 10½ x 11						
988	3¢ Samuel Gompers, Jan. 27	.15	.15	.30	(4)	1.00	128,478,000

Americans Volunteer to Put Out Fires

Most small towns and rural areas in the United States depend on citizen volunteers for fire protection (#971). At the sound of their community fire sirens, these heroic men and women drop everything to combat local fires. Small towns in western New York hold Firemen's Field Days during the summer. Main streets turn into fairs complete with bingo games, pony rides and Ferris wheels. Proceeds are used to purchase and maintain local fire-fighting equipment and firehouses.

968

969

970

971

972

973

974

975

976

977

978

979

980

981

982

983

984

985

986

987

988

989

990

991

992

993

994

995

996

997

998

999

1000

1001

1002

1003

1004

1005

1006

1007

	1950 continued	Un	U	PB	#	FDC	Q
	National Capital Sesquicentennial Issue, Perf. 10½ x 11, 11 x 10½						
989	3¢ Statue of Freedom on Capitol Dome, Apr. 20	.15	.15	.30	(4)	1.00	132,090,000
990	3¢ Executive Mansion, June 12	.15	.15	.38	(4)	1.00	130,050,000
991	3¢ Supreme Court, Aug. 2	.15	.15	.30	(4)	1.00	131,350,000
992	3¢ U.S. Capitol, Nov. 22	.15	.15	.38	(4)	1.00	129,980,000
	Gripper cracks	1.00	.50				
	Perf. 11 x 10½						
993	3¢ Railroad Engineers, Apr. 29	.15	.15	.30	(4)	1.00	122,315,000
994	3¢ Kansas City, MO, June 3	.15	.15	.30	(4)	1.00	122,170,000
995	3¢ Boy Scouts, June 30	.15	.15	.35	(4)	2.00	131,635,000
996	3¢ Indiana Territory, July 4	.15	.15	.30	(4)	1.00	121,860,000
997	3¢ California Statehood, Sept. 9	.15	.15	.30	(4)	1.00	121,120,000
	Issues of 1951						
998	3¢ United Confederate Veterans, May 30	.15	.15	.30	(4)	1.00	119,120,000
999	3¢ Nevada Settlement, July 14	.15	.15	.30	(4)	1.00	112,125,000
1000	3¢ Landing of Cadillac, July 24	.15	.15	.30	(4)	1.00	114,140,000
1001	3¢ Colorado Statehood, Aug. 1	.15	.15	.30	(4)	1.00	114,490,000
1002	3¢ American Chemical Society, Sept. 4	.15	.15	.30	(4)	1.00	117,200,000
1003	3¢ Battle of Brooklyn, Dec. 10	.15	.15	.30	(4)	1.00	116,130,000
	Issues of 1952						
1004	3¢ Betsy Ross, Jan. 2	.15	.15	.35	(4)	1.00	116,175,000
1005	3¢ 4-H Club, Jan. 15	.15	.15	.30	(4)	1.00	115,945,000
1006	3¢ B&O Railroad, Feb. 28	.15	.15	.35	(4)	1.25	112,540,000
1007	3¢ American Automobile Association, Mar. 4	.15	.15	.30	(4)	.85	117,415,000

Betsy Ross Flag: Fact or Folklore?

Born in Philadelphia in 1752, Betsy Griscom married upholsterer John Ross in 1773. An accomplished seamstress, Mrs. Ross eventually became an official flagmaker for the Pennsylvania Navy. But did she sew the first United States flag? According to a paper written in 1870 by her grandson William J. Canby, Betsy Ross was asked to make the first official flag by a committee headed by George Washington. Historians, however, are divided as to whether Canby's account is fact or fiction. One thing is certain: Congress adopted the flag's stars-and-stripes design on June 14, 1777. (#1004)

	1952 continued, Perf. 11 x 10½	Un	U	PB	#	FDC	Q
1008	3¢ NATO, Apr. 4	.15	.15	.30	(4)	.85	2,899,580,000
1009	3¢ Grand Coulee Dam, May 15	.15	.15	.30	(4)	.85	114,540,000
1010	3¢ Arrival of Lafayette, June 13	.15	.15	.30	(4)	.85	113,135,000
	Perf. 10½ x 11						
1011	3¢ Mt. Rushmore Memorial, Aug. 11	.15	.15	.35	(4)	.85	116,255,000
	Perf. 11 x 10½						
1012	3¢ Engineering, Sept. 6	.15	.15	.30	(4)	.85	113,860,000
1013	3¢ Service Women, Sept. 11	.15	.15	.30	(4)	.85	124,260,000
1014	3¢ Gutenberg Bible, Sept. 30	.15	.15	.30	(4)	.85	115,735,000
1015	3¢ Newspaper Boys, Oct. 4	.15	.15	.30	(4)	.85	115,430,000
1016	3¢ International Red Cross, Nov. 21	.15	.15	.30	(4)	.85	136,220,000
	Issues of 1953						
1017	3¢ National Guard, Feb. 23	.15	.15	.35	(4)	.85	114,894,000
1018	3¢ Ohio Statehood, Mar. 2	.15	.15	.35	(4)	.85	118,706,000
1019	3¢ Washington Territory, Mar. 2	.15	.15	.30	(4)	.85	114,190,000
1020	3¢ Louisiana Purchase, Apr. 30	.15	.15	.30	(4)	.85	113,990,000
1021	5¢ Opening of Japan, July 14	.15	.15	.90	(4)	.85	89,289,600
1022	3¢ American Bar Association, Aug. 24	.15	.15	.30	(4)	.85	114,865,000
1023	3¢ Sagamore Hill, Sept. 14	.15	.15	.30	(4)	.90	115,780,000
1024	3¢ Future Farmers, Oct. 13	.15	.15	.30	(4)	.85	115,244,600
1025	3¢ Trucking Industry, Oct. 27	.15	.15	.30	(4)	.85	123,709,600
1026	3¢ General George S. Patton, Nov. 11	.15	.15	.40	(4)	.85	114,798,600
1027	3¢ New York City, Nov. 20	.15	.15	.35	(4)	.85	115,759,600
1028	3¢ Gadsden Purchase, Dec. 30	.15	.15	.30	(4)	.85	116,134,600
	Issue of 1954						
1029	3¢ Columbia University, Jan. 4	.15	.15	.30	(4)	.85	118,540,000

WOMEN PLAY ACTIVE ROLE IN U.S. MILITARY

In 1948, American women became a permanent part of regular and reserved armed forces units, a status honored on a stamp in 1952 (#1013). Their previous service, notably during World Wars I and II, had been on an "emergency" or auxiliary basis. During the Desert Shield/Desert Storm military operation, U.S. women served alongside men in the midst of desert warfare and earned the service medal depicted on new stamp #2551.

1008

1009

1010

1011

1012

1013

1014

1015

1016

1017

1018

1019

1020

1021

1022

1023

1024

1025

1026

1027

1028

1029

1030

1031

1031A

1032

1033

1034

1035

1036

1037

1038

1039

1040

1041

1042

1042A

1043

1044

1044A

1045

1046

1047

1048

1049

1050

1051

1052

1053

	Issues of 1954-67	Un	U	PB	#	FDC
	Liberty Issue, Perf. 11 x 10½, 10½ x 11					
1030	½¢ Franklin, Oct. 20, 1954	.15	.15	.25	(4)	.85
1031	1¢ Washington, Aug. 26, 1954	.15	.15	.25	(4)	.85
	Pair with full vertical or horizontal gutter between	*150.00*				
b	Wet printing	.15	.15			
1031A	1¼¢ Palace of the Governors, June 17, 1960	.15	.15	.45	(4)	.85
1032	1½¢ Mt. Vernon, Feb. 22, 1956	.15	.15	2.00	(4)	.60
1033	2¢ Jefferson, Sept. 15, 1954	.15	.15	.25	(4)	.60
	Pair with full vertical or horizontal gutter between	—				

	1954-67 continued, Perf. 11 x 10½ , 10½ x 11					
		Un	U	PB	#	FDC
1034	2½¢ Bunker Hill, June 17, 1959	.15	.15	.50	(4)	.60
1035	3¢ Statue of Liberty, June 24, 1954	.15	.15	.30	(4)	.60
a	Booklet pane of 6, June 30, 1954	3.00	*.50*			5.00
b	Tagged, July 6, 1966	.25	.20	5.00	(4)	15.00
c	Imperf. pair	*1,500.00*				
d	Horizontal pair, imperf. between	*800.00*				
e	Wet printing	.15	.15			
f	As "a," dry printing	4.00	*.60*			
1036	4¢ Lincoln, Nov. 19, 1954	.15	.15	.35	(4)	.60
a	Booklet pane of 6, July 31, 1958	2.25	*.50*			4.00
b	Tagged, Nov. 2, 1963	.48	.16	7.00	(4)	50.00
c	Wet printing	.15	.15			
1037	4½¢ The Hermitage, Mar. 16, 1959	.15	.15	.50	(4)	.60
1038	5¢ James Monroe, Dec. 2, 1954	.15	.15	.50	(4)	.60
	Pair with full vertical gutter between	*200.00*				
1039	6¢ T. Roosevelt, Nov. 18, 1955	.25	.15	1.25	(4)	.65
a	Wet printing	.42	.15			
1040	7¢ Wilson, Jan. 10, 1956	.20	.15	1.00	(4)	.70
	Perf. 11					
1041	8¢ Statue of Liberty, Apr. 9, 1954	.24	.15	2.50	(4)	.80
a	Carmine double impression	*650.00*				
1042	8¢ Statue of Liberty, redrawn, Mar. 22, 1958	.25	.15	1.25	(4)	.60
	Perf. 11 x 10½, 10½ x 11					
1042A	8¢ Gen. John J. Pershing, Nov. 17, 1961	.22	.15	1.10	(4)	.60
1043	9¢ The Alamo, June 14, 1956	.28	.15	1.40	(4)	1.50
1044	10¢ Independence Hall, July 4, 1956	.22	.15	1.10	(4)	.90
b	Tagged, July 6, 1966	1.20	1.00	7.50	(4)	15.00
	Perf. 11					
1044A	11¢ Statue of Liberty, June 15, 1961	.30	.15	1.50	(4)	.90
c	Tagged, Jan. 11, 1967	2.00	1.60	9.00	(4)	22.50
	Perf. 11 x 10½, 10½ x 11					
1045	12¢ Benjamin Harrison, June 6, 1959	.32	.15	1.60	(4)	.90
a	Tagged, 1968	.45	.15	3.00	(4)	25.00
1046	15¢ John Jay, Dec. 12, 1958	.90	.15	5.00	(4)	1.00
a	Tagged, July 6, 1966	1.10	.22	6.00	(4)	20.00
1047	20¢ Monticello, Apr. 13, 1956	.50	.15	2.50	(4)	1.20
1048	25¢ Paul Revere, Apr. 18, 1958	1.50	.15	7.50	(4)	1.30
1049	30¢ Robert E. Lee, Sept. 21, 1955	1.00	.15	5.25	(4)	1.50
a	Wet printing	1.75	.15			
1050	40¢ John Marshall, Sept. 24, 1955	2.00	.15	10.00	(4)	1.75
a	Wet printing	2.50	.25			
1051	50¢ Susan B. Anthony, Aug. 25, 1955	1.75	.15	8.75	(4)	6.00
a	Wet printing	2.50	.15			
1052	$1 Patrick Henry, Oct. 7, 1955	5.50	.15	25.00	(4)	10.00
a	Wet printing	5.50	.15			
	Perf. 11					
1053	$5 Alexander Hamilton, Mar. 19, 1956	75.00	6.75	325.00	(4)	50.00

	Issues of 1954-73, Coil Stamps, Perf. 10 Vertically						
		Un	U	PB/LP	#	FDC	Q
1054	1¢ dark green Washington (1031), Oct. 8, 1954	.18	.15	.75	(2)	.75	
b	Imperf. pair	*2,000.00*					
c	Wet printing	.35	.16				
	Coil Stamp, Perf. 10 Horizontally						
1054A	1 1/4¢ turquoise Palace of the Governors (1031A), June 17, 1960	.15	.15	2.00	(2)	1.00	
	Coil Stamps, Perf. 10 Vertically						
1055	2¢ rose carmine Jefferson (1033), Oct. 22, 1954	.15	.15	.45	(2)	.75	
a	Tagged, May 6, 1968	.15	.15		(2)	11.00	
b	Imperf. pair (Bureau precanceled)		*500.00*				
c	As "a," imperf. pair	*600.00*					
d	Wet printing	.16	.15				
1056	2 1/2¢ gray blue Bunker Hill (1034), Sept. 9, 1959	.30	.25	3.50	(2)	2.00	
1057	3¢ deep violet Statue of Liberty (1035), July 20, 1954	.15	.15	.55	(2)	.75	
a	Imperf. pair	*750.00*	—	*1,000.00*	(2)		
b	Tagged, Oct. 1966	.50	.25				
c	Wet printing	.24	.15				
1058	4¢ red violet Lincoln (1036), July 31, 1958	.15	.15	.60	(2)	.75	
a	Imperf. pair	90.00	70.00	200.00	(2)		
b	Wet printing (Bureau precanceled)		.50				
	Coil Stamp, Perf. 10 Horizontally						
1059	4 1/2¢ blue green The Hermitage (1037), May 1, 1959	1.50	1.20	12.00	(2)	1.75	
	Coil Stamp, Perf. 10 Vertically						
1059A	25¢ green Revere (1048), Feb. 25, 1965	.50	.30	1.75	(2)	1.20	
b	Tagged, Apr. 3, 1973	.55	.20			14.00	
	Dull finish gum	.55					
c	Imperf. pair	*45.00*					
	Issues of 1954, Perf. 11 x 10 1/2						
1060	3¢ Nebraska Territory, May 7	.15	.15	.30	(4)	.75	115,810,000
1061	3¢ Kansas Territory, May 31	.15	.15	.30	(4)	.75	113,603,700
	Perf. 10 1/2 x 11						
1062	3¢ George Eastman, July 12	.15	.15	.35	(4)	.75	128,002,000
	Perf. 11 x 10 1/2						
1063	3¢ Lewis and Clark Expedition, July 28	.15	.15	.35	(4)	.75	116,078,150
	Issues of 1955, Perf. 10 1/2 x 11						
1064	3¢ Pennsylvania Academy of the Fine Arts, Jan. 15	.15	.15	.30	(4)	.75	116,139,800
	Perf. 11 x 10 1/2						
1065	3¢ Land-Grant Colleges, Feb. 12	.15	.15	.30	(4)	.75	120,484,800
1066	8¢ Rotary International, Feb. 23	.16	.15	.90	(4)	1.10	53,854,750
1067	3¢ Armed Forces Reserve, May 21	.15	.15	.30	(4)	.75	176,075,000
	Perf. 10 1/2 x 11						
1068	3¢ New Hampshire, June 21	.15	.15	.35	(4)	.75	125,944,400
	Perf. 11 x 10 1/2						
1069	3¢ Soo Locks, June 28	.15	.15	.30	(4)	.75	122,284,600
1070	3¢ Atoms for Peace, July 28	.15	.15	.40	(4)	.75	133,638,850
1071	3¢ Fort Ticonderoga, Sept. 18	.15	.15	.40	(4)	.75	118,664,600

1060

1061

1062

1063

1064

1065

1066

1067

1068

1069

1070

1071

1072

1073

1074

1075

1076

1077

1078

1079

1080

1081

1082

1083

1084

1085

1086

	1955 continued, Perf. 10½ x 11	Un	U	PB	#	FDC	Q
1072	3¢ Andrew W. Mellon, Dec. 20	.15	.15	.30	(4)	.75	112,434,000
	Issues of 1956						
1073	3¢ Benjamin Franklin, Jan. 17	.15	.15	.30	(4)	.75	129,384,550
	Perf. 11 x 10½						
1074	3¢ Booker T. Washington, Apr. 5	.15	.15	.30	(4)	.75	121,184,600
	Fifth International Philatelic Exhibition Issues, Souvenir Sheet, Imperf.						
1075	Sheet of 2 stamps (1035, 1041), Apr. 28	2.25	2.00			5.00	2,900,731
a	3¢ (1035), single stamp from sheet	.90	.80				
b	8¢ (1041), single stamp from sheet	1.25	1.00				
	Perf. 11 x 10½						
1076	3¢ New York Coliseum and Columbus Monument, Apr. 30	.15	.15	.30	(4)	.75	119,784,200
	Wildlife Conservation Issue						
1077	3¢ Wild Turkey, May 5	.15	.15	.35	(4)	1.10	123,159,400
1078	3¢ Pronghorn Antelope, June 22	.15	.15	.35	(4)	1.10	123,138,800
1079	3¢ King Salmon, Nov. 9	.15	.15	.35	(4)	1.10	109,275,000
	Perf. 10½ x 11						
1080	3¢ Pure Food and Drug Laws, June 27	.15	.15	.30	(4)	.80	112,932,200
	Perf. 11 x 10½						
1081	3¢ Wheatland, Aug. 5	.15	.15	.30	(4)	.80	125,475,000
	Perf. 10½ x 11						
1082	3¢ Labor Day, Sept. 3	.15	.15	.30	(4)	.80	117,855,000
	Perf. 11 x 10½						
1083	3¢ Nassau Hall, Sept. 22	.15	.15	.30	(4)	.80	122,100,000
	Perf. 10½ x 11						
1084	3¢ Devils Tower, Sept. 24	.15	.15	.30	(4)	.80	118,180,000
	Pair with full horizontal gutter between	—					
	Perf. 11 x 10½						
1085	3¢ Children's Stamp, Dec. 15	.15	.15	.30	(4)	.80	100,975,000
	Issues of 1957						
1086	3¢ Alexander Hamilton, Jan. 11	.15	.15	.30	(4)	.80	115,299,450

History Dwells in Nassau Hall
Nassau Hall has seen its share of America's historic moments. The hall's capture by George Washington's troops on January 3, 1777, ended the Battle of Princeton and marked a turning point of the Revolutionary War. When the Congress of the Confederation met there for five months in 1783, Nassau Hall served as the new nation's capitol. Completed in 1756, Nassau Hall is the the oldest building on New Jersey's Princeton University campus. (#1083)

	1957 continued, Perf. 10½ x 11	Un	U	PB	#	FDC	Q
1087	3¢ Polio, Jan. 15	.15	.15	.30	(4)	.80	186,949,627
	Perf. 11 x 10½						
1088	3¢ Coast and Geodetic Survey, Feb. 11	.15	.15	.30	(4)	.80	115,235,000
1089	3¢ American Institute of Architects, Feb. 23	.15	.15	.30	(4)	.80	106,647,500
	Perf. 10½ x 11						
1090	3¢ Steel Industry, May 22	.15	.15	.30	(4)	.80	112,010,000
1091	3¢ International Naval Review-Jamestown Festival, June 10	.15	.15	.30	(4)	.80	118,470,000
1092	3¢ Oklahoma Statehood, June 14	.15	.15	.35	(4)	.80	102,230,000
1093	3¢ School Teachers, July 1	.15	.15	.30	(4)	.80	102,410,000
	Perf. 11						
1094	4¢ Flag, July 4	.15	.15	.35	(4)	.80	84,054,400
	Perf. 10½ x 11						
1095	3¢ Shipbuilding, Aug. 15	.15	.15	.30	(4)	.80	126,266,000
	Champion of Liberty Issue, Ramon Magsaysay, Aug. 31, Perf. 11						
1096	8¢ Bust of Magsaysay on Medal	.16	.15	.75	(4)	1.00	39,489,600
	Plate block of 4, ultramine P# omitted			—			
	Perf. 10½ x 11						
1097	3¢ Lafayette, Sept. 6	.15	.15	.30	(4)	.80	122,990,000
	Perf. 11						
1098	3¢ Wildlife Conservation, Nov. 22	.15	.15	.35	(4)	1.00	174,372,800
	Perf. 10½ x 11						
1099	3¢ Religious Freedom, Dec. 27	.15	.15	.30	(4)	.80	114,365,000
	Issues of 1958						
1100	3¢ Gardening-Horticulture, Mar. 15	.15	.15	.30	(4)	.80	122,765,200
1101-03	not assigned						
	Perf. 11 x 10½						
1104	3¢ Brussels Universal and International Exhibition, Apr. 17	.15	.15	.30	(4)	.80	113,660,200
1105	3¢ James Monroe, Apr. 28	.15	.15	.30	(4)	.80	120,196,580
1106	3¢ Minnesota Statehood, May 11	.15	.15	.30	(4)	.80	120,805,200
	Perf. 11						
1107	3¢ International Geophysical Year, May 31	.15	.15	.35	(4)	.80	125,815,200
	Perf. 11 x 10½						
1108	3¢ Gunston Hall, June 12	.15	.15	.30	(4)	.80	108,415,200
	Perf. 10½ x 11						
1109	3¢ Mackinac Bridge, June 25	.15	.15	.30	(4)	.80	107,195,200
	Champion of Liberty Issue, Simon Bolivar, July 24						
1110	4¢ Bust of Bolivar on Medal	.15	.15	.35	(4)	.80	115,745,280
	Perf. 11						
1111	8¢ Bust of Bolivar on Medal	.16	.15	1.50	(4)	1.00	39,743,640
	Plate block of four, ocher P# only			—			

Minimum value listed for a stamp is 15 cents. This minimum represents a fair-market price for having a dealer locate and provide a single stamp from his or her stock. Dealers may charge less per stamp for a group of such stamps, or less for a single stamp.

1087

1088

1089

1090

1091

1092

1093

1094

1095

1096

1097

1098

1099

1100

1104

1105

1106

1107

1108

1109

1110

CHAMPION OF LIBERTY
SIMON BOLIVAR · THE LIBERATOR
8¢
UNITED STATES POSTAGE

1111

1112

1115

1116

1113

1114

1120

1117

1118

1119

1123

1124

1121

1122

1128

1125

1126

1127

1129

1130

1131

	1958 continued, Perf. 11 x 10½	Un	U	PB	#	FDC	Q
1112	4¢ Atlantic Cable, Aug. 15	.15	.15	.40	(4)	.80	114,570,200
	Issues of 1958-59, Lincoln Sesquicentennial Issue, Perf. 10½ x 11, 11 x 10½						
1113	1¢ Portrait by George Healy, Feb. 12, 1959	.15	.15	.25	(4)	.80	120,400,200
1114	3¢ Sculptured Head by Gutzon Borglum, Feb. 27, 1959	.15	.15	.30	(4)	.80	91,160,200
1115	4¢ Lincoln and Stephen Douglas Debating, by Joseph Boggs Beale, Aug. 27, 1958	.15	.15	.40	(4)	.80	114,860,200
1116	4¢ Statue in Lincoln Memorial by Daniel Chester French, May 30, 1959	.15	.15	.40	(4)	.80	126,500,000
	1958 continued, Champion of Liberty Issue, Lajos Kossuth, Sept. 19, Perf. 10½ x 11						
1117	4¢ Bust of Kossuth on Medal	.15	.15	.40	(4)	.80	120,561,280
	Perf. 11						
1118	8¢ Bust of Kossuth on Medal	.16	.15	1.25	(4)	1.00	44,064,576
	Perf. 10½ x 11						
1119	4¢ Freedom of the Press, Sept. 22	.15	.15	.40	(4)	.80	118,390,200
	Perf. 11 x 10½						
1120	4¢ Overland Mail, Oct. 10	.15	.15	.40	(4)	.80	125,770,200
	Perf. 10½ x 11						
1121	4¢ Noah Webster, Oct. 16	.15	.15	.40	(4)	.80	114,114,280
	Perf. 11						
1122	4¢ Forest Conservation, Oct. 27	.15	.15	.40	(4)	.80	156,600,200
	Perf. 11 x 10½						
1123	4¢ Fort Duquesne, Nov. 25	.15	.15	.40	(4)	.80	124,200,200
	Issues of 1959						
1124	4¢ Oregon Statehood, Feb. 14	.15	.15	.40	(4)	.80	120,740,200
	Champion of Liberty Issue, José de San Martin, Feb. 25, Perf. 10½ x 11						
1125	4¢ Bust of San Martin on Medal	.15	.15	.40	(4)	.80	133,623,280
a	Horizontal pair, imperf. between	*1,250.00*					
	Perf. 11						
1126	8¢ Bust of San Martin on Medal	.15	.15	.80	(4)	1.00	45,569,088
	Perf. 10½ x 11						
1127	4¢ NATO, Apr. 1	.15	.15	.40	(4)	.80	122,493,280
	Perf. 11 x 10½						
1128	4¢ Arctic Explorations, Apr. 6	.15	.15	.40	(4)	.80	131,260,200
1129	8¢ World Peace Through World Trade, Apr. 20	.16	.15	.75	(4)	.80	47,125,200
1130	4¢ Silver Centennial, June 8	.15	.15	.40	(4)	.80	123,105,000
	Perf. 11						
1131	4¢ St. Lawrence Seaway, June 26	.15	.15	.40	(4)	.80	126,105,050
	Pair with full horizontal gutter between	—					

	1959 continued, Perf. 11	Un	U	PB	#	FDC	Q
1132	4¢ 49-Star Flag, July 4	.15	.15	.40	(4)	.80	209,170,000
1133	4¢ Soil Conservation, Aug. 26	.15	.15	.40	(4)	.80	120,835,000
1134	4¢ Petroleum Industry, Aug. 27	.15	.15	.40	(4)	.80	115,715,000
	Perf. 11 x 10½						
1135	4¢ Dental Health, Sept. 14	.15	.15	.40	(4)	.80	118,445,000
	Champion of Liberty Issue, Ernst Reuter, Sept. 29, Perf. 10½ x 11						
1136	4¢ Bust of Reuter on Medal	.15	.15	.40	(4)	.80	111,685,000
	Perf. 11						
1137	8¢ Bust of Reuter on Medal	.16	.15	.80	(4)	1.00	43,099,200
	Perf. 10½ x 11						
1138	4¢ Dr. Ephraim McDowell, Dec. 3	.15	.15	.40	(4)	.80	115,444,000
a	Vertical pair, imperf. between	*500.00*					
b	Vertical pair, imperf. horizontally	*400.00*					
	Issues of 1960-61, American Credo Issue, Perf. 11						
1139	4¢ Quotation from Washington's Farewell Address, Jan. 20, 1960	.15	.15	.40	(4)	.90	126,470,000
1140	4¢ Benjamin Franklin Quotation, Mar. 31, 1960	.15	.15	.40	(4)	.90	124,560,000
1141	4¢ Thomas Jefferson Quotation, May 18, 1960	.15	.15	.45	(4)	.90	115,455,000
1142	4¢ Francis Scott Key Quotation, Sept. 14, 1960	.15	.15	.45	(4)	.90	122,060,000
1143	4¢ Abraham Lincoln Quotation, Nov. 19, 1960	.15	.15	.50	(4)	.90	120,540,000
	Pair with full horizontal gutter between	—					
1144	4¢ Patrick Henry Quotation, Jan. 11, 1961	.15	.15	.60	(4)	.90	113,075,000
	Issues of 1960						
1145	4¢ Boy Scouts, Feb. 8	.15	.15	.40	(4)	.90	139,325,000
	Olympic Winter Games Issue, Feb. 18, Perf. 10½ x 11						
1146	4¢ Olympic Rings and Snowflake	.15	.15	.40	(4)	.80	124,445,000
	Champion of Liberty Issue, Thomas G. Masaryk, Mar. 7						
1147	4¢ Bust of Masaryk on Medal	.15	.15	.40	(4)	.80	113,792,000
a	Vertical pair, imperf. between	*2,250.00*					
	Perf. 11						
1148	8¢ Bust of Masaryk on Medal	.16	.15	1.10	(4)	1.00	44,215,200
a	Horizontal pair, imperf. between	—					
	Perf. 11 x 10½						
1149	4¢ World Refugee Year, Apr. 7	.15	.15	.40	(4)	.80	113,195,000
	Perf. 11						
1150	4¢ Water Conservation, Apr. 18	.15	.15	.40	(4)	.80	121,805,000
	Perf. 10½ x 11						
1151	4¢ SEATO, May 31	.15	.15	.40	(4)	.80	115,353,000
a	Vertical pair, imperf. between	*150.00*					

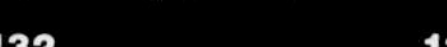

1132

1133

1134

1135

1136

1137

1138

1139

1140

1141

1142

1143

1144

1145

1146

1147

1148

1149

1150

1151

1960

1152

1153

1154

1155

1156

1157

1158

1159

1160

1161

1162

1163

1164

1165

1166

1167

1168

1169

1170

1171

1172

1173

	1960 continued, Perf. 11 x 10½	Un	U	PB	#	FDC	Q
1152	4¢ American Woman, June 2	.15	.15	.40	(4)	.80	111,080,000
	Perf. 11						
1153	4¢ 50-Star Flag, July 4	.15	.15	.40	(4)	.80	153,025,000
	Perf. 11 x 10½						
1154	4¢ Pony Express, July 19	.15	.15	.40	(4)	.80	119,665,000
	Perf. 10½ x 11						
1155	4¢ Employ the Handicapped, Aug. 28	.15	.15	.40	(4)	.80	117,855,000
1156	4¢ World Forestry Congress, Aug. 29	.15	.15	.40	(4)	.80	118,185,000
	Perf. 11						
1157	4¢ Mexican Independence, Sept. 16	.15	.15	.40	(4)	.80	112,260,000
1158	4¢ U.S.-Japan Treaty, Sept. 28	.15	.15	.40	(4)	.80	125,010,000
	Champion of Liberty Issue, Ignacy Jan Paderewski, Oct. 8, Perf. 10½ x 11						
1159	4¢ Bust of Paderewski on Medal	.15	.15	.40	(4)	.80	119,798,000
	Perf. 11						
1160	8¢ Bust of Paderewski on Medal	.16	.15	1.10	(4)	1.00	42,696,000
	Perf. 10½ x 11						
1161	4¢ Sen. Robert A. Taft Memorial, Oct. 10	.15	.15	.40	(4)	.80	106,610,000
	Perf. 11 x 10½						
1162	4¢ Wheels of Freedom, Oct. 15	.15	.15	.40	(4)	.80	109,695,000
	Perf. 11						
1163	4¢ Boys' Club of America, Oct. 18	.15	.15	.40	(4)	.80	123,690,000
1164	4¢ First Automated Post Office, Oct. 20	.15	.15	.40	(4)	.80	123,970,000
	Champion of Liberty Issue, Gustaf Mannerheim, Oct. 26, Perf. 10½ x 11						
1165	4¢ Bust of Mannerheim on Medal	.15	.15	.40	(4)	.80	124,796,000
	Perf. 11						
1166	8¢ Bust of Mannerheim on Medal	.16	.15	.80	(4)	1.00	42,076,800
1167	4¢ Camp Fire Girls, Nov. 1	.15	.15	.40	(4)	.80	116,210,000
	Champion of Liberty Issue, Giusseppe Garibaldi, Nov. 2, Perf. 10½ x 11						
1168	4¢ Bust of Garibaldi on Medal	.15	.15	.40	(4)	.80	126,252,000
	Perf. 11						
1169	8¢ Bust of Garibaldi on Medal	.16	.15	.80	(4)	1.00	42,746,400
	Perf. 10½ x 11						
1170	4¢ Sen. Walter F. George Memorial, Nov. 5	.15	.15	.40	(4)	.80	124,117,000
1171	4¢ Andrew Carnegie, Nov. 25	.15	.15	.40	(4)	.80	119,840,000
1172	4¢ John Foster Dulles Memorial, Dec. 6	.15	.15	.40	(4)	.80	117,187,000
	Perf. 11 x 10½						
1173	4¢ Echo 1-Communications for Peace, Dec. 15	.18	.15	1.10	(4)	2.00	124,390,000

	Issues of 1961	Un	U	PB	#	FDC	Q
	Champion of Liberty Issue, Mahatma Gandhi, Jan. 26, Perf. 10½ x 11						
1174	4¢ Bust of Gandhi on Medal	.15	.15	.40	(4)	.80	112,966,000
	Perf. 11						
1175	8¢ Bust of Gandhi on Medal	.16	.15	1.25	(4)	1.00	41,644,200
1176	4¢ Range Conservation, Feb. 2	.15	.15	.40	(4)	.75	110,850,000
	Perf. 10½ x 11						
1177	4¢ Horace Greeley, Feb. 3	.15	.15	.40	(4)	.75	98,616,000
	Issues of 1961-65, Civil War Centennial Issue, Perf. 11 x 10½						
1178	4¢ Fort Sumter, Apr. 12, 1961	.15	.15	.60	(4)	1.25	101,125,000
1179	4¢ Shiloh, Apr. 7, 1962	.15	.15	.50	(4)	1.25	124,865,000
	Perf. 11						
1180	5¢ Gettysburg, July 1, 1963	.15	.15	.60	(4)	1.25	79,905,000
1181	5¢ The Wilderness, May 5, 1964	.15	.15	.60	(4)	1.25	125,410,000
1182	5¢ Appomattox, Apr. 9, 1965	.18	.15	.60	(4)	1.25	112,845,000
a	Horizontal pair, imperf. vertically	*4,500.00*					
	1961 continued						
1183	4¢ Kansas Statehood, May 10	.15	.15	.40	(4)	.75	106,210,000
	Perf. 11 x 10½						
1184	4¢ Sen. George W. Norris, July 11	.15	.15	.40	(4)	.75	110,810,000
1185	4¢ Naval Aviation, Aug. 20	.15	.15	.40	(4)	.90	116,995,000
	Perf. 10½ x 11						
1186	4¢ Workmen's Compensation, Sept. 4	.15	.15	.40	(4)	.75	121,015,000
	With plate # inverted			.60	(4)		
	Perf. 11						
1187	4¢ Frederic Remington, Oct. 4	.15	.15	.40	(4)	.75	111,600,000
	Perf. 10½ x 11						
1188	4¢ Republic of China, Oct. 10	.15	.15	.40	(4)	.75	110,620,000
1189	4¢ Naismith-Basketball, Nov. 6	.15	.15	.40	(4)	1.50	109,110,000
	Perf. 11						
1190	4¢ Nursing, Dec. 28	.15	.15	.40	(4)	.75	145,350,000
	Issues of 1962						
1191	4¢ New Mexico Statehood, Jan. 6	.15	.15	.40	(4)	.75	112,870,000
1192	4¢ Arizona Statehood, Feb. 14	.15	.15	.40	(4)	.75	121,820,000
1193	4¢ Project Mercury, Feb. 20	.15	.15	.40	(4)	2.00	289,240,000
1194	4¢ Malaria Eradication, Mar. 30	.15	.15	.40	(4)	.75	120,155,000
	Perf. 10½ x 11						
1195	4¢ Charles Evans Hughes, Apr. 11	.15	.15	.40	(4)	.75	124,595,000

From Basket to Big Time

Throw a soccer ball into a peach basket and what have you got? A basketball! Dr. James Naismith invented the game in just this way in December 1891. A faculty member at the International YMCA Training School in Springfield, Massachusetts, Naismith—a Canadian—came up with basketball to fill the hiatus between football and baseball seasons. Tremendously popular in the United States today, basketball also is played internationally. (#1189 and a new 1991 issue, #2534)

1174

1175

1176

1177

1178

1179

1180

1181

1182

1183

1184

1185

1186

1187

1188

1189

1190

1191

1192

1193

1194

1195

1196

1197

1198

1199

1200

1201

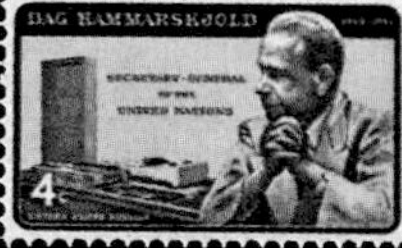

1202

1203

1205

1206

1207

1208

1209

1213

1230

1231

1232

1233

1234

1235

	1962 continued, Perf. 11	Un	U	PB/LP	#	FDC	Q
1196	4¢ Seattle World's Fair, Apr. 25	.15	.15	.40	(4)	.75	147,310,000
1197	4¢ Louisiana Statehood, Apr. 30	.15	.15	.40	(4)	.75	118,690,000
	Perf. 11 x 10½						
1198	4¢ Homestead Act, May 20	.15	.15	.40	(4)	.75	122,730,000
1199	4¢ Girl Scouts, July 24	.15	.15	.40	(4)	1.00	126,515,000
	Pair with full vertical gutter between	*250.00*					
1200	4¢ Sen. Brien McMahon, July 28	.15	.15	.40	(4)	.75	130,960,000
1201	4¢ Apprenticeship, Aug. 31	.15	.15	.40	(4)	.75	120,055,000
	Perf. 11						
1202	4¢ Sam Rayburn, Sept. 16	.15	.15	.40	(4)	.75	120,715,000
1203	4¢ Dag Hammarskjold, Oct. 23	.15	.15	.40	(4)	.75	121,440,000
1204	4¢ black, brown and yellow Dag Hammarskjold, Special Printing (yellow inverted), Nov. 16	.15	.15	1.25	(4)	6.00	40,270,000
	Christmas Issue, Nov. 1						
1205	4¢ Wreath and Candles	.15	.15	.40	(4)	.75	861,970,000
1206	4¢ Higher Education, Nov. 14	.15	.15	.40	(4)	.75	120,035,000
1207	4¢ Winslow Homer, Dec. 15	.15	.15	.50	(4)	.75	117,870,000
a	Horizontal pair, imperf. between	—					
	Issue of 1963-66						
1208	5¢ Flag over White House, Jan. 9, 1963	.15	.15	.50	(4)	.75	
a	Tagged, Aug. 25, 1966	.16	.15	.80	(4)	11.50	
b	As "a," horizontal pair, imperf. between	*1,250.00*					
	Issues of 1962-66, Perf. 11 x 10½						
1209	1¢ Andrew Jackson, Mar. 22, 1963	.15	.15	.25	(4)	.75	
a	Tagged, July 6, 1966	.15	.15	.30	(4)	5.75	
b	Horizontal pair, imperf. between, tagged	—					
1210-12	not assigned						
1213	5¢ George Washington, Nov. 23, 1962	.15	.15	.60	(4)	.75	
a	Booklet pane of 5 + label	5.00	*1.50*			4.00	
b	Tagged, Oct. 28, 1963	.50	.22	3.00	(4)	5.75	
c	As "a," tagged	3.00	*1.50*				
1214-24	not assigned						
	Coil Stamps, Perf. 10 Vertically						
1225	1¢ green Jackson (1209), May 31, 1963	.15	.15	2.25	(2)	.75	
a	Tagged, July 6, 1966	.15	.15	5.75	(2)	5.00	
1226-28	not assigned						
1229	5¢ dark blue gray Washington (1213), Nov. 23, 1962	1.00	.15	3.50	(2)	.75	
a	Tagged, Oct. 28, 1963	1.25	.15			20.00	
b	Imperf. pair	*375.00*					
	Issues of 1963, Perf. 11						
1230	5¢ Carolina Charter, Apr. 6	.15	.15	.50	(4)	.75	129,945,000
1231	5¢ Food for Peace-Freedom from Hunger, June 4	.15	.15	.50	(4)	.75	135,620,000
1232	5¢ West Virginia Statehood, June 20	.15	.15	.50	(4)	.75	137,540,000
1233	5¢ Emancipation Proclamation, Aug. 16	.15	.15	.50	(4)	.75	132,435,000
1234	5¢ Alliance for Progress, Aug. 17	.15	.15	.50	(4)	.75	135,520,000
	Perf. 10½ x 11						
1235	5¢ Cordell Hull, Oct. 5	.15	.15	.50	(4)	.75	131,420,000

	1963 continued, Perf. 11 x 10½	Un	U	PB	#	FDC	Q
1236	5¢ Eleanor Roosevelt, Oct. 11	.15	.15	.50	(4)	.75	133,170,000
	Perf. 11						
1237	5¢ The Sciences, Oct. 14	.15	.15	.50	(4)	.75	130,195,000
1238	5¢ City Mail Delivery, Oct. 26	.15	.15	.50	(4)	.75	128,450,000
1239	5¢ International Red Cross, Oct. 29	.15	.15	.50	(4)	.75	118,665,000
	Christmas Issue, Nov. 1						
1240	5¢ National Christmas Tree and White House	.15	.15	.50	(4)	.75	1,291,250,000
a	Tagged, Nov. 2	.65	.25	5.00	(4)	60.00	
	Pair with full horizontal gutter between	—					
1241	5¢ John James Audubon, Dec. 7 (see also #C71)	.15	.15	.50	(4)	.75	175,175,000
	Issues of 1964, Perf. 10½ x 11						
1242	5¢ Sam Houston, Jan. 10	.15	.15	.50	(4)	.75	125,995,000
	Perf. 11						
1243	5¢ Charles M. Russell, Mar. 19	.15	.15	.50	(4)	.75	128,925,000
	Perf. 11 x 10½						
1244	5¢ New York World's Fair, Apr. 22	.15	.15	.50	(4)	.75	145,700,000
	Perf. 11						
1245	5¢ John Muir, Apr. 29	.15	.15	.50	(4)	.75	120,310,000
	Perf. 11 x 10½						
1246	5¢ President John Fitzgerald Kennedy Memorial, May 29	.15	.15	.50	(4)	1.00	511,750,000
	Perf. 10½ x 11						
1247	5¢ New Jersey Settlement, June 15	.15	.15	.50	(4)	.75	123,845,000
	Perf. 11						
1248	5¢ Nevada Statehood, July 22	.15	.15	.50	(4)	.75	122,825,000
1249	5¢ Register and Vote, Aug. 1	.15	.15	.50	(4)	.75	453,090,000
	Perf. 10½ x 11						
1250	5¢ Shakespeare, Aug. 14	.15	.15	.50	(4)	.75	123,245,000
1251	5¢ Doctors Mayo, Sept. 11	.15	.15	.50	(4)	.75	123,355,000
	Perf. 11						
1252	5¢ American Music, Oct. 15	.15	.15	.50	(4)	.75	126,970,000
a	Blue omitted	*1,250.00*					
1253	5¢ Homemakers, Oct. 26	.15	.15	.50	(4)	.75	121,250,000

"TREES THAT . . . STAND IN PERFECT STRENGTH AND BEAUTY . . ."
John Muir (#1245) considered America's primeval forests a national treasure, for—once cut—the centuries-old trees they contain can never be replaced. A naturalist and conservationist, Muir was instrumental in influencing Congress to establish Yosemite and Sequoia National Parks. Since his death in 1914, Muir's work has been continued by the Sierra Club, a conservation group he founded. Now a national organization, the Sierra Club celebrates its 100th anniversary in 1992.

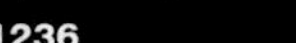

1236

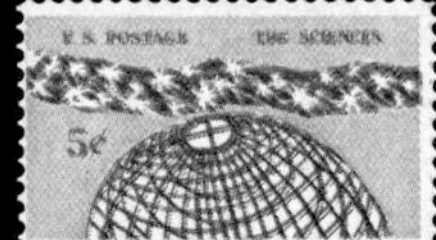

1237

1238

1239

1240

1241

1242

1243

1244

1245

1246

1247

1248

1249

1250

1251

1252

1253

1254 1255 1257b
1256 1257

1258

1259

1260

1261

1262

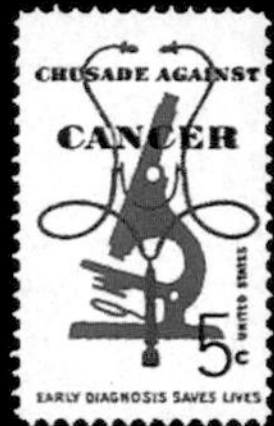

1263

1264

1265

1266

1267

1268

1269

1270

1271

1272

1273

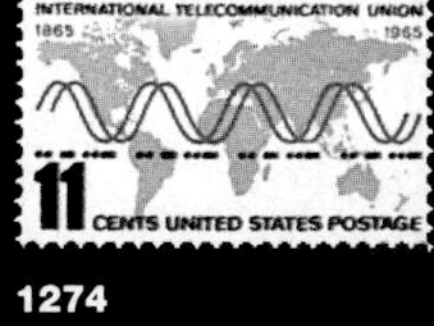

1274

1275

1276

	1964 continued	Un	U	PB	#	FDC	Q
	Christmas Issue, Nov. 9, Perf. 10½ x 11						
1254	5¢ Holly	.30	.15	1.50	(4)	.75	351,940,000
1255	5¢ Mistletoe	.30	.15	1.50	(4)	.75	351,940,000
1256	5¢ Poinsettia	.30	.15	1.50	(4)	.75	351,940,000
1257	5¢ Sprig of Conifer	.30	.15	1.50	(4)	.75	351,940,000
b	Block of four, #1254-57	1.25	1.00			3.00	
c	As "b," tagged, Nov. 10	4.25	2.00	5.00	(4)	57.50	
	Perf. 10½ x 11						
1258	5¢ Verrazano-Narrows Bridge, Nov. 21	.15	.15	.50	(4)	.75	120,005,000
	Perf. 11						
1259	5¢ Fine Arts, Dec. 2	.15	.15	.50	(4)	.75	125,800,000
	Perf. 10½ x 11						
1260	5¢ Amateur Radio, Dec. 15	.15	.15	.50	(4)	.75	122,230,000
	Issues of 1965, Perf. 11						
1261	5¢ Battle of New Orleans, Jan. 8	.15	.15	.50	(4)	.75	115,695,000
1262	5¢ Physical Fitness-Sokols, Feb. 15	.15	.15	.50	(4)	.75	115,095,000
1263	5¢ Crusade Against Cancer, Apr. 1	.15	.15	.50	(4)	.75	119,560,000
	Perf. 10½ x 11						
1264	5¢ Winston Churchill Memorial, May 13	.15	.15	.50	(4)	.75	125,180,000
	Perf. 11						
1265	5¢ Magna Carta, June 15	.15	.15	.50	(4)	.75	120,135,000
	Corner block of four, black PB# omitted			—			
1266	5¢ International Cooperation Year-United Nations, June 26	.15	.15	.50	(4)	.75	115,405,000
1267	5¢ Salvation Army, July 2	.15	.15	.50	(4)	.75	115,855,000
	Perf. 10½ x 11						
1268	5¢ Dante, July 17	.15	.15	.50	(4)	.75	115,340,000
1269	5¢ President Herbert Hoover Memorial, Aug. 10	.15	.15	.50	(4)	.75	114,840,000
	Perf. 11						
1270	5¢ Robert Fulton, Aug. 19	.15	.15	.50	(4)	.75	116,140,000
1271	5¢ Florida Settlement, Aug. 28	.15	.15	.50	(4)	.75	116,900,000
a	Yellow omitted	*700.00*					
1272	5¢ Traffic Safety, Sept. 3	.15	.15	.50	(4)	.75	114,085,000
1273	5¢ John Singleton Copley, Sept. 17	.15	.15	.50	(4)	.75	114,880,000
1274	11¢ International Telecommunication Union, Oct. 6	.32	.16	6.00	(4)	.75	26,995,000
1275	5¢ Adlai E. Stevenson Memorial, Oct. 23	.15	.15	.50	(4)	.75	128,495,000
	Christmas Issue, Nov. 2						
1276	5¢ Angel with Trumpet (1840 Weathervane)	.15	.15	.50	(4)	.75	1,139,930,000
a	Tagged, Nov. 15	.75	.15	7.50	(4)	42.50	
1277	not assigned						

The stamp listings contain a number of "a," "b," "c," etc. additions which include recognized varieties and errors. These listings are as complete as space permits.

	Issues of 1965-78	Un	U	PB	#	FDC
	Prominent Americans Issue, Perf. 11 x 10½, 10½ x 11					
1278	1¢ Jefferson, Jan. 12, 1968	.15	.15	.25	(4)	.60
a	Booklet pane of 8	1.00	*.25*			2.50
b	Bklt. pane of 4 + 2 labels, May 10, 1971	.75	*.20*			12.50
c	Untagged (Bureau precanceled)		.15			
1279	1¼¢ Albert Gallatin, Jan. 30, 1967	.15	.15	12.00	(4)	.60
1280	2¢ Frank Lloyd Wright, Jan. 8, 1968	.15	.15	.25	(4)	.60
a	Booklet pane of 5 + label	1.20	*.40*			4.00
b	Untagged (Bureau precanceled)		.15			
c	Booklet pane of 6, May 7, 1971	1.00	*.35*			15.00
	Pair with full vertical gutter between	—				
1281	3¢ Francis Parkman, Sept. 16, 1967	.15	.15	.30	(4)	.60
a	Untagged (Bureau precanceled)		.15			
1282	4¢ Lincoln, Nov. 19, 1965	.15	.15	.40	(4)	.60
a	Tagged, Dec. 1, 1965	.15	.15	.50	(4)	20.00
	Pair with full horizontal gutter between	—				
1283	5¢ Washington, Feb. 22, 1966	.15	.15	.50	(4)	.60
a	Tagged, Feb. 23, 1966	.15	.15	.60	(4)	22.50
1283B	5¢ redrawn, Nov. 17, 1967	.15	.15	.50	(4)	.50
d	Untagged (Bureau precanceled)		.15			
1284	6¢ Roosevelt, Jan. 29, 1966	.15	.15	.60	(4)	.50
a	Tagged, Dec. 29, 1966	.15	.15	.80	(4)	20.00
b	Booklet pane of 8, Dec. 28, 1967	1.50	*.50*			3.00
c	Booklet pane of 5 + label, Jan. 9, 1968	1.25	*.50*			100.00
1285	8¢ Albert Einstein, Mar. 14, 1966	.20	.15	1.00	(4)	.50
a	Tagged, July 6, 1966	.16	.15	.90	(4)	14.00
1286	10¢ Jackson, Mar. 15, 1967	.20	.15	1.00	(4)	.60
b	Untagged (Bureau precanceled)		.20			
1286A	12¢ Henry Ford, July 30, 1968	.28	.15	1.40	(4)	.50
c	Untagged (Bureau precanceled)		.25			
1287	13¢ John F. Kennedy, May 29, 1967	.24	.15	1.20	(4)	.65
a	Untagged (Bureau precanceled)		.25			
1288	15¢ Oliver Wendell Holmes, Mar. 8, 1968	.30	.15	1.50	(4)	.60
a	Untagged (Bureau precanceled)		.30			
	Perf. 10					
1288B	15¢ dark rose claret Holmes (1288), Single from booklet	.30	.15			.65
c	Booklet pane of 8, June 14, 1978	2.40	*1.25*			3.00
	Perf. 11 x 10½, 10½ x 11					
1289	20¢ George C. Marshall, Oct. 24, 1967	.42	.15	2.10	(4)	.80
a	Tagged, Apr. 3, 1973	.40	.15	2.00	(4)	12.50
1290	25¢ Frederick Douglass, Feb. 14, 1967	.55	.15	2.75	(4)	1.00
a	Tagged, Apr. 3, 1973	.50	.15	2.50	(4)	14.00

1278  1279  1280  1281  1282

1283  1283B  1284  1285  1286

1286A  1287  1288  1289  1290

1291  1292  1293  1294  1295

	Issues of 1965-78 continued, Perf. 11 x 10½, 10½ x 11					
	Prominent Americans Issue continued					
		Un	U	PB	#	FDC
1291	30¢ John Dewey, Oct. 21, 1968	.65	.15	3.25	(4)	1.20
a	Tagged, Apr. 3, 1973	.60	.15	3.00	(4)	14.00
292	40¢ Thomas Paine, Jan. 29, 1968	.85	.15	4.25	(4)	1.60
a	Tagged, Apr. 3, 1973	.80	.15	4.00	(4)	15.00
293	50¢ Lucy Stone, Aug. 13, 1968	1.00	.15	5.00	(4)	3.25
a	Tagged, Apr. 3, 1973	1.00	.15	5.00	(4)	20.00
294	$1 Eugene O'Neill, Oct. 16, 1967	2.50	.15	12.50	(4)	7.50
a	Tagged, Apr. 3, 1973	2.00	.15	10.00	(4)	22.50
295	$5 John Bassett Moore, Dec. 3, 1966	12.50	2.00	62.50	(4)	40.00
a	Tagged, Apr. 3, 1973	9.00	2.00	45.00	(4)	65.00
296	not assigned					

1305

1306

1307

1308

1309

1310

1312

1313

1311

1314

1315

	Issues of 1966-75, Coil Stamps, Perf. 10 Horizontally					
		Un	U	PB/LP	#	FDC
1297	3¢ violet Parkman (1281), Nov. 4, 1975	.15	.15	.45	(2)	.75
a	Imperf. pair	*30.00*		*50.00*	(2)	
b	Untagged (Bureau precanceled)		.15			
c	As "b," Imperf. pair		10.00			
1298	6¢ gray brown Roosevelt (1284), Dec. 28, 1967	.15	.15	1.25	(2)	.75
a	Imperf. pair	*2,000.00*				

	Issues of 1966-81, Coil Stamps, Perf. 10 Vertically	Un	U	PB/LP	#	FDC	Q
1299	1¢ green Jefferson (1278), Jan. 12, 1968	.15	.15	.20	(2)	.75	
a	Untagged (Bureau precanceled)		.15				
b	Imperf. pair	*40.00*		*65.00*	(2)		
1300-02	not assigned						
1303	4¢ black Lincoln (1282), May 28, 1966	.15	.15	.75	(2)	.75	
a	Untagged (Bureau precanceled)		.15				
b	Imperf. pair	*500.00*		*750.00*	(2)		
1304	5¢ blue Washington (1283), Sept. 8, 1966	.15	.15	.40	(2)	.75	
a	Untagged (Bureau precanceled)		.15				
b	Imperf. pair	*200.00*		*325.00*	(2)		
e	As "a," imperf. pair		*300.00*				
1304C	5¢ redrawn (1283B), 1981	.15	.15	.60	(2)		
d	Imperf. pair	—					
1305	6¢ Roosevelt, Feb. 28, 1968	.15	.15	.55	(2)	.75	
a	Imperf. pair	*75.00*		*100.00*	(2)		
b	Untagged (Bureau precanceled)		.20				
1305E	15¢ rose claret Holmes (1288), June 14, 1978	.25	.15	1.25	(2)	.75	
	Dull finish gum	.60					
f	Untagged (Bureau precanceled)		.30				
g	Imperf. pair	*30.00*		*90.00*	(2)		
h	Pair, imperf. between	*200.00*					
1305C	$1 dull purple Eugene O'Neill (1294), Jan. 12, 1973	1.50	.20	5.00	(2)	5.00	
d	Imperf. pair	*2,000.00*		—			
	Issues of 1966, Perf. 11						
1306	5¢ Migratory Bird Treaty, Mar. 16	.15	.15	.50	(4)	.75	116,835,000
1307	5¢ Humane Treatment of Animals, Apr. 9	.15	.15	.50	(4)	.75	117,470,000
1308	5¢ Indiana Statehood, Apr. 16	.15	.15	.50	(4)	.75	123,770,000
1309	5¢ American Circus, May 2	.15	.15	.50	(4)	.75	131,270,000
	Sixth International Philatelic Exhibition Issue						
1310	5¢ Stamped Cover, May 21	.15	.15	.50	(4)	.75	122,285,000
	Souvenir Sheet, Imperf.						
1311	5¢ Stamped Cover (1310) and Washington, D.C., Scene, May 23	.15	.15			.75	14,680,000
	Perf. 11						
1312	5¢ The Bill of Rights, July 1	.15	.15	.50	(4)	.75	114,160,000
	Perf. 10½ x 11						
1313	5¢ Poland's Millennium, July 30	.15	.15	.50	(4)	.75	128,475,000
	Perf. 11						
1314	5¢ National Park Service, Aug. 25	.15	.15	.50	(4)	.75	119,535,000
a	Tagged, Aug. 26	.30	.15	2.00	(4)	20.00	
1315	5¢ Marine Corps Reserve, Aug. 29	.15	.15	.50	(4)	.75	125,110,000
a	Tagged	.30	.15	2.00	(4)	20.00	
b	Black and bister omitted	—					

	1966 continued, Perf. 11	Un	U	PB	#	FDC	Q
1316	5¢ General Federation of Women's Clubs, Sept. 12	.15	.15	.50	(4)	.75	114,853,200
a	Tagged, Sept. 13	.30	.15	2.00	(4)	22.50	
	American Folklore Issue, Johnny Appleseed, Sept. 24						
1317	5¢ Appleseed Carrying Shovel and Seed Sack, Apple in Background	.15	.15	.50	(4)	.75	124,290,000
a	Tagged, Sept. 26	.30	.15	2.00	(4)	22.50	
1318	5¢ Beautification of America, Oct. 5	.15	.15	.50	(4)	.75	128,460,000
a	Tagged	.30	.15	1.50	(4)	20.00	
1319	5¢ Great River Road, Oct. 21	.15	.15	.50	(4)	.75	127,585,000
a	Tagged, Oct. 22	.30	.15	2.00	(4)	22.50	
1320	5¢ Savings Bond-Servicemen, Oct. 26	.15	.15	.50	(4)	.75	115,875,000
a	Tagged, Oct. 27	.30	.15	2.00	(4)	22.50	
b	Red, dark blue and black omitted	*4,000.00*					
	Christmas Issue, Nov. 1						
1321	5¢ Madonna and Child, by Hans Memling	.15	.15	.50	(4)	.75	1,173,547,000
a	Tagged, Nov. 2	.30	.15	1.90	(4)	9.50	
1322	5¢ Mary Cassatt, Nov. 17	.15	.15	.60	(4)	.75	114,015,000
a	Tagged	.25	.15	1.75	(4)	20.00	
	Issues of 1967						
1323	5¢ National Grange, Apr. 17	.15	.15	.50	(4)	.75	121,105,000
1324	5¢ Canada, May 25	.15	.15	.50	(4)	.75	132,045,000
1325	5¢ Erie Canal, July 4	.15	.15	.50	(4)	.75	118,780,000
1326	5¢ Search for Peace-Lions International, July 5	.15	.15	.50	(4)	.75	121,985,000
1327	5¢ Henry David Thoreau, July 12	.15	.15	.50	(4)	.75	111,850,000
1328	5¢ Nebraska Statehood, July 29	.15	.15	.50	(4)	.75	117,225,000
1329	5¢ Voice of America, Aug. 1	.15	.15	.50	(4)	.75	111,515,000
	American Folklore Issue, Davy Crockett, Aug. 17						
1330	5¢ Davy Crockett with Rifle, and Scrub Pine	.15	.15	.50	(4)	.75	114,270,000
a	Vertical pair, imperf. between	—					
b	Green omitted	—					
c	Black and green omitted	—					
d	Yellow and green omitted	—					
	Accomplishments in Space Issue, Sept. 29						
1331	5¢ Space-Walking Astronaut	.65	.15	3.50	(4)	3.00	60,432,500
a	Attached pair, #1331-32	1.40	1.25			8.00	
1332	5¢ Gemini 4 Capsule and Earth	.65	.15	3.50	(4)	3.00	60,432,500
1333	5¢ Urban Planning, Oct. 2	.15	.15	.50	(4)	.75	110,675,000
1334	5¢ Finland Independence, Oct. 6	.15	.15	.50	(4)	.75	110,670,000

Minimum value listed for a stamp is 15 cents. This minimum represents a fair-market price for having a dealer locate and provide a single stamp from his or her stock. Dealers may charge less per stamp for a group of such stamps, or less for a single stamp.

1316

1317

1318

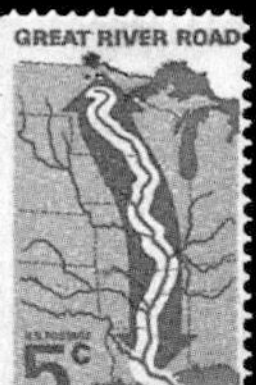

1319

1320

1321

1322

1323

1324

1325

1326

1327

1328

1329

1330

1331 1332 1331a

1333

1334

1335

1336

1337

1338

1339

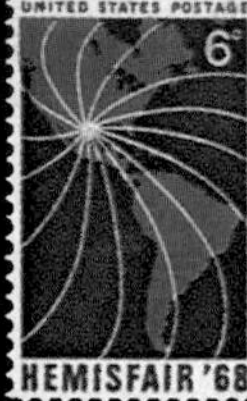

1340

1341

1342

1343

1344

1345

1346

1347

1348

1349

1350

1351

1352

1353

1354

1355

	1967 continued, Perf. 12	Un	U	PB	#	FDC	Q
1335	5¢ Thomas Eakins, Nov. 2	.15	.15	.50	(4)	.75	113,825,000
	Christmas Issue, Nov. 6, Perf. 11						
1336	5¢ Madonna and Child, by Hans Memling	.15	.15	.45	(4)	.75	1,208,700,000
1337	5¢ Mississippi Statehood, Dec. 11	.15	.15	.50	(4)	.75	113,330,000
	Issues of 1968-1971						
1338	6¢ Flag over White House design 19 x 22mm, Jan. 24, 1968	.15	.15	.45	(4)	.75	
k	Vertical pair, imperf. between	*400.00*					
	Perf. 11 x 10½						
1338D	6¢ dark blue, red and green (1338),						
	design 18¼ x 21mm, Aug. 7, 1970	.15	.15	2.60	(20)	.75	
e	Horizontal pair, imperf. between	*150.00*					
1338F	8¢ dark blue, red and slate green (1338), May 10, 1971	.16	.15	3.50	(20)	.75	
i	Imperf. pair	*65.00*					
j	Horizontal pair, imperf. between	*50.00*					
	Coil Stamps, Perf. 10 Vertically						
1338A	6¢ dark blue, red and green (1338), May 30, 1969	.15	.15			.75	
b	Imperf. pair	*500.00*					
1338G	8¢ dark blue, red and slate green (1338), May 10, 1971	.18	.15			.75	
h	Imperf. pair	*55.00*					
	Issues of 1968, Perf. 11						
1339	6¢ Illinois Statehood, Feb. 12	.15	.15	.55	(4)	.75	141,350,000
1340	6¢ HemisFair '68, Mar. 30	.15	.15	.55	(4)	.75	144,345,000
a	White omitted	*1,250.00*					
1341	$1 Airlift, Apr. 4	2.50	1.25	14.00	(4)	6.50	
	Pair with full horizontal gutter between		—				
1342	6¢ Support Our Youth-Elks, May 1	.15	.15	.55	(4)	.75	147,120,000
1343	6¢ Law and Order, May 17	.15	.15	.55	(4)	.75	130,125,000
1344	6¢ Register and Vote, June 27	.15	.15	.55	(4)	.75	158,700,000
	Historic Flag Issue, July 4						
1345	6¢ Fort Moultrie Flag, 1776	.50	.25			3.00	23,153,000
1346	6¢ U.S. Flag, 1795-1818 (Ft. McHenry Flag)	.35	.25			3.00	23,153,000
1347	6¢ Washington's Cruisers Flag, 1775	.30	.25			3.00	23,153,000
1348	6¢ Bennington Flag, 1777	.30	.25			3.00	23,153,000
1349	6¢ Rhode Island Flag, 1775	.30	.25			3.00	23,153,000
1350	6¢ First Stars and Stripes, 1777	.30	.25			3.00	23,153,000
1351	6¢ Bunker Hill Flag, 1775	.30	.25			3.00	23,153,000
1352	6¢ Grand Union Flag, 1776	.30	.25			3.00	23,153,000
1353	6¢ Philadelphia Light Horse Flag, 1775	.30	.25			3.00	23,153,000
1354	6¢ First Navy Jack, 1775	.30	.25			3.00	23,153,000
a	Strip of 10, #1345-54	3.25	3.00	6.75	(20)	12.00	
	Perf. 12						
1355	6¢ Walt Disney, Sept. 11	.16	.15	.75	(4)	1.00	153,015,000
a	Ocher omitted	*850.00*					
b	Vertical pair, imperf. horizontally	*725.00*					
c	Imperf. pair	*800.00*					
d	Black omitted	*1,750.00*					
e	Horizontal pair, imperf. between	*3,250.00*					
f	Blue omitted	*2,000.00*					

	1968 continued, Perf. 11	Un	U	PB	#	FDC	Q
1356	6¢ Father Marquette, Sept. 20	.15	.15	.55	(4)	.75	132,560,000
	American Folklore Issue, Daniel Boone, Sept. 26						
1357	6¢ Pennsylvania Rifle, Powder Horn, Tomahawk, Pipe and Knife	.15	.15	.55	(4)	.75	130,385,000
1358	6¢ Arkansas River Navigation, Oct. 1	.15	.15	.55	(4)	.75	132,265,000
1359	6¢ Leif Erikson, Oct. 9	.15	.15	.55	(4)	.75	128,710,000
	Perf. 11 x 10½						
1360	6¢ Cherokee Strip, Oct. 15	.15	.15	.55	(4)	.75	124,775,000
	Perf. 11						
1361	6¢ John Trumbull, Oct. 18	.15	.15	.60	(4)	.75	128,295,000
1362	6¢ Waterfowl Conservation, Oct. 24	.15	.15	.70	(4)	.75	142,245,000
a	Vertical pair, imperf. between	*600.00*					
b	Red and dark blue omitted	*1,700.00*					
	Christmas Issue, Nov. 1						
1363	6¢ Angel Gabriel, from "The Annunciation," by Jan van Eyck	.15	.15	2.25	(10)	.75	1,410,580,000
a	Untagged, Nov. 2	.20	.15	2.25	(10)	6.50	
b	Imperf. pair (tagged)	*275.00*					
c	Light yellow omitted	*150.00*					
d	Imperf. pair (untagged)	*400.00*					
1364	6¢ American Indian, Nov. 4	.16	.15	.70	(4)	.75	125,100,000
	Issues of 1969, Beautification of America Issue, Jan. 16						
1365	6¢ Capitol, Azaleas and Tulips	.40	.15	2.25	(4)	1.50	48,142,500
1366	6¢ Washington Monument, Potomac River and Daffodils	.40	.15	2.25	(4)	1.50	48,142,500
1367	6¢ Poppies and Lupines along Highway	.40	.15	2.25	(4)	1.50	48,142,500
1368	6¢ Blooming Crabapple Trees Lining Avenue	.40	.15	2.25	(4)	1.50	48,142,500
a	Block of 4, #1365-68	1.70	1.25			4.00	
1369	6¢ American Legion, Mar. 15	.15	.15	.55	(4)	.75	148,770,000
	American Folklore Issue, Grandma Moses, May 1						
1370	6¢ "July Fourth," by Grandma Moses	.15	.15	.55	(4)	.75	139,475,000
a	Horizontal pair, imperf. between	*275.00*					
b	Black and Prussian blue omitted	*950.00*					
1371	6¢ Apollo 8, May 5	.15	.15	.65	(4)	2.50	187,165,000
a	Imperf. pair	—					
1372	6¢ W.C. Handy, May 17	.15	.15	.55	(4)	.75	125,555,000
1373	6¢ California Settlement, July 16	.15	.15	.55	(4)	.75	144,425,000
1374	6¢ John Wesley Powell, Aug. 1	.15	.15	.55	(4)	.75	135,875,000
1375	6¢ Alabama Statehood, Aug. 2	.15	.15	.55	(4)	.75	151,110,000

1356

1357

1358

1359

1360

1361

1362

1363

1364

1365 1366 1368a
1367 1368

1369

1370

1371

1372

1374

1375

1376 1377 1379a

1378 1379

1380

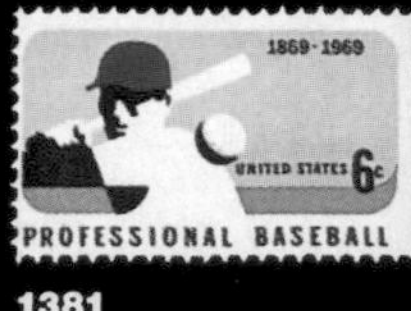

1381

1382

1383

1384

1384a

1385

1386

1387 1388 1390a

1391

1392

	1969 continued, Perf. 11	Un	U	PB	#	FDC	Q
	Botanical Congress Issue, Aug. 23						
1376	6¢ Douglas Fir (Northwest)	.75	.15	3.50	(4)	1.50	39,798,750
1377	6¢ Lady's Slipper (Northeast)	.75	.15	3.50	(4)	1.50	39,798,750
1378	6¢ Ocotillo (Southwest)	.75	.15	3.50	(4)	1.50	39,798,750
1379	6¢ Franklinia (Southeast)	.75	.15	3.50	(4)	1.50	39,798,750
a	Block of 4, #1376-79	3.00	3.00			5.00	
	Perf. 10½ x 11						
1380	6¢ Dartmouth College Case, Sept. 22	.15	.15	.55	(4)	.75	129,540,000
	Perf. 11						
1381	6¢ Professional Baseball, Sept. 24	.45	.15	1.50	(4)	1.50	130,925,000
a	Black omitted	*1,350.00*					
1382	6¢ College Football, Sept. 26	.15	.15	.70	(4)	1.50	139,055,000
1383	6¢ Dwight D. Eisenhower, Oct. 14	.15	.15	.55	(4)	.75	150,611,200
	Christmas Issue, Nov. 3, Perf. 11 x 10½						
1384	6¢ Winter Sunday in Norway, Maine	.15	.15	1.40	(10)	.75	1,709,795,000
	Precanceled	.30	.15				
b	Imperf. pair	*1,250.00*					
c	Light green omitted	*30.00*					
d	Light green and yellow omitted	*1,200.00*	—				
e	Yellow omitted	—					
	Precanceled versions issued on an experimental basis in four cities whose names appear on the stamps: Atlanta, GA; Baltimore, MD; Memphis, TN, and New Haven, CT.						
	Perf. 11						
1385	6¢ Hope for the Crippled, Nov. 20	.15	.15	.55	(4)	.75	127,545,000
1386	6¢ William M. Harnett, Dec. 3	.15	.15	.55	(4)	.75	145,788,800
	Issues of 1970, Natural History Issue, May 6						
1387	6¢ American Bald Eagle	.15	.15	.65	(4)	1.50	50,448,550
1388	6¢ African Elephant Herd	.15	.15	.65	(4)	1.50	50,448,550
1389	6¢ Tlingit Chief in Haida Ceremonial Canoe	.15	.15	.65	(4)	1.50	50,448,550
1390	6¢ Brontosaurus, Stegosaurus and Allosaurus from Jurassic Period	.15	.15	.65	(4)	1.50	50,448,550
a	Block of 4, #1387-90	.50	.50			4.00	
1391	6¢ Maine Statehood, July 9	.15	.15	.55	(4)	.75	171,850,000
	Perf. 11 x 10½						
1392	6¢ Wildlife Conservation, July 20	.15	.15	.55	(4)	.90	142,205,000

BATTER UP!
American colonists played early forms of baseball as early as 1778. In 1869, the Cincinnati Red Stockings became the first openly all-professional club, despite the National Association of Base Ball Players' strict prohibition of payment for play. Today, professional baseball attracts millions of Americans to ballparks each year. (#1381)

	Issues of 1970-74, Perf. 11 x 10½	Un	U	PB/LP	#	FDC	Q
1393	6¢ Eisenhower, Aug. 6, 1970	.15	.15	.55	(4)	.75	
a	Booklet pane of 8	1.25	*.50*			3.00	
b	Booklet pane of 5 + label	1.50	*.50*			1.50	
c	Untagged (Bureau precanceled)		.15				
	Perf. 10½ x 11						
1393D	7¢ Franklin, Oct. 20, 1972	.15	.15	.65	(4)	.75	
e	Untagged (Bureau precanceled)		.15				
	Perf. 11						
1394	8¢ Eisenhower, May 10, 1971	.16	.15	.70	(4)	.75	
	Pair with full vertical gutter between	—					
	Perf. 11 x 10½						
1395	8¢ deep claret Eisenhower (1394), Single from booklet	.16	.15			.75	
a	Booklet pane of 8, May 10, 1971	1.80	*1.25*			3.00	
b	Booklet pane of 6, May 10, 1971	1.25	*.75*			3.00	
c	Booklet pane of 4 + 2 labels, Jan. 28, 1972	1.40	*.50*			2.25	
d	Booklet pane of 7 + label, Jan. 28, 1972	1.60	*1.00*			2.00	
1396	8¢ U.S. Postal Service, July 1, 1971	.15	.15	2.00	(12)	.75	
1397	14¢ Fiorello H. LaGuardia, Apr. 24, 1972	.25	.15	1.15	(4)	.85	
a	Untagged (Bureau precanceled)		.25				
1398	16¢ Ernie Pyle, May 7, 1971	.30	.15	1.40	(4)	.75	
a	Untagged (Bureau precanceled)		.35				
1399	18¢ Dr. Elizabeth Blackwell, Jan. 23, 1974	.32	.15	1.40	(4)	1.00	
1400	21¢ Amadeo P. Giannini, June 27, 1973	.35	.15	1.60	(4)	1.00	
	Coil Stamps, Perf. 10 Vertically						
1401	6¢ dark blue gray Eisenhower (1393), Aug. 6, 1970	.15	.15	.50	(2)	.75	
a	Untagged (Bureau precanceled)		.15				
b	Imperf. pair	*1,200.00*					
1402	8¢ deep claret Eisenhower (1394), May 10, 1971	.15	.15	.45	(2)	.75	
a	Imperf. pair	45.00		80.00	(2)		
b	Untagged (Bureau precanceled)		.15				
c	Pair, imperf. between	—					
1403-04	not assigned						
	Issues of 1970, Perf. 11						
1405	6¢ Edgar Lee Masters, Aug. 22	.15	.15	.55	(4)	.75	137,660,000
1406	6¢ Woman Suffrage, Aug. 26	.15	.15	.55	(4)	.75	135,125,000
1407	6¢ South Carolina Settlement, Sept. 12	.15	.15	.55	(4)	.75	135,895,000
1408	6¢ Stone Mountain Memorial, Sept. 19	.15	.15	.55	(4)	.75	132,675,000
1409	6¢ Fort Snelling, Oct. 17	.15	.15	.55	(4)	.75	134,795,000
	Anti-Pollution Issue, Oct. 28, Perf. 11 x 10½						
1410	6¢ Save Our Soil-Globe and Wheat Field	.22	.15	1.05	(10)	1.25	40,400,000
1411	6¢ Save Our Cities-Globe and City Playground	.22	.15	1.05	(10)	1.25	40,400,000
1412	6¢ Save Our Water-Globe and Bluegill Fish	.22	.15			1.25	40,400,000
1413	6¢ Save Our Air-Globe and Seagull	.22	.15			1.25	40,400,000
a	Block of 4, #1410-13	1.00	1.00			3.00	

1393

1393D

1394

1396

1397

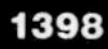

1398

1399

1400

1405

1406

SOUTH CAROLINA 1670 1970 US POSTAGE 6c

1407

1408

1409

1410 1411 1413a

1412 1413

1414

1414a

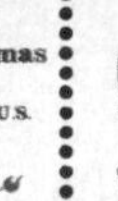

1415 1416 1418b

1417 1418

1419

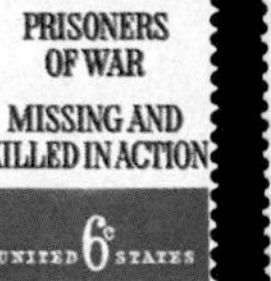

1420 1421 1422 1421a 1423

1425 1426

1424

1427 1428 1430a

	1970 continued	Un	U	PB	#	FDC	Q
	Christmas Issue, Nov. 5, Perf. 10½ x 11						
1414	6¢ Nativity, by Lorenzo Lotto	.15	.15	1.15	(8)	1.40	638,730,000
a	Precanceled	.15	.15				358,245,000
b	Black omitted	*650.00*					
c	As "a," blue omitted	*2,000.00*					
	#1414a-18a were furnished to 68 cities. Unused prices are for copies with gum and used prices are for copies with or without gum but with an additional cancellation.						
	Perf. 11 x 10½						
1415	6¢ Tin and Cast-iron Locomotive	.40	.15	3.75	(8)	1.40	122,313,750
a	Precanceled	.90	.15	7.75	(8)		109,912,500
b	Black omitted	*800.00*					
1416	6¢ Toy Horse on Wheels	.40	.15	3.75	(8)	1.40	122,313,750
a	Precanceled	.90	.15	7.75	(8)		109,912,500
b	Black omitted	—					
c	Imperf. pair		—				
1417	6¢ Mechanical Tricycle	.40	.15			1.40	122,313,750
a	Precanceled	.90	.15				109,912,500
b	Black omitted	—					
1418	6¢ Doll Carriage	.40	.15			1.40	122,313,750
a	Precanceled	.90	.15				109,912,500
b	Block of 4, #1415-18	1.90	1.75			3.50	
c	Block of 4, #1415a-18a	3.75	3.50				
d	Black omitted	—					
	Perf. 11						
1419	6¢ United Nations, Nov. 20	.15	.15	.55	(4)	.75	127,610,000
	Pair with full horizontal gutter between	—					
1420	6¢ Landing of the Pilgrims, Nov. 21	.15	.15	.55	(4)	.75	129,785,000
a	Orange and yellow omitted	*1,400.00*					
	Disabled American Veterans and Servicemen Issue, Nov. 24						
1421	6¢ Disabled American Veterans Emblem	.15	.15	1.00	(4)	.75	67,190,000
a	Attached pair, #1421-22	.25	.25			1.20	
1422	6¢ U.S. Servicemen	.15	.15	1.00	(4)	.75	67,190,000
	Issues of 1971						
1423	6¢ American Wool Industry, Jan. 19	.15	.15	.55	(4)	.75	136,305,000
1424	6¢ Gen. Douglas MacArthur, Jan. 26	.15	.15	.55	(4)	.75	134,840,000
1425	6¢ Blood Donor, Mar. 12	.15	.15	.55	(4)	.75	130,975,000
	Perf. 11 x 10½						
1426	8¢ Missouri Statehood, May 8	.15	.15	2.00	(12)	.75	161,235,000
	Wildlife Conservation Issue, June 12, Perf. 11						
1427	8¢ Trout	.16	.15	.75	(4)	1.25	43,920,000
1428	8¢ Alligator	.16	.15	.75	(4)	1.25	43,920,000
1429	8¢ Polar Bear	.16	.15	.75	(4)	1.25	43,920,000
1430	8¢ California Condor	.16	.15	.75	(4)	1.25	43,920,000
a	Block of 4, #1427-30	.65	.65			3.00	
b	As "a," light green and dark green omitted from #1427-28	*3,500.00*					
c	As "a", red omitted from #1427, 1429-30	—					

	1971 continued, Perf. 11	Un	U	PB	#	FDC	Q
1431	8¢ Antarctic Treaty, June 23	.15	.15	.70	(4)	.75	138,700,000
	American Bicentennial Issue, American Revolution, July 4						
1432	8¢ Bicentennial Commission Emblem	.16	.15	.80	(4)	.75	138,165,000
a	Gray and black omitted	*650.00*					
b	Gray omitted	*1,100.00*					
1433	8¢ John Sloan, Aug. 2	.15	.15	.70	(4)	.75	152,125,000
	Space Achievement Decade Issue, Aug. 2						
1434	8¢ Earth, Sun and Landing Craft on Moon	.15	.15	.70	(4)		88,147,500
a	Attached pair, #1434-35	.30	.25	.70		1.75	
b	As "a," blue and red omitted	*1,250.00*					
1435	8¢ Lunar Rover and Astronauts	.15	.15	.70	(4)		88,147,500
1436	8¢ Emily Dickinson, Aug. 28	.15	.15	.70	(4)	.75	142,845,000
a	Black and olive omitted	*1,100.00*					
b	Pale rose omitted	—					
1437	8¢ San Juan, Puerto Rico, Sept. 12	.15	.15	.70	(4)	.75	148,755,000
	Perf. 10½ x 11						
1438	8¢ Prevent Drug Abuse, Oct. 4	.15	.15	1.00	(6)	.75	139,080,000
1439	8¢ CARE, Oct. 27	.15	.15	1.25	(8)	.75	130,755,000
b	Black omitted	—					
	Historic Preservation Issue, Oct. 29, Perf. 11						
1440	8¢ Decatur House, Washington, D.C.	.16	.15	.75	(4)	1.25	42,552,000
1441	8¢ Whaling Ship *Charles W. Morgan*, Mystic, Connecticut	.16	.15	.75	(4)	1.25	42,552,000
1442	8¢ Cable Car, San Francisco	.16	.15	.75	(4)	1.25	42,552,000
1443	8¢ San Xavier del Bac Mission, Tucson, Arizona	.16	.15	.75	(4)	1.25	42,552,000
a	Block of 4, #1440-43	.65	.65			3.00	
b	As "a," black brown omitted	*3,000.00*					
c	As "a," ocher omitted	—					
	Christmas Issue, Nov. 10, Perf. 10½ x 11						
1444	8¢ Adoration of the Shepherds, by Giorgione	.15	.15	2.00	(12)	.75	1,074,350,000
a	Gold omitted	*575.00*					
1445	8¢ Partridge in a Pear Tree	.15	.15	2.00	(12)	.75	979,540,000
	Issues of 1972, Perf. 11						
1446	8¢ Sidney Lanier, Feb. 3	.15	.15	.70	(4)	.75	137,355,000
	Perf. 10½ x 11						
1447	8¢ Peace Corps, Feb. 11	.15	.15	1.00	(6)	.75	150,400,000

The stamp listings contain a number of "a," "b," "c," etc. additions which include recognized varieties and errors. These listings are as complete as space permits.

1431

1432

John
Sloan
American
Artist
United
States
8 cents

1433

1434 1435 1434a

1436

1437

1438

1439

1440 1441 1443a
1442 1443

1444

1445

1446

1447

1972

1448 1449
1450 1451

1451a

National Parks Centennial
U.S. 6c
Wolf Trap Farm • Virginia

1452

1453

1454

1455

1456 1457 1459a
1458 1459

1460

1461

1462

1463

1464 1465 1467a
1466 1467

	1972 continued	Un	U	PB	#	FDC	Q
	National Parks Centennial Issue, Cape Hatteras, Apr. 5, Perf. 11 (see also #C84)						
1448	2¢ Hull of Ship	.15	.15	.45	(4)		172,730,000
1449	2¢ Cape Hatteras Lighthouse	.15	.15	.45	(4)		172,730,000
1450	2¢ Laughing Gulls on Driftwood	.15	.15	.45	(4)		172,730,000
1451	2¢ Laughing Gulls and Dune	.15	.15	.45	(4)		172,730,000
a	Block of 4, #1448-51	.20	.20			1.25	
b	As "a," black omitted	*2,000.00*					
	Wolf Trap Farm, June 26						
1452	6¢ Performance at Shouse Pavilion	.15	.15	.55	(4)	.75	104,090,000
	Yellowstone, Mar. 1						
1453	8¢ Old Faithful, Yellowstone	.15	.15	.70	(4)	.75	164,096,000
	Mount McKinley, July 28						
1454	15¢ View of Mount McKinley in Alaska	.30	.18	1.30	(4)	1.00	53,920,000
	Note: Beginning with this National Parks Centennial issue, the USPS began to offer stamp collectors first day cancellations affixed to 8" x 10½" souvenir pages. The pages are similar to the stamp announcements that have appeared on Post Office bulletin boards beginning with Scott #1132.						
1455	8¢ Family Planning, Mar. 18	.15	.15	.70	(4)	.75	153,025,000
a	Yellow omitted	—					
	American Bicentennial Issue, Colonial American Craftsmen, July 4, Perf. 11 x 10½						
1456	8¢ Glassblower	.16	.15	.75	(4)	1.00	50,472,500
1457	8¢ Silversmith	.16	.15	.75	(4)	1.00	50,472,500
1458	8¢ Wigmaker	.16	.15	.75	(4)	1.00	50,472,500
1459	8¢ Hatter	.16	.15	.75	(4)	1.00	50,472,500
a	Block of 4, #1456-59	.65	.65			2.50	
	Olympic Games Issue, Aug. 17 (see also #C85)						
1460	8¢ Bicycling and Olympic Rings	.15	.15	1.25	(10)	.75	67,335,000
	Plate flaw (broken red ring)	7.50					
1461	8¢ Bobsledding and Olympic Rings	.15	.15	1.60	(10)	.85	179,675,000
1462	15¢ Running and Olympic Rings	.28	.18	3.00	(10)	1.00	46,340,000
1463	8¢ Parent Teachers Association, Sept. 15	.15	.15	.70	(4)	.75	180,155,000
	Wildlife Conservation Issue, Sept. 20, Perf. 11						
1464	8¢ Fur Seal	.16	.15	.75	(4)	1.50	49,591,200
1465	8¢ Cardinal	.16	.15	.75	(4)	1.50	49,591,200
1466	8¢ Brown Pelican	.16	.15	.75	(4)	1.50	49,591,200
1467	8¢ Bighorn Sheep	.16	.15	.75	(4)	1.50	49,591,200
a	Block of 4, #1464-67	.65	.65			3.00	
b	As "a," brown omitted	*3,500.00*					
c	As "a," green and blue omitted	—					
	Note: With this Wildlife Conservation issue the USPS introduced the "American Commemorative Series" Stamp Panels. Each panel contains a block of four mint stamps with text and background illustrations.						

	1972 continued, Perf. 11 x 10½	Un	U	PB	#	FDC	Q
1468	8¢ Mail Order Business, Sept. 27	.15	.15	1.90	(12)	.75	185,490,000
	Perf. 10½ x 11						
1469	8¢ Osteopathic Medicine, Oct. 9	.15	.15	1.00	(6)	.75	162,335,000
	American Folklore Issue, Tom Sawyer, Oct. 13, Perf. 11						
1470	8¢ Tom Sawyer Whitewashing a Fence, by Norman Rockwell	.15	.15	.70	(4)	.75	162,789,950
a	Horizontal pair, imperf. between	*2,500.00*					
b	Red and black omitted	*1,500.00*					
c	Yellow and tan omitted	*1,500.00*					
	Christmas Issue, Nov. 9, Perf. 10½ x 11						
1471	8¢ Angels from "Mary, Queen of Heaven," by the Master of the St. Lucy Legend	.15	.15	1.90	(12)	.75	1,003,475,000
a	Pink omitted	*400.00*					
b	Black omitted	*4,000.00*					
1472	8¢ Santa Claus	.15	.15	1.90	(12)	.75	1,017,025,000
	Perf. 11						
1473	8¢ Pharmacy, Nov. 10	.15	.15	.70	(4)	.75	165,895,000
a	Blue and orange omitted	*1,150.00*					
b	Blue omitted	*2,000.00*					
1474	8¢ Stamp Collecting, Nov. 17	.15	.15	.70	(4)	.75	166,508,000
a	Black omitted	*1,250.00*					
	Issues of 1973, Perf. 11 x 10½						
1475	8¢ Love, Jan. 26	.15	.15	1.00	(6)	.75	320,055,000
	American Bicentennial Issues, Communications in Colonial Times, Perf. 11						
1476	8¢ Printer and Patriots Examining Pamphlet, Feb. 16	.15	.15	.70	(4)	.75	166,005,000
1477	8¢ Posting a Broadside, Apr. 13	.15	.15	.70	(4)	.75	163,050,000
	Pair with full horizontal gutter between	—					
1478	8¢ Post Rider, June 22	.15	.15	.70	(4)	.75	159,005,000
1479	8¢ Drummer, Sept. 28	.15	.15	.70	(4)	.75	147,295,000
	Boston Tea Party, July 4						
1480	8¢ British Merchantman	.15	.15	.70	(4)	1.50	49,068,750
1481	8¢ British Three-Master	.15	.15	.70	(4)	1.50	49,068,750
1482	8¢ Boats and Ship's Hull	.15	.15	.70	(4)	1.50	49,068,750
1483	8¢ Boat and Dock	.15	.15	.70	(4)	1.50	49,068,750
a	Block of 4, #1480-83	.60	.45			3.00	
b	As "a," black (engraved) omitted	*2,000.00*					
c	As "a," black (lithographed) omitted	*1,500.00*					

1468

1469

1470

1471

1472

1473

1474

1475

1476

1477

1478

1479

1480 1481 1483a

1482 1483

1484

1485

1486

1487

1488

Nearly 27 billion U.S. stamps are sold yearly to carry your letters to every corner of the world.

People Serving You

Mail is picked up from nearly a third of a million local collection boxes, as well as your mailbox.

People Serving You

More than 87 billion letters and packages are handled yearly—almost 300 million every delivery day.

People Serving You

The People in your Postal Service handle and deliver more than 500 million packages yearly.

People Serving You

Thousands of machines, buildings, and vehicles must be operated and maintained to keep your mail moving.

People Serving You

1489 1490 1491 1492 1493

The skill of sorting mail manually is still vital to delivery of your mail.

People Serving You

Employees use modern, high-speed equipment to sort and process huge volumes of mail in central locations.

People Serving You

Thirteen billion pounds of mail are handled yearly by postal employees as they speed your letters and packages.

People Serving You

Our customers include 54 million urban and 12 million rural families, plus 9 million businesses.

People Serving You

Employees cover 4 million miles each delivery day to bring mail to your home or business.

People Serving You

1498a

1494 1495 1496 1497 1498

	1973 continued, Perf. 11	Un	U	PB	#	FDC	Q
	American Arts Issue						
1484	8¢ George Gershwin and Scene from "Porgy and Bess," Feb. 28	.15	.15	1.85	(12)	.75	139,152,000
a	Vertical pair, imperf. horizontally	*275.00*					
1485	8¢ Robinson Jeffers, Man and Children of Carmel with Burro, Aug. 13	.15	.15	1.85	(12)	.75	128,048,000
a	Vertical pair, imperf. horizontally	*325.00*					
1486	8¢ Henry Ossawa Tanner, Palette and Rainbow, Sept. 10	.15	.15	1.85	(12)	.75	146,008,000
1487	8¢ Willa Cather, Pioneer Family and Covered Wagon, Sept. 20	.15	.15	1.85	(12)	1.00	139,608,000
a	Vertical pair, imperf. horizontally	*350.00*					
1488	8¢ Nicolaus Copernicus, Apr. 23	.15	.15	.70	(4)	.75	159,475,000
a	Orange omitted	*1,100.00*					
b	Black omitted	*2,000.00*					
	Postal Service Employees Issue, Apr. 30, Perf. 10½ x 11						
1489	8¢ Stamp Counter	.15	.15			1.00	48,602,000
1490	8¢ Mail Collection	.15	.15			1.00	48,602,000
1491	8¢ Letter-Facing on Conveyor	.15	.15			1.00	48,602,000
1492	8¢ Parcel Post Sorting	.15	.15			1.00	48,602,000
1493	8¢ Mail Canceling	.15	.15			1.00	48,602,000
1494	8¢ Manual Letter Routing	.15	.15			1.00	48,602,000
1495	8¢ Electronic Letter Routing	.15	.15			1.00	48,602,000
1496	8¢ Loading Mail on Truck	.15	.15			1.00	48,602,000
1497	8¢ Carrier Delivering Mail	.15	.15			1.00	48,602,000
1498	8¢ Rural Mail Delivery	.15	.15			1.00	48,602,000
a	Strip of 10, #1489-98	1.50	1.00	3.10	(20)	5.00	
	#1489-98 were the first United States stamps to have printing on the back. (see also #1559-62)						

COPERNICUS POINTED WAY TO THE STARS

Nicolaus Copernicus (#1488) is considered the father of modern astronomy. Born in Poland in 1473, Copernicus challenged the commonly accepted notion that the Earth was the center of the universe. Instead, he proposed that all of the planets, including the Earth, revolve around the sun. Inspired by theories of early Greek astronomers, Copernicus published his own theories in a book entitled On the Revolutions of the Heavenly Spheres. *Later astronomers proved that the theories of Copernicus were correct.*

	1973 continued, Perf. 11	Un	U	PB	#	FDC	Q
1499	8¢ Harry S. Truman, May 8	.15	.15	.65	(4)	.75	157,052,800
	Progress in Electronics Issue, July 10 (see also #C86)						
1500	6¢ Marconi's Spark Coil and Gap	.15	.15	.55	(4)	.75	53,005,000
1501	8¢ Transistors and Printed Circuit Board	.15	.15	.70	(4)	.75	159,775,000
a	Black omitted	*850.00*					
b	Tan and lilac omitted	*1,500.00*					
1502	15¢ Microphone, Speaker, Vacuum Tube, TV Camera Tube	.28	.15	1.20	(4)	.85	39,005,000
a	Black omitted	*1,600.00*					
1503	8¢ Lyndon B. Johnson, Aug. 27	.15	.15	1.85	(12)	.75	152,624,000
a	Horizontal pair, imperf. vertically	*375.00*					
	Issues of 1973-74, Rural America Issue						
1504	8¢ Angus and Longhorn Cattle, by F.C. Murphy, Oct. 5, 1973	.15	.15	.70	(4)	.75	145,840,000
a	Green and red brown omitted	*1,000.00*					
b	Vertical pair, imperf. between		—				
1505	10¢ Chautauqua Tent and Buggies, Aug. 6, 1974	.18	.15	.80	(4)	.75	151,335,000
1506	10¢ Wheat Fields and Train, Aug. 16, 1974	.18	.15	.80	(4)	.75	141,085,000
a	Black and blue omitted	*850.00*					
	Issues of 1973, Christmas Issue, Nov. 7, Perf. 10½ x 11						
1507	8¢ Small Cowper Madonna, by Raphael	.15	.15	1.85	(12)	.75	885,160,000
	Pair with full vertical gutter between	—					
1508	8¢ Christmas Tree in Needlepoint	.15	.15	1.85	(12)	.75	939,835,000
a	Vertical pair, imperf. between	*675.00*					
	Pair with full horizontal gutter between	—					

KNOWLEDGE AND CULTURE ARE CHAUTAUQUA TRADEMARKS
The chautauqua movement began in 1874, when Methodist ministers John H. Vincent and Lewis Miller organized a two-week summer camp to train Methodist Sunday School teachers. Held by a lake in Chautauqua, New York, the course was so successful that it was expanded the following year. Secular topics were added and courses were open to people of all denominations. Each summer thereafter, thousands flocked to Chautauqua for classes, lectures and concerts. Other "chautauquas" sprang up in several hundred towns, and tent chautauquas traveled across the nation. (#1505)

1499

1500

1501

1502

1503

1504

1505

1506

1507

1508

1509

1510

1511

1518

1525

1526

1527

1528

1529

1530 1531 1532 1533 1537a

1534 1535 1536 1537

	Issue of 1973, Perf. 11 x 10½	Un	U	PB	#	FDC
1509	10¢ 50-Star and 13-Star Flags, Dec. 8, 1973	.18	.15	3.75	(20)	.75
a	Horizontal pair, imperf. between	*60.00*				
b	Blue omitted	*200.00*				
c	Imperf. pair	*1,000.00*				

	Issues of 1973-74, Perf. 11 x 10½	Un	U	PB/LP	#	FDC	Q
1510	10¢ Jefferson Memorial, Dec. 14, 1973	.18	.15	.80	(4)	.75	
a	Untagged (Bureau precanceled)		.18				
b	Booklet pane of 5 + label	1.50	*.30*			2.25	
c	Booklet pane of 8	1.65	*.30*			2.50	
d	Booklet pane of 6, Aug. 5, 1974	4.25	*.30*			3.00	
e	Vertical pair, imperf. horizontally	*250.00*					
f	Vertical pair, imperf. between	—					
1511	10¢ ZIP Code, Jan. 4, 1974	.18	.15	1.50	(8)	.75	
a	Yellow omitted	*50.00*					
	Pair with full horizontal gutter between	—					
1512-17	not assigned						
	Coil Stamps, Perf. 10 Vertically						
1518	6.3¢ Liberty Bell, Oct. 1, 1974	.15	.15	.65	(2)	1.00	
a	Untagged (Bureau precanceled)		.15				
b	Imperf. pair	*300.00*					
c	As "a," imperf. pair		*150.00*				
1519	10¢ red and blue Flags (1509), Dec. 8, 1973	.18	.15			.75	
a	Imperf. pair	40.00					
1520	10¢ blue Jefferson Memorial (1510), Dec. 14, 1973	.18	.15	.55	(2)	.75	
a	Untagged (Bureau precanceled)		.25				
b	Imperf. pair	*47.50*		—	(2)		
1521-24	not assigned						
	Issues of 1974, Perf. 11						
1525	10¢ Veterans of Foreign Wars, Mar. 11	.18	.15	.80	(4)	.75	149,930,000
	Perf. 10½ x 11						
1526	10¢ Robert Frost, Mar. 26	.18	.15	.80	(4)	.75	145,235,000
	Perf. 11						
1527	10¢ Expo '74 World's Fair, Apr. 18	.18	.15	2.20	(12)	.75	135,052,000
	Perf. 11 x 10½						
1528	10¢ Horse Racing, May 4	.18	.15	2.20	(12)	.75	156,750,000
a	Blue omitted	*1,300.00*					
b	Red omitted	—					
	Perf. 11						
1529	10¢ Skylab, May 14	.18	.15	.80	(4)	1.25	164,670,000
a	Vertical pair, imperf. between	—					
	Universal Postal Union Issue, June 6						
1530	10¢ Michelangelo, from "School of Athens," by Raphael	.20	.15	3.50	(16)	1.00	23,769,600
1531	10¢ "Five Feminine Virtues," by Hokusai	.20	.15			1.00	23,769,600
1532	10¢ "Old Scraps," by John Fredrick Peto	.20	.15			1.00	23,769,600
1533	10¢ "The Lovely Reader," by Jean Etienne Liotard	.20	.15	3.50	(16)	1.00	23,769,600
1534	10¢ "Lady Writing Letter," by Gerard Terborch	.20	.15	3.50	(16)	1.00	23,769,600
1535	10¢ Inkwell and Quill, from "Boy with a Top," by Jean-Baptiste Simeon Chardin	.20	.15			1.00	23,769,600
1536	10¢ Mrs. John Douglas, by Thomas Gainsborough	.20	.15			1.00	23,769,600
1537	10¢ Don Antonio Noriega, by Francisco de Goya	.20	.15	3.50	(16)	1.00	23,769,600
a	Block of 8, #1530-37	1.60	1.50			3.00	
b	As "a," imperf. vertically	*6,000.00*					

	1974 continued, Perf. 11	Un	U	PB	#	FDC	Q
	Mineral Heritage Issue, June 13						
1538	10¢ Petrified Wood	.18	.15	.85	(4)	1.10	41,803,200
a	Light blue and yellow omitted	—					
1539	10¢ Tourmaline	.18	.15	.85	(4)	1.10	41,803,200
a	Light blue omitted	—					
b	Black and purple omitted	—					
1540	10¢ Amethyst	.18	.15	.85	(4)	1.10	41,803,200
a	Light blue and yellow omitted	—					
1541	10¢ Rhodochrosite	.18	.15	.85	(4)	1.10	41,803,200
a	Block of 4, #1538-41	.75	.75			2.50	
b	As "a," light blue and yellow omitted	*2,400.00*					
c	Light blue omitted	—					
d	Black and red omitted	—					
1542	10¢ First Kentucky Settlement-Fort Harrod, June 15	.18	.15	.80	(4)	.75	156,265,000
a	Dull black omitted	*1,250.00*					
b	Green, black and blue omitted	*2,500.00*					
c	Green omitted	—					
d	Green and black omitted	—					
	American Bicentennial Issue, First Continental Congress, July 4						
1543	10¢ Carpenters' Hall	.18	.15	.85	(4)	.90	48,896,250
1544	10¢ "We Ask but for Peace, Liberty and Safety"	.18	.15	.85	(4)	.90	48,896,250
1545	10¢ "Deriving their Just Powers from the Consent of the Governed"	.18	.15	.85	(4)	.90	48,896,250
1546	10¢ Independence Hall	.18	.15	.85	(4)	.90	48,896,250
a	Block of 4, #1543-46	.75	.75			2.75	
1547	10¢ Energy Conservation, Sept. 23	.18	.15	.80	(4)	.75	148,850,000
a	Blue and orange omitted	*1,100.00*					
b	Orange and green omitted	*1,100.00*					
c	Green omitted	*950.00*					
	American Folklore Issue, The Legend of Sleepy Hollow, Oct. 10						
1548	10¢ Headless Horseman and Ichabod Crane	.18	.15	.80	(4)	.75	157,270,000
1549	10¢ Retarded Children, Oct. 12	.18	15	.80	(4)	.75	150,245,000
	Christmas Issue						
1550	10¢ Angel from Perussis Altarpiece, Oct. 23	.18	.15	1.85	(10)	.75	835,180,000
1551	10¢ "The Road-Winter," by Currier and Ives, Oct. 23	.18	.15	2.20	(12)	.75	882,520,000
	Precanceled Self-Adhesive, Imperf.						
1552	10¢ Dove Weather Vane atop Mount Vernon, Nov. 15	.18	.15	3.70	(20)	.75	213,155,000
	Issues of 1975, American Arts Issues, Perf. 10½ x 11						
1553	10¢ Benjamin West, Self-Portrait, Feb. 10	.18	.15	1.85	(10)	.75	156,995,000
	Perf. 11						
1554	10¢ Paul Laurence Dunbar and Lamp, May 1	.18	.15	1.85	(10)	.75	146,365,000
a	Imperf. pair	*1,100.00*					
1555	10¢ D.W. Griffith and Motion-Picture Camera, May 27	.18	.15	.80	(4)	.75	148,805,000
a	Brown omitted	*900.00*					

1538

1539

1540

1541 1541a

1542

1543 1544 1546a

1545 1546

1547

1548

1549

1550

1551

1552

1553

Paul Laurence Dunbar
American poet
10 cents U.S. postage

1554

1555

1556

MARINER 10 ★ VENUS/MERCURY
US 10c

1557

1558

YOUTHFUL HEROINE
On the dark night of April 26, 1777, 16-year-old Sybil Ludington rode her horse "Star" alone through the Connecticut countryside rallying her father's militia to repel a raid by the British on Danbury.

1559

GALLANT SOLDIER
The conspicuously courageous actions of black foot soldier Salem Poor at the Battle of Bunker Hill on June 17, 1775, earned him citations for his bravery and leadership ability.

1560

FINANCIAL HERO
Businessman and broker Haym Salomon was responsible for raising most of the money needed to finance the American Revolution and later to save the new nation from collapse.

1561

FIGHTER EXTRAORDINARY
Peter Francisco's strength and bravery made him a legend around campfires. He fought with distinction at Brandywine, Yorktown and Guilford Court House.

1562

1563

1564

1565 1566 1568a
1567 1568

1569 1569a
1570

	1975 continued, Perf. 11	Un	U	PB	#	FDC	Q
	Space Issues						
1556	10¢ Pioneer 10 Passing Jupiter, Feb. 28	.18	.15	.80	(4)	1.25	173,685,000
a	Red and yellow omitted	*1,500.00*					
b	Blue omitted	*1,250.00*					
c	Imperf. pair	—					
1557	10¢ Mariner 10, Venus and Mercury, Apr. 4	.18	.15	.80	(4)	1.25	158,600,000
a	Red omitted	*800.00*					
b	Ultramarine and bister omitted	*2,000.00*					
1558	10¢ Collective Bargaining, Mar. 13	.18	.15	1.60	(8)	.75	153,355,000
	Imperfs. of #1558 exist from printer's waste.						
	American Bicentennial Issues, Contributors to the Cause, Mar. 25, Perf. 11 x 10½						
1559	8¢ Sybil Ludington Riding Horse	.16	.15	1.65	(10)	.75	63,205,000
a	Back inscription omitted	*350.00*					
1560	10¢ Salem Poor Carrying Musket	.18	.15	1.85	(10)	.75	157,865,000
a	Back inscription omitted	*300.00*					
1561	10¢ Haym Salomon Figuring Accounts	.18	.15	1.85	(10)	.75	166,810,000
a	Back inscription omitted	*350.00*					
b	Red omitted	*250.00*					
1562	18¢ Peter Francisco Shouldering Cannon	.35	.20	3.60	(10)	.75	44,825,000
	Battle of Lexington & Concord, Apr. 19, Perf. 11						
1563	10¢ "Birth of Liberty," by Henry Sandham	.18	.15	2.20	(12)	.75	144,028,000
a	Vertical pair, imperf. horizontally	*500.00*					
	Battle of Bunker Hill, June 17						
1564	10¢ "Battle of Bunker Hill," by John Trumbull	.18	.15	2.20	(12)	.75	139,928,000
	Military Services, July 4						
1565	10¢ Soldier with Flintlock Musket, Uniform Button	.18	.15	2.30	(12)	.90	44,963,750
1566	10¢ Sailor with Grappling Hook, First Navy Jack, 1775	.18	.15			.90	44,963,750
1567	10¢ Marine with Musket, Full-Rigged Ship	.18	.15	2.30	(12)	.90	44,963,750
1568	10¢ Militiaman with Musket, Powder Horn	.18	.15			.90	44,963,750
a	Block of 4, #1565-68	.75	.75			2.50	
	Apollo Soyuz Space Issue, July 15						
1569	10¢ Apollo and Soyuz after Docking, and Earth	.18	.15	2.20	(12)	1.25	80,931,600
a	Attached pair, #1569-70	.36	.25			4.00	
b	As "a," vertical pair, imperf. horizontally	*1,200.00*					
	Pair with full horizontal gutter between	—					
1570	10¢ Spacecraft before Docking, Earth and Project Emblem	.18	.15			1.25	80,931,600

	1975 continued, Perf. 11 x 10½	Un	U	PB	#	FDC	Q
1571	10¢ International Women's Year, Aug. 26	.18	.15	1.15	(6)	.75	145,640,000
	Postal Service Bicentennial Issue, Sept. 3						
1572	10¢ Stagecoach and Trailer Truck	.18	.15	2.30	(12)	.75	42,163,750
1573	10¢ Old and New Locomotives	.18	.15	2.30	(12)	.75	42,163,750
1574	10¢ Early Mail Plane and Jet	.18	.15			.75	42,163,750
1575	10¢ Satellite for Transmission of Mailgrams	.18	.15			.75	42,163,750
a	Block of 4, #1572-75	.75	.75			2.40	
b	As "a," red "10¢" omitted	—					
	Perf. 11						
1576	10¢ World Peace Through Law, Sept. 29	.18	.15	.80	(4)	.75	146,615,000
	Banking and Commerce Issue, Oct. 6						
1577	10¢ Engine Turning, Indian Head Penny and Morgan Silver Dollar	.18	.15	.80	(4)	.75	73,098,000
a	Attached pair, #1577-78	.36	.20			1.00	
b	Brown and blue omitted	*1,200.00*					
1578	10¢ Seated Liberty Quarter, $20 Gold Piece and Engine Turning	.18	.15	.80	(4)	.75	73,098,000
	Christmas Issue, Oct. 14						
1579	(10¢) Madonna and Child, by Domenico Ghirlandaio	.18	.15	2.20	(12)	.75	739,430,000
a	Imperf. pair	*125.00*					
	Plate flaw ("d" damaged)	5.00	—				
1580	(10¢) Christmas Card, by Louis Prang, 1878	.18	.15	2.20	(12)	.75	878,690,000
a	Imperf. pair	*125.00*					
b	Perf. 10½ x 11	.60	.15	7.25	(12)		
	Issues of 1975-81, Americana Issue, Perf. 11 x 10½ (Designs 18½ x 22½mm; #1590-90a, 17½ x 20mm; see also #1596-99, 1603-06, 1608, 1610-19, 1622-23e, 1625, 1811, 1813, 1816)						
1581	1¢ Inkwell & Quill, Dec. 8, 1977	.15	.15	.25	(4)	.60	
a	Untagged (Bureau precanceled)		.15				
1582	2¢ Speaker's Stand, Dec. 8, 1977	.15	.15	.25	(4)	.60	
a	Untagged (Bureau precanceled)		.15				
1583	not assigned						
1584	3¢ Early Ballot Box, Dec. 8, 1977	.15	.15	.28	(4)	.60	
a	Untagged (Bureau precanceled)		.15				
1585	4¢ Books, Bookmark, Eyeglasses, Dec. 8, 1977	.15	.15	.38	(4)	.60	
a	Untagged (Bureau precanceled)		.15				
1586-89	not assigned						
1590	9¢ Capitol Dome (1591), single from booklet (#1623a), Mar. 11, 1977	.50	.20			1.00	
	Perf. 10						
a	Single (1591) from booklet (1623b)	18.50	10.00				
	#1590 is on white paper; #1591 is on grey paper.						
	Perf. 11 x 10½						
1591	9¢ Capitol Dome, Nov. 24, 1975	.16	.15	.70	(4)	.60	
a	Untagged (Bureau precanceled)		.18				
1592	10¢ Contemplation of Justice, Nov. 17, 1977	.18	.15	.90	(4)	.60	
a	Untagged (Bureau precanceled)		.25				
1593	11¢ Printing Press, Nov. 13, 1975	.20	.15	.90	(4)	.60	
1594	12¢ Torch, Apr. 8, 1981	.22	.15	1.25	(4)	.60	

1571

1572 1573 1575a

1574 1575

1576

1577 1578 1577a

1579 1580

1581 1582

1584 1585

1591 1592

1593 1594

1595

1596

1597

1599

1603

1604

1605

1606

1608

1610

1611

1612

1613

1614

1615

1615C

	Issues of 1975-78	Un	U	PB/LP	#	FDC
	Americana Issue continued, Perf. 11 x 10½					
159	3¢ Liberty Bell, single from booklet	.26	.15			.60
a	Booklet pane of 6, Oct. 31, 1975	1.90	*.50*			2.00
b	Booklet pane of 7 + label	2.00	*.50*			2.75
c	Booklet pane of 8	2.25	*.50*			2.50
d	Booklet pane of 5 + label, Apr. 2, 1976	1.30	*.50*			2.25
	Perf. 11					
159	3¢ Eagle and Shield, Dec. 1, 1975	.26	.15	3.25	(12)	.60
a	Imperf. pair	*45.00*				
b	Yellow omitted	*175.00*				
1597	5¢ Fort McHenry Flag, June 30, 1978	.28	.15	1.75	(6)	.65
a	Imperf. pair	*17.50*				
b	Gray omitted	—				
	Perf. 11 x 10½					
1598	15¢ Fort McHenry Flag (1597), single from booklet	.30	.15			.65
a	Booklet pane of 8, June 30, 1978	3.50	*.60*			2.50
1599	6¢ Head of Liberty, Mar. 31, 1978	.34	.15	1.90	(4)	.65
1600-02 not assigned						
1603	24¢ Old North Church, Nov. 14, 1975	.45	.15	1.90	(4)	.75
1604	28¢ Fort Nisqually, Aug. 11, 1978	.55	.15	2.30	(4)	1.25
	Dull finish gum	1.50				
160	29¢ Sandy Hook Lighthouse, Apr. 14, 1978	.55	.15	2.60	(4	.10
	Dull finish gum	3.00				

	Issues of 1975-79	Un	U	PB/LP	#	FDC
	Americana Issue continued, Perf. 11 x 10½					
1606	30¢ One-Room Schoolhouse, Aug. 27, 1979	.55	.15	2.30	(4)	1.10
1607	not assigned					
1608	50¢ Whale Oil Lamp, Sept. 11, 1979	.95	.15	4.00	(4)	1.50
a	Black omitted	*550.00*				
b	Vertical pair, imperf. horizontally	—				
1609	not assigned					
1610	$1 Candle and Rushlight Holder, July 2, 1979	1.75	.20	7.50	(4)	3.00
a	Brown omitted	*425.00*				
b	Tan, orange and yellow omitted	*400.00*				
c	Brown inverted	—				
1611	$2 Kerosene Table Lamp, Nov. 16, 1978	3.75	.45	15.50	(4)	5.00
1612	$5 Railroad Lantern, Aug. 23, 1979	9.00	1.50	37.50	(4)	12.50
	For additional Americana Series, see #1581-82, 1583-85, 1590-95d, 1811, 1813 and 1816.					
	Coil Stamps, Perf. 10 Vertically					
1613	3.1¢ Guitar, Oct. 25, 1979	.15	.15	1.50	(2)	.60
a	Untagged (Bureau precanceled)		.40			
b	Imperf. pair	*1,100.00*				
1614	7.7¢ Saxhorns, Nov. 20, 1976	.18	.15	1.00	(2)	.60
a	Untagged (Bureau precanceled)		.35			
b	As "a," imperf. pair		*1,100.00*			
1615	7.9¢ Drum, Apr. 23, 1976	.15	.15	.65	(2)	.60
a	Untagged (Bureau precanceled)		.16			
b	Imperf. pair	*800.00*				
1615C	8.4¢ Piano, July 13, 1978	.22	.15	3.25	(2)	.60
d	Untagged (Bureau precanceled)		.16			
e	As "d," pair, imperf. between		60.00	—	(2)	
f	As "d," imperf. pair		15.00			
1616	9¢ slate green Capitol Dome (1591), Mar. 5, 1976	.20	.15	.90	(2)	.60
a	Imperf. pair	*110.00*				
b	Untagged (Bureau precanceled)		.28			
c	As "b," imperf. pair		*190.00*			
1617	10¢ purple Contemplation of Justice (1592), Nov. 4, 1977	.24	.15	1.10	(2)	.60
a	Untagged (Bureau precanceled)		.25			
b	Imperf. pair	*60.00*				
1618	13¢ brown Liberty Bell (1595), Nov. 25, 1975	.25	.15	.60	(2)	.65
a	Untagged (Bureau precanceled)		.38			
b	Imperf. pair	25.00		—	(2)	
g	Pair, imperf. between	200.00				
1618C	15¢ Fort McHenry Flag (1597), June 30, 1978	.40	.15			.65
d	Imperf. pair	20.00				
e	Pair, imperf. between	150.00				
f	Gray omitted	*40.00*				
1619	16¢ blue Head of Liberty (1599), Mar. 31, 1978	.32	.15	1.50	(2)	.60
a	Huck Press printing (white background with a bluish tinge, fraction of a millimeter smaller)	.50	.15			

	Issues of 1975-81	Un	U	PB	#	FDC	Q
	Americana Issue continued, Perf. 11 x 10½						
1620-21	not assigned						
1622	13¢ Flag over Independence Hall, Nov. 15, 1975	.24	.15	5.75	(20)	.65	
a	Horizontal pair, imperf. between	60.00					
b	Imperf. pair	—					
c	Perf. 11, 1981	.65	.15	*50.00*	(20)		
d	As "c," imperf. pair	—					
1623	13¢ Flag over Capitol, Single from booklet (1623a)	.22	.15			1.00	
a	Booklet pane of 8, (1 #1590 and 7 #1623), Mar. 11, 1977	2.00	*.60*			25.00	
	Perf. 10						
b	13¢ Single from booklet	1.00	1.00				
c	Booklet pane of 8, (1 #1590 and 7 #1623b)	27.50	—			12.50	
	#1623, 1623b issued only in booklets. All stamps are imperf. at one side or imperf. at one side and bottom.						
	Perf. 11 x 10½						
d	Attached pair, #1590 and #1623	.75	—				
	Perf. 10						
e	Attached pair, #1509a and #1623b	20.00	—				
1624	not assigned						
	Coil Stamp, Perf. 10 Vertically						
1625	13¢ Flag over Independence Hall (1622), Nov. 15, 1975	.30	.15			.65	
a	Imperf. pair	22.50					
	Issues of 1976, American Bicentennial Issues, The Spirit of '76, Jan. 1, Perf. 11						
1629	13¢ Drummer Boy	.25	.15			.65	72,822,000
1630	13¢ Old Drummer	.25	.15			.65	72,822,000
1631	13¢ Fife Player	.25	.15			.65	72,822,000
a	Strip of 3, #1629-31	.75	.60	3.10	(12)	1.25	
b	As "a," imperf.	*1,500.00*					
c	Imperf. pair, #1631	*800.00*					
1632	13¢ Interphil 76, Jan. 17	.24	.15	1.05	(4)	.65	157,825,000
	State Flags, Feb. 23						
1633	13¢ Delaware	.24	.20			1.00	8,720,100
1634	13¢ Pennsylvania	.24	.20			1.00	8,720,100
1635	13¢ New Jersey	.24	.20			1.00	8,720,100
1636	13¢ Georgia	.24	.20			1.00	8,720,100
1637	13¢ Connecticut	.24	.20			1.00	8,720,100
1638	13¢ Massachusetts	.24	.20			1.00	8,720,100
1639	13¢ Maryland	.24	.20			1.00	8,720,100
1640	13¢ South Carolina	.24	.20			1.00	8,720,100
1641	13¢ New Hampshire	.24	.20			1.00	8,720,100
1642	13¢ Virginia	.24	.20			1.00	8,720,100
1643	13¢ New York	.24	.20			1.00	8,720,100
1644	13¢ North Carolina	.24	.20			1.00	8,720,100

1622

1623a

1629 1630 1631 1631a

1632

1633  1634  1635

1636  1637  1638

1639  1640  1641

1642  1643  1644

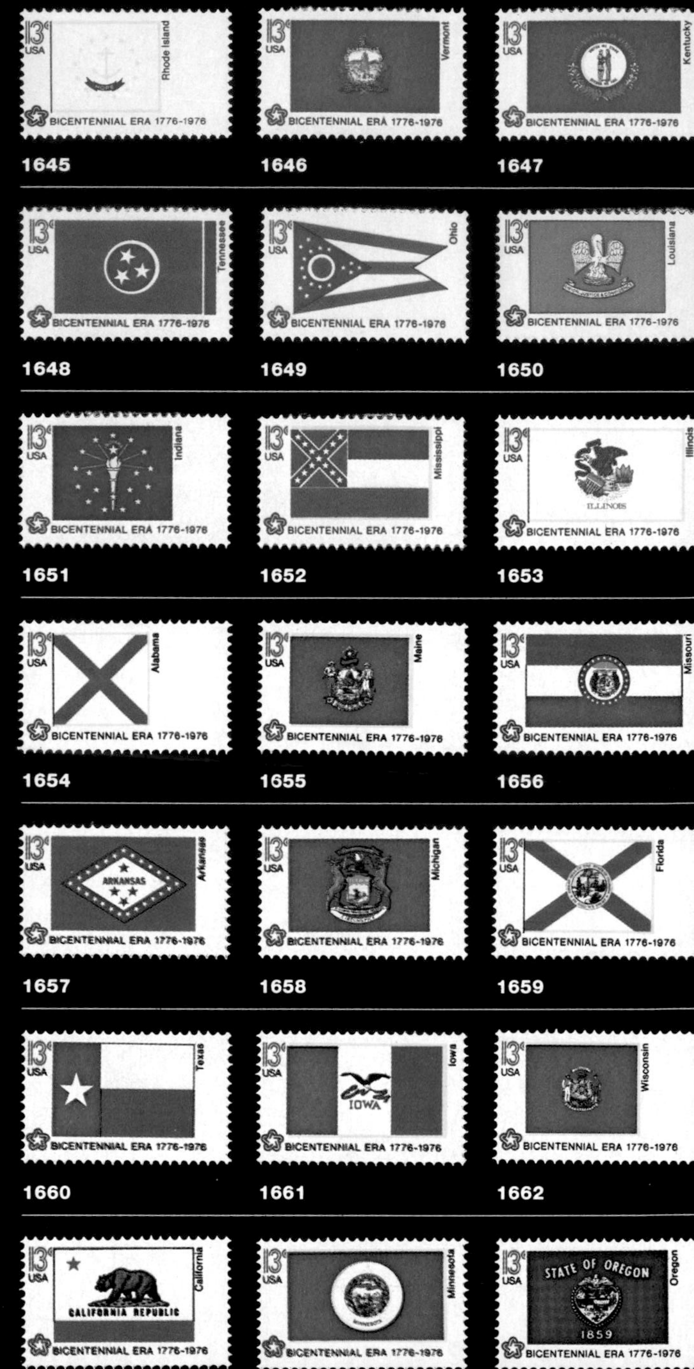

1645 1646 1647

1648 1649 1650

1651 1652 1653

1654 1655 1656

1657 1658 1659

1660 1661 1662

	1976 continued, Perf. 11	Un	U	FDC	Q
	American Bicentennial Issue continued, State Flags, Feb. 23				
1645	13¢ Rhode Island	.24	.20	1.00	8,720,100
1646	13¢ Vermont	.24	.20	1.00	8,720,100
1647	13¢ Kentucky	.24	.20	1.00	8,720,100
1648	13¢ Tennessee	.24	.20	1.00	8,720,100
1649	13¢ Ohio	.24	.20	1.00	8,720,100
1650	13¢ Louisiana	.24	.20	1.00	8,720,100
1651	13¢ Indiana	.24	.20	1.00	8,720,100
1652	13¢ Mississippi	.24	.20	1.00	8,720,100
1653	13¢ Illinois	.24	.20	1.00	8,720,100
1654	13¢ Alabama	.24	.20	1.00	8,720,100
1655	13¢ Maine	.24	.20	1.00	8,720,100
1656	13¢ Missouri	.24	.20	1.00	8,720,100
1657	13¢ Arkansas	.24	.20	1.00	8,720,100
1658	13¢ Michigan	.24	.20	1.00	8,720,100
1659	13¢ Florida	.24	.20	1.00	8,720,100
1660	13¢ Texas	.24	.20	1.00	8,720,100
1661	13¢ Iowa	.24	.20	1.00	8,720,100
1662	13¢ Wisconsin	.24	.20	1.00	8,720,100
1663	13¢ California	.24	.20	1.00	8,720,100
1664	13¢ Minnesota	.24	.20	1.00	8,720,100
1665	13¢ Oregon	.24	.20	1.00	8,720,100

LOUISIANA RICH IN NAMES

Named in 1682 by French explorer de la Salle for his king, Louis XIV, Louisiana (#1650) is also known as the Pelican State and the Bayou State. Brown pelicans once were plentiful along the state's coast, while Louisiana's slow-moving bayous—inlets or outlets of rivers and lakes—still harbor a diversity of wildlife. Like the state itself, New Orleans—Louisiana's largest city—also was named for a Frenchman, the Duke of Orleans. New Orleans is famous for its Mardi Gras, a pre-Easter carnival.

	1976 continued, Perf. 11	Un	U	PB	#	FDC	Q
	American Bicentennial Issue continued, State Flags, Feb. 23						
1666	13¢ Kansas	.24	.20			1.00	8,720,100
1667	13¢ West Virginia	.24	.20			1.00	8,720,100
1668	13¢ Nevada	.24	.20			1.00	8,720,100
1669	13¢ Nebraska	.24	.20			1.00	8,720,100
1670	13¢ Colorado	.24	.20			1.00	8,720,100
1671	13¢ North Dakota	.24	.20			1.00	8,720,100
1672	13¢ South Dakota	.24	.20			1.00	8,720,100
1673	13¢ Montana	.24	.20			1.00	8,720,100
1674	13¢ Washington	.24	.20			1.00	8,720,100
1675	13¢ Idaho	.24	.20			1.00	8,720,100
1676	13¢ Wyoming	.24	.20			1.00	8,720,100
1677	13¢ Utah	.24	.20			1.00	8,720,100
1678	13¢ Oklahoma	.24	.20			1.00	8,720,100
1679	13¢ New Mexico	.24	.20			1.00	8,720,100
1680	13¢ Arizona	.24	.20			1.00	8,720,100
1681	13¢ Alaska	.24	.20			1.00	8,720,100
1682	13¢ Hawaii	.24	.20			1.00	8,720,100
a	Pane of 50, #1633-82	12.00		12.00	(50)	27.50	
1683	13¢ Telephone Centennial, Mar. 10	.24	.15	1.05	(4)	.65	158,915,000
1684	13¢ Commercial Aviation, Mar. 19	.24	.15	2.50	(10)	.65	156,960,000
1685	13¢ Chemistry, Apr. 6	.24	.15	3.00	(12)	.65	158,470,000
	Pair with full vertical gutter between	—					

"The Most Wonderful Thing in America"
Alexander Graham Bell invented the telephone in 1876. Shortly thereafter, British scientist Sir William Thomson called it "the most wonderful thing in America." Today telephones exist in many forms, including radiophones, cordless phones and speakerphones. Hundreds of millions of telephones enable people to communicate with each other almost anywhere on Earth. Bell's invention has become the cornerstone of a worldwide system of communication. (#1683)

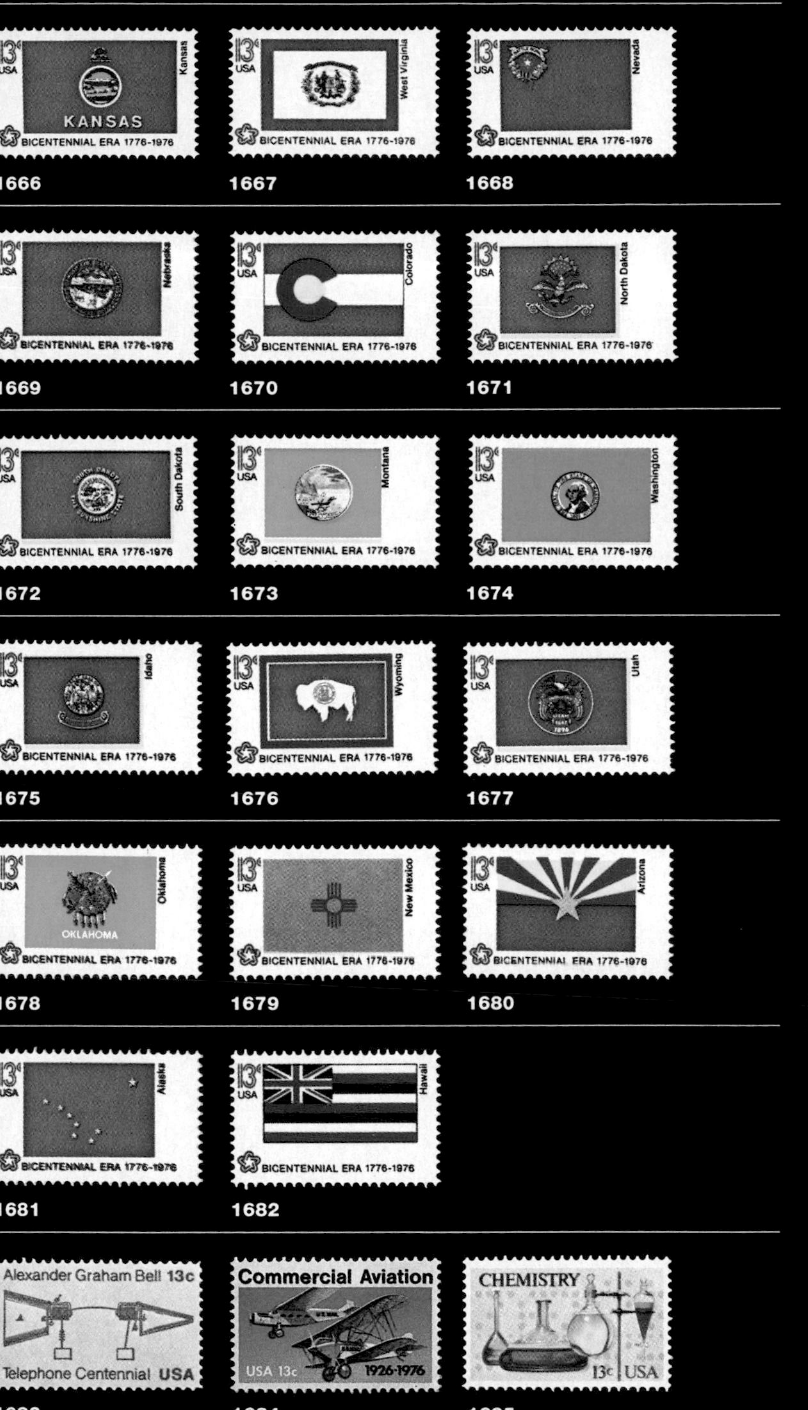

1666 1667 1668

1669 1670 1671

1672 1673 1674

1675 1676 1677

1678 1679 1680

1681 1682

1683 1684 1685

1976

1686

1687

	1976 continued, Perf. 11	Un	U	FDC	Q
	American Bicentennial Issue, Souvenir Sheets, May 29, 5 stamps each				
1686	13¢ The Surrender of Lord Cornwallis at Yorktown, by John Trumbull	3.25		6.00	1,990,000
a	13¢ Two American Officers	.45	.40		1,990,000
b	13¢ Gen. Benjamin Lincoln	.45	.40		1,990,000
c	13¢ George Washington	.45	.40		1,990,000
d	13¢ John Trumbull, Col. David Cobb, General Friedrich von Steuben, Marquis de Lafayette and Thomas Nelson	.45	.40		1,990,000
e	13¢ Alexander Hamilton, John Laurens and Walter Stewart	.45	.40		1,990,000
f	"USA/13¢" omitted on "b, "c" and "d," imperf.	—	*1,500.00*		
g	"USA/13¢" omitted on "a" and "e"	—	—		
h	Imperf. (untagged)		*1,750.00*		
i	"USA/13¢" omitted on "b," "c" and "d"	—			
j	"USA/13¢" double on "b"	—			
k	"USA/13¢" omitted on "c" and "d"	—			
l	"USA/13¢" omitted on "e"	—			
m	"USA/13¢" omitted, imperf. (untaggged)		—		
1687	18¢ The Declaration of Independence, 4 July 1776 at Philadelphia, by John Trumbull	4.25		7.50	1,983,000
a	18¢ John Adams, Roger Sherman and Robert R. Livingston	.55	.55		1,983,000
b	18¢ Thomas Jefferson and Benjamin Franklin	.55	.55		1,983,000
c	18¢ Thomas Nelson, Jr., Francis Lewis, John Witherspoon and Samuel Huntington	.55	.55		1,983,000
d	18¢ John Hancock and Charles Thomson	.55	.55		1,983,000
e	18¢ George Read, John Dickinson and Edward Rutledge	.55	.55		1,983,000
f	Design and marginal inscriptions omitted	*2,250.00*			
g	"USA/18¢" omitted on "a" and "c"	—			
h	"USA/18¢" omitted on "b," "d" and "e"	—			
i	"USA/18¢" omitted on "d"	—			
j	Black omitted in design	*800.00*			
k	"USA/18¢" omitted, imperf. (untagged)	—			
m	"USA/18¢" omitted on "b" and "e"	*1,750.00*			

	1976 continued, Perf. 11	Un	U	FDC	Q
	American Bicentennial Issue continued, Souvenir Sheets, May 29, 5 stamps each				
1688	24¢ Washington Crossing the Delaware, by Emanuel Leutze/ Eastman Johnson	5.25		8.50	1,953,000
a	24¢ Boatmen	.70	.70		1,953,000
b	24¢ George Washington	.70	.70		1,953,000
c	24¢ Flagbearer	.70	.70		1,953,000
d	24¢ Men in Boat	.70	.70		1,953,000
e	24¢ Steersman and Men on Shore	.70	.70		1,953,000
f	"USA/24¢" omitted, imperf.	*1,750.00*			
g	"USA/24¢" omitted on "d" and "e"	—	—		
h	Design and marginal inscriptions omitted	*2,250.00*			
i	"USA/24¢" omitted on "a," "b" and "c"	—	—		
j	Imperf. (untagged)	*1,750.00*			
k	"USA/24¢" inverted on "d" and "e"	—			
1689	31¢ Washington Reviewing His Ragged Army at Valley Forge, by William T. Trego	6.25		9.50	1,903,000
a	31¢ Two Officers	.85	.85		1,903,000
b	31¢ George Washington	.85	.85		1,903,000
c	31¢ Officer and Brown Horse	.85	.85		1,903,000
d	31¢ White Horse and Officer	.85	.85		1,903,000
e	31¢ Three Soldiers	.85	.85		1,903,000
f	"USA/31¢" omitted, imperf.	—			
g	"USA/31¢" omitted on "a" and "c"	—			
h	"USA/31¢" omitted on "b," "d" and "e"	—	—		
i	"USA/31¢" omitted on "e"	—			
j	Black omitted in design	*900.00*			
k	Imperf. (untagged)		*1,600.00*		
l	"USA/31¢" omitted on "b" and "d"	—			
m	"USA/31¢" omitted on "a," "b" and "e"	—			
n	As "m," imperf. (untagged)	—			
p	As "h," imperf. (untagged)		*1,750.00*		
q	As "g," imperf. (untagged)	*1,750.00*			

Washington Crossing the Delaware

From a Painting by Emanuel Leutze / Eastman Johnson

Washington Reviewing His Ragged Army at Valley Forge

From a Painting by William T. Trego

1690

1691 1692 1693 1694 1694a

1695 1696 1698a
1697 1698

1699

1700

1701

1702

1703

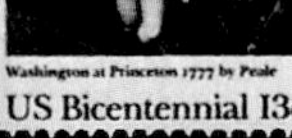

1704

1705

	1976 continued, Perf.11	Un	U	PB	#	FDC	Q
	American Bicentennial Issues, Benjamin Franklin, June 1						
1690	13¢ Bust of Franklin, Map of North America, 1776	.20	.15	.90	(4)	.65	164,890,000
a	Light blue omitted	*525.00*					
	Declaration of Independence, by John Trumbull, July 4						
1691	13¢ Delegates	.22	.15	4.75	(20)	.65	52,008,750
1692	13¢ Delegates and John Adams	.22	.15			.65	52,008,750
1693	13¢ Roger Sherman, Robert R. Livingston, Thomas Jefferson and Benjamin Franklin	.22	.15			.65	52,008,750
1694	13¢ John Hancock, Charles Thomson, George Read, John Dickinson and Edward Rutledge	.22	.15	4.75	(20)	.65	52,008,750
a	Strip of 4, #1691-94	.95	.75			2.00	
	Olympic Games Issue, July 16						
1695	13¢ Diver and Olympic Rings	.28	.15	3.50	(12)	.75	46,428,750
1696	13¢ Skier and Olympic Rings	.28	.15			.75	46,428,750
1697	13¢ Runner and Olympic Rings	.28	.15	3.50	(12)	.75	46,428,750
1698	13¢ Skater and Olympic Rings	.28	.15			.75	46,428,750
a	Block of 4, #1695-98	1.15	.85			2.00	
b	As "a," imperf.	*800.00*					
1699	13¢ Clara Maass, Aug. 18	.26	.15	3.40	(12)	.75	130,592,000
a	Horizontal pair, imperf. vertically	*475.00*					
1700	13¢ Adolph S. Ochs, Sept. 18	.24	.15	1.05	(4)	.75	158,332,800
	Christmas Issue, Oct. 27						
1701	13¢ Nativity, by John Singleton Copley	.24	.15	3.00	(12)	.65	809,955,000
a	Imperf. pair	*95.00*					
1702	13¢ "Winter Pastime," by Nathaniel Currier	.24	.15	2.50	(10)	.65	481,685,000
a	Imperf. pair	*120.00*					
1703	13¢ as #1702	.24	.15	5.00	(20)	.65	481,685,000
a	Imperf. pair	*140.00*					
b	Vertical pair, imperf. between	—					

#1702 has overall tagging. Lettering at base is black and usually 1/2mm below design. As a rule, no "snowflaking" in sky or pond. Pane of 50 has margins on 4 sides with slogans. #1703 has block tagging the size of the printed area. Lettering at base is gray black and usually 3/4mm below design. "Snowflaking" generally in sky and pond. Pane of 50 has margin only at right or left and no slogans.

	Issues of 1977, American Bicentennial Issue, Washington at Princeton, Jan. 3	Un	U	PB	#	FDC	Q
1704	13¢ Washington, Nassau Hall, Hessian Prisoners and 13-star Flag, by Charles Willson Peale	.24	.15	2.50	(10)	.65	150,328,000
a	Horizontal pair, imperf. vertically	*500.00*					
1705	13¢ Sound Recording, Mar. 23	.24	.15	1.05	(4)	.65	176,830,000

	1977 continued, Perf. 11	Un	U	PB	#	FDC	Q
	American Folk Art Issue, Pueblo Pottery, Apr. 13						
1706	13¢ Zia Pot	.24	.15	2.50	(10)	.75	48,994,000
1707	13¢ San Ildefonso Pot	.24	.15			.75	48,994,000
1708	13¢ Hopi Pot	.24	.15			.75	48,994,000
1709	13¢ Acoma Pot	.24	.15			.75	48,994,000
a	Block of 4, #1706-09	1.00	.60			2.00	
b	As "a," imperf. vertically	*2,500.00*					
1710	13¢ Solo Transatlantic Flight, May 20	.24	.15	3.00	(12)	.75	208,820,000
a	Imperf. pair	*1,400.00*					
1711	13¢ Colorado Statehood, May 21	.24	.15	3.00	(12)	.65	192,250,000
a	Horizontal pair, imperf. between	—					
b	Horizontal pair, imperf. vertically	—					
c	Perf. 11.2	.35	.25				
	Butterflies Issue, June 6						
1712	13¢ Swallowtail	.24	.15	3.10	(12)	.75	54,957,500
1713	13¢ Checkerspot	.24	.15	3.10	(12)	.75	54,957,500
1714	13¢ Dogface	.24	.15			.75	54,957,500
1715	13¢ Orange-Tip	.24	.15			.75	54,957,500
a	Block of 4, #1712-15	1.00	.60			2.00	
b	As "a," imperf. horizontally	—					
	American Bicentennial Issues, Lafayette's Landing in South Carolina, June 13						
1716	13¢ Marquis de Lafayette	.24	.15	1.05	(4)	.65	159,852,000
	Skilled Hands for Independence, July 4						
1717	13¢ Seamstress	.24	.15	3.10	(12)	.65	47,077,500
1718	13¢ Blacksmith	.24	.15	3.10	(12)	.65	47,077,500
1719	13¢ Wheelwright	.24	.15			.65	47,077,500
1720	13¢ Leatherworker	.24	.15			.65	47,077,500
a	Block of 4, #1717-20	1.00	.80			1.75	
	Perf. 11 x 10½						
1721	13¢ Peace Bridge, Aug. 4	.24	.15	1.05	(4)	.65	163,625,000

PUEBLO ARTISTS CONTINUE TRADITION
Following an artistic tradition that is very old, Pueblo Indians of the American Southwest continue to produce many distinctive pieces, including the Acoma pot shown here. In 1977, the U.S. Postal Service commemorated Pueblo art with a block of four stamps, each showing an example of pottery produced by a different Pueblo tribe: Zia (#1706), San Idlefonso (#1707), Hopi (#1708) and Acoma (#1709).

1706 1707 1709a
1708 1709

1710

1711

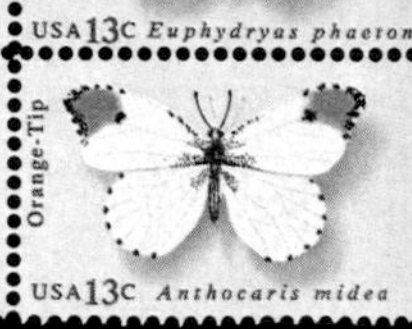

1712 1713 1715a
1714 1715

1716

1717 1718 1720a
1719 1720

1721

1722

1723 1723a
1724

1725

1726

1727

1728

1729

1730

1731

1732 1732a

1734

1735

1737

	1977 continued	Un	U	PB	#	FDC	Q
	American Bicentennial Issue, Battle of Oriskany, Aug. 6, Perf. 11						
1722	13¢ Herkimer at Oriskany, by Frederick Yohn	.24	.15	2.50	(10)	.65	156,296,000
	Energy Issue, Oct. 20						
1723	13¢ Energy Conservation	.24	.15	3.00	(12)	.65	79,338,000
a	Attached pair, #1723-24	.48	.40			1.00	
1724	13¢ Energy Development	.24	.15	3.00	(12)	.65	79,338,000
1725	13¢ First Civil Settlement-Alta, California, Sept. 9	.24	.15	1.05	(4)	.65	154,495,000
	American Bicentennial Issue, Articles of Confederation, Sept. 30						
1726	13¢ Members of Continental Congress in Conference	.24	.15	1.05	(4)	.65	168,050,000
1727	13¢ Talking Pictures, Oct. 6	.24	.15	1.05	(4)	.75	156,810,000
	American Bicentennial Issue, Surrender at Saratoga, Oct. 7						
1728	13¢ Surrender of Burgoyne, by John Trumbull	.24	.15	2.50	(10)	.65	153,736,000
	Christmas Issue, Oct. 21						
1729	13¢ Washington at Valley Forge, by J.C. Leyendecker	.24	.15	5.75	(20)	.65	882,260,000
a	Imperf. pair	*90.00*					
1730	13¢ Rural Mailbox	.24	.15	2.50	(10)	.65	921,530,000
a	Imperf. pair	*250.00*					
	Issues of 1978						
1731	13¢ Carl Sandburg, Jan. 6	.24	.15	1.05	(4)	.65	156,560,000
	Capt. Cook Issue, Jan. 20						
1732	13¢ Capt. James Cook–Alaska, by Nathaniel Dance	.24	.15	1.10	(4)	.75	101,095,000
a	Attached pair, #1732-33	.50	.30			1.50	
b	As "a," imperf. between	*4,000.00*					
1733	13¢ Resolution and Discovery–Hawaii, by John Webber	.24	.15	1.10	(4)	.75	101,095,000
a	Vertical pair, imperf. horizontally	—					
1734	13¢ Indian Head Penny, Jan. 11	.24	.15	1.50	(4)	1.00	
	Pair with full horizontal gutter between	—					
a	Horizontal pair, imperf. vertically	*300.00*					
1735	(15¢) A Stamp, May 22	.24	.15	1.05	(4)	.65	
a	Imperf. pair	*80.00*					
b	Vertical pair, imperf. horizontally	*300.00*					
	Perf. 11 x 10½						
1736	(15¢) orange Eagle (1735), Single from booklet	.25	.15			.65	
a	Booklet pane of 8, May 22	2.40	*.60*			2.50	
	Roses Booklet Issue, July 11, Perf. 10						
1737	15¢ Roses, Single from booklet	.25	.15			.65	
a	Booklet pane of 8	2.50	*.60*			2.50	
b	As "a," imperf.	—					
	#1737 issued only in booklets. All stamps have one side imperf. or one side and bottom imperf.						

Minimum value listed for a stamp is 15 cents. This minimum represents a fair-market price for having a dealer locate and provide a single stamp from his or her stock. Dealers may charge less per stamp for a group of such stamps, or less for a single stamp.

	Issues of 1980	Un	U	PB	#	FDC	Q
	Windmills Booklet Issue, Feb. 7, Perf. 11						
1738	15¢ Virginia, 1720	.30	.15			.65	
1739	15¢ Rhode Island, 1790	.30	.15			.65	
1740	15¢ Massachusetts, 1793	.30	.15			.65	
1741	15¢ Illinois, 1860	.30	.15			.65	
1742	15¢ Texas, 1890	.30	.15			.65	
a	Booklet pane of 10, #1738-42	3.60	*.60*			3.50	
	#1737-42 issued only in booklets. All stamps have one or two imperf. edges.						
	Issues of 1978, Coil Stamp, Perf. 10 Vertically						
1743	(15¢) orange Eagle (1735), May 22	.25	.15	.65	(2)	.65	
a	Imperf. pair	*100.00*		—	(2)		
	Black Heritage Issue, Harriet Tubman, Feb. 1, Perf. 10½ x 11						
1744	13¢ Harriet Tubman and Cart Carrying Slaves	.24	.15	3.00	(12)	1.00	156,525,000
	American Folk Art Issue, Quilts, Mar. 8, Perf. 11						
1745	13¢ Basket design, red & orange	.24	.15	3.10	(12)	.75	41,295,600
1746	13¢ Basket design, red	.24	.15	3.10	(12)	.75	41,295,600
1747	13¢ Basket design, orange	.24	.15			.75	41,295,600
1748	13¢ Basket design, brown	.24	.15			.75	41,295,600
a	Block of 4, #1745-48	1.00	.60			2.00	
	American Dance Issue, Apr. 26						
1749	13¢ Ballet	.24	.15	3.10	(12)	.75	39,399,600
1750	13¢ Theater	.24	.15	3.10	(12)	.75	39,399,600
1751	13¢ Folk	.24	.15			.75	39,399,600
1752	13¢ Modern	.24	.15			.75	39,399,600
a	Block of 4, #1749-52	1.00	.60			1.75	
	American Bicentennial Issue, French Alliance, May 4						
1753	13¢ King Louis XVI and Benjamin Franklin, by Charles Gabriel Sauvage	.24	.15	1.05	(4)	.65	102,920,000
	Perf. 10½ x 11						
1754	13¢ Early Cancer Detection, May 18	.24	.15	1.05	(4)	.65	152,355,000
	Performing Arts Issues, Jimmie Rodgers, May 24, Perf. 11						
1755	13¢ Jimmie Rodgers with Locomotive, Guitar and Brakeman's Cap	.24	.15	3.00	(12)	.65	94,625,000
	George M. Cohan, July 3						
1756	15¢ George M. Cohan, "Yankee Doodle Dandy" and Stars	.28	.15	3.50	(12)	.65	151,570,000

TUBMAN RODE THE FREEDOM TRAIN

Harriet Tubman (#1744) began life as a slave, probably in the year 1820, in Bucktown, Maryland. Aided by the underground railroad—an anti-slavery group that helped slaves escape to free states in the North or to Canada—Tubman escaped to Philadelphia and freedom in 1849. A year later, Congress passed the Fugitive Slave Act, making it a crime to help runaway slaves. Tubman nevertheless returned to Maryland many times, eventually helping to guide some 300 slaves—including her parents—to freedom.

1738 1739 1740 1741 1742

1742a

1744

1745 1746 1748a

1747 1748

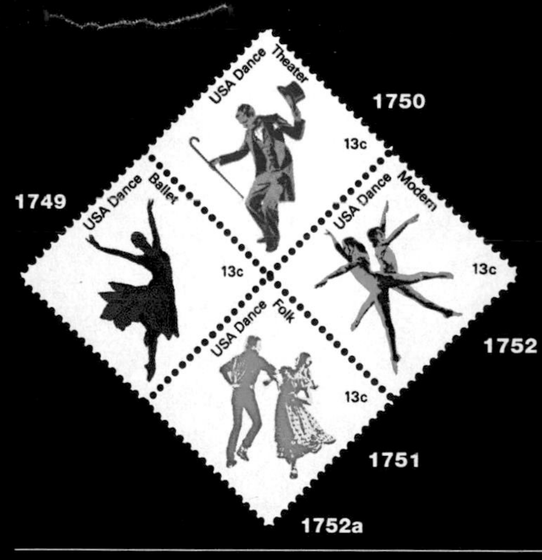

1749 1750 1751 1752

1752a

1753

1754

1755

1756

1757a, b, c, d

1757e, f, g, h

1757

1758

1759

1763a

1760 1761

1762 1763

1764 1765 1767a

1766 1767

1768

1769

	1978 continued, Perf. 11	Un	U	PB	#	FDC	Q
	CAPEX '78, Souvenir Sheet, June 10						
1757	13¢ Souvenir sheet of 8	1.65	1.65	1.90	(8)	2.75	15,170,400
a	13¢ Cardinal	.20	.15				
b	13¢ Mallard	.20	.15				
c	13¢ Canada Goose	.20	.15				
d	13¢ Blue Jay	.20	.15				
e	13¢ Moose	.20	.15				
f	13¢ Chipmunk	.20	.15				
g	13¢ Red Fox	.20	.15				
h	13¢ Raccoon	.20	.15				
i	Yellow, green, red, brown and black (litho.) omitted	*3,500.00*					
1758	15¢ Photography, June 26	.26	.15	3.25	(12)	.65	163,200,000
1759	15¢ Viking Missions to Mars, July 20	.28	.15	1.20	(4)	1.10	158,880,000
	Wildlife Conservation Issue, American Owls, Aug. 26						
1760	15¢ Great Gray Owl	.28	.15	1.25	(4)	.75	46,637,500
1761	15¢ Saw-Whet Owl	.28	.15	1.25	(4)	.75	46,637,500
1762	15¢ Barred Owl	.28	.15	1.25	(4)	.75	46,637,500
1763	15¢ Great Horned Owl	.28	.15	1.25	(4)	.75	46,637,500
a	Block of 4, #1760-63	1.15	.85			2.00	
	American Trees Issue, Oct. 9						
1764	15¢ Giant Sequoia	.28	.15	3.50	(12)	.75	42,034,000
1765	15¢ White Pine	.28	.15	3.50	(12)	.75	42,034,000
1766	15¢ White Oak	.28	.15			.75	42,034,000
1767	15¢ Gray Birch	.28	.15			.75	42,034,000
a	Block of 4, #1764-67	1.15	.85			2.00	
b	As "a," imperf. horizontally	*12,500.00*					
	Christmas Issue, Oct. 18						
1768	15¢ Madonna and Child with Cherubim, by Andrea della Robbia	.28	.15	3.50	(12)	.65	963,370,000
a	Imperf. pair	*100.00*					
1769	15¢ Child on Hobby Horse and Christmas Trees	.28	.15	3.50	(12)	.65	916,800,000
a	Imperf. pair	*100.00*					
b	Vertical pair, imperf. horizontally	—					
	Pair with full horizontal gutter between	—					

	Issues of 1979, Perf. 11	Un	U	PB	#	FDC	Q
1770	15¢ Robert F. Kennedy, Jan. 12	.28	.15	1.20	(4)	.65	159,297,600
	Black Heritage Issue, Martin Luther King, Jr., Jan. 13						
1771	15¢ Martin Luther King, Jr., and Civil Rights Marchers	.28	.15	3.50	(12)	.65	166,435,000
a	Imperf. pair	—					
1772	15¢ International Year of the Child, Feb. 15	.28	.15	1.20	(4)	.65	162,535,000
	Literary Arts Issue, John Steinbeck, Feb. 27, Perf. 10½ x 11						
1773	15¢ John Steinbeck, by Philippe Halsman	.28	.15	1.20	(4)	.65	155,000,000
1774	15¢ Albert Einstein, Mar. 4	.28	.15	1.20	(4)	.65	157,310,000
	Pair with full horizontal gutter between	—					
	American Folk Art Issue, Pennsylvania Toleware, Apr. 19, Perf. 11						
1775	15¢ Straight-spout Coffeepot	.28	.15	2.90	(10)	.75	43,524,000
1776	15¢ Tea Caddy	.28	.15			.75	43,524,000
1777	15¢ Sugar Bowl	.28	.15			.75	43,524,000
1778	15¢ Curved-spout Coffeepot	.28	.15			.75	43,524,000
a	Block of 4, #1775-78	1.15	.85			2.00	
b	As "a," imperf. horizontally	—					
	American Architecture Issue, June 4						
1779	15¢ Virginia Rotunda, by Thomas Jefferson	.28	.15	1.25	(4)	.75	41,198,400
1780	15¢ Baltimore Cathedral, by Benjamin Latrobe	.28	.15	1.25	(4)	.75	41,198,400
1781	15¢ Boston State House, by Charles Bulfinch	.28	.15	1.25	(4)	.75	41,198,400
1782	15¢ Philadelphia Exchange, by William Strickland	.28	.15	1.25	(4)	.75	41,198,400
a	Block of 4, #1779-82	1.15	.85			2.00	
	Endangered Flora Issue, June 7						
1783	15¢ Persistent Trillium	.28	.15	3.50	(12)	.75	40,763,750
1784	15¢ Hawaiian Wild Broadbean	.28	.15			.75	40,763,750
1785	15¢ Contra Costa Wallflower	.28	.15	3.50	(12)	.75	40,763,750
1786	15¢ Antioch Dunes Evening Primrose	.28	.15			.75	40,763,750
a	Block of 4, #1783-86	1.15	.85			2.00	
b	As "a," imperf.	*750.00*					
	As "b," full vertical gutter between	—					

FROM HUMBLE OBJECTS, FOLK ART SPRANG

During the first half of the 19th century, southeastern Pennsylvania Germans, or "Dutch," created toleware coffee pots, trays and other household items that were both beautiful and useful. Made of varnished tin, Pennsylvania toleware was typically decorated with rural motifs such as flowers, fruit and birds. Red was a favorite background color. (#1775-78a)

1770

1771

1772

1773

1774

1775 1776 1778a

1777 1778

1779 1780 1782a

1781 1782

1786a

1783 1784

1785 1786

1787

Special Olympics
Skill · Sharing · Joy
USA 15c

1788

1789

1790

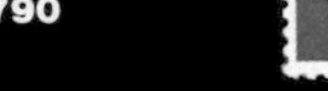

1791 1792 1794a

1793 1794

1795 1796 1798b

1797 1798

1799

1800

1801

USA · 15c
HONORING VIETNAM VETERANS
NOV · 11 · 1979

1802

1803

1804

	1979 continued, Perf. 11	Un	U	PB	#	FDC	Q
1787	15¢ Seeing Eye Dogs, June 15	.28	.15	5.75	(20)	.65	161,860,000
a	Imperf. pair	*400.00*					
1788	15¢ Special Olympics, Aug. 9	.28	.15	2.90	(10)	.65	165,775,000
	American Bicentennial Issue, John Paul Jones, Sept. 23, Perf. 11 x 12						
1789	15¢ John Paul Jones, by Charles Willson Peale	.28	.15	2.90	(10)	.65	160,000,000
a	Perf. 11	.30	.15	3.10	(10)		
b	Perf. 12	*2,000.00*	*1,000.00*				
c	Vertical pair, imperf. horizontally	*240.00*					
d	As "a," vertical pair, imperf. horizontally	*200.00*					
	Numerous varieties of printer's waste of #1789 exist.						
	Olympic Summer Games Issues, Sept. 5, Perf. 11 (see also #C97)						
1790	10¢ Javelin Thrower	.20	.20	2.50	(12)	1.00	67,195,000
	Sept. 28						
1791	15¢ Runner	.28	.15	3.50	(12)	.75	46,726,250
1792	15¢ Swimmer	.28	.15	3.50	(12)	.75	46,726,250
1793	15¢ Rowers	.28	.15			.75	46,726,250
1794	15¢ Equestrian Contestant	.28	.15			.75	46,726,250
a	Block of 4, #1791-94	1.15	.85			2.00	
b	As "a," imperf.	*1,850.00*					
	Issues of 1980, Olympic Winter Games Issue, Feb. 1, Perf. 11 x 10½						
1795	15¢ Speed Skater	.32	.15	4.00	(12)	.75	52,073,750
1796	15¢ Downhill Skier	.32	.15	4.00	(12)	.75	52,073,750
1797	15¢ Ski Jumper	.32	.15			.75	52,073,750
1798	15¢ Hockey Goaltender	.32	.15			.75	52,073,750
a	Perf. 11	1.05	—	13.00	(12)		
b	Block of 4, #1795-98	1.30	1.00			2.00	
c	Block of 4, #1795a-98a	4.25	—				
	1979 continued, Christmas Issue, Oct. 18, Perf. 11						
1799	15¢ Virgin and Child with Cherubim, by Gerard David	.28	.15	3.40	(12)	.65	873,710,000
a	Imperf. pair	*125.00*					
b	Vertical pair, imperf. horizontally	*850.00*					
c	Vertical pair, imperf. between	—					
1800	15¢ Santa Claus, Christmas Tree Ornament	.28	.15	3.40	(12)	1.00	931,880,000
a	Green and yellow omitted	*750.00*					
b	Green, yellow and tan omitted	*800.00*					
	Performing Arts Issue, Will Rogers, Nov. 4						
1801	15¢ Will Rogers Portrait and Rogers as a Cowboy Humorist	.28	.15	3.40	(12)	.65	161,290,000
a	Imperf. pair	*275.00*					
1802	15¢ Vietnam Veterans, Nov. 11	.28	.15	2.90	(10)	1.25	172,740,000
	1980 continued, Performing Arts Issue, W.C. Fields, Jan. 29						
1803	15¢ W.C. Fields Portrait and Fields as a Juggler	.28	.15	3.40	(12)	.65	168,995,000
	Black Heritage Issue, Benjamin Banneker, Feb. 15						
1804	15¢ Benjamin Banneker Portrait and Banneker as Surveyor	.28	.15	3.40	(12)	.65	160,000,000
a	Horizontal pair, imperf. vertically	—					

	1980 continued, Perf. 11	Un	U	PB/LP	#	FDC	Q
	Letter Writing Issue, Feb. 25						
1805	15¢ Letters Preserve Memories	.28	.15	10.50	(36)	.65	38,933,000
1806	15¢ purple P.S. Write Soon	.28	.15			.65	38,933,000
1807	15¢ Letters Lift Spirits	.28	.15			.65	38,933,000
1808	15¢ green P.S. Write Soon	.28	.15			.65	38,933,000
1809	15¢ Letters Shape Opinions	.28	.15			.65	38,933,000
1810	15¢ red and blue P.S. Write Soon	.28	.15	10.50	(36)	.65	38,933,000
a	Vertical Strip of 6, #1805-10	1.70	1.50			2.50	
	Issues of 1980-81, Americana Issue, Coil Stamps, Perf. 10 Vertically (see also #1581-82, 1584-85, 1590-99, 1603-06, 1608, 1610-19, 1622-23e, 1625)						
1811	1¢ dark blue, *greenish* Inkwell & Quill (1581), Mar. 6, 1980	.15	.15	.30	(2)	.60	
a	Imperf. pair	*225.00*		—	(2)		
1812, 1814-15,1817 not assigned							
1813	3.5¢ Weaver Violins, June 23, 1980	.15	.15	.90	(2)	.60	
a	Untagged (Bureau precanceled)		.15				
b	Imperf. pair	*300.00*		—	(2)		
1816	12¢ red brown, *beige* Torch from Statue of Liberty (1594), Apr. 8, 1981	.24	.15	1.25	(2)	.60	
a	Untagged (Bureau precanceled)		.25				
b	Imperf. pair	*225.00*		—	(2)		
	Issues of 1981, Perf. 11 x 10½						
1818	(18¢) B Stamp, Mar. 15	.32	.15	1.50	(4)	.75	
	Perf. 10						
1819	(18¢) B Stamp (1818), single from booklet	.40	.15			.75	
a	Booklet pane of 8, Mar. 15	4.50	*1.50*			3.00	
	Coil Stamp, Perf. 10 Vertically						
1820	(18¢) B Stamp (1818), Mar. 15	.40	.15	1.60	(2)	.75	
a	Imperf. pair	*110.00*		—	(2)		
	1980 continued, Perf. 10½ x 11						
1821	15¢ Frances Perkins, April 10	.28	.15	1.20	(4)	.65	163,510,000
	Perf. 11						
1822	15¢ Dolley Madison, May 20	.28	.15	1.40	(4)	.65	256,620,000
1823	15¢ Emily Bissell, May 31	.28	.15	1.20	(4)	.65	95,695,000
a	Vertical pair, imperf. horizontally	*300.00*					
1824	15¢ Helen Keller/Anne Sullivan, June 27	.28	.15	1.20	(4)	.80	153,975,000
1825	15¢ Veterans Administration, July 21	.28	.15	1.20	(4)	.65	160,000,000
a	Horizontal pair, imperf. vertically	*500.00*					
	American Bicentennial Issue, General Bernardo de Galvez, July 23						
1826	15¢ General Bernardo de Galvez and Revolutionary Flag at Battle of Mobile	.28	.15	1.20	(4)	.65	103,855,000
a	Red, brown and blue omitted	*900.00*					
b	Blue, brown, red and yellow omitted	*1,400.00*					
	Coral Reefs Issue, Aug. 26						
1827	15¢ Brain Coral, Beaugregory Fish	.30	.15	3.65	(12)	.85	51,291,250
1828	15¢ Elkhorn Coral, Porkfish	.30	.15			.85	51,291,250
1829	15¢ Chalice Coral, Moorish Idol	.30	.15	3.65	(12)	.85	51,291,250
1830	15¢ Finger Coral, Sabertooth Blenny	.30	.15			.85	51,291,250
a	Block of 4, #1827-30	1.20	.85			2.00	
b	As "a," imperf.	*1,600.00*					
c	As "a," imperf. between, vertically	—					
d	As "a," imperf. vertically	*3,000.00*					

1805
1806

1807
1808

1809
1810

1813

1816

1818

1821

1822

1823

1824

1825

1826

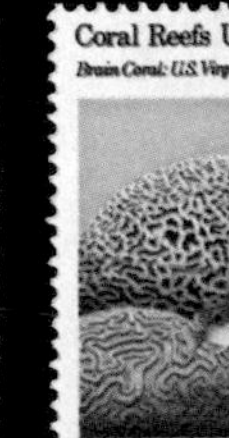

1827 1828 1830a
1829 1830

1980

1831

1832

USA 15c
Learning never ends

1833

1834 1835 1837a
1836 1837

1838 1839 1841a
1840 1841

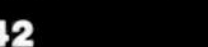

1842

USA 15c
Season's Greetings

1843

	1980 continued, Perf. 11	Un	U	PB	#	FDC	Q
1831	15¢ Organized Labor, Sept. 1	.28	.15	3.50	(12)	.65	166,590,000
a	Imperf. pair	*450.00*					
	Literary Arts Issue, Edith Wharton, Sept. 5, Perf. 10½ x 11						
1832	15¢ Edith Wharton Reading Letter	.28	.15	1.20	(4)	.65	163,275,000
	Perf. 11						
1833	15¢ Education, Sept. 12	.28	.15	1.70	(6)	.65	160,000,000
a	Horizontal pair, imperf. vertically	*300.00*					
	American Folk Art Issue, Pacific Northwest Indian Masks, Sept. 25						
1834	15¢ Heiltsuk, Bella Bella Tribe	.30	.15			.75	38,101,000
1835	15¢ Chilkat Tlingit Tribe	.30	.15			.75	38,101,000
1836	15¢ Tlingit Tribe	.30	.15			.75	38,101,000
1837	15¢ Bella Coola Tribe	.30	.15			.75	38,101,000
a	Block of 4, #1834-37	1.20	.85	3.10	(10)	2.00	
	American Architecture Issue, Oct. 9						
1838	15¢ Smithsonian Institution, by James Renwick	.30	.15			.75	38,756,000
1839	15¢ Trinity Church, by Henry Hobson Richardson	.30	.15			.75	38,756,000
1840	15¢ Pennsylvania Academy of Fine Arts, by Frank Furness	.30	.15			.75	38,756,000
1841	15¢ Lyndhurst, by Alexander Jefferson Davis	.30	.15			.75	38,756,000
a	Block of 4, #1838-41	1.20	.85	1.30	(4)	2.00	
	Christmas Issue, Oct. 31						
1842	15¢ Madonna and Child from Epiphany Window, Washington Cathedral	.28	.15	3.40	(12)	.65	693,250,000
a	Imperf. pair	*100.00*					
	Pair with full vertical gutter between	—					
1843	15¢ Wreath and Toys	.28	.15	5.75	(20)	.65	718,715,000
a	Imperf. pair	*100.00*					
b	Buff omitted	—					

Trinity Church Is Major Work
Completed in 1877, Trinity Church (#1839) is the first major work by Henry Hobson Richardson, who dominated American architecture during the 1870s and '80s. Located on Copley Square in Boston, Massachusetts, the church's large, round-arched openings are typical of what has become known as Richardsonian Romanesque architecture.

	Issues of 1980-85	Un	U	PB	#	FDC
	Great Americans Issue, Perf. 11 (see also #2168-72, 2176-80, 2182-84, 2188, 2191-97)					
1844	1¢ Dorothea Dix, Sept. 23, 1983	.15	.15	.35	(6)	.60
a	Imperf. pair	*350.00*				
b	Vertical pair, imperf. between	—				
	Perf. 10½ x 11					
1845	2¢ Igor Stravinsky, Nov. 18, 1982	.15	.15	.25	(4)	.60
1846	3¢ Henry Clay, July 13, 1983	.15	.15	.30	(4)	.60
1847	4¢ Carl Schurz, June 3, 1983	.15	.15	.32	(4)	.60
1848	5¢ Pearl Buck, June 25, 1983	.15	.15	.40	(4)	.60
	Perf. 11					
1849	6¢ Walter Lippman, Sept. 19, 1985	.15	.15	.75	(6)	.60
a	Vertical pair, imperf. between	—				
1850	7¢ Abraham Baldwin, Jan. 25, 1985	.15	.15	.75	(6)	.60
1851	8¢ Henry Knox, July 25, 1985	.15	.15	.70	(4)	.60
1852	9¢ Sylvanus Thayer, June 7, 1985	.16	.15	1.00	(6)	.60
1853	10¢ Richard Russell, May 31, 1984	.18	.15	1.10	(6)	.65
a	Vertical pair, imperf. between	*1,100.00*				
b	Horizontal pair, imperf. between	—				
1854	11¢ Alden Partridge, Feb. 12, 1985	.20	.15	.95	(4)	.65
	Perf. 10½ x 11					
1855	13¢ Crazy Horse, Jan. 15, 1982	.24	.15	1.35	(4)	.65
	Perf. 11					
1856	14¢ Sinclair Lewis, Mar. 21, 1985	.25	.15	1.55	(6)	.65
a	Vertical pair, imperf. horizontally	*150.00*				
b	Horizontal pair, imperf. between	10.00				
c	Vertical pair, imperf. between	*2,000.00*				
	Perf. 10½ x 11					
1857	17¢ Rachel Carson, May 28, 1981	.32	.15	1.40	(4)	.75
1858	18¢ George Mason, May 7, 1981	.32	.15	2.00	(4)	.75
1859	19¢ Sequoyah, Dec. 27, 1980	.35	.15	2.00	(4)	.80
1860	20¢ Ralph Bunche, Jan. 12, 1982	.40	.15	2.50	(4)	.75
1861	20¢ Thomas H. Gallaudet, June 10, 1983	.38	.15	2.50	(4)	.75
	Perf. 11					
1862	20¢ Harry S. Truman, Jan. 26, 1984	.38	.15	2.40	(6)	.75
1863	22¢ John J. Audubon, Apr. 23, 1985	.40	.15	2.50	(6)	.80
a	Vertical pair, imperf. horizontally	—				
b	Vertical pair, imperf. between	—				
c	Horizontal pair, imperf. between	—				
1864	30¢ Frank C. Laubach, Sept. 2, 1984	.55	.15	3.50	(6)	.85
	Perf. 10½ x 11					
1865	35¢ Charles R. Drew, MD, June 3, 1981	.65	.15	2.75	(4)	1.00
1866	37¢ Robert Millikan, Jan. 26, 1982	.70	.15	2.90	(4)	1.00
	Perf. 11					
1867	39¢ Grenville Clark, May 20, 1985	.70	.15	4.25	(6)	1.00
a	Vertical pair, imperf. horizontally	*700.00*				
b	Vertical pair, imperf. between	*1,100.00*				
1868	40¢ Lillian M. Gilbreth, Feb. 24, 1984	.70	.15	4.60	(6)	1.00
1869	50¢ Chester W. Nimitz, Feb. 22, 1985	.90	.15	4.50	(4)	1.25
1870-73	not assigned					

1844  1845  1846  1847

1848  1849  1850  1851

1852  1853  1854  1855  1856

1857  1858  1859  1860  1861

1862

1863

1864

1865

1866 1867 1868 1869

1874

1875

1876 1877 1879a
1878 1879

1880 1881
1882 1883
1884 1885
1886 1887
1888 1889

1890

1891

1889a

1892 1893a
1893

1894

	Issues of 1981, Perf. 11	Un	U	PB	#	FDC	Q
1874	15¢ Everett Dirksen, Jan. 4	.28	.15	1.20	(4)	.65	160,155,000
	Black Heritage Issue, Whitney Moore Young, Jan. 30						
1875	15¢ Whitney Moore Young at Desk	.28	.15	1.25	(4)	.65	159,505,000

	1981 continued, Perf. 11	Un	U	PB/PNC	#	FDC	Q
	Flower Issue, April 23						
1876	18¢ Rose	.35	.15			.75	52,658,250
1877	18¢ Camellia	.35	.15			.75	52,658,250
1878	18¢ Dahlia	.35	.15			.75	52,658,250
1879	18¢ Lily	.35	.15			.75	52,658,250
a	Block of 4, #1876-79	1.40	.85	1.50	(4)	2.50	
	Wildlife Booklet Issue, May 14						
1880	18¢ Bighorn Sheep	.35	.15			.75	
1881	18¢ Puma	.35	.15			.75	
1882	18¢ Harbor Seal	.35	.15			.75	
1883	18¢ Bison	.35	.15			.75	
1884	18¢ Brown Bear	.35	.15			.75	
1885	18¢ Polar Bear	.35	.15			.75	
1886	18¢ Elk (Wapiti)	.35	.15			.75	
1887	18¢ Moose	.35	.15			.75	
1888	18¢ White-Tailed Deer	.35	.15			.75	
1889	18¢ Pronghorn Antelope	.35	.15			.75	
a	Booklet pane of 10, #1880-89	9.00				5.00	
	#1880-89 issued only in booklets. All stamps are imperf. at one side or imperf. at one side and bottom.						
	Flag and Anthem Issue, April 24						
1890	18¢ "...for amber waves of grain"	.32	.15	9.00	(20)	.75	
a	Imperf. pair	100.00					
b	Vertical pair, imperf. horizontally	—					
	Coil Stamp, Perf. 10 Vertically						
1891	18¢ "...from sea to shining sea"	.36	.15	4.50	(3)	.75	
a	Imperf. pair	20.00					
	Beginning with #1891, all coil stamps except #1947 feature a small plate number at the bottom of the design at varying intervals in a roll, depending on the press used. The basic "plate number coil" (PNC) collecting unit is a strip of three stamps, with the plate number appearing on the middle stamp.						
	Perf. 11						
1892	6¢ USA Circle of Stars, single from booklet (1893a)	.55	.15			.75	
1893	18¢ "...for purple mountain majesties," single from booklet (1893a)	.32	.15			.75	
a	Booklet pane of 8, (2 #1892 & 6 #1893)	3.25				2.50	
b	As "a," imperf. vertically between	*80.00*					
	#1892-93 issued only in booklets. All stamps are imperf. at one side or imperf. at one side and bottom.						
	Flag over Supreme Court Issue, Dec. 17 (except #1896b, issued June 1, 1982)						
1894	20¢ Flag over Supreme Court	.35	.15	7.25	(20)	.75	
a	Imperf. pair	35.00					
b	Vertical pair, imperf. horizontally	*650.00*					
c	Dark blue omitted	*225.00*					
d	Black omitted	*300.00*					
	Coil Stamp, Perf. 10 Vertically						
1895	20¢ Flag over Supreme Court (1894)	.35	.15	4.00	(3)	.75	
a	Imperf. pair	10.00					
b	Black omitted	*65.00*					
c	Blue omitted	—					
e	Untagged (Bureau precanceled)	.48	.48	18.75	(3)		
	Perf. 11 x 10½						
1896	20¢ Flag over Supreme Court (1894), single from booklet	.35	.15			.75	
a	Booklet pane of 6	2.60				6.00	
b	Booklet pane of 10, June 1, 1982	4.00				*10.00*	

	Issues of 1981-84	Un	U	PB/PNC	#	FDC	Q
	Coil Stamps, Transportation Issue, Perf. 10 Vertically (see also #2123-36, 2225-26, 2228, 2231, 2252-66)						
1897	1¢ Omnibus 1880s, Aug. 19, 1983	.15	.15	.50	(3)	.60	
a	Imperf. pair	*700.00*		—	(3)		
1897A	2¢ Locomotive 1870s, May 20, 1982	.15	.15	.55	(3)	.60	
e	Imperf. pair	*85.00*		—	(3)		
1898	3¢ Handcar 1880s, Mar. 25, 1983	.15	.15	.70	(3)	.60	
1898A	4¢ Stagecoach 1890s, Aug. 19, 1982	.15	.15	1.40	(3)	.60	
b	Untagged (Bureau precanceled)	.15	.15	2.50	(3)	.60	
c	As "b," imperf. pair	*900.00*					
1899	5¢ Motorcycle 1913, Oct. 10, 1983	.15	.15	1.35	(3)	.60	
a	Imperf. pair	—					
1900	5.2¢ Sleigh 1880s, Mar. 21, 1983	.15	.15	8.50	(3)	.60	
a	Untagged (Bureau precanceled)	.15	.15	10.50	(3)	.60	
1901	5.9¢ Bicycle 1870s, Feb. 17, 1982	.18	.15	11.00	(3)	.60	
a	Untagged (Bureau precanceled)	.18	.18	13.00	(3)	.60	
b	As "a," imperf. pair	*300.00*		—	(3)		
1902	7.4¢ Baby Buggy 1880s, April 7, 1984	.18	.15	9.00	(3)	.75	
a	Untagged (Bureau precanceled)	.20	.20	3.25	(3)	.75	
1903	9.3¢ Mail Wagon 1880s, Dec. 15, 1981	.25	.15	10.50	(3)	.75	
a	Untagged (Bureau precanceled)	.22	.22	3.50	(3)	.75	
b	As "a," imperf. pair	*165.00*		—	(3)		
1904	10.9¢ Hansom Cab 1890s, Mar. 26, 1982	.24	.15	21.00	(3)	.60	
a	Untagged (Bureau precanceled)	.24	.24	20.00	(3)	.60	
b	As "a," imperf. pair	*225.00*		—	(3)		
1905	11¢ RR Caboose 1890s, Feb. 3, 1984	.24	.15	3.75	(3)	.65	
a	Untagged (Bureau precanceled)	.24	.24	3.50	(3)	.65	
1906	17¢ Electric Auto 1917, June 25, 1981	.32	.15	3.00	(3)	.75	
a	Untagged (Bureau precanceled)	.35	.35	5.00	(3)	.75	
b	Imperf. pair	*200.00*		—	(3)		
c	As "a," imperf. pair	*750.00*		—	(3)		
1907	18¢ Surrey 1890s, May 18, 1981	.34	.15	3.75	(3)	.75	
a	Imperf. pair	*170.00*					
1908	20¢ Fire Pumper 1860s, Dec. 10, 1981	.32	.15	2.75	(3)	.65	
a	Imperf. pair	*150.00*					
	Values for plate # coil strips of 3 stamps for #1897-#1908 are for the most common plate numbers. Other plate #s and strips of 5 stamps may have higher values.						
	Issue of 1983, Express Mail Booklet Issue, Perf. 10 Vertically, Aug. 12						
1909	$9.35 Eagle and Moon, single from booklet	24.00	12.50			45.00	
a	Booklet pane of 3	72.50				*100.00*	
	#1909 issued only in booklets. All stamps are imperf. at top and bottom or imperf. at top, bottom and one side.						
	Issues of 1981, Perf. 10½ x 11						
1910	18¢ American Red Cross, May 1	.32	.15	1.35	(4)	.75	165,175,000
	Perf. 11						
1911	18¢ Savings and Loans, May 8	.32	.15	1.40	(4)	.75	107,240,000

1897

1897A

1898

1898A

1899

1900

1901

1902

1903

1904

1905

1906

1907

1908

1909

1910

1911

1919a

1912 1913 1914 1915

1916 1917 1918 1919

1920

1924a

1921 1922

1923 1924

1925

1926

1927

	1981 continued, Perf. 11	Un	U	PB	#	FDC	Q
	Space Achievement Issue, May 21						
1912	18¢ Exploring the Moon-Moon Walk	.32	.15			.75	42,227,375
1913	18¢ Benefiting Mankind (upper left)-Columbia Space Shuttle	.32	.15			.75	42,227,375
1914	18¢ Benefiting Mankind (upper right)	.32	.15			.75	42,227,375
1915	18¢ Understanding the Sun-Skylab	.32	.15			.75	42,227,375
1916	18¢ Probing the Planets-Pioneer II	.32	.15			.75	42,227,375
1917	18¢ Benefiting Mankind (lower left)-Columbia Space Shuttle	.32	.15			.75	42,227,375
1918	18¢ Benefiting Mankind (lower right)	.32	.15			.75	42,227,375
1919	18¢ Comprehending the Universe-Telescope	.32	.15			.75	42,227,375
a	Block of 8, #1912-19	3.00	2.75	3.00	(8)	4.00	
b	As "a," imperf.	*8,000.00*					
1920	18¢ Professional Management, June 18	.32	.15	1.40	(4)	.75	99,420,000
	Preservation of Wildlife Habitats Issue, June 26						
1921	18¢ Save Wetland Habitats-Great Blue Heron	.35	.15			.75	44,732,500
1922	18¢ Save Grassland Habitats-Badger	.35	.15			.75	44,732,500
1923	18¢ Save Mountain Habitats-Grizzly Bear	.35	.15			.75	44,732,500
1924	18¢ Save Woodland Habitats-Ruffled Grouse	.35	.15			.75	44,732,500
a	Block of 4, #1921-24	1.40	1.00	1.50	(4)	2.50	
1925	18¢ International Year of the Disabled, June 29	.32	.15	1.40	(4)	.75	100,265,000
a	Vertical pair, imperf. horizontally	*2,250.00*					
1926	18¢ Edna St. Vincent Millay, July 10	.32	.15	1.40	(4)	.75	99,615,000
a	Black omitted	*650.00*					
1927	18¢ Alcoholism, Aug. 19	.42	.15	45.00	(20)	.75	97,535,000
a	Imperf. pair	*350.00*					

SURVIVAL OF WETLANDS IS KEY
Wetlands are a vital natural resource. In addition to offering refuge to many wildlife species, wetlands help control erosion and filter humankind's pollution. Many ecologists believe that the disappearance of wetlands will contribute to global warming. Yet more than 100 million acres of primitive United States wetlands have been drained and filled. Conservation groups are attempting to protect the rest. (#1921)

	1981 continued, Perf. 11	Un	U	PB	#	FDC	Q
	American Architecture Issue, Aug. 28						
1928	18¢ NYU Library, by Sanford White	.42	.15			.75	41,827,000
1929	18¢ Biltmore House, by Richard Morris Hunt	.42	.15			.75	41,827,000
1930	18¢ Palace of the Arts, by Bernard Maybeck	.42	.15			.75	41,827,000
1931	18¢ National Farmer's Bank, by Louis Sullivan	.42	.15			.75	41,827,000
a	Block of 4, #1928-31	1.75	1.00	1.85	(4)	1.00	
	American Sports Issue, Babe Zaharias and Bobby Jones, Sept. 22, Perf. 10½ x 11						
1932	18¢ Babe Zaharias Holding Trophy	.32	.15	1.75	(4)	.75	101,625,000
1933	18¢ Bobby Jones Teeing off	.32	.15	1.50	(4)	.75	99,170,000
	Perf. 11						
1934	18¢ Frederic Remington, Oct. 9	.32	.15	1.50	(4)	.75	101,155,000
a	Vertical pair, imperf. between	*300.00*					
b	Brown omitted	*600.00*					
1935	18¢ James Hoban, Oct. 13	.32	.15	1.60	(4)	.75	101,200,000
1936	20¢ James Hoban, Oct. 13	.35	.15	1.65	(4)	.75	167,360,000
	American Bicentennial Issue, Yorktown-Virginia Capes, Oct. 16						
1937	18¢ Battle of Yorktown 1781	.35	.15	1.60	(4)	.75	81,210,000
1938	18¢ Battle of the Virginia Capes 1781	.35	.15			.75	81,210,000
a	Attached pair, #1937-38	.70	.15	1.60	(4)	1.00	
b	As "a," black omitted	*550.00*					
	Christmas Issue, Oct. 28						
1939	20¢ Madonna and Child, by Botticelli	.38	.15	1.60	(4)	.75	597,720,000
a	Imperf. pair	*110.00*					
b	Vertical pair, imperf. horizontally	—					
1940	20¢ Felt Bear on Sleigh	.38	.15	1.60	(4)	.75	792,600,000
a	Imperf. pair	*250.00*					
b	Vertical pair, imperf. horizontally	—					
1941	20¢ John Hanson, Nov. 5	.38	.15	1.60	(4)	.75	167,130,000

REMINGTON CAPTURED OLD WEST

An "Easterner" born in Canton, New York, in 1861, Frederic Remington set out as a young man to explore the American West. There, he worked as a cowboy, rancher and saloon operator before returning East to create a visual record of what he had seen. Remington succeeded to an amazing degree, leaving 2,739 pictures and 25 sculptures by the time of his death in 1909. The U.S. Postal Service has honored Remington three times: in 1940, as part of the Famous American Series (#888); in 1961, the centennial of his birth (#1187), and in 1981, as "Frederic Remington, American Sculptor" (#1934).

1928 1929 1931a

1930 1931

1932

1933

1934

1935

1936

1937 1938 1938a

1939

1940

John Hanson
President Continental Congress
USA 20c

1941

1942 1943 1944 1945 1945a

1946

1949

1950

1951

1952

	1981 continued, Perf. 11	Un	U	PB/LP	#	FDC	Q
	Desert Plants Issue, Dec. 11						
1942	20¢ Barrel Cactus	.35	.15			.75	47,890,000
1943	20¢ Agave	.35	.15			.75	47,890,000
1944	20¢ Beavertail Cactus	.35	.15			.75	47,890,000
1945	20¢ Saguaro	.35	.15			.75	47,890,000
a	Block of 4, #1942-45	1.50	.85	1.60	(4)	2.50	
b	As "a," deep brown omitted	*7,500.00*					
c	#1945 imperf. pair	—					
	Perf. 11 x 10½						
1946	(20¢) C Stamp, Oct. 11	.38	.15	1.85	(4)	.75	
	Coil Stamp, Perf. 10 Vertically						
1947	(20¢) brown Eagle (1946), Oct. 11	.60	.15	1.50	(2)	.75	
a	Imperf. pair	*1,500.00*		—	(2)		
	Perf. 11 x 10½						
1948	(20¢) brown Eagle (1946), single from booklet	.38	.15			.75	
a	Booklet pane of 10, Oct. 11	4.50	—			*3.50*	
	Issues of 1982, Bighorn Sheep Booklet Issue, Jan. 8, Perf. 11						
1949	20¢ Bighorn Sheep, single from booklet	.50	.15			.75	
a	Booklet pane of 10	5.00				*6.00*	
b	As "a," imperf. between	*125.00*					
	#1949 issued only in booklets. All stamps are imperf. at one side or imperf. at one side and bottom.						
1950	20¢ Franklin D. Roosevelt, Jan. 30	.38	.15	1.60	(4)	.75	163,939,200
	Perf. 11 x 10½						
1951	20¢ Love, Feb. 1	.38	.15	1.60	(4)	.75	446,745,000
a	Perf. 11	.48	.15	2.00	(4)		
b	Imperf. pair	*275.00*					
c	Blue omitted	*200.00*					
	Perf. 11						
1952	20¢ George Washington, Feb. 22	.38	.15	1.60	(4)	.75	180,700,000

BARREL CACTUS IS DESERT MARVEL
A common sight in the American Southwest and Mexico, the barrel cactus (#1942) is a marvel of adaptation. Its shallow, widespreading roots efficiently seek out moisture, which the cactus stores in its barrel-shaped stalk. The outside of the stalk is fluted, enabling it to expand or contract according to the amount of water it contains. Folklore credits the barrel cactus for saving many travelers from dying of thirst. Although there may be some truth to such stories, extracting liquid from the tough-skinned, spiny plant is hard work.

	1982 continued	Un	U	FDC	Q
	State Birds & Flowers Issue, Apr. 14, Perf 10½ x 11				
1953	20¢ Alabama	.40	.25	1.00	13,339,900
1954	20¢ Alaska	.40	.25	1.00	13,339,900
1955	20¢ Arizona	.40	.25	1.00	13,339,900
1956	20¢ Arkansas	.40	.25	1.00	13,339,900
1957	20¢ California	.40	.25	1.00	13,339,900
1958	20¢ Colorado	.40	.25	1.00	13,339,900
1959	20¢ Connecticut	.40	.25	1.00	13,339,900
1960	20¢ Delaware	.40	.25	1.00	13,339,900
1961	20¢ Florida	.40	.25	1.00	13,339,900
1962	20¢ Georgia	.40	.25	1.00	13,339,900
1963	20¢ Hawaii	.40	.25	1.00	13,339,900
1964	20¢ Idaho	.40	.25	1.00	13,339,900
1965	20¢ Illinois	.40	.25	1.00	13,339,900
1966	20¢ Indiana	.40	.25	1.00	13,339,900
1967	20¢ Iowa	.40	.25	1.00	13,339,900
1968	20¢ Kansas	.40	.25	1.00	13,339,900
1969	20¢ Kentucky	.40	.25	1.00	13,339,900
1970	20¢ Louisiana	.40	.25	1.00	13,339,900
1971	20¢ Maine	.40	.25	1.00	13,339,900
1972	20¢ Maryland	.40	.25	1.00	13,339,900
1973	20¢ Massachusetts	.40	.25	1.00	13,339,900
1974	20¢ Michigan	.40	.25	1.00	13,339,900
1975	20¢ Minnesota	.40	.25	1.00	13,339,900
1976	20¢ Mississippi	.40	.25	1.00	13,339,900
1977	20¢ Missouri	.40	.25	1.00	13,339,900

Bluebirds Compete for Nesting Space

Found east of the Rocky Mountains throughout the United States and southern Canada, the eastern bluebird has experienced a sharp decline in its population since the early 1900s. Many biologists believe the bird, which must compete with starlings and sparrows for nesting holes, is suffering from loss of habitat. The eastern bluebird is the state bird of Missouri (#1977) and New York (#1984), and appears on a 1991 definitive stamp (#2482).

1953

Alaska
USA 20c
Willow Ptarmigan & Forget-Me-Not

1954

1955

1956

1957

1958

1959

Delaware
USA 20c
Blue Hen Chicken & Peach Blossom

1960

1961

1962

1963

1964

1965

1966

1967

Kansas
USA 20c
Western Meadowlark & Sunflower

1968

1969

1970

1971

1972

1973

1974

1975

1976

1977

1982

1978 1979 1980 1981 1982

1983 1984 1985 1986 1987

1988 1989 1990 1991 1992

1993 1994 1995 1996 1997

1998 1999 2000 2001 2002

	1982 continued, Perf. 10½ x 11	Un	U	PB	#	FDC	Q
	State Birds & Flowers Issue continued, Apr. 14						
1978	20¢ Montana	.40	.25			1.00	13,339,900
1979	20¢ Nebraska	.40	.25			1.00	13,339,900
1980	20¢ Nevada	.40	.25			1.00	13,339,900
1981	20¢ New Hampshire	.40	.25			1.00	13,339,900
1982	20¢ New Jersey	.40	.25			1.00	13,339,900
1983	20¢ New Mexico	.40	.25			1.00	13,339,900
1984	20¢ New York	.40	.25			1.00	13,339,900
1985	20¢ North Carolina	.40	.25			1.00	13,339,900
1986	20¢ North Dakota	.40	.25			1.00	13,339,900
1987	20¢ Ohio	.40	.25			1.00	13,339,900
1988	20¢ Oklahoma	.40	.25			1.00	13,339,900
1989	20¢ Oregon	.40	.25			1.00	13,339,900
1990	20¢ Pennsylvania	.40	.25			1.00	13,339,900
1991	20¢ Rhode Island	.40	.25			1.00	13,339,900
1992	20¢ South Carolina	.40	.25			1.00	13,339,900
1993	20¢ South Dakota	.40	.25			1.00	13,339,900
1994	20¢ Tennessee	.40	.25			1.00	13,339,900
1995	20¢ Texas	.40	.25			1.00	13,339,900
1996	20¢ Utah	.40	.25			1.00	13,339,900
1997	20¢ Vermont	.40	.25			1.00	13,339,900
1998	20¢ Virginia	.40	.25			1.00	13,339,900
1999	20¢ Washington	.40	.25			1.00	13,339,900
2000	20¢ West Virginia	.40	.25			1.00	13,339,900
2001	20¢ Wisconsin	.40	.25			1.00	13,339,900
2002	20¢ Wyoming	.40	.25			1.00	13,339,900
a	Any single, perf. 11	.45	.30				
b	Pane of 50	20.00		20.00	(50)	30.00	
c	Pane of 50, perf. 11	22.50	—	22.50	(50)		
d	Pane of 50, imperf.	—					

Sweet Violets

Ranging in color from blue and purple to yellow and white, the violet is found throughout much of the world. Still grown in Europe as a source of perfume essence, this charming plant also has been used to make wines, syrups and cosmetic washes. Sometimes used in salads, the flower has a peppery flavor. Candied violets may be eaten as confections or used to decorate cakes. The violet is the state flower of New Jersey (#1982), Rhode Island (#1991) and Wisconsin (#2001), as well as Illinois (#1965).

	1982 continued, Perf. 11	Un	U	PB/PNC	#	FDC	Q
2003	20¢ USA/The Netherlands, Apr. 20	.38	.15	11.50	(20)	.75	109,245,000
a	Imperf. pair	*475.00*					
2004	20¢ Library of Congress, Apr. 21	.38	.15	1.60	(4)	.75	112,535,000
	Coil Stamp, Perf. 10 Vertically						
2005	20¢ Consumer Education, Apr. 27	.75	.15	35.00	(3)	.75	
a	Imperf. pair	*125.00*		—	(3)		
	Value for plate no. coil strip of 3 stamps is for most common plate nos. Other plate nos. and strips of 5 stamps may have higher values.						
	Knoxville World's Fair Issue, Apr. 29, Perf. 11						
2006	20¢ Solar Energy	.38	.15			.75	31,160,000
2007	20¢ Synthetic Fuels	.38	.15			.75	31,160,000
2008	20¢ Breeder Reactor	.38	.15			.75	31,160,000
2009	20¢ Fossil Fuels	.38	.15			.75	31,160,000
a	Block of 4, #2006-09	1.55	.85	1.65	(4)	2.50	
2010	20¢ Horatio Alger, Apr. 30	.38	.15	1.60	(4)	.75	107,605,000
2011	20¢ Aging Together, May 21	.38	.15	1.60	(4)	.75	173,160,000
	Performing Arts Issue, The Barrymores, June 8						
2012	20¢ Portraits of John, Ethel and Lionel Barrymore	.38	.15	1.60	(4)	.75	107,285,000
2013	20¢ Dr. Mary Walker, June 10	.38	.15	1.60	(4)	.75	109,040,000
2014	20¢ International Peace Garden, June 30	.38	.15	1.60	(4)	.75	183,270,000
a	Black, green and brown omitted	*300.00*					
2015	20¢ America's Libraries, July 13	.38	.15	1.60	(4)	.75	169,495,000
a	Vertical pair, imperf. horizontally	*300.00*					
	Black Heritage Issue, Jackie Robinson, Aug. 2, Perf. 10 1/2 x 11						
2016	20¢ Jackie Robinson Portrait and Robinson Stealing Home Plate	.75	.15	2.00	(4)	.75	164,235,000
	Perf. 11						
2017	20¢ Touro Synagogue, Aug. 22	.38	.15	11.50	(20)	.85	110,130,000
a	Imperf. pair	*800.00*					
2018	20¢ Wolf Trap Farm Park, Sept. 1	.38	.15	1.60	(4)	.75	110,995,000
	American Architecture Issue, Sept. 30						
2019	20¢ Fallingwater, by Frank Lloyd Wright	.38	.15			.75	41,335,000
2020	20¢ Illinois Institute of Technology, by Mies van der Rohe	.38	.15			.75	41,335,000
2021	20¢ Gropius House, by Walter Gropius	.38	.15			.75	41,335,000
2022	20¢ Dulles Airport, by Eeno Saarinen	.38	.15			.75	41,335,000
a	Block of 4, #2019-22	1.90	1.00	1.65	(4)	1.00	

The stamp listings contain a number of "a," "b," "c," etc. additions which include recognized varieties and errors. These listings are as complete as space permits.

2003

2004

2005

2006 2007 2009a
2008 2009

2010

2012

2011

2013

2014

2015

2016

2017

2018

2019 2020 2022a
2021 2022

2023

2024

2025

2026

2027 2028 2030a

2029 2030

2031

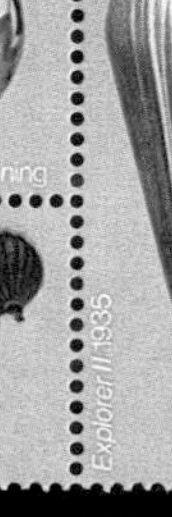

2032 2033 2035 2035a

2034

2036

2037

	1982 continued, Perf. 11	Un	U	PB	#	FDC	Q
2023	20¢ Francis of Assisi, Oct. 7	.38	.15	1.60	(4)	.75	174,180,000
2024	20¢ Ponce de Leon, Oct. 12	.38	.15	11.50	(20)	.75	110,261,000
a	Imperf. pair	*750.00*					
	Christmas Issue						
2025	13¢ Puppy and Kitten, Nov. 3	.24	.15	1.05	(4)	.75	234,010,000
a	Imperf. pair	*500.00*					
2026	20¢ Madonna and Child, by Tiepolo, Oct. 28	.38	.15	11.00	(20)	.75	703,295,000
a	Imperf. pair	*175.00*					
b	Horizontal pair, imperf. vertically	—					
c	Vertical pair, imperf. horizontally	—					
	Seasons Greetings Issue, Oct. 28						
2027	20¢ Children Sledding	.45	.15			.75	197,220,000
2028	20¢ Children Building a Snowman	.45	.15			.75	197,220,000
2029	20¢ Children Skating	.45	.15			.75	197,220,000
2030	20¢ Children Trimming a Tree	.45	.15			.75	197,220,000
a	Block of 4, #2027-30	1.85	1.00	2.00	(4)	2.50	
b	As "a," imperf.	*2,750.00*					
c	As "a," imperf. horizontally	—					
	Issues of 1983						
2031	20¢ Science & Industry, Jan. 19	.38	.15	1.60	(4)	.75	118,555,000
a	Black omitted	*1,400.00*					
	Balloons Issue, March 31						
2032	20¢ Intrepid, 1861	.38	.15			.75	56,557,000
2033	20¢ Hot Air Ballooning (wording lower right)	.38	.15			.75	56,557,000
2034	20¢ Hot Air Ballooning (wording upper left)	.38	.15			.75	56,557,000
2035	20¢ Explorer II, 1935	.38	.15			.75	56,557,000
a	Block of 4, #2032-35	1.55	1.00	1.65	(4)	2.50	
b	As "a," imperf.	*2,500.00*					
2036	20¢ U.S./Sweden Treaty, Mar. 24	.38	.15	1.60	(4)	.75	118,225,000
2037	20¢ Civilian Conservation Corps, Apr. 5	.38	.15	1.60	(4)	.75	114,290,000
a	Imperf. pair	*2,250.00*					

St. Francis Devoted to the Poor
The son of a prosperous merchant, Frances of Assisi (#2023) renounced his inheritance in 1205 to embrace a life of poverty. Four years later, in 1209, he founded the Franciscans, a religious order of the Catholic Church. Born in Assisi, Italy, Francis was declared a saint by the Catholic Church in 1228. He is remembered for his devotion to the poor and his love of peace and all living creatures.

	1983 continued, Perf. 11	Un	U	PB	#	FDC	Q
2038	20¢ Joseph Priestley, Apr. 13	.38	.15	1.60	(4)	.75	165,000,000
2039	20¢ Volunteerism, Apr. 20	.38	.15	11.00	(20)	.75	120,430,000
a	Imperf. pair	*1,000.00*					
2040	20¢ Concord-German Immigration, Apr. 29	.38	.15	1.60	(4)	.75	117,025,000
2041	20¢ Brooklyn Bridge, May 17	.38	.15	1.60	(4)	.75	181,700,000
2042	20¢ Tennessee Valley Authority, May 18	.38	.15	11.50	(20)	.75	114,250,000
2043	20¢ Physical Fitness, May 14	.38	.15	11.00	(20)	.75	111,775,000
	Black Heritage Issue, Scott Joplin, June 9						
2044	20¢ Scott Joplin Portrait and Joplin Playing the Piano	.38	.15	1.60	(4)	.75	115,200,000
a	Imperf. pair	*500.00*					
2045	20¢ Medal of Honor, June 7	.38	.15	1.65	(4)	.75	108,820,000
a	Red omitted	*325.00*					
	American Sports Issue, Babe Ruth, July 6, Perf. 10½ x 11						
2046	20¢ Babe Ruth Hitting a Home Run	.60	.15	2.00	(4)	.75	184,950,000
	Literary Arts Issue, Nathaniel Hawthorne, July 8, Perf. 11						
2047	20¢ Nathaniel Hawthorne, by Cephus Giovanni Thompson	.38	.15	1.60	(4)	.75	110,925,000
	Olympic Summer Games Issue, July 28 (see also #2082-85, C101-112)						
2048	13¢ Discus Thrower	.28	.15			.75	98,856,250
2049	13¢ High Jumper	.28	.15			.75	98,856,250
2050	13¢ Archer	.28	.15			.75	98,856,250
2051	13¢ Boxers	.28	.15			.75	98,856,250
a	Block of 4, #2048-51	1.20	.80	1.30	(4)	2.50	
	American Bicentennial Issue, Treaty of Paris, Sept. 2						
2052	20¢ Signing of Treaty of Paris (John Adams, Benjamin Franklin and John Jay observing David Hartley), by Benjamin West	.38	.15	1.60	(4)	.75	104,340,000
2053	20¢ Civil Service, Sept. 9	.38	.15	11.00	(20)	.75	114,725,000
2054	20¢ Metropolitan Opera, Sept. 14	.38	.15	1.65	(4)	.75	112,525,000

TREATY OF PARIS DEFINED NEW NATION

On September 3, 1783, the United States and Great Britain signed a peace treaty in Paris that formally ended the Revolutionary War. Negotiating for the United States were three of colonial America's finest statesmen: Benjamin Franklin, John Adams and John Jay. The Treaty of Paris (#2052) established the borders of the United States: north to Canada, south almost to Florida, east to the Atlantic Ocean and west to the Mississippi.

2038

2039

2040

2041

2042

2043

2044

2045

2046

2047

2048 2049 2051a

2050 2051

2052

2053

2054

1983

2055 2056 2058a
2057 2058

2059 2060 2062a
2061 2062

2063

2064

2065

	1983 continued, Perf. 11	Un	U	PB	#	FDC	Q
	American Inventors Issue, Sept. 21						
2055	20¢ Charles Steinmetz and Curve on Graph	.38	.15			.75	48,263,750
2056	20¢ Edwin Armstrong and Frequency Modulator	.38	.15			.75	48,263,750
2057	20¢ Nikola Tesla and Induction Motor	.38	.15			.75	48,263,750
2058	20¢ Philo T. Farnsworth and First Television Camera	.38	.15			.75	48,263,750
a	Block of 4, #2055-58	1.55	1.00	1.65	(4)	2.50	
b	As "a," black omitted	*400.00*					
	Streetcars Issue, Oct. 8						
2059	20¢ First American Streetcar	.38	.15			.75	51,931,250
2060	20¢ Early Electric Streetcar	.38	.15			.75	51,931,250
2061	20¢ "Bobtail" Horsecar	.38	.15			.75	51,931,250
2062	20¢ St. Charles Streetcar	.38	.15			.75	51,931,250
a	Block of 4, #2059-62	1.55	1.00	1.65	(4)	2.50	
b	As "a," black omitted	*550.00*					
	Christmas Issue, Oct. 28						
2063	20¢ Niccolini-Cowper Madonna, by Raphael	.38	.15	1.65	(4)	.75	715,975,000
2064	20¢ Santa Claus	.38	.15	11.50	(20)	.75	848,525,000
a	Imperf. pair	*165.00*					
2065	20¢ Martin Luther, Nov. 11	.38	.15	1.60	(4)	.75	165,000,000

Raphael's Genius Graced Italian Renaissance

One of the greatest of Italian Renaissance painters, Raphael was born in Urbino, Italy, in 1483. Among his most popular works are Raphael's paintings of the Madonna. His Niccolini-Cowper Madonna (#2063) and his Small Cowper Madonna (#1507) appear on U.S. postal issues. A third stamp (#1530) shows Michaelangelo as portrayed in the Raphael masterpiece, "School of Athens."

	Issues of 1984, Perf. 11	Un	U	PB	#	FDC	Q
2066	20¢ Alaska Statehood, Jan. 3	.38	.15	1.65	(4)	.75	120,000,000
	Olympic Winter Games Issue, Jan. 6, Perf. 10½ x 11						
2067	20¢ Ice Dancers	.42	.15			.75	79,918,750
2068	20¢ Alpine Skiers	.42	.15			.75	79,918,750
2069	20¢ Nordic Skiers	.42	.15			.75	79,918,750
2070	20¢ Hockey Player	.42	.15			.75	79,918,750
a	Block of 4, #2067-70	1.70	1.00	1.95	(4)	2.50	
	Perf. 11						
2071	20¢ Federal Deposit Insurance Corporation, Jan. 12	.38	.15	1.60	(4)	.75	103,975,000
	Perf. 11 x 10½						
2072	20¢ Love, Jan. 31	.38	.15	11.50	(20)	.75	554,675,000
a	Horizontal pair, imperf. vertically	*200.00*					
	Black Heritage Issue, Carter G. Woodson, Feb. 1, Perf. 11						
2073	20¢ Carter G. Woodson Holding History Book	.42	.15	1.80	(4)	.75	120,000,000
a	Horizontal pair, imperf. vertically	*1,200.00*					
2074	20¢ Soil and Water Conservation, Feb. 6	.38	.15	1.75	(4)	.75	106,975,000
2075	20¢ Credit Union Act, Feb. 10	.38	.15	1.60	(4)	.75	107,325,000
	Orchids Issue, Mar. 5						
2076	20¢ Wild Pink	.38	.15			.75	76,728,000
2077	20¢ Yellow Lady's-Slipper	.38	.15			.75	76,728,000
2078	20¢ Spreading Pogonia	.38	.15			.75	76,728,000
2079	20¢ Pacific Calypso	.38	.15			.75	76,728,000
a	Block of 4, #2076-79	1.55	1.00	1.65	(4)	2.50	
2080	20¢ Hawaii Statehood, Mar. 12	.38	.15	1.60	(4)	.75	120,000,000
2081	20¢ National Archives, Apr. 16	.38	.15	1.60	(4)	.75	108,000,000

ARCHIVES HOLD HISTORIC TREASURES
Visitors to the National Archives' Exhibition Hall In Washington, D.C., may view historic American treasures, including the original Declaration of Independence, Constitution and Bill of Rights. Each is encased in a sealed bronze-and-glass case that can be lowered instantly to a fireproof and shockproof safe. The National Archives Building opened in 1935 and houses a vast collection of maps, letters, pictures and documents. John Russell Pope designed the building, which features bronze entrance doors weighing 10 tons and a system of temperature and humidity control that protects the precious contents of the Archives. (#2081)

2066

2070a

2067 2068
2069 2070

2071

LOVE
LOVE
LOVE
LOVE
LOVE
USA 20c

2072

2073

2074

2075

Yellow lady's-slipper Cypripedium calceolus

2079a

2076 2077
2078 2079

2080

2081

2082 2083 2085a
2084 2085

2086

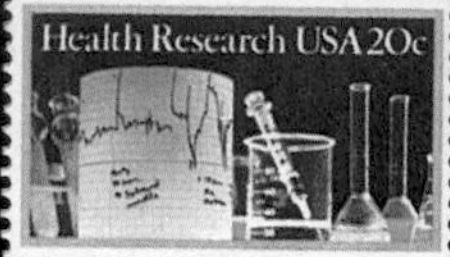

2087

2088

2089

2090

2091

2092

2093

2094

2095

	1984 continued, Perf. 11	Un	U	PB	#	FDC	Q
	Olympic Summer Games Issue, May 4 (see also #2048-52, C101-112)						
2082	20¢ Diver	.40	.15			.75	78,337,500
2083	20¢ Long Jumper	.40	.15			.75	78,337,500
2084	20¢ Wrestlers	.40	.15			.75	78,337,500
2085	20¢ Kayaker	.40	.15			.75	78,337,500
a	Block of 4, #2082-85	2.50	1.00	2.25	(4)	2.50	
2086	20¢ Louisiana World Exposition, May 11	.38	.15	1.60	(4)	.75	130,320,000
2087	20¢ Health Research, May 17	.38	.15	1.60	(4)	.75	120,000,000
	Performing Arts Issue, May 23						
2088	20¢ Douglas Fairbanks Portrait and Fairbanks in Swashbuckling Pirate Role	.38	.15	11.50	(20)	.75	117,050,000
	American Sports Issue, Jim Thorpe, May 24						
2089	20¢ Jim Thorpe on Football Field	.38	.15	1.75	(4)	.75	115,725,000
	Performing Arts Issue, John McCormack, June 6						
2090	20¢ John McCormack Portrait and McCormack in Tenor Role	.38	.15	1.75	(4)	.75	116,600,000
2091	20¢ St. Lawrence Seaway, June 26	.38	.15	1.60	(4)	.75	120,000,000
2092	20¢ Migratory Bird Hunting & Preservation Act, July 2	.38	.15	1.60	(4)	.75	123,575,000
a	Horizontal pair, imperf. vertically	*575.00*					
2093	20¢ Roanoke Voyages, July 13	.38	.15	1.60	(4)	.75	120,000,000
	Pair with full horizontal gutter between	—					
	Literary Arts Issue, Herman Melville, Aug. 1						
2094	20¢ Herman Melville, by Joseph Eaton	.38	.15	1.60	(4)	.75	117,125,000
2095	20¢ Horace Moses, Aug. 6	.38	.15	11.00	(20)	.75	117,225,000

After 70 Years, Committee Returned Thorpe's Medals

Generally considered one of the world's most outstanding all-around athletes, Jim Thorpe won the pentathlon and decathlon in the 1912 Olympic Games. He was the first athlete ever to win both events. However, when Olympic officials learned that Thorpe had been paid for playing baseball prior to competing in the Games, he was declared ineligible for Olympic competition. As a result, his medals were taken away. Thorpe nevertheless pursued an outstanding career, first in major league baseball and then in football (#2089). In 1982, nearly 30 years after his death, the Olympic Committee restored Jim Thorpe's medals.

	1984 continued, Perf. 11	Un	U	PB	#	FDC	Q
2096	20¢ Smokey the Bear, Aug. 13	.38	.15	1.75	(4)	.75	95,525,000
a	Horizontal pair, imperf. between	*300.00*					
b	Vertical pair, imperf. between	*225.00*	.15				
c	Block of 4, imperf. between vertically and horizontally	*3,500.00*					
	American Sports Issue, Roberto Clemente, Aug. 17						
2097	20¢ Roberto Clemente Wearing Pittsburgh Pirates Cap, Puerto Rican Flag in Background	.45	.15	2.00	(4)	2.00	119,125,000
a	Horizontal pair, imperf. vertically	*1,600.00*					
	American Dogs Issue, Sept. 7						
2098	20¢ Beagle and Boston Terrier	.38	.15			.75	54,065,000
2099	20¢ Chesapeake Bay Retriever and Cocker Spaniel	.38	.15			.75	54,065,000
2100	20¢ Alaskan Malamute and Collie	.38	.15			.75	54,065,000
2101	20¢ Black and Tan Coonhound and American Foxhound	.38	.15			.75	54,065,000
a	Block of 4, #2098-2101	1.55	1.00	1.65	(4)	2.50	
2102	20¢ Crime Prevention, Sept. 26	.38	.15	1.70	(4)	.75	120,000,000
2103	20¢ Hispanic Americans, Oct. 31	.38	.15	1.60	(4)	.75	108,140,000
a	Vertical pair, imperf. horizontally	*1,500.00*					
2104	20¢ Family Unity, Oct. 1	.38	.15	12.00	(20)	.75	117,625,000
a	Horizontal pair, imperf. vertically	*600.00*					
2105	20¢ Eleanor Roosevelt, Oct. 11	.38	.15	1.60	(4)	.75	112,896,000
2106	20¢ A Nation of Readers, Oct. 16	.38	.15	1.60	(4)	.75	116,500,000
	Christmas Issue, Oct. 30						
2107	20¢ Madonna and Child, by Fra Filippo Lippi	.40	.15	1.70	(4)	.75	751,300,000
2108	20¢ Santa Claus	.40	.15	1.70	(4)	.75	786,225,000
a	Horizontal pair, imperf. vertically	*1,250.00*					
	Perf. 10½						
2109	20¢ Vietnam Veterans' Memorial, Nov. 10	.38	.15	1.60	(4)	.75	105,300,000

ROYALTY'S PET AND AMERICA'S DARLING

Collie dogs were first bred in Scotland, probably about 400 years ago. Intelligent and keen of eye, they were set to work guarding sheep. With their nearly weatherproof coats of long, thick hair, collies were superbly suited to the task. Collies traveled with British colonists to America in the 1700s. There, some two centuries later, a Hollywood film based on Eric Knight's novel Lassie Come-Home *endeared a collie named Lassie to children everywhere. (#2100)*

2096

2097

2098 2099 2101a
2100 2101

2102

2103

2104

2105

2106

2107

2108

2109

2110

2111

2114

2115b

2116

2117

2118

2119

2120

2121

2121a

2122

	Issues of 1985	Un	U	PB/PNC	#	FDC	Q
	Performing Arts Issue, Jerome Kern, Jan. 23, Perf. 11						
2110	22¢ Jerome Kern Portrait and Kern Studying Sheet Music	.40	.15	1.75	(4)	.80	124,500,000
2111	(22¢) D Stamp, Feb. 1	.60	.15	15.00	(20)	.80	
a	Imperf. pair	*75.00*					
b	Vertical pair, imperf. horizontally	—					
	Coil Stamp, Perf. 10 Vertically						
2112	(22¢) green Eagle (2111), Feb. 1	.60	.15	5.25	(3)	.80	
a	Imperf. pair	60.00					
	Perf. 11						
2113	(22¢) green Eagle (2111), single from booklet	.60	.15			.80	
a	Booklet pane of 10, Feb. 1	6.50				*7.50*	
	Issue of 1985-87, Flag over Capitol Issue						
2114	22¢ Flag over Capitol, Mar. 29, 1985	.40	.15	1.80	(4)	.80	
	Pair with full horizontal gutter between	—					
	Coil Stamp, Perf. 10 Vertically						
2115	22¢ Flag over Capitol (2114), Mar. 29, 1985	.40	.15	3.25	(3)	.80	
a	Imperf. pair	17.50					
b	22¢ Flag over Capitol, May 23, 1987	.48	.15	3.10	(3)	.80	
c	Black field of stars	—	—				
	#2115b issued for test on pre-phosphored paper. Paper is whiter and colors are brighter than on #2115.						
	Perf. 10 Horizontally						
2116	22¢ Flag over Capitol, single from booklet	.48	.15			.80	
a	Booklet pane of 5, Mar. 29, 1985	2.50	—			3.50	
	#2116 issued only in booklets. All stamps are imperf. at both sides or imperf. at both sides and bottom.						
	1985 continued, Seashells Booklet Issue, Apr. 4, Perf. 10						
2117	22¢ Frilled Dogwinkle	.40	.15			.80	
2118	22¢ Reticulated Helmet	.40	.15			.80	
2119	22¢ New England Neptune	.40	.15			.80	
2120	22¢ Calico Scallop	.40	.15			.80	
2121	22¢ Lightning Whelk	.40	.15			.80	
a	Booklet pane of 10, #2117-21	4.25				*7.50*	
b	As "a," violet omitted on both #2120s	*1,100.00*					
c	As "a," imperf. between vertically	*800.00*					
d	As "a," imperf.		—				
e	Strip of 5, #2117-21	2.00	—				
	#2117-21 issued only in booklets. All stamps are imperf. at one side or imperf. at one side and bottom.						
	Express Mail Booklet Issue, Apr. 29, Perf. 10 Vertically						
2122	$10.75 Eagle and Moon, single from booklet	20.00	6.75			40.00	
a	Booklet pane of 3	62.50	—			*85.00*	
	#2122 issued only in booklets. All stamps are imperf. at top and bottom or imperf. at top, bottom and one side.						

	Issues of 1985-89, Coil Stamps, Transportation Issue, Perf. 10 Vertically (see also #1897-1908, 2225-26, 2228, 2231, 2252-66)	Un	U	PB/PNC	#	FDC	Q
2123	3.4¢ School Bus 1920s, June 8, 1985	.15	.15	1.05	(3)	1.00	
a	Untagged (Bureau precanceled)	.15	.15	1.50	(3)	1.00	
2124	4.9¢ Buckboard 1880s, June 21, 1985	.15	.15	1.05	(3)	1.00	
a	Untagged (Bureau precanceled)	.15	.15	1.75	(3)		
2125	5.5¢ Star Route Truck 1910s, Nov. 1, 1986	.15	.15	1.30	(3)	1.00	
a	Untagged (Bureau precanceled)	.15	.15	1.40	(3)	1.00	
2126	6¢ Tricycle 1880s, May 6, 1985	.15	.15	1.15	(3)	1.00	
a	Untagged (Bureau precanceled)	.15	.15	1.90	(3)		
b	As "a," imperf. pair		*225.00*				
2127	7.1¢ Tractor 1920s, Feb. 6, 1987	.15	.15	1.85	(3)	1.00	
a	Untagged (Bureau precanceled "Nonprofit org.")	.15	.15	2.00	(3)	1.00	
	Untagged (Bureau precanceled "Nonprofit 5-Digit ZIP + 4"), May 26, 1989	.15	.15	2.50	(3)	1.00	
2128	8.3¢ Ambulance 1860s, June 21, 1985	.18	.15	1.50	(3)	1.00	
a	Untagged (Bureau precanceled)	.18	.15	1.50	(3)		
2129	8.5¢ Tow Truck 1920s, Jan. 24, 1987	.16	.15	2.50	(3)	1.00	
a	Untagged (Bureau precanceled)	.16	.15	2.75	(3)		
2130	10.1¢ Oil Wagon 1890s, Apr. 18, 1985	.22	.15	2.25	(3)	1.00	
a	Untagged (Bureau precanceled, black)	.22	.22	2.50	(3)	1.00	
	Untagged (Bureau precanceled, red)	.22	.22	2.35	(3)	1.00	
b	As "a," black precancel, imperf. pair	15.00					
b	As "a," red precancel, imperf. pair	15.00					
2131	11¢ Stutz Bearcat 1933, June 11, 1985	.22	.15	1.60	(3)	1.00	
2132	12¢ Stanley Steamer 1909, Apr. 2, 1985	.24	.15	1.75	(3)	1.00	
a	Untagged (Bureau precanceled)	.24	.24	2.50	(3)	1.00	
2133	12.5¢ Pushcart 1880s, Apr. 18, 1985	.25	.15	2.50	(3)	1.00	
a	Untagged (Bureau precanceled)	.25	.25	3.00	(3)	1.00	
b	As "a," imperf. pair	*75.00*					
2134	14¢ Iceboat 1880s, Mar. 23, 1985	.28	.15	1.50	(3)	1.10	
a	Imperf. pair	150.00					
2135	17¢ Dog Sled 1920s, Aug. 20, 1986	.30	.15	2.75	(3)	1.00	
a	Imperf. pair	*800.00*					
2136	25¢ Bread Wagon 1880s, Nov. 22, 1986	.45	.15	4.00	(3)	.85	
a	Imperf. pair	15.00					
b	Pair, imperf. between	—					
	Issues of 1985, Black Heritage Issue, Mary McLeod Bethune, Mar. 5, Perf. 11						
2137	22¢ Mary McLeod Bethune Portrait	.40	.15	1.70	(4)	.80	120,000,000
	American Folk Art Issue, Duck Decoys, Mar. 22						
2138	22¢ Broadbill Decoy	.42	.15			.80	75,000,000
2139	22¢ Mallard Decoy	.42	.15			.80	75,000,000
2140	22¢ Canvasback Decoy	.42	.15			.80	75,000,000
2141	22¢ Redhead Decoy	.42	.15			.80	75,000,000
a	Block of 4, #2138-41	2.00	1.00	2.20	(4)	2.75	
2142	22¢ Winter Special Olympics, Mar. 25	.40	.15	1.70	(4)	.80	120,580,000
a	Vertical pair, imperf. horizontally	*800.00*					
2143	22¢ Love, Apr. 17	.40	.15	1.70	(4)	.80	729,700,000
a	Imperf. pair	*2,250.00*					
2144	22¢ Rural Electrification Administration, May 11	.40	.15	14.00	(20)	.80	124,750,000

2123

2124

2125

2126

2127

2128

2129

2130

2131

2132

2133

2134

2135

2136

2137

2138 2139 2141a

2140 2141

2142

2143

2144

2145

2146

2147

2149

2150

2152

2153

2154

2155 2156 2158a
2157 2158

2159

2160 2161 2163a
2162 2163

	1985 continued, Perf. 11	Un	U	PB/PNC	#	FDC	Q
2145	22¢ AMERIPEX '86, May 25	.40	.15	1.70	(4)	.80	203,496,000
a	Red, black and blue omitted	*275.00*					
b	Red and black omitted	—					
2146	22¢ Abigail Adams, June 14	.40	.15	1.80	(4)	.80	126,325,000
a	Imperf. pair	*350.00*					
2147	22¢ Frederic A. Bartholdi, July 18	.40	.15	1.80	(4)	.80	130,000,000
2148	not assigned						
	Coil Stamps, Perf. 10 Vertically						
2149	18¢ George Washington, Washington Monument, Nov. 6	.32	.15	2.75	(3)	1.00	
a	Bureau precanceled	.35	.35	3.50	(3)	1.00	
b	Imperf. pair	*1,250.00*					
c	As "a," imperf. pair	*600.00*					
2150	21.1¢ Sealed Envelopes, Oct. 22	.40	.15	3.25	(3)	1.00	
a	Bureau precanceled	.38	.38	3.75	(3)	1.00	
2151	not assigned						
	Perf. 11						
2152	22¢ Korean War Veterans, July 26	.40	.15	1.70	(4)	.80	119,975,000
2153	22¢ Social Security Act, Aug. 14	.40	.15	1.70	(4)	.80	120,000,000
2154	22¢ World War I Veterans, Aug. 26	.40	.15	1.70	(4)	.80	119,975,000
	American Horses Issue, Sept. 25						
2155	22¢ Quarter Horse	.40	.15			.80	36,985,000
2156	22¢ Morgan	.40	.15			.80	36,985,000
2157	22¢ Saddlebred	.40	.15			.80	36,985,000
2158	22¢ Appaloosa	.40	.15			.80	36,985,000
a	Block of 4, #2155-58	2.00	1.00	2.20	(4)	2.50	
2159	22¢ Public Education, Oct. 1	.40	.15	1.70	(4)	.80	120,000,000
	International Youth Year Issue, Oct. 7						
2160	22¢ YMCA Youth Camping	.42	.15			.80	32,500,000
2161	22¢ Boy Scouts	.42	.15			.80	32,500,000
2162	22¢ Big Brothers/Big Sisters	.42	.15			.80	32,500,000
2163	22¢ Camp Fire	.42	.15			.80	32,500,000
a	Block of 4, #2160-63	2.00	1.00	2.20	(4)	1.25	

BIG BROTHERS
BIG SISTERS OF AMERICA®
Because you have so much to share℠

When You Need a Friend . . .
Big Brothers/Big Sisters of America has been making a difference in the lives of young people for more than 80 years. This nonprofit organization carefully matches adult volunteers with school-age children in need of grown-up friends. Each Big Brother or Big Sister volunteer agrees to spend between four and six hours each week providing one-to-one friendship for at least one year. (#2162)

	1985 continued, Perf. 11	Un	U	PB	#	FDC	Q
2164	22¢ Help End Hunger, Oct. 15	.40	.15	1.70	(4)	.80	120,000,000
	Christmas Issue, Oct. 30						
2165	22¢ Genoa Madonna, by Luca della Robbia	.40	.15	1.70	(4)	.80	759,200,000
a	Imperf. pair	*130.00*					
2166	22¢ Poinsettia Plants	.40	.15	1.70	(4)	.80	757,600,000
a	Imperf. pair	*175.00*					
	Issues of 1986						
2167	Arkansas Statehood, Jan. 3	.40	.15	1.70	(4)	.80	130,000,000
a	Vertical pair, imperf. horizontally	—					
	Issues of 1986-90, Great Americans Issue (see also #1844-69)						
2168	1¢ Margaret Mitchell, June 30, 1986	.15	.15	.25	(4)	.80	
2169	2¢ Mary Lyon, Feb. 28, 1987	.15	.15	.25	(4)	.80	
2170	3¢ Paul Dudley White, MD, Sept. 15, 1986	.15	.15	.25	(4)	.80	
2171	4¢ Father Flanagan, July 14, 1986	.15	.15	.35	(4)	.80	
2172	5¢ Hugo L. Black, Feb. 27, 1986	.15	.15	.40	(4)	.80	
2173	5¢ Luis Munoz Marin, Feb. 18, 1990	.15	.15	.50	(4)	.85	
2174-75	not assigned						
2176	10¢ Red Cloud, Aug. 15, 1987	.18	.15	.85	(4)	.80	
2177	14¢ Julia Ward Howe, Feb. 12, 1987	.25	.15	1.10	(4)	.80	
2178	15¢ Buffalo Bill Cody, June 6, 1988	.28	.15	1.20	(4)	.75	
2179	17¢ Belva Ann Lockwood, June 18, 1986	.30	.15	1.45	(4)	.80	
2180	21¢ Chester Carlson, Oct. 21, 1988	.38	.15	1.65	(4)	.80	
2181	not assigned						
2182	23¢ Mary Cassatt, Nov. 4, 1988	.42	.15	1.75	(4)	.80	
2183	25¢ Jack London, Jan. 11, 1986	.45	.15	2.00	(4)	.85	
a	Booklet pane of 10, May 3, 1988	4.75				6.00	
2184	28¢ Sitting Bull, Sept. 28, 1989	.56	.15	2.80	(4)	.90	
2185	not assigned						
2186	40¢ Claire Lee Chennault, Sept. 6, 1990	.80	.15		(4)	1.00	
2187	not assigned						
2188	45¢ Harvey Cushing, MD, June 17, 1988	.80	.15	3.50	(4)	1.05	
2189-90	not assigned						
2191	56¢ John Harvard, Sept. 3, 1986	1.00	.15	4.25	(4)	1.25	
2192	65¢ H.H. 'Hap' Arnold, Nov. 5, 1988	1.20	.18	5.00	(4)	1.50	
2193	not assigned						
2194	$1 Bernard Revel, Sept. 23, 1986	1.75	.50	7.25	(4)	2.00	
2194A	$1 Johns Hopkins, June 7, 1989	1.75	.50	7.25	(4)	2.00	
2195	$2 William Jennings Bryan, Mar. 19, 1986	3.50	.50	15.00	(4)	4.00	
2196	$5 Bret Harte, Aug. 25, 1987	7.75	1.00	32.50	(4)	12.00	
	Perf. 10						
2197	25¢ Jack London (2183), single from booklet	.45	.15				
a	Booklet pane of 6, May 3, 1988	3.00				4.00	

2164

2165

2166

2167

2168

2169

2170

2171

2172

2173

2176

2177

2178

2179

2180

2182

2183

2184

2186

2188

2191

2192

2194

2194A

2195

2196

2198 2199 2200 2201 2201a

2202 2203 2204

2205

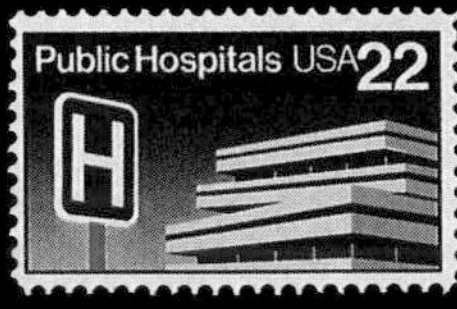

2210

2211

2206

Largemouth Bass 22 USA

2207

2208

2209

	1986 continued, Perf. 10 Vertically	Un	U	PB	#	FDC	Q
	United States-Sweden Stamp Collecting Booklet Issue, Jan. 23						
2198	22¢ Handstamped Cover	.40	.15			.80	16,999,200
2199	22¢ Boy Examining Stamp Collection	.40	.15			.80	16,999,200
2200	22¢ #836 Under Magnifying Glass	.40	.15			.80	16,999,200
2201	22¢ 1986 Presidents Miniature Sheet	.40	.15			.80	16,999,200
a	Booklet pane of 4, #2198-2201	2.00				3.00	
b	As "a," black omitted on #2198, 2201	50.00					
c	As "a," blue omitted on #2198-2200	—					
d	As "a," buff omitted	—					
	#2198-2201 issued only in booklets. All stamps are imperf. at top and bottom or imperf. at top, bottom and one side.						
	Perf. 11						
2202	22¢ Love, Jan. 30	.40	.15	1.70	(4)	.80	948,860,000
	Black Heritage Issue, Sojourner Truth, Feb. 4						
2203	22¢ Sojourner Truth Portrait and Truth Lecturing	.40	.15	1.70	(4)	.80	130,000,000
2204	22¢ Republic of Texas 150th Anniversary, Mar. 2	.40	.15	1.70	(4)	.80	136,500,000
a	Horizontal pair, imperf. vertically	*950.00*					
	Fish Booklet Issue, Mar. 21, Perf. 10 Horizontally						
2205	22¢ Muskellunge	.40	.15			.80	43,998,000
2206	22¢ Atlantic Cod	.40	.15			.80	43,998,000
2207	22¢ Largemouth Bass	.40	.15			.80	43,998,000
2208	22¢ Bluefin Tuna	.40	.15			.80	43,998,000
2209	22¢ Catfish	.40	.15			.80	43,998,000
a	Booklet pane of 5, #2205-09	2.75				2.50	
	#2205-09 issued only in booklets. All stamps are imperf. at sides or imperf. at sides and bottom.						
	Perf. 11						
2210	22¢ Public Hospitals, Apr. 11	.40	.15	1.70	(4)	.80	130,000,000
a	Vertical pair, imperf. horizontally	*425.00*					
b	Horizontal pair, imperf. vertically	*1,000.00*					
	Performing Arts Issue, Duke Ellington, Apr. 29						
2211	22¢ Duke Ellington Portrait and Piano Keys	.40	.15	1.70	(4)	.80	130,000,000
a	Vertical pair, imperf. horizontally	*1,000.00*					
2212-15	not assigned						

Minimum value listed for a stamp is 15 cents. This minimum represents a fair-market price for having a dealer locate and provide a single stamp from his or her stock. Dealers may charge less per stamp for a group of such stamps, or less for a single stamp.

	1986 continued, Perf. 11	Un	U	FDC	Q
	AMERIPEX '86 Issue, Presidents Miniature Sheets, May 22				
2216	Sheet of 9	3.50		4.00	5,825,050
a	22¢ George Washington				
b	22¢ John Adams				
c	22¢ Thomas Jefferson				
d	22¢ James Madison				
e	22¢ James Monroe				
f	22¢ John Quincy Adams				
g	22¢ Andrew Jackson				
h	22¢ Martin Van Buren				
i	22¢ William H. Harrison				
	a-i, any single	.38	.20	.80	
j	Blue omitted	—			
k	Black inscription omitted	*1,250.00*			
l	Imperf.	*9,000.00*			
2217	Sheet of 9	3.50		4.00	5,825,050
a	22¢ John Tyler				
b	22¢ James Polk				
c	22¢ Zachary Taylor				
d	22¢ Millard Fillmore				
e	22¢ Franklin Pierce				
f	22¢ James Buchanan				
g	22¢ Abraham Lincoln				
h	22¢ Andrew Johnson				
i	22¢ Ulysses S. Grant				
	a-i, any single	.38	.20	.80	

U.S. Grant Was Reluctant Hero

Ulysses S. Grant (#2217i) served two terms as President of the United States, from 1869 to 1877. Yet Grant is perhaps best remembered for his role in the Civil War as commander of the Union armies. An unlikely candidate for heroism and fame, Grant was quiet and unassuming. Although he graduated from West Point, he disliked army life and resigned his commission in 1854. However, when the Civil War broke out, Grant's strong sense of duty prompted him to join the Union army. Grant proved to be a decisive and aggressive leader and, in 1864, Lincoln placed all Union armies under his command.

2216a  2216b  2216c  2216d  2216e

2216f  2216g  2216h  2216i

2217a  2217b  2217c  2217d  2217e

2217f 2217g 2217h 2217i

2218a

2218b

2218c

2218d

2218e

2218f

2218g

2218h

2218i

2219a

2219b

2219c

2219d

2219e

2219f

2219g

2219h

2219i

	1986 continued, Perf. 11	Un	U	FDC	Q
	AMERIPEX '86 Issue continued, Presidents Miniature Sheets, May 22				
2218	Sheet of 9	3.50		4.00	5,825,050
a	22¢ Rutherford B. Hayes				
b	22¢ James A. Garfield				
c	22¢ Chester A. Arthur				
d	22¢ Grover Cleveland				
e	22¢ Benjamin Harrison				
f	22¢ William McKinley				
g	22¢ Theodore Roosevelt				
h	22¢ William H. Taft				
i	22¢ Woodrow Wilson				
	a-i, any single	.38	.20	.80	
j	Brown omitted	—			
k	Black inscription omitted	*2,000.00*			
2219	Sheet of 9	3.50		4.00	5,825,050
a	22¢ Warren G. Harding				
b	22¢ Calvin Coolidge				
c	22¢ Herbert Hoover				
d	22¢ Franklin D. Roosevelt				
e	22¢ White House				
f	22¢ Harry S. Truman				
g	22¢ Dwight D. Eisenhower				
h	22¢ John F. Kennedy				
i	22¢ Lyndon B. Johnson				
	a-i, any single	.38	.20	.80	

COOLIDGE KEPT SILENT WHILE TWENTIES ROARED

Shy and austere by nature, President Calvin Coolidge offered a marked contrast with the fun-loving mood of the nation during his administration (1923-1929). Coolidge was the second U.S. President born in Vermont. The first was Chester A. Arthur. Both of these Vermont-born Presidents were elected to the vice presidency and both served out terms of Presidents who died in office. Vice President Arthur succeeded President James Garfield when he died from an assassin's bullet in 1881. Coolidge succeeded President Warren G. Harding in 1923. Coolidge (#2219b) and Arthur (2218c) each appear on a U.S. commemorative stamp. A 1991 stamp honors their home state, Vermont. (#2533)

	1986 continued, Perf. 11	Un	U	PB/PNC	#	FDC	Q
	Polar Explorers Issue, May 28						
2220	22¢ Elisha Kent Kane	.45	.15			.80	32,500,000
2221	22¢ Adolphus W. Greely	.45	.15			.80	32,500,000
2222	22¢ Vilhjalmur Stefansson	.45	.15			.80	32,500,000
2223	22¢ Robert E. Peary, Matthew Henson	.45	.15			.80	32,500,000
a	Block of 4, #2220-23	2.00	1.00	2.05	(4)	2.25	
b	As "a," black omitted	—					
2224	22¢ Statue of Liberty, July 4	.40	.15	1.80	(4)	.80	220,725,000
	Issues of 1986-87, Reengraved Transportation Issues, Coil Stamps, Perf. 10 Vertically (see also #1897-1908, 2123-36, 2252-66)						
2225	1¢ Omnibus, Nov. 26, 1986	.05	.15	.60	(3)	1.00	
2226	2¢ Locomotive, Mar. 6, 1987	.05	.15	.80	(3)	1.00	
2227, 2229-30, 2232-34 not assigned							
2228	4¢ Stagecoach (1898A), Aug. 1986	.08	.15	1.00	(3)		
2231	8.3¢ Ambulance (2128, precancel), Aug. 29, 1986	.16	.16	3.50	(3)		
	On #2228, "Stagecoach 1890s" is 17 mm long; on #1898A, it is 19 1/2mm long. On #2231, "Ambulance 1860s" is 18 mm long; on #2128, it is 18 1/2mm long.						
	American Folk Art Issue, Navajo Blankets, Sept. 4, Perf. 11						
2235	22¢ Navajo Blanket, black and white lines dominate	.40	.15			.80	60,131,250
2236	22¢ Navajo Blanket, black and white diamonds dominate	.40	.15			.80	60,131,250
2237	22¢ Navajo Blanket, white diamonds dominate	.40	.15			.80	60,131,250
2238	22¢ Navajo Blanket, black-and-white bordered patterns dominate	.40	.15			.80	60,131,250
a	Block of 4, #2235-38	1.65	1.00	1.90	(4)	2.25	
b	As "a," black omitted	*350.00*					
	Literary Arts Issue, T.S. Eliot, Sept. 26						
2239	22¢ T.S. Eliot Portrait	.40	.15	1.90	(4)	.80	131,700,000
	American Folk Art Issue, Wood-Carved Figurines, Oct. 1						
2240	22¢ Highlander Figure	.40	.15			.80	60,000,000
2241	22¢ Ship Figurehead	.40	.15			.80	60,000,000
2242	22¢ Nautical Figure	.40	.15			.80	60,000,000
2243	22¢ Cigar-Store Figure	.40	.15			.80	60,000,000
a	Block of 4, #2240-43	1.65	1.00	1.90	(4)	2.25	
b	As "a," imperf. vertically	*2,000.00*					
	Christmas Issue, Oct. 24						
2244	22¢ Madonna and Child, by Perugino	.40	.15	1.90	(4)	.80	690,100,000
2245	22¢ Village Scene	.40	.15	1.90	(4)	.80	882,150,000
	Issues of 1987						
2246	22¢ Michigan Statehood, Jan. 26	.40	.15	1.90	(4)	.85	167,430,000
	Pair with full vertical gutter between	—					
2247	22¢ Pan American Games, Jan. 29	.40	.15	1.90	(4)	.85	166,550,000
a	Silver omitted	*1,500.00*					
	Perf. 11 1/2 x 11						
2248	22¢ Love, Jan. 30	.40	.15	1.90	(4)	.85	842,360,000
	Black Heritage Issue, Jean Baptiste Point Du Sable, Feb. 20, Perf. 11						
2249	22¢ Portrait of Du Sable and Chicago Settlement	.40	.15	1.90	(4)	.85	142,905,000
	Performing Arts Issue, Enrico Caruso, Feb. 27						
2250	22¢ Caruso as the Duke of Mantua in *Rigoletti*	.40	.15	1.90	(4)	.85	130,000,000
a	Black omitted	—					
2251	22¢ Girl Scouts, Mar. 12	.40	.15	1.90	(4)	.85	149,980,000

2220 2221 2223a
2222 2223

2224

2225

2226

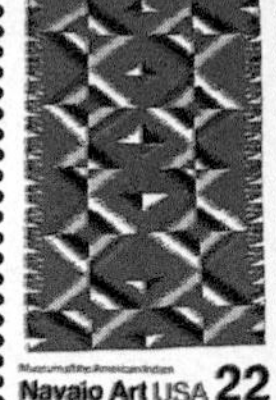

2235 2236 2238a
2237 2238

2239

2240 2241 2243a
2242 2243

2244

2245

1837-1987 Michigan Statehood

2246

2247

2248

2249

2250

2251

1987-1988

2252 2253 2254

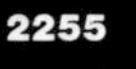

2255 2256 2257

2258 2259 2260

2261 2262 2263

2264 2265 2266

	Issues of 1987-88	Un	U	PNC	#	FDC	Q
	Coil Stamps, Transportation Issue, Perf 10. Vertically (see also #1897-1908, 2123-36, 2225-26, 2228, 2231)						
2252	3¢ Conestoga Wagon 1800s, Feb. 29, 1988	.15	.15	.80	(3)	1.00	
2253	5¢ Milk Wagon 1900s, Sept. 25, 1987	.15	.15	1.15	(3)	1.00	
2254	5.3¢ Elevator 1900s, Bureau precanceled, Sept. 16, 1988	.15	.15	1.25	(3)	1.00	
2255	7.6¢ Carreta 1770s, Bureau precanceled, Aug. 30, 1988	.15	.15	1.80	(3)	1.00	
2256	8.4¢ Wheel Chair 1920s, Bureau precanceled, Aug. 12, 1988	.15	.15	2.50	(3)	1.00	
a	Imperf. pair	—					
2257	10¢ Canal Boat 1880s, Apr. 11, 1987	.18	.15	1.40	(3)	1.00	
2258	13¢ Patrol Wagon 1880s, Bureau precanceled, Oct. 29, 1988	.22	.22	2.50	(3)	1.00	
2259	13.2¢ Coal Car 1870s, Bureau precanceled, July 19, 1988	.22	.22	2.50	(3)	1.00	
a	Imperf. pair	*200.00*					
2260	15¢ Tugboat 1900s, July 12, 1988	.24	.15	2.50	(3)	1.00	
2261	16.7¢ Popcorn Wagon 1902, Bureau precanceled, July 7, 1988	.28	.28	3.50	(3)	1.00	
a	Imperf. pair	*325.00*					
2262	17.5¢ Racing Car 1911, Sept. 25, 1987	.30	.15	3.50	(3)	1.00	
a	Untagged (Bureau precanceled)	.30	.30	3.50	(3)	1.00	
b	Imperf. pair	*1,500.00*					
2263	20¢ Cable Car 1880s, Oct. 28, 1988	.35	.15	3.25	(3)	1.00	
a	Imperf. pair	—					
2264	20.5¢ Fire Engine 1920s, Bureau precanceled, Sept. 28, 1988	.38	.38	3.25	(3)	1.00	
2265	21¢ Railroad Mail Car 1920s, Bureau precanceled, Aug. 16, 1988	.38	.38	3.50	(3)	1.00	
a	Imperf. pair	325.00					
2266	24.1¢ Tandem Bicycle 1890s, Bureau precanceled, Oct. 26, 1988	.42	.42	3.75	(3)	1.00	
	Special Occasions Booklet Issue, Apr. 20, 1987, Perf. 10						
2267	22¢ Congratulations!	.40	.15			.80	1,222,140,000
2268	22¢ Get Well!	.40	.15			.80	611,070,000
2269	22¢ Thank you!	.40	.15			.80	611,070,000
2270	22¢ Love You, Dad!	.40	.15			.80	611,070,000
2271	22¢ Best Wishes!	.40	.15			.80	611,070,000
2272	22¢ Happy Birthday!	.40	.15			.80	1,222,140,000
2273	22¢ Love You, Mother!	.40	.15			.80	611,070,000
2274	22¢ Keep In Touch!	.40	.15			.80	611,070,000
a	Booklet pane of 10, #2268-71, 2273-74 and 2 each of #2267-72	4.25	—			5.00	
	#2267-74 issued only in booklets. All stamps are imperf. at one or two sides or imperf. at sides and bottom.						

	1987 continued, Perf. 11	Un	U	PB/PNC	#	FDC	Q
2275	United Way, Apr. 28	.40	.15	1.90	(4)	.80	156,995,000
2276	Flag with Fireworks, May 9	.40	.15	1.90	(4)	.80	
a	Booklet pane of 20, Nov. 30	8.50	—			12.00	
	Issues of 1988-89 (All issued in 1988 except #2280 on prephosphored paper)						
2277	(25¢) E Stamp, Mar. 22	.45	.15	1.90	(4)	.85	
2278	25¢ Flag with Clouds, May 6	.40	.15	1.90	(4)	.85	
	Pair with full vertical gutter between	—					
	Coil Stamps, Perf. 10 Vertically						
2279	(25¢) E Stamp (2277), Mar. 22	.45	.15	3.00	(3)	.85	
a	Imperf. pair	*160.00*					
2280	25¢ Flag over Yosemite, May 20	.45	.15	4.25	(3)	.85	
	Prephosphored paper, Feb. 14, 1989	.45	.15	3.85	(3)		
a	Imperf. pair	*25.00*					
b	Black trees	—	—				
2281	25¢ Honeybee, Sept. 2	.45	.15	3.00	(3)	.85	
a	Imperf. pair	*32.50*					
b	Black omitted	*125.00*					
d	Pair, imperf. between	—					
	Perf. 10						
2282	(25¢) E Stamp (2277), single from booklet	.45	.15			.85	
a	Booklet pane of 10, Mar. 22	4.75	—			6.00	
	Perf. 11						
2283	25¢ Pheasant, single from booklet	.45	.15			.85	
a	Booklet pane of 10, Apr. 29	4.75	—			6.00	
d	As "a," imperf. horizontally between	—					
	#2283 issued only in booklets. All stamps have one or two imperf. edges. Imperf. and part perf. pairs and panes exist from printer's waste.						
	Perf. 10						
2284	25¢ Owl, single from booklet	.45	.15			.85	
2285	25¢ Grosbeak, single from booklet	.45	.15			.85	
b	Booklet pane of 10, 5 each of #2284, 2285, May 28	4.75	—			6.00	
	#2284-85 issued only in booklets. All stamps are imperf. at one side or imperf. at one side and bottom.						
2285A	25¢ Flag with Clouds (2278), single from booklet	.45	.15			.85	
c	Booklet pane of 6, July 5	2.75	—			4.00	

2275

2276

2277

2278

2280

2281

2283

2283a

2285b

2284 2285

2286 2287 2288 2289 2290

2291 2292 2293 2294 2295

2296 2297 2298 2299 2300

2301 2302 2303 2304 2305

2306

2307

2308

2309

2310

	Issues of 1987	Un	U	FDC	Q
	American Wildlife Issue, June 13, Perf. 11				
2286	22¢ Barn Swallow	.40	.15	.80	12,952,500
2287	22¢ Monarch	.40	.15	.80	12,952,500
2288	22¢ Bighorn Sheep	.40	.15	.80	12,952,500
2289	22¢ Broad-tailed Hummingbird	.40	.15	.80	12,952,500
2290	22¢ Cottontail	.40	.15	.80	12,952,500
2291	22¢ Osprey	.40	.15	.80	12,952,500
2292	22¢ Mountain Lion	.40	.15	.80	12,952,500
2293	22¢ Luna Moth	.40	.15	.80	12,952,500
2294	22¢ Mule Deer	.40	.15	.80	12,952,500
2295	22¢ Gray Squirrel	.40	.15	.80	12,952,500
2296	22¢ Armadillo	.40	.15	.80	12,952,500
2297	22¢ Eastern Chipmunk	.40	.15	.80	12,952,500
2298	22¢ Moose	.40	.15	.80	12,952,500
2299	22¢ Black Bear	.40	.15	.80	12,952,500
2300	22¢ Tiger Swallowtail	.40	.15	.80	12,952,500
2301	22¢ Bobwhite	.40	.15	.80	12,952,500
2302	22¢ Ringtail	.40	.15	.80	12,952,500
2303	22¢ Red-winged Blackbird	.40	.15	.80	12,952,500
2304	22¢ American Lobster	.40	.15	.80	12,952,500
2305	22¢ Black-tailed Jack Rabbit	.40	.15	.80	12,952,500
2306	22¢ Scarlet Tanager	.40	.15	.80	12,952,500
2307	22¢ Woodchuck	.40	.15	.80	12,952,500
2308	22¢ Roseate Spoonbill	.40	.15	.80	12,952,500
2309	22¢ Bald Eagle	.40	.15	.80	12,952,500
2310	22¢ Alaskan Brown Bear	.40	.15	.80	12,952,500

Mountain Lion Has Many Names

Called cougar by the early American settlers, the mountain lion (#2292) also is known as puma, catamount and panther. Mountain lions once roamed in profusion throughout the United States and southern Canada. Then settlers greatly reduced their numbers. As a result, mountain lions in the United States and Canada now live primarily in the western states and provinces.

	1987 continued, Perf. 11	Un	U	PB	#	FDC	Q
	American Wildlife Issue continued, June 13						
2311	22¢ Iiwi	.40	.15			.80	12,952,500
2312	22¢ Badger	.40	.15			.80	12,952,500
2313	22¢ Pronghorn	.40	.15			.80	12,952,500
2314	22¢ River Otter	.40	.15			.80	12,952,500
2315	22¢ Ladybug	.40	.15			.80	12,952,500
2316	22¢ Beaver	.40	.15			.80	12,952,500
2317	22¢ White-tailed Deer	.40	.15			.80	12,952,500
2318	22¢ Blue Jay	.40	.15			.80	12,952,500
2319	22¢ Pika	.40	.15			.80	12,952,500
2320	22¢ Bison	.40	.15			.80	12,952,500
2321	22¢ Snowy Egret	.40	.15			.80	12,952,500
2322	22¢ Gray Wolf	.40	.15			.80	12,952,500
2323	22¢ Mountain Goat	.40	.15			.80	12,952,500
2324	22¢ Deer Mouse	.40	.15			.80	12,952,500
2325	22¢ Black-tailed Prairie Dog	.40	.15			.80	12,952,500
2326	22¢ Box Turtle	.40	.15			.80	12,952,500
2327	22¢ Wolverine	.40	.15			.80	12,952,500
2328	22¢ American Elk	.40	.15			.80	12,952,500
2329	22¢ California Sea Lion	.40	.15			.80	12,952,500
2330	22¢ Mockingbird	.40	.15			.80	12,952,500
2331	22¢ Raccoon	.40	.15			.80	12,952,500
2332	22¢ Bobcat	.40	.15			.80	12,952,500
2333	22¢ Black-footed Ferret	.40	.15			.80	12,952,500
2334	22¢ Canada Goose	.40	.15			.80	12,952,500
2335	22¢ Red Fox	.40	.15			.80	12,952,500
a	Pane of 50, #2286-2335	20.00		20.00	(50)	—	
	Any single, red omitted	—					

SNOWY EGRET DWELLS FAR FROM SNOW

Named for its pure white feathers, the snowy egret (#2321) is most at home in the warm climate of the southern United States. A member of the heron family, the egret has the long neck and legs and the long, thin bill characteristic of the heron. Like other herons, egrets most often live near water, where they feed on frogs, fish and other small animals. They frequently nest in colonies.

2311 2312 2313 2314 2315

2316 2317 2318 2319 2320

2321 2322 2323 2324 2325

2326 2327 2328 2329 2330

2331 2332 2333 2334 2335

2336 2337 2338 2339 2340

2341 2342 2343 2344

2345 2346 2347 2348

2349 2350

2351 2352 2354a
2353 2354

	Issues of 1987-90	Un	U	PB	#	FDC	Q
	Constitution Bicentennial Issues, Statehood, Perf. 11						
2336	22¢ Delaware, July 4, 1987	.40	.15	1.70	(4)	.80	168,000,000
2337	22¢ Pennsylvania, Aug. 26, 1987	.40	.15	1.70	(4)	.80	186,575,000
2338	22¢ New Jersey, Sept. 11, 1987	.40	.15			.80	184,325,000
2339	22¢ Georgia, Jan. 6, 1988	.40	.15	1.70	(4)	.80	168,845,000
2340	22¢ Connecticut, Jan. 9, 1988	.40	.15	1.70	(4)	.80	155,170,000
2341	22¢ Massachusetts, Feb. 6, 1988	.40	.15	1.70	(4)	.80	102,100,000
2342	22¢ Maryland, Feb. 15, 1988	.40	.15	1.70	(4)	.80	103,325,000
2343	25¢ South Carolina, May 23, 1988	.45	.15	1.90	(4)	.85	162,045,000
2344	25¢ New Hampshire, June 21, 1988	.45	.15	1.90	(4)	.85	153,295,000
2345	25¢ Virginia, June 25, 1988	.45	.15	1.90	(4)	.85	160,245,000
2346	25¢ New York, July 26, 1988	.45	.15	1.90	(4)	.85	183,790,000
2347	25¢ North Carolina, Aug. 22, 1989	.45	.15	1.90	(4)	.85	
2348	25¢ Rhode Island, May 29, 1990	.50	.15	2.50	(4)	.85	164,130,000
	1987 continued						
2349	22¢ Friendship with Morocco, July 17	.40	.15	1.70	(4)	.80	157,475,000
a	Black omitted	*450.00*					
	Literary Arts Issue, William Faulkner, Aug. 3						
2350	22¢ Portrait of Faulkner	.40	.15	1.70	(4)	.80	156,225,000
	American Folk Art Issue, Lacemaking, Aug. 14						
2351	22¢ Squash Blossoms	.40	.15			.80	40,995,000
2352	22¢ Floral Piece	.40	.15			.80	40,995,000
2353	22¢ Floral Piece	.40	.15			.80	40,995,000
2354	22¢ Dogwood Blossoms	.40	.15			.80	40,995,000
a	Block of 4, #2351-54	1.65	1.00	1.75	(4)	2.75	
b	As "a," white omitted	*1,750.00*					

Small State First in History

Delaware—home to the earliest U.S. beauty contest and other firsts—is known as the First State. This nickname dates back to December 7, 1787, when Delaware was the first to ratify the United States Constitution. In 1880, Thomas Edison helped select the first "Miss United States" at Delaware's Rehoboth Beach. Other U.S. firsts credited to Delaware include the appearance of log cabins (in 1638) and the sale of Christmas seals (in 1907). (#2336)

	1987 continued	Un	U	PB	#	FDC	Q
	Constitution Bicentennial Issues, Drafting of the Constitution Booklet Issue, Aug. 28, Perf. 10 Horizontally						
2355	22¢ "The Bicentennial..."	.40	.15			.80	121,944,000
2356	22¢ "We the people..."	.40	.15			.80	121,944,000
2357	22¢ "Establish justice..."	.40	.15			.80	121,944,000
2358	22¢ "And secure..."	.40	.15			.80	121,944,000
2359	22¢ "Do ordain..."	.40	.15			.80	121,944,000
a	Booklet pane of 5, #2355-59	2.10	—			3.00	
	#2355-59 issued only in booklets. All stamps are imperf. at sides or imperf. at sides and bottom.						
	Signing of the Constitution, Sept. 17, Perf. 11						
2360	22¢ Constitution and Signer's Hand Holding Quill Pen, Sept. 17	.40	.15	1.70	(4)	.80	168,995,000
2361	22¢ Certified Public Accountants, Sept. 21	.40	.15	1.70	(4)	.80	163,145,000
a	Black omitted	*600.00*					
	Locomotives Booklet Issue, Oct. 1, Perf. 10 Horizontally						
2362	22¢ Stourbridge Lion, 1829	.40	.15			.80	142,501,200
2363	22¢ Best Friend of Charleston, 1830	.40	.15			.80	142,501,200
2364	22¢ John Bull, 1831	.40	.15			.80	142,501,200
2365	22¢ Brother Jonathan, 1832	.40	.15			.80	142,501,200
2366	22¢ Gowan & Marx, 1839	.40	.15			.80	142,501,200
a	Booklet pane of 5, #2362-66	2.10	—			3.00	
b	As "a," black omitted on #2366	—					
	#2362-66 issued only in booklets. All stamps are imperf. at sides or imperf. at sides and bottom.						
	Christmas Issue, Oct. 23, Perf. 11						
2367	22¢ Madonna and Child, by Moroni	.40	.15	1.70	(4)	.80	528,790,000
2368	22¢ Christmas Ornaments	.40	.15	1.70	(4)	.80	978,340,000
	Pair with full vertical gutter between	—					

JOHN BULL MADE HISTORIC RUN
John Bull (#2364) was, in 1831, the first locomotive to travel on the railway line between Camden and Amboy, New Jersey. Imported from England, John Bull was one of a number of English engines ordered by American railways. John Bull is the oldest surviving locomotive in the United States.

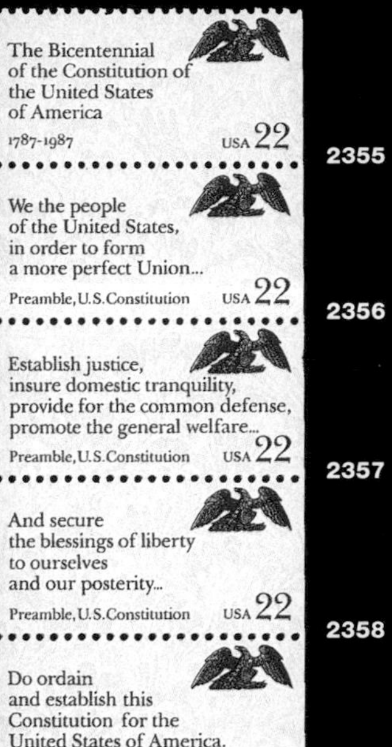

2355

2356

2357

2358

2359

2359a

2360 2361

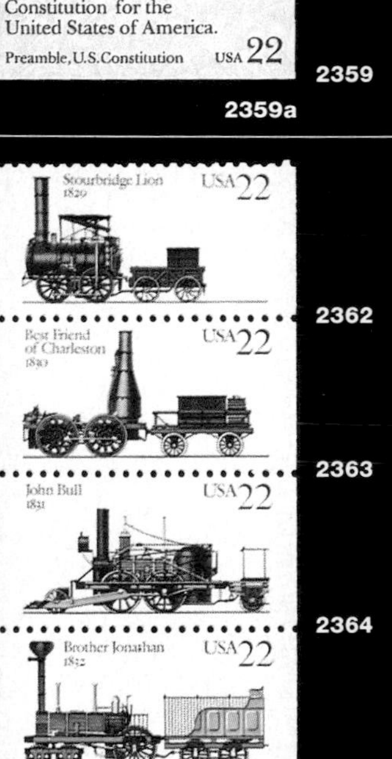

2362

2363

2364

2365

2366

2366a

2367 2368

2369

2370

2371

2372 2373 2375a
2374 2375

2376

2377

2378

2379

2380

	Issues of 1988	Un	U	PB	#	FDC	Q
	Olympic Winter Games Issue, Jan. 10, Perf. 11						
2369	22¢ Skier and Olympic Rings	.40	.15	1.70	(4)	.80	158,870,000
2370	22¢ Australia Bicentennial, Jan. 26	.40	.15	1.70	(4)	.80	145,560,000
	Black Heritage Issue, James Weldon Johnson, Feb. 2						
2371	22¢ Portrait of Johnson and Music from "Lift Ev'ry Voice and Sing"	.40	.15	1.70	(4)	.80	97,300,000
	American Cats Issue, Feb. 5						
2372	22¢ Siamese and Exotic Shorthair	.40	.15			.80	39,639,000
2373	22¢ Abyssinian and Himalayan	.40	.15			.80	39,639,000
2374	22¢ Maine Coon and Burmese	.40	.15			.80	39,639,000
2375	22¢ American Shorthair and Persian	.40	.15			.80	39,639,000
a	Block of 4, #2372-75	1.65	1.00	1.75	(4)	2.75	
	American Sports Issues, Knute Rockne, Mar. 9						
2376	22¢ Rockne Holding Football on Field	.40	.15	1.70	(4)	.80	97,300,000
	Francis Ouimet, June 13						
2377	25¢ Portrait of Ouimet and Ouimet Hitting Fairway Shot	.45	.15	1.90	(4)	.85	153,045,000
2378	25¢ Love, July 4	.45	.15	1.90	(4)	.85	762,090,000
2379	45¢ Love, Aug. 8	.65	.20	3.00	(4)	1.00	179,553,550
	Olympic Summer Games Issue, Aug. 19						
2380	25¢ Gymnast on Rings	.45	.15	1.90	(4)	.85	157,215,000

GYMNASTS COMPETED AT FIRST MODERN GAMES

Gymnastics has been part of the modern Olympic Games since they first were held in 1896. Male gymnasts compete in six categories, including the rings. A separate competition for women comprises four events. The "Gymnast on Rings" depicted on a 1988 U.S. postal issue (#2380) commemorates the 1988 Summer Olympic Games. The U.S. Postal Service is a sponsor of the 1992 Olympic Games.

	1988 continued	Un	U	PB	#	FDC	Q
	Classic Cars Booklet Issue, Aug. 25, Perf. 10 Horizontally						
2381	25¢ 1928 Locomobile	.45	.15			.85	131,661,600
2382	25¢ 1929 Pierce-Arrow	.45	.15			.85	127,047,600
2383	25¢ 1931 Cord	.45	.15			.85	127,047,600
2384	25¢ 1932 Packard	.45	.15			.85	127,047,600
2385	25¢ 1935 Duesenberg	.45	.15			.85	127,047,600
a	Booklet pane of 5, #2381-85	2.30	—			3.00	
	#2381-85 issued only in booklets. All stamps are imperf. at sides or imperf. at sides and bottom.						
	Antarctic Explorers Issue, Sept. 14, Perf. 11						
2386	25¢ Nathaniel Palmer	.45	.15			.85	40,535,000
2387	25¢ Lt. Charles Wilkes	.45	.15			.85	40,535,000
2388	25¢ Richard E. Byrd	.45	.15			.85	40,535,000
2389	25¢ Lincoln Ellsworth	.45	.15			.85	40,535,000
a	Block of 4, #2386-89	1.85	1.00	2.00	(4)	3.00	
b	As "a," black omitted	*2,000.00*					
c	As "a," imperf. horizontally	—					
	American Folk Art Issue, Carousel Animals, Oct. 1						
2390	25¢ Deer	.45	.15			.85	76,253,750
2391	25¢ Horse	.45	.15			.85	76,253,750
2392	25¢ Camel	.45	.15			.85	76,253,750
2393	25¢ Goat	.45	.15			.85	76,253,750
a	Block of 4, #2390-93	1.85	1.00	2.00	(4)	3.00	

CAROUSEL ART GOES 'ROUND AND 'ROUND

The carousel was a favorite amusement in the United States from 1880 to 1930. In 1988, the U.S. Postal Service commemorated four outstanding examples of American carousel art: Gustav Dentzel's graceful 1895 deer, complete with real antlers (#2390); a rare, long-horned goat carved by Charles Looff around 1880 (#2393); a bejeweled camel produced by Looff's company in 1917 (#2392); and a "lead" or "king" horse, created by Daniel C. Muller (#2391).

2381 2385a
2382
2383
2384
2385

2386 2387 2389a
2388 2389

2390 2391 2393a
2392 2393

2394

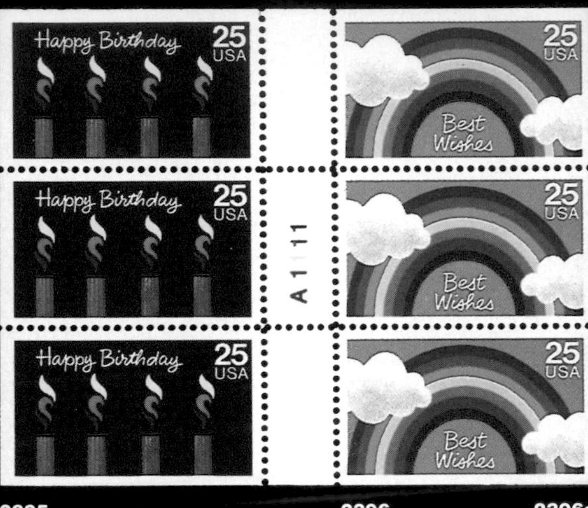

2395 2396 2396a

2397 2398 2398a

2399

2400

	1988 continued, Perf. 11	Un	U	PB	#	FDC	Q
2394	$8.75 Express Mail, Oct. 4	15.00	7.75	60.00	(4)	25.00	
	Special Occasions Booklet Issue, Oct. 22						
2395	25¢ Happy Birthday	.45	.15			.85	120,000,000
2396	25¢ Best Wishes	.45	.15			.85	120,000,000
a	Booklet pane of 6, 3 #2395 and 3 #2396 with gutter between	2.75					
2397	25¢ Thinking of You	.45	.15			.85	120,000,000
2398	25¢ Love You	.45	.15			.85	120,000,000
a	Booklet pane of 6, 3 #2397 and 3 #2398 with gutter between	2.75					
	Christmas Issue, Oct. 20, Perf. 11						
2399	25¢ Madonna and Child, by Botticelli	.45	.15	1.90	(4)	.85	843,835,000
a	Gold omitted	50.00					
2400	25¢ One-Horse Open Sleigh and Village Scene	.45	.15	1.90	(4)	.85	1,037,610,000
	Pair with full vertical gutter between	—					

Greetings by the Millions
Greeting cards express wishes for every conceivable occasion—weddings, birthdays, religious holidays and many others. The first greeting cards were valentines. Initally made by hand, valentines first were produced commercially in the early 19th century. Not long after, in 1843, John C. Horsley created the first Christmas card. Published in London, it sold about 1,000 copies. In 1847, Esther A. Howland began manufacturing greeting cards in the United States. Inspired by English valentines, this Massachusetts resident set up an assembly line for card production. U.S. mail carriers have since carried greetings of all kinds to millions of households. In 1988, the U.S. Postal Service issued four stamps celebrating popular greetings: "Happy Birthday" (#2395), "Best Wishes" (#2396), "Thinking of You" (#2397) and "Love You" (#2398).

	Issues of 1989, Perf. 11	Un	U	PB	#	FDC	Q
2401	25¢ Montana Statehood, Jan. 15	.45	.15	1.90	(4)	.85	165,495,000
	Black Heritage Issue, A. Philip Randolph, Feb. 3						
2402	25¢ Portrait of Randolph, Pullman Porters and Railroad Cars	.45	.15	1.90	(4)	.85	151,675,000
2403	25¢ North Dakota Statehood, Feb. 21	.45	.15	1.90	(4)	.85	163,000,000
2404	25¢ Washington Statehood, Feb. 22	.45	.15	1.90	(4)	.85	264,625,000
	Steamboats Booklet Issue, Mar. 3, Perf. 10						
2405	25¢ Experiment 1788-90	.45	.15			.85	159,154,200
2406	25¢ Phoenix 1809	.45	.15			.85	159,154,200
2407	25¢ New Orleans 1812	.45	.15			.85	159,154,200
2408	25¢ Washington 1816	.45	.15			.85	159,154,200
2409	25¢ Walk in the Water 1818	.45	.15			.85	159,154,200
a	Booklet pane of 5, #2405-09	2.25	—			4.00	
	#2405-09 issued only in booklets. All stamps are imperf. at sides or imperf. at sides and bottom.						
2410	25¢ WORLD STAMP EXPO '89, Mar. 16	.45	.15	1.90	(4)	.85	163,984,000
	Performing Arts Issue, Arturo Toscanini, Mar. 25						
2411	25¢ Portrait of Toscanini Conducting with Baton	.45	.15	1.90	(4)	.85	152,250,000
	Issues of 1989-90, Constitution Bicentennial Issues						
2412	25¢ U.S. House of Representatives, Apr. 4, 1989	.45	.15	1.90	(4)	.85	138,760,000
2413	25¢ U.S. Senate, Apr. 6, 1989	.45	.15	1.90	(4)	.85	137,985,000
2414	25¢ Executive Branch, Apr. 16, 1989	.45	.15	1.90	(4)	.85	138,580,000
2415	25¢ Supreme Court, Feb. 2, 1990	.45	.15	1.90	(4)	.85	150,545,000
	1989 continued, Perf. 11						
2416	25¢ South Dakota Statehood, May 3	.45	.15	1.90	(4)	.85	164,680,000
	American Sports Issue, Lou Gehrig, June 10						
2417	25¢ Portrait of Gehrig, Gehrig Swinging Bat	.45	.15	2.50	(4)	2.00	262,755,000
	Literary Arts Issue, Ernest Hemingway, July 17						
2418	25¢ Portrait of Hemingway, African Landscape in Background	.45	.15	1.90	(4)	.85	191,755,000

"WESTWARD HO"
A combined clipper and steamboat, Walk in the Water *(#2409) is one of five early steamboats commemorated by the U.S. Postal Service in 1989. During the 19th century, steamboats hastened westward expansion by transforming America's waterways into the first superhighways.*

2401

2402

North Dakota 1889
USA25

2403

2404

2405 2409a
2406
2407
2408
2409

2410

USA25
Toscanini

2411

2412

2413

2414

2415

2416

2417

2418

2419

2420

2421

2422 2423 2425a

2424 2425

2426

2427

2428

2431

2433

	1989 continued	Un	U	PB	#	FDC	Q
	Priority Mail Issue, July 20, Perf. 11 x 11 1/2						
2419	$2.40 Moon Landing	3.75	1.90	17.50	(4)	5.00	
	Perf. 11						
a	Black omitted	—					
b	Imperf. pair	—					
2420	25¢ Letter Carriers, Aug. 30	.45	.15	1.90	(4)	.85	188,400,000
	Constitution Bicentennial Issue, Drafting of the Bill of Rights, Sept. 25						
2421	25¢ Stylized U.S. Flag, Eagle With Quill Pen in Mouth	.45	.15	1.90	(4)	.85	191,860,000
a	Black omitted	*300.00*					
	Prehistoric Animals Issue, Oct. 1						
2422	25¢ Tryannosaurus Rex	.45	.15			.85	101,747,000
2423	25¢ Pteranodon	.45	.15			.85	101,747,000
2424	25¢ Stegosaurus	.45	.15			.85	101,747,000
2425	25¢ Brontosaurus	.45	.15			.85	101,747,000
a	Block of 4, #2422-25	1.80	1.00	1.90	(4)	3.00	
b	As "a," black omitted	—					
	America/PUAS Issue, Oct. 12						
2426	25¢ Southwest Carved Figure (A.D. 1150-1350), Emblem of the Postal Union of the Americas (see also #C121)	.45	.15	2.50	(4)	.85	137,410,000
	Christmas Issue, Oct. 19, Perf. 11 1/2 x 11						
2427	25¢ Madonna and Child, by Caracci	.45	.15	1.90	(4)	.85	609,465,000
a	Booklet Pane of 10	4.50	—			6.00	
2428	25¢ Sleigh Full of Presents	.45	.15	1.90	(4)	.85	900,000,000
a	Vertical pair, imperf. horizontally	—					
2429	25¢ Single from booklet pane (#2428)	.45	.15				
a	Booklet pane of 10	5.00				6.00	
b	As "a," imperf. horizontally between	—					
c	As "a," red omitted	—					
	In #2429, runners on sleigh are twice as thick as in #2428; bow on package at rear of sleigh is same color as package; board running underneath sleigh is pink.						
2430	not assigned						
	Self-Adhesive, Die-Cut						
2431	25¢ Eagle and Shield, Nov. 10	.50	.20			1.00	75,441,000
a	Booklet pane of 18	9.00					
b	Vertical pair, no diecutting between	—					
2432	not assigned						
	WORLD STAMP EXPO '89 Issue, Souvenir Sheet, Nov. 17, Imperf.						
2433	Reproduction of #122, 90¢ Lincoln, and three essays of #122	6.00	6.00			5.00	2,227,600

	1989 continued	Un	U	PB	#	FDC	Q
	20th UPU Congress Issues, Classic Mail Transportation, Nov. 19, Perf. 11						
2434	25¢ Stagecoach	.45	.15			.85	40,956,000
2435	25¢ Paddlewheel Steamer	.45	.15			.85	40,956,000
2436	25¢ Biplane	.45	.15			.85	40,956,000
2437	25¢ Depot-hack Type Automobile	.45	.15			.85	40,956,000
a	Block of 4, #2434-37	1.80	1.00	2.50	(4)	3.00	
b	As "a," dark blue omitted	—					
	Souvenir Sheet, Nov. 27, Imperf. (see also #C122-C126)						
2438	Designs of #2434-37	2.00	1.75			2.00	
	Issues of 1990, Perf. 11						
2439	25¢ Idaho Statehood, Jan. 6	.45	.15	2.50	(4)	.85	173,000,000
	Perf. 12½ x 13						
2440	25¢ Love, January 18	.45	.15	2.50	(4)	.85	886,220,000
a	Imperf. pair	—					
	Perf. 11½						
2441	25¢ Love, single from booklet	.45	.15			.85	995,178,000
a	Booklet pane of 10, Jan. 18	4.50	—				
b	As "a," bright pink omitted	—					
	Black Heritage Issue, Ida B. Wells, Feb. 1						
2442	25¢ Portrait of Ida B. Wells, Marchers in Background	.45	.15	2.50	(4)	.85	153,125,000
	Perf. 11½ x 11						
2443	15¢ Beach Umbrella, single from booklet	.28	.15			.75	
a	Booklet pane of 10, Feb. 3	2.80	—				
b	As "a," blue omitted	—					

VERSATILE BIPLANE FIRST TO TAKE FLIGHT

On December 17, 1903, a biplane changed the course of transportation history. Designed and built by the Wright brothers, the Wright Flyer *was the first heavier-than-air machine to make a controlled flight. After World War I, the biplane—with its open cockpit and "double-decker" wings—became a source of entertainment. Barnstorming pilots executed aerial acrobatics or sometimes flew with daredevils performing on the plane's wings. When the U.S. Post Office began providing airmail service in 1918, the biplane became an early form of mail transportation. (#2436)*

2434 **2435** **2437a**
2436 **2437**

2438

2439

2440

2442

2443

1990

2444

2445 2446 2448a

2447 2448

2449

2452

2468

2470 2471 2472 2473 2474 2474a

2475

2476

2496 2497 2498 2499 2500 2500a

	1990 continued, Perf. 11	Un	U	PB	#	FDC	Q
2444	Wyoming Statehood, Feb. 23	.45	.15	2.50	(4)	.85	169,495,000
	Classic Films Issue, Mar. 23						
2445	25¢ The Wizard of Oz	.45	.15	2.50	(4)	.85	44,202,000
2446	25¢ Gone With the Wind	.45	.15	2.50	(4)	.85	44,202,000
2447	25¢ Beau Geste	.45	.15	2.50	(4)	.85	44,202,000
2448	25¢ Stagecoach	.45	.15	2.50	(4)	.85	44,202,000
a	Block of 4, #2445-48	1.80	1.00			2.50	
	Literary Arts Issue, Marianne Moore, Apr. 18						
2449	25¢ Portrait of Marianne Moore	.50	.15	2.50	(4)	.85	150,000,000
2450-51	not assigned						
	Coil Stamps, Transportation Issue, Perf. 10 Vertically						
2452	5¢ Circus Wagon 1900s, Aug. 31	.15	.15	1.20	(3)	.85	
2453-67	not assigned						
2468	$1 Seaplane 1914, Apr. 20	2.00	.50	6.50	(3)	1.75	
	Lighthouses Booklet Issue, Apr. 26, Perf. 10						
2470	25¢ Admiralty Head, WA	.50	.15			.85	146,721,600
2471	25¢ Cape Hatteras, NC	.50	.15			.85	146,721,600
2472	25¢ West Quoddy Head, ME	.50	.15			.85	146,721,600
2473	25¢ American Shoals, FL	.50	.15			.85	146,721,600
2474	25¢ Sandy Hook, NJ	.50	.15			.85	146,721,600
a	Booklet pane of 5, #2470-74	2.50	—			3.00	
b	As "a," white ("USA 25") omitted	*125.00*					
	#2470-74 issued only in booklets. All stamps are imperf. top and bottom or top, bottom and right edge.						
	Self-Adhesive, Die-Cut						
2475	25¢ Flag, single from pane	.50	.25			1.00	36,168,000
a	Pane of 12, May 18	6.00					
	Sold only in panes of 12; available for test in which panes were dispensed from bank automatic teller machines.						
	Perf. 11						
2476	$2 Bobcat, June 1	4.00	.50	17.50	(4)	3.00	
2477-95	not assigned						
	Olympians Issue, July 6						
2496	25¢ Jesse Owens	.50	.15	5.50	(10)	.90	35,717,500
2497	25¢ Ray Ewry	.50	.15			.90	35,717,500
2498	25¢ Hazel Wightman	.50	.15			.90	35,717,500
2499	25¢ Eddie Eagan	.50	.15			.90	35,717,500
2500	25¢ Helene Madison	.50	.15	5.50	(10)	.90	35,717,500
a	Strip of 5, #2496-2500	2.50	—			3.00	

	1990 continued, Perf. 11	Un	U	PB	#	FDC	Q
	Indian Headdresses Booklet Issue, Aug. 17						
2501	25¢ Assiniboine Headdress	.50	.15			.85	123,825,600
2502	25¢ Cheyenne Headdress	.50	.15			.85	123,825,600
2503	25¢ Comanche Headdress	.50	.15			.85	123,825,600
2504	25¢ Flathead Headdress	.50	.15			.85	123,825,600
2505	25¢ Shoshone Headdress	.50	.15			.85	123,825,600
a	Booklet pane of 10, 2 each of #2501-05	5.00	—			6.00	
b	As "a," black omitted	—					
	#2501-05 issued only in booklets. All stamps imperf. top or bottom, or top or bottom and right side.						
	Micronesia/Marshall Islands Issue, Sept. 28						
2506	25¢ Canoe and Flag of the Federated States of Micronesia	.50	.15	2.50	(4)	.85	75,715,000
2507	25¢ Stick Chart, Canoe and Flag of the Marshall Islands	.50	.15	2.50	(4)	.85	75,715,000
a	Pair, #2506-07	1.00	.16			1.50	
	Creatures of the Sea Issue, Oct. 1						
2508	25¢ Killer Whale	.50	.15	2.50	(4)	.85	69,476,000
2509	25¢ Northern Sea Lion	.50	.15	2.50	(4)	.85	69,476,000
2510	25¢ Sea Otter	.50	.15	2.50	(4)	.85	69,476,000
2511	25¢ Common Dolphin	.50	.15	2.50	(4)	.85	69,476,000
a	Block of 4, #2508-11	2.00	—			2.50	
b	As "a," black omitted	—					
	America/PUAS Issue, Oct. 12 (see also #C127)						
2512	25¢ Grand Canyon	.50	.15	2.50	(4)	.85	150,760,000
2513	25¢ Dwight D. Eisenhower	.50	.15	2.50	(4)	.85	
	Christmas Issue, Oct. 18						
2514	25¢ Madonna and Child, by Antonello	.50	.15	2.50	(4)	.85	
a	Booklet pane of 10	5.00					
2515	25¢ Christmas Tree	.50	.15	2.50	(4)	.85	
2516	Single (2515) from booklet pane	.50	.15				
a	Booklet pane of 10	5.00					

2501 2502 2503 2504 2505 2505a

2506 2507 2507a

2508 2509 2511a
2510 2511

2512

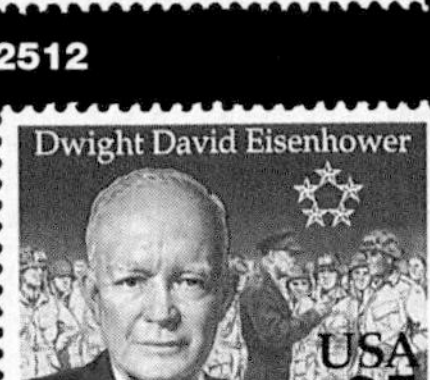

2513

2514 2515

1991 Issues
Commemoratives and Specials

Switzerland (50¢, #2532)
Date of Issue: February 22, 1991
Place of Issue: Washington, DC
Designer: Hans Hartmann
Printing: Gravure
This joint issue, featuring the Swiss Parliament and the U.S. Capitol, honors Switzerland's 700th anniversary.

Vermont Statehood (29¢, #2533)
Date of Issue: March 1, 1991
Place of Issue: Bennington, Vermont
Designer: Sabra Field
Printing: Gravure
An independent republic until 1791, Vermont celebrated its bicentennial as a state with the issuance of this stamp.

Savings Bonds (29¢, #2534)
Date of Issue: April 30, 1991
Place of Issue: Washington, DC
Designer: Primo Angeli
Printing: Gravure
The Series E Savings Bonds were created in 1941 to help finance the nation's defense effort during World War II.

Love (29¢, #2535 sheet; #2536-36a booklet single, pane of 10)
Date of Issue: May 9, 1991
Place of Issue: Honolulu, Hawaii
Designer: Harry Zelenko
Printing: Gravure
The latest Love stamp gives a new dimension to affection by depicting a heart-shaped Earth.

Love (52¢, #2537)
Date of Issue: May 9, 1991
Place of Issue: Honolulu, Hawaii
Designer: Nancy Krause
Printing: Gravure
A pair of Fischer's lovebirds adorns the Love stamp issued to cover the two-ounce First-Class letter rate.

William Saroyan (29¢ #2538)
Date of Issue: May 22, 1991
Place of Issue: Fresno, California
Designer: Ren Wicks
Printing: Gravure
This acclaimed writer's exuberant, impressionistic style earned him a Pulitzer Prize and an Academy Award.

Fishing Flies (29¢, #2545-49a booklet singles, pane of 5)
Date of Issue: May 31, 1991
Place of Issue: Cuddebackville, New York
Designer: Chuck Ripper
Printing: Offset/Intaglio
Five popular types of lures used in the sport of fly fishing are depicted in these booklet pane designs.

Cole Porter (29¢, #2550)
Date of Issue: June 8, 1991
Place of Issue: Peru, Indiana
Designer: Jim Sharpe
Printing: Gravure
Porter wrote such famous musicals as *Kiss Me, Kate, Can-Can* and *Silk Stockings* and such songs as "Night and Day," "Begin the Beguine" and "Let's Do It."

Desert Shield/Desert Storm (29¢, #2551 sheet; #2552-52a booklet single, pane of 5)
Date of Issue: July 2, 1991
Place of Issue: Washington, DC
Designer: Jack Williams
Printing: Gravure
This stamp depicts the medal presented to all military personnel who helped achieve victory in the Persian Gulf War.

Summer Olympics (29¢, #2553-57)
Date of Issue: July 12, 1991
Place of Issue: Los Angeles, California
Designer: Joni Carter
Printing: Gravure
The electric motion of five events is captured on these stamps which focus attention on the '92 Summer Olympics.

Numismatics (29¢, #2558)
Date of Issue: August 13, 1991
Place of Issue: Chicago, Illinois
Designer: V. Jack Ruther
Printing: Offset/Intaglio
The hobby of coin and currency collecting earns tribute in the centennial year of the American Numismatic Association.

Basketball (29¢, #2560)
Date of Issue: August 28, 1991
Place of Issue: Springfield, Massachusetts
Designer: Lon Busch
Printing: Gravure
The 100th anniversary of the invention of the popular sport of basketball is commemorated with this graphic design.

Comedians (29¢, #2562-66a)
Date of Issue: August 29, 1991
Place of Issue: Hollywood, California
Designer: Al Hirschfeld
Printing: Offset/Intaglio
These comedians brought laughter to millions of Americans.

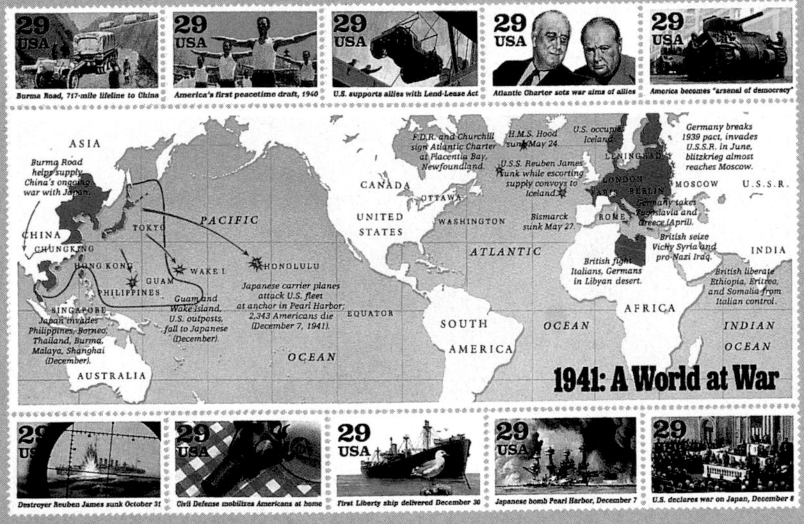

World War II (29¢, #2559-59h singles, sheet of 10)
Date of Issue: September 3, 1991
Place of Issue: Phoenix, Arizona
Designer: Bill Bond
Printing: Offset/Intaglio
This miniature sheet featuring key 1941 events and activities is the first of five such World War II annual issues.

District of Columbia (29¢, #2561)
Date of Issue: September 7, 1991
Place of Issue: Washington, DC
Designer: Pierre Mion
Printing: Offset/Intaglio
A turn-of-the-century street scene highlights the design commemorating the bicentennial of the nation's capital.

Jan Matzeliger (29¢, #2567)
Date of Issue: September 15, 1991
Place of Issue: Lynn, Massachusetts
Designer: Higgins Bond
Printing: Gravure
Matzeliger's ingenuity resulted in machinery which revolutionized the shoe manufacturing industry in America.

Space Exploration (29¢, #2568-77a booklet singles, pane of 10)
Date of Issue: October 1, 1991
Place of Issue: Pasadena, California
Designer: Ron Miller
Printing: Offset/Intaglio
These booklet designs focus on the planets and missions to them which resulted in important discoveries.

Christmas Traditional (Nondenominated, #2578 sheet; #2580-80a booklet single, pane of 10)
Date of Issue: October 17, 1991
Place of Issue: Houston, Texas
Designer: Bradbury Thompson
Printing: Offset/Intaglio
The Madonna and Child portrait is from a painting by Antoniazzo which is in Houston's Museum of Fine Arts.

Designs not available at press time.

Christmas Contemporary
(Nondenominated, #2579 sheet; 2581-85a booklet singles, panes of 4)
Date of Issue: October 17, 1991
Place of Issue: Santa, Idaho
Designer: John Berkey
Printing: Gravure
The five Santa Claus renditions mark the first multi-design Christmas Contemporary booklet issued by the Postal Service.

1991 Issues
Definitives and Airmails

"F" (29¢, #2517 sheet; #2518 coil; #2519-19a BEP-printed booklet single, pane of 10; #2520-20a KCS-printed booklet single, pane of 10)
Date of Issue: January 22, 1991
Place of Issue: Washington, DC
Designer: Wallace Marosek
Printing: Gravure
This is the sixth "letter" stamp used in conjunction with postage rate changes.

This U.S. stamp, along with 25¢ of additional U.S. postage, is equivalent to the 'F' stamp rate

Makeup (4¢, #2521)
Date of Issue: January 22, 1991
Place of Issue: Washington, DC
Designer: Dick Sheaff
Printing: Offset
This nondenominated stamp was issued for use with any 25-cent stamp to meet the new First-Class letter rate.

Flag ATM Stamp (29¢, #2522-22a booklet single, pane of 12)
Date of Issue: January 22, 1991
Place of Issue: Washington, DC
Designer: Harry Zelenko
Printing: Gravure
The nondenominated ATM stamp is for purchase from automatic teller machines.

Steam Carriage (4¢, #2451)
Date of Issue: January 25, 1991
Place of Issue: Tucson, Arizona
Designer: Richard Schlecht
Printing: Intaglio
Steam carriages were mechanically successful but took more than 30 years to become popular transportation.

Fawn (19¢, #2487)
Date of Issue: March 11, 1991
Place of Issue: Washington, DC
Designer: Peter Cocci
Printing: Gravure
A fawn taking its first steps graces this First-Class postcard-rate issue.

Intaglio

Gravure

Flag over Mount Rushmore (29¢, #2523-23A coils of 100-3,000, coils of 10,000)
Dates of Issue: March 29, 1991 (100-3,000), July 4, 1991 (10,000)
Place of Issue:
Mount Rushmore, South Dakota
Designer: Peter Cocci
Printing: Intaglio (100-3,000)/
Gravure (10,000)
This issue helps note the 50th anniversary of Mount Rushmore National Memorial.

Dennis Chavez (35¢, #2185)
Date of Issue: April 3, 1991
Place of Issue: Albuquerque, New Mexico
Designer: Chris Calle
Printing: Intaglio
Chavez, of New Mexico, was the first American-born Hispanic in the U.S. Senate.

29 USA

Slit-perf.

Flower (29¢, #2524 sheet; #2525 slit-perf. coil; #2526 regular-perf. coil; #2427-27a booklet single, pane of 10)
Date of Issue: April 5, 1991
(slit-perf., August 16, 1991)
Place of Issue: Rochester, New York
Designer: Wallace Marosek
Printing: Gravure
This is the denominated version of the "F" rate-change First-Class stamp.

Lunch Wagon (23¢, #2464)
Date of Issue: April 12, 1991
Place of Issue: Columbus, Ohio
Designer: Robert Brangwynne
Printing: Intaglio
Lunch wagons later evolved into an American institution—the diner.

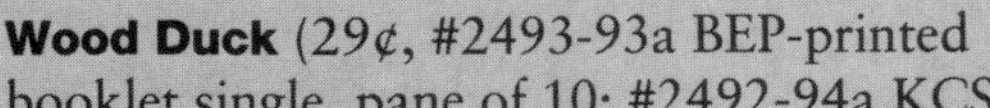

Wood Duck (29¢, #2493-93a BEP-printed booklet single, pane of 10; #2492-94a KCS-printed booklet single, pane of 10)
Date of Issue: April 12, 1991
Place of Issue: Columbus, Ohio
Designer: Robert Giusti
Printing: Gravure
The BEP stamp is printed with black lettering and numbers; the KCS version features lettering and numbers printed in red.

Flag with Olympic Rings (29¢, #2528-28a booklet single, pane of 10)
Date of Issue: April 21, 1991
Place of Issue: Atlanta, Georgia
Designer: John Boyd
Printing: Gravure
This design helps meet demand for flag stamps and publicizes the 1992 Olympic Games, of which the USPS is a sponsor.

Harriet Quimby (50¢, #C128)
Date of Issue: April 27, 1991
Place of Issue: Plymouth, Michigan
Designer: Howard Koslow
Printing: Gravure
Quimby was the first American woman to receive a pilot's license and the first woman to fly the English Channel solo.

Ballooning (19¢, #2530-30a booklet single, pane of 10)
Date of Issue: May 17, 1991
Place of Issue: Denver, Colorado
Designer: Pierre Mion
Printing: Gravure
This postcard-rate design pays tribute to the popular sport of ballooning.

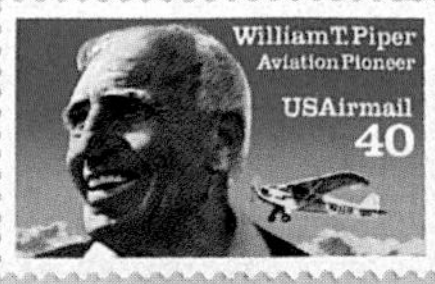

William T. Piper (40¢, #C129)
Date of Issue: May 17, 1991
Place of Issue: Denver, Colorado
Designer: Ren Wicks
Printing: Gravure
The "Henry Ford of aviation" brought flying to the masses.

Intaglio

Gravure design not available at press time.

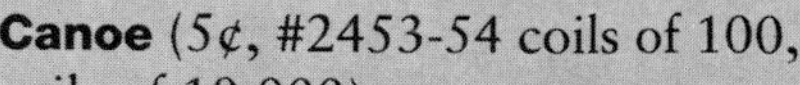

Canoe (5¢, #2453-54 coils of 100, coils of 10,000)
Dates of Issue: May 25, 1991 (100), (10,000 date not available)
Place of Issue: Secaucus, New Jersey
Designer: Paul Calle
Printing: Intaglio (100)/Gravure (10,000)
A birchbark canoe similar to those used by the Chippewa Indians in Minnesota graces this nonprofit-rate stamp.

Tractor-Trailer (10¢, #2457)
Date of Issue: May 25, 1991
Place of Issue: Secaucus, New Jersey
Designer: David K. Stone
Printing: Intaglio
Tractor-trailers long have been major movers of material and key factors in the progress of U.S. commerce.

Flags on Parade (29¢, #2531)
Date of Issue: May 30, 1991
Place of Issue: Waterloo, New York
Designers: Frank Waslick, Peter Cocci
Printing: Gravure
This issue represents part of the Postal Service's effort to provide the public with a variety of popular flag stamps.

Hubert H. Humphrey (52¢, #2190)
Date of Issue: June 3, 1991
Place of Issue: Minneapolis, Minnesota
Designer: John Berkey
Printing: Intaglio
The 38th U.S. Vice President and four-term Senator championed civil rights and many other causes.

Express Mail ($9.95, #2541)
Date of Issue: June 16, 1991
Place of Issue: Sacramento, California
Designer: Terry McCaffrey
Printing: Offset/Intaglio
The new stamp for the basic domestic overnight delivery rate is one of several linked to the '92 Olympic Games.

Antarctic Treaty (50¢, #C130)
Date of Issue: June 21, 1991
Place of Issue: Washington, DC
Designer: Howard Koslow
Printing: Gravure
Signed in 1961, the Antarctic Treaty supported peaceful exploration and scientific cooperation in the region.

Kestral (1¢, #2481)
Date of Issue: June 22, 1991
Place of Issue: Aurora, Colorado
Designer: Michael Matherly
Printing: Gravure
This new definitive stamp depicts a male American kestral (also called a "sparrow hawk") sitting on a cedar branch.

Bluebird (3¢, #2482)
Date of Issue: June 22, 1991
Place of Issue: Aurora, Colorado
Designer: Michael Matherly
Printing: Gravure
This stamp, a departure from recent definitive issues, features a male Eastern bluebird on a crabapple branch.

Cardinal (30¢, #2489)
Date of Issue: June 22, 1991
Place of Issue: Aurora, Colorado
Designer: Robert Giusti
Printing: Gravure
The closeup of a male cardinal graces a stamp whose denomination covers the postcard rate to Canada and Mexico.

Liberty Torch (29¢, #2531A-31Ab booklet single, pane of 18)
Date of Issue: June 25, 1991
Place of Issue: New York, New York
Designer: Harry Zelenko
Printing: Gravure
Easy-to-use self-adhesive stamps are playing an expanding role in providing convenience for the mailing public.

Priority Mail ($2.90, #2540)
Date of Issue: July 7, 1991
Place of Issue: San Diego, California
Designer: Terry McCaffrey
Printing: Offset/Intaglio
This second-ever Priority Mail issue is the fifth issue featuring the American bald eagle on a special rate stamp.

Fishing Boat (19¢, #2529)
Date of Issue: August 8, 1991
Place of Issue: Washington, DC
Designer: Pierre Mion
Printing: Gravure
This stamp, with its idyllic setting, signals a departure from the one-color Transportation Series.

Express Mail ($14, #2542)
Date of Issue: August 31, 1991
Place of Issue: Baltimore, Maryland
Designer: Tim Knepp
Printing: Offset/Intaglio
This issue, continuing the eagle-with-Olympic-rings theme, covers the basic international Express Mail rate.

Design not available at press time.

Stars & Stripes (23¢, #2607)
Date of Issue: September 26, 1991
Place of Issue: Washington, DC
Designer: Terry McCaffrey
Printing: Gravure
This new base-rate stamp for First-Class presort mailings brings to five the 1991 issues carrying a flag theme.

Design not available at press time.

USPS/Olympic Logo ($1, #2539)
Date of Issue: September 29, 1991
Place of Issue: Orlando, Florida
Designer: Terry McCaffrey
Printing: Offset/Intaglio
This "commemorative-sized" definitive issue calls attention to Postal Service sponsorship of the 1992 Olympic Games.

Design not available at press time.

America (50¢, #C131)
Date of Issue: October 12, 1991
Place of Issue: Anchorage, Alaska
Designer: Richard Schlecht
Printing: Gravure
This issue focuses on the population of early North America via the Bering Land Bridge.

Design not available at press time.

Eagle & Shield (nondenominated, #2604)
Date of Issue: Not available
Place of Issue: Not available
Designer: Chris Calle
Printing: Gravure
This coil stamp, to cover the nonprofit bulk base rate, is similar to a 25-cent self-adhesive stamp issued in 1989.

Wonderful Keepsakes of Stamp Ceremonies

- Programs feature biography or background of stamp subject
- Complete with stamp, postal card or other philatelic item issued

Some of the best moments in philatelic history happen when the Postal Service dedicates the issuance of a new stamp at one of its exciting stamp ceremonies. Often held at well-known sites such as Disney World, the Baseball Hall of Fame or Notre Dame, First Day Ceremonies are attended by a wide variety of celebrities.

Share the Moment

You can share the excitement of ceremonies in 1991 and the future! Subscribe to the First Day Ceremony Program now. The price for these *limited-edition* programs averages approximately $6.00 per program, available by subscription service only.

Subscription Benefits

Colorful, top-quality programs include a list of participants in the ceremonies, a biography or background on the stamp subject *and* the actual stamp, postal card, stamped envelope or aerogramme affixed and postmarked right in the program.

For More Information

To learn more about the First Day Ceremony Program subscription service, use the postage-paid request card in this book or write to:

USPS GUIDE
CEREMONY PROGRAMS
SUBSCRIPTION SERVICE
PHILATELIC SALES DIVISION
UNITED STATES POSTAL SERVICE
BOX 449980
KANSAS CITY MO 64144-9980

Airmail and Special Delivery Stamps

1918-1938

C1 C2 C3 C4 C5

C6 C7 C10

C11

C12

C13 C14

C15

C18

C21

C23

	Issues of 1918, Perf. 11	Un	U	PB	#	FDC	Q
	For prepayment of postage on all mailable matter sent by airmail. All unwatermarked.						
C1	6¢ Curtiss Jenny, Dec. 10	62.50	26.00	750.00	(6)	*17,500.00*	3,395,854
	Double transfer	87.50	40.00				
C2	16¢ Curtiss Jenny, July 11	90.00	27.50	1,250.00	(6)	*22,500.00*	3,793,887
C3	24¢ Curtiss Jenny, May 13	85.00	32.50	1,600.00	(12)	*27,500.00*	2,134,888
a	Center Inverted	*135,000.00*					
	Issues of 1923						
C4	8¢ Airplane Radiator and Wooden Propeller, Aug. 15	25.00	12.00	275.00	(6)	300.00	6,414,576
C5	16¢ Air Service Emblem, Aug. 17	85.00	30.00	2,150.00	(6)	500.00	5,309,275
C6	24¢ De Havilland Biplane, Aug. 21	90.00	24.00	2,600.00	(6)	600.00	5,285,775
	Issues of 1926-27						
C7	10¢ Map of U.S. and Two Mail Planes, Feb. 13, 1926	2.25	.25	40.00	(6)	55.00	42,092,800
	Double transfer	5.00	1.00				
C8	15¢ olive brown (C7), Sept. 18, 1926	2.75	1.90	45.00	(6)	75.00	15,597,307
C9	20¢ yellow green (C7), Jan. 25, 1927	8.00	1.65	95.00	(6)	100.00	17,616,350
	Issue of 1927-28						
C10	10¢ Lindbergh's "Spirit of St. Louis," June 18, 1927	6.75	1.65	140.00	(6)	20.00	20,379,179
a	Booklet pane of 3, May 26, 1928	90.00	*50.00*			825.00	
	Issue of 1928						
C11	5¢ Beacon on Rocky Mountains, July 25	3.50	.40	45.00	(6)	50.00	106,887,675
	Recut frame line at left	6.00	1.00				
	Issues of 1930						
C12	5¢ Winged Globe, Feb. 10	8.00	.25	160.00	(6)	10.00	97,641,200
a	Horizontal pair, imperf. between	*4,500.00*					
	Graf Zeppelin Issue, Apr. 19						
C13	65¢ Zeppelin over Atlantic Ocean	275.00	200.00	2,250.00	(6)	1,500.00	93,536
C14	$1.30 Zeppelin Between Continents	625.00	400.00	5,750.00	(6)	1,100.00	72,428
C15	$2.60 Zeppelin Passing Globe	950.00	600.00	8,500.00	(6)	1,300.00	61,296
	Issues of 1931-32, Perf. 10½ x 11						
C16	5¢ violet (C12), Aug. 19, 1931	4.75	.30	75.00	(4)	175.00	57,340,050
C17	8¢ olive bistre (C12), Sept. 26, 1932	1.90	.20	30.00	(4)	15.00	76,648,803
	Issue of 1933, Century of Progress Issue, Oct. 2, Perf. 11						
C18	50¢ Zeppelin, Federal Building at Chicago Exposition and Hangar at Friedrichshafen	80.00	65.00	800.00	(6)	200.00	324,070
	Beginning with #C19, unused values are for never-hinged stamps.						
	Issue of 1934, Perf. 10½ x 11						
C19	6¢ dull orange (C12), June 30	2.25	.15	27.50	(4)	*175.00*	302,205,100
	Issues of 1935-37, Trans-Pacific Issue, Perf. 11						
C20	25¢ China Clipper over Pacific, Nov. 22, 1935	1.10	.75	22.50	(6)	20.00	10,205,400
C21	20¢ China Clipper over Pacific, Feb. 15, 1937	8.50	1.25	110.00	(6)	20.00	12,794,600
C22	50¢ carmine (C21), Feb. 15, 1937	8.00	4.00	130.00	(6)	20.00	9,285,300
	Issue of 1938						
C23	6¢ Eagle Holding Shield, Olive Branch and Arrows, May 14	.40	.15	8.00	(4)	15.00	349,946,500
a	Vertical pair, imperf. horizontally	275.00					
b	Horizontal pair, imperf. vertically	*10,000.00*					
c	6¢ ultramarine and carmine	150.00					

	Issue of 1939	Un	U	PB\LP	#	FDC	Q
	Trans-Atlantic Issue, May 16, Perf. 11						
C24	30¢ Winged Globe	7.50	1.00	175.00	(6)	45.00	19,768,150
	Issues of 1941-44, Perf. 11 x 10½						
C25	6¢ Twin-Motor Transport, June 25, 1941	.15	.15	.80	(4)	2.25	4,476,527,700
a	Booklet pane of 3, Mar. 18, 1943	4.00	*1.00*			25.00	
	Singles of #C25a are imperf. at sides or imperf. at sides and bottom.						
b	Horizontal pair, imperf. between	*1,500.00*					
C26	8¢ olive green (C25), Mar. 21, 1944	.16	.15	1.40	(4)	3.75	1,744,878,650
C27	10¢ violet (C25), Aug. 15, 1941	1.10	.20	9.00	(4)	8.00	67,117,400
C28	15¢ brown carmine (C25), Aug. 19, 1941	2.25	.35	12.00	(4)	10.00	78,434,800
C29	20¢ bright green (C25), Aug. 27, 1941	1.75	.30	11.00	(4)	12.50	42,359,850
C30	30¢ blue (C25), Sept. 25, 1941	2.00	.30	12.00	(4)	20.00	59,880,850
C31	50¢ orange (C25), Oct. 29, 1941	10.00	3.75	75.00	(4)	40.00	11,160,600
	Issue of 1946						
C32	5¢ DC-4 Skymaster, Sept. 25	.15	.15	.50	(4)	2.00	864,753,100
	Issues of 1947, Perf. 10½ x 11						
C33	5¢ DC-4 Skymaster, Mar. 26	.15	.15	.50	(4)	2.00	971,903,700
	Perf. 11 x 10½						
C34	10¢ Pan American Union Building, Washington, D.C. and Martin 2-0-2, Aug. 30	.25	.15	1.25	(4)	2.00	207,976,550
C35	15¢ Statue of Liberty, N.Y. Skyline and Lockheed Constellation, Aug. 20	.35	.15	2.00	(4)	2.00	756,186,350
a	Horizontal pair, imperf. between	*1,500.00*					
b	Dry printing	.55	.15				
C36	25¢ San Francisco-Oakland Bay Bridge and Boeing Stratocruiser, July 30	.85	.15	4.25	(4)	2.75	132,956,100
	Issues of 1948, Coil Stamp, Perf. 10 Horizontally						
C37	5¢ carmine (C33), Jan. 15	.80	.75	8.50	(2)	2.00	
	Perf. 11 x 10½						
C38	5¢ New York City, July 31	.15	.15	6.50	(4)	1.75	38,449,100
	Issues of 1949, Perf. 10½ x 11						
C39	6¢ carmine (C33), Jan. 18	.15	.15	.60	(4)	1.50	5,070,095,200
a	Booklet pane of 6, Nov. 18	9.50	*4.00*			9.00	
b	Dry printing	.50	.15				
c	As "a," dry printing	15.00	—				
	Perf. 11 x 10½						
C40	6¢ Alexandria, Virginia, May 11	.15	.15	.60	(4)	1.25	75,085,000
	Coil Stamp, Perf. 10 Horizontally						
C41	6¢ carmine (C33), Aug. 25	2.75	.15	12.00	(2)	1.25	
	Universal Postal Union Issue, Perf. 11 x 10½						
C42	10¢ Post Office Dept. Bldg., Nov. 18	.20	.18	1.50	(4)	1.75	21,061,300
C43	15¢ Globe and Doves Carrying Messages, Oct. 7	.30	.25	1.50	(4)	2.25	36,613,100
C44	25¢ Boeing Stratocruiser and Globe, Nov. 30	.50	.40	5.75	(4)	3.00	16,217,100
C45	6¢ Wright Brothers, Dec. 17	.15	.15	.65	(4)	3.50	80,405,000
	Issue of 1952						
C46	80¢ Diamond Head, Honolulu, Hawaii, Mar. 26	6.00	1.00	30.00	(4)	17.50	18,876,800
	Issue of 1953						
C47	6¢ Powered Flight, May 29	.15	.15	.50	(4)	1.50	78,415,000

C24

C25

C32

C33

C34

C35

C36

C38

C40

C42

C43

C44

C45

C46

C47

1954-1964

C48

C49

C51

C53

C54

C55

C56

C57

C58

C59

C62

C63

C64

C66

C67

C68

C69

	Issue of 1954, Perf. 11 x 10½	Un	U	PB/LP	#	FDC	Q
C48	4¢ Eagle in Flight, Sept. 3	.15	.15	2.00	(4)	.75	50,483,977
	Issue of 1957						
C49	6¢ Air Force, Aug. 1	.15	.15	.75	(4)	1.75	63,185,000
	Issues of 1958						
C50	5¢ rose red (C48), July 31	.15	.15	2.00	(4)	.80	72,480,000
	Perf. 10½ x 11						
C51	7¢ Jet Airliner, July 31	.15	.15	.60	(4)	.75	1,326,960,000
a	Booklet pane of 6	11.00	*6.00*			9.50	
	Coil Stamp, Perf. 10 Horizontally						
C52	7¢ blue (C51), July 31	2.25	.15	14.00	(2)	.90	157,035,000
	Issues of 1959, Perf. 11 x 10½						
C53	7¢ Alaska Statehood, Jan. 3	.15	.15	.75	(4)	.75	90,055,200
	Perf. 11						
C54	7¢ Balloon Jupiter, Aug. 17	.15	.15	.75	(4)	1.10	79,290,000
	Perf. 11 x 10½						
C55	7¢ Hawaii Statehood, Aug. 21	.15	.15	.75	(4)	1.00	84,815,000
	Perf. 11						
C56	10¢ Pan American Games, Aug. 27	.24	.24	1.75	(4)	.90	38,770,000
	Issues of 1959-60						
C57	10¢ Liberty Bell, June 10, 1960	1.40	.70	7.25	(4)	1.25	39,960,000
C58	15¢ Statue of Liberty, Nov. 20, 1959	.35	.15	1.50	(4)	1.25	98,160,000
C59	25¢ Abraham Lincoln, Apr. 22, 1960	.48	.15	2.00	(4)	1.75	
a	Tagged, Dec. 29, 1966	.50	.20	2.25	(4)	12.50	
	Issues of 1960, Perf. 10½ x 11						
C60	7¢ Jet Airliner, Aug. 12	.15	.15	.60	(4)	.75	1,289,460,000
	Pair with full horizontal gutter between	—					
a	Booklet pane of 6, Aug. 19	14.50	*7.00*			9.50	
	Coil Stamp, Perf. 10 Horizontally						
C61	7¢ carmine (C60), Oct. 22	4.00	.25	32.50	(2)	1.00	87,140,000
	Issues of 1961-67, Perf. 11						
C62	13¢ Liberty Bell, June 28, 1961	.40	.15	1.65	(4)	.80	
a	Tagged, Feb. 15, 1967	.70	.50			10.00	
C63	15¢ Statue of Liberty, Jan. 13, 1961	.30	.15	1.20	(4)	1.00	
a	Tagged, Jan. 11, 1967	.32	.15			12.50	
b	As "a," hor. pair, imperf. vertically *15,000.00*						
	#C63 has a gutter between the two parts of the design; #C58 does not.						
	Issues of 1962-65, Perf. 10½ x 11						
C64	8¢ Jetliner over Capitol, Dec. 5, 1962	.15	.15	.70	(4)	.75	
a	Tagged, Aug. 1, 1963	.18	.15	.75	(4)	1.00	
b	Bklt. pane of 5 + label, Dec. 5, 1962	4.75	*2.50*			2.75	
c	As "b," tagged, 1964	1.75	*.50*			2.50	
	Coil Stamp, Perf. 10 Horizontally						
C65	8¢ carmine (C64), Dec. 5, 1962	.40	.15	4.25	(2)	.80	
a	Tagged, Jan. 14, 1965	.35	.15			—	
	Issue of 1963, Perf. 11						
C66	15¢ Montgomery Blair, May 3	.60	.55	3.25	(4)	1.10	42,245,000
	Issues of 1963-67, Perf. 11 x 10½						
C67	6¢ Bald Eagle, July 12, 1963	.15	.15	1.80	(4)	.75	
a	Tagged, Feb. 15, 1967	2.75	.50			12.50	
	1963 continued, Perf. 11						
C68	8¢ Amelia Earhart, July 24	.20	.15	1.25	(4)	1.75	63,890,000
	Issue of 1964						
C69	8¢ Robert H. Goddard, Oct. 5	.48	.15	2.00	(4)	1.75	62,255,000

	Issues of 1967, Perf. 11	Un	U	PB/LP	#	FDC	Q
C70	8¢ Alaska Purchase, Mar. 30	.24	.15	1.50	(4)	.75	55,710,000
C71	20¢ "Columbia Jays," by Audubon, Apr. 26 (see also #1241)	.80	.15	3.75	(4)	2.00	165,430,000
	Issues of 1968, Perf. 11 x 10½						
C72	10¢ 50-Star Runway, Jan. 5	.20	.15	1.00	(4)	.75	
b	Booklet pane of 8	2.00	.75			2.50	
c	Booklet pane of 5 + label, Jan. 6	3.75	.75			115.00	
	Coil Stamp, Perf. 10 Vertically						
C73	10¢ carmine (C72), Jan. 5	.32	.05	1.70	(2)	.75	
a	Imperf. pair	*600.00*					
	Perf. 11						
C74	10¢ U.S. Air Mail Service, May 15	.25	.15	2.75	(4)	1.50	
a	Red (tail stripe) omitted		—				
C75	20¢ USA and Jet, Nov. 22	.48	.15	2.25	(4)	1.10	
	Issue of 1969						
C76	10¢ Moon Landing, Sept. 9	.20	.15	.95	(4)	3.50	152,364,800
a	Rose red omitted	*500.00*					
	Issues of 1971-73, Perf. 10½ x 11, 11 x 10½						
C77	9¢ Plane, May 15, 1971	.18	.15	.80	(4)	.75	
C78	11¢ Silhouette of Jet, May 7, 1971	.20	.15	.90	(4)	.75	
a	Booklet pane of 4 + 2 labels	1.25	*.75*			1.75	
C79	13¢ Winged Airmail Envelope, Nov. 16, 1973	.22	.15	1.05	(4)	.75	
a	Booklet pane of 5 + label, Dec. 27, 1973	1.35	*.75*			1.75	
b	Untagged (Bureau precanceled)		.28				
	Perf. 11						
C80	17¢ Statue of Liberty, July 13, 1971	.35	.15	1.70	(4)	.75	
	Perf. 11 x 10½						
C81	21¢ USA and Jet, May 21, 1971	.40	.15	1.70	(4)	.75	
	Coil Stamps, Perf. 10 Vertically						
C82	11¢ carmine (C78), May 7, 1971	.25	.15	.80	(2)	.75	
a	Imperf. pair	*250.00*		*300.00*			
C83	13¢ carmine (C79), Dec. 27, 1973	.22	.15	1.00	(2)	.50	
a	Imperf. pair	125.00		160.00	(2)		
	Issues of 1972, National Parks Centennial Issue, May 3, Perf. 11 (see also #1448-54)						
C84	11¢ Kii Statue and Temple at City of Refuge Historical National Park, Honaunau, Hawaii	.20	.15	.95	(4)	.75	78,210,000
a	Blue and green omitted	*1,400.00*					
	Olympic Games Issue, Aug. 17, Perf. 11 x 10½ (see also #1460-62)						
C85	11¢ Skiers and Olympic Rings	.22	.15	2.25	(10)	.75	96,240,000
	Issue of 1973, Progress in Electronics Issue, July 10, Perf. 11 (see also #1500-02)						
C86	11¢ DeForest Audions	.22	.15	.95	(4)	.75	58,705,000
a	Vermilion and green omitted	*2,250.00*					
	Issues of 1974						
C87	18¢ Statue of Liberty, Jan. 11	.40	.25	1.70	(4)	.75	
C88	26¢ Mount Rushmore National Memorial, Jan. 2	.48	.15	2.00	(4)	.85	
	Issues of 1976						
C89	25¢ Plane and Globes, Jan. 2	.45	.15	2.10	(4)	.85	
C90	31¢ Plane, Globes and Flag, Jan. 2	.55	.15	2.30	(4)	.85	

C70

C71

C72

C74

C75

C76

C77

C78

C79

C80

C81

C84

C85

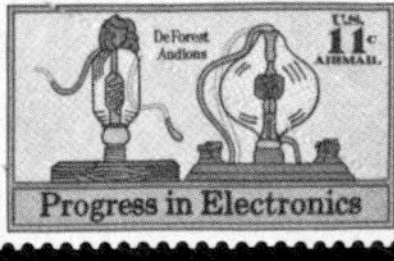
C86

C87

C88

C89

C90

C97

C98

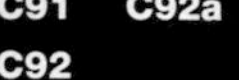

C91 C92a C93 C94a C95 C96a

C92 C94 C96

C99 C100

C105 C106 C108a

C107 C108

C101 C102 C104a

C103 C104

C113

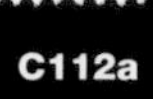

C110 C112a

C112

C114

	Issues of 1978	Un	U	PB	#	FDC	Q
	Wright Brothers Issue, Sept. 23, Perf. 11						
C91	31¢ Orville and Wilbur Wright, Flyer A	.65	.30			2.00	157,445,000
C92	31¢ Wright Brothers, Flyer A and Shed	.65	.30			2.00	157,445,000
a	Attached pair, #C91-C92	1.30	.85	3.00	(4)	2.35	
b	As "a," ultramarine and black omitted	*1,250.00*					
d	As "a," black, yellow, magenta, blue and brown omitted	*2,000.00*					
	Issues of 1979, Octave Chanute Issue, Mar. 29						
C93	21¢ Chanute and Biplane Hang-Glider	.70	.32			1.00	29,012,500
C94	21¢ Biplane Hang-Glider and Chanute	.70	.32			1.00	29,012,500
a	Attached pair, #C93-C94	1.40	.95	3.50	(4)	1.75	
b	As "a," ultramarine and black omitted	*3,500.00*					
	Wiley Post Issue, Nov. 20						
C95	25¢ Wiley Post and "Winnie Mae"	1.10	.35			1.00	32,005,000
C96	25¢ NR-105-W, Post in Pressurized Suit and Portrait	1.10	.35			1.00	32,005,000
a	Attached pair, #C95-C96	2.25	.95	9.50	(4)	2.00	
	Olympic Summer Games Issue, Nov. 1 (see also #1790-94)						
C97	31¢ High Jumper	.65	.30	9.50	(12)	1.15	47,200,000
	Issues of 1980-82						
C98	40¢ Philip Mazzei, Oct. 13, 1980	.70	.15	8.75	(12)	1.35	80,935,000
a	Perf. 10½ x 11, 1982	3.00	—				
b	Imperf. pair	*3,250.00*					
C99	28¢ Blanche Stuart Scott, Dec. 30, 1980	.55	.15	6.75	(12)	1.10	20,190,000
C100	35¢ Glenn Curtiss, Dec. 30, 1980	.60	.15	8.00	(12)	1.25	22,945,000
	Issues of 1983, Olympic Summer Games Issue, June 17, Perf. 11 (see also #2048-51, 2082-85)						
C101	28¢ Gymnast	.60	.28			1.10	42,893,750
C102	28¢ Hurdler	.60	.28			1.10	42,893,750
C103	28¢ Basketball Player	.60	.28			1.10	42,893,750
C104	28¢ Soccer Player	.60	.28	3.50	(4)	1.10	42,893,750
a	Block of 4, #C101-C104	2.50	1.75			3.75	
b	As "a," imperf. vertically	—					
	Olympic Summer Games Issue, Apr. 8 (see also #2048-51 and 2082-85)						
C105	40¢ Shotputter	.90	.40			1.35	66,573,750
C106	40¢ Gymnast	.90	.40			1.35	66,573,750
C107	40¢ Swimmer	.90	.40			1.35	66,573,750
C108	40¢ Weightlifter	.90	.40	5.25	(4)	1.35	66,573,750
a	Block of 4, #C105-C108	3.60	2.00			5.00	
b	as "a," imperf.	*1,350.00*					
d	As "a," perf. 11 x 10½	4.25	—	6.50			
	Olympic Summer Games Issue, Nov. 4 (see also #2048-51 and 2082-85)						
C109	35¢ Fencer	.90	.35			1.25	42,587,500
C110	35¢ Bicyclist	.90	.35			1.25	42,587,500
C111	35¢ Volleyball Players	.90	.35			1.25	42,587,5
C112	35¢ Pole Vaulter	.90	.35	3.60	(4)	1.25	42,58
a	Block of 4, #C109-C112	3.60	1.85			4.50	
	Issues of 1985						
C113	33¢ Alfred V. Verville, Feb. 13	.60	.20	3.00	(4)	1.25	[illegible]
a	Imperf. pair	*1,100.00*					
C114	39¢ Lawrence & Elmer Sperry, Feb. 13	.70	.20	3.25	(4)	1.35	
a	Imperf, pair	*1,500.00*					

	1985 continued, Perf. 11	Un	U	PB	#	FDC	Q
C115	44¢ Transpacific Airmail, Feb. 15	.80	.20	3.75	(4)	1.35	209,025,000
a	Imperf. pair	*1,100.00*					
C116	44¢ Junipero Serra, Aug. 22	.80	.20	5.00	(4)	1.35	164,350,000
a	Imperf. pair	—					
	Issues of 1988						
C117	44¢ New Sweden, Mar. 29	1.25	.20	5.25	(4)	1.35	136,900,000
C118	45¢ Samuel P. Langley, May 14	.80	.20	3.75	(4)	1.40	390,600,000
C119	36¢ Igor Sikorsky, June 23	.65	.20	3.10	(4)	1.30	174,300,000
	Issues of 1989, Perf. 11½ x 11						
C120	45¢ French Revolution, July 14	.80	.22	4.50	(4)	1.40	38,922,000
	America/PUAS Issue, Oct. 12, Perf. 11						
C121	45¢ Southeast Carved Wood Figure, Key Marco Cat (A.D. 700-1450), Emblem of the Postal Union of the Americas and Spain (see also #2426)	.80	.22	4.50	(4)	1.40	39,325,000
	20th UPU Congress Issues, Future Mail Transportation, Nov. 28						
C122	45¢ Hypersonic Airliner	.90	.30			1.00	26,590,000
C123	45¢ Air-Cushion Vehicle	.90	.30			1.00	26,590,000
C124	45¢ Surface Rover	.90	.30			1.00	26,590,000
C125	45¢ Shuttle	.90	.30			1.00	26,590,000
a	Block of 4, #C122-C125	3.60	2.25	4.50	(4)	3.00	
b	As "a," light blue omitted	*3,000.00*					
	Souvenir Sheet, Nov. 24, Imperf.						
C126	Designs of #C122-C125	3.60	2.25			3.00	2,182,400
	1990 Issue, American/PUAS Issue, Oct. 12 (see also #2512)						
C127	45¢ Tropical Coast	.90	.22	4.50	(4)	1.00	
	Airmail Special Delivery Stamps						
	Issue of 1934						
CE1	16¢ Great Seal of the United States, Aug. 30	.65	.85	16.00	(6)	25.00	
	For imperforate variety see #771.						
	Issue of 1936						
CE2	16¢ carmine and blue (CE1), Feb. 10	.40	.25	8.50	(4)	17.50	
a	Horizontal pair, imperf. vertically	*3,750.00*					

Shuttle May Bring Future Mail

Mail delivery by space shuttle may not be as farfetched as it seems. The U.S. Postal Service has consistently used the quickest, most reliable means of transportation available for delivering mail. In the early 1860s, that meant the Pony Express—relays of riders on fast ponies. Today, mail is carried by supersonic jets. In anticipation of mail dis-
ibution methods to come, the U.S. Postal
vice's 1989 issues included four potential
s of future mail delivery. In addition
pace shuttle (#C125), they are the
ic airliner (#C122), the air-cushion
C123) and—for those living on
s—the surface rover (#C124).

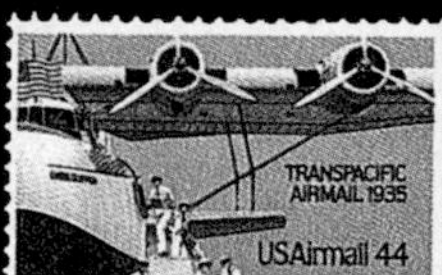

C115

Junipero Serra USAirmail 44

C116

C117

C118

C119

C120

C121

C122 C123 C125a

C124 C125

20th Universal Postal Congress

A glimpse at several potential mail delivery methods of the future is the theme of these four stamps issued by the U.S. in commemoration of the convening of the 20th Universal Postal Congress in Washington, D.C. from November 13 through December 14, 1989. The United States, as host nation to the Congress for the first time in ninety-two years, welcomed more than 1,000 delegates from most of the member nations of the Universal Postal Union to the major international event.

©USPS 1989

C126

C127

CE1

E1

E3

E4

E6

E7

E12

E13

E14

E17

E18

E20

E21

E22

E23

	Special Delivery Stamps	Un	U	PB	#	FDC
	Issue of 1885, Oct. 1, Unwmkd., Perf. 12					
E1	10¢ Messenger Running	175.00	27.50	*12,000.00*	(8)	*8,000.00*
	Issue of 1888, Sept. 6					
E2	10¢ blue Messenger Running (E3)	175.00	5.00	*12,000.00*	(8)	
	Issue of 1893, Jan. 24					
	10¢ Messenger Running	110.00	11.00	*7,250.00*	(8)	
	Issue of 1894, Oct. 10, Line under "Ten Cents"					
	10¢ Messenger Running	450.00	14.00	*14,500.00*	(6)	

	Issue of 1895, Aug. 16, Wmkd. (191)	Un	U	PB	#	FDC
E5	10¢ blue Messenger Running (E4)	85.00	1.90	*4,500.00*	(6)	
	Double transfer	—	15.00			
	Line of color through "POSTAL DELIVERY"	125.00	9.00			
	Issue of 1902, Dec. 9					
E6	10¢ Messenger on Bicycle	52.50	1.90	*3,000.00*	(6)	
	Damaged transfer under "N" of "CENTS"	85.00	3.00			
	Issue of 1908, Dec. 12					
E7	10¢ Mercury Helmet and Olive Branch	45.00	24.00	925.00	(6)	
	Issue of 1911, Jan., Wmkd. (190)					
E8	10¢ ultramarine Messenger on Bicycle (E6)	55.00	2.50	*2,750.00*	(6)	
	Top frame line missing	72.50	3.25			
	Issue of 1914, Sept., Perf. 10					
E9	10¢ ultramarine Messenger on Bicycle (E6)	110.00	3.00	*5,000.00*	(6)	
	Issue of 1916, Oct. 19, Unwmkd.					
E10	10¢ ultramarine Messenger on Bicycle (E6)	200.00	14.00	6,250.00	(6)	
	Issue of 1917, May 2, Perf. 11					
E11	10¢ ultramarine Messenger on Bicycle (E6)	10.00	.25	850.00	(6)	
c	Blue	20.00	.60			
d	Perf. 10 at left	—				
	Issue of 1922, July 12					
E12	10¢ Postman and Motorcycle	18.00	.15	275.00	(6)	400.00
a	10¢ deep ultramarine	25.00	.20			
	Double transfer	35.00	1.00			
	Issues of 1925					
E13	15¢ Postman and Motorcycle, Apr. 11	15.00	.50	150.00	(6)	225.00
E14	20¢ Post Office Truck, Apr. 25	1.65	.85	25.00	(6)	90.00
	Issue of 1927, Nov. 29, Perf. 11 x 10½					
E15	10¢ gray violet Postman and Motorcycle (E12)	.60	.15	4.00	(4)	90.00
c	Horizontal pair, imperf. between	275.00				
	Cracked plate	35.00				
	Issue of 1931, Aug. 13					
E16	15¢ orange Postman and Motorcycle (E13)	.70	.15	3.50	(4)	125.00
	Beginning with #E17, unused values are for never-hinged stamps.					
	Issues of 1944, Oct. 30					
E17	13¢ Postman and Motorcycle	.60	.15	3.00	(4)	12.00
E18	17¢ Postman and Motorcycle	2.75	1.25	22.50	(4)	12.00
	Issue of 1951, Nov. 30					
E19	20¢ black Post Office Truck (E14)	1.20	.15	5.00	(4)	5.00
	Issues of 1954-57					
E20	20¢ Delivery of Letter, Oct. 13, 1954	.40	.15	1.90	(4)	3[illegible]
E21	30¢ Delivery of Letter, Sept. 3, 1957	.48	.15	2.40	(4)	[illegible]
	Issues of 1969-71, Perf. 11					
E22	45¢ Arrows, Nov. 21, 1969	1.10	.15	5.50	[illegible]	[illegible]
E23	60¢ Arrows, May 10, 1971	.85	.15	4.2[illegible]	[illegible]	[illegible]

Registration, Certified Mail and Postage Due Stamps

1879-1959

F1

FA1

J2

J19

J25

J33

J69

J78

J88

J98

J101

Registration Stamp
Issued for the prepayment of registry; not usable for postage. Sale discontinued May 28, 1913.

Issues of 1911, Wmkd. (190), Perf. 12

		Un	U	PB	#	FDC	Q
F1	10¢ Bald Eagle, Dec. 11	55.00	2.25	*1,350.00*	(6)	*8,000.00*	

Certified Mail Stamp
For use on First-Class mail for which no indemnity value was claimed, but for which proof of mailing and proof of delivery were available at less cost than registered mail.

Issues of 1955, Perf. 10½ x 11

		Un	U	PB	#	FDC	Q
FA1	15¢ Letter Carrier, June 6	.28	.20	4.00	(4)	3.25	54,460,300

Postage Due Stamps For affixing by a postal clerk to any mail to denote amount to be collected from addressee because of insufficient prepayment of postage.

Issues of 1879, Printed by American Bank Note Co., Design of J2, Perf. 12, Unwmkd.

		Un	U
J1	1¢ brown	30.00	5.00
J2	2¢ Figure of Value	200.00	4.00
J3	3¢ brown	25.00	2.50
J4	5¢ brown	300.00	25.00
J5	10¢ brown, Sept. 19	350.00	12.50
a	Imperf. pair	*1,600.00*	
J6	30¢ brown, Sept. 19	175.00	25.00
J7	50¢ brown, Sept. 19	225.00	30.00
	Special Printing, Soft, Porous Paper		
J8	1¢ deep brown	*5,750.00*	—
J9	2¢ deep brown	*3,750.00*	—
J10	3¢ deep brown	*3,500.00*	
J11	5¢ deep brown	*3,000.00*	—
J12	10¢ deep brown	*1,850.00*	—
J13	30¢ deep brown	*1,850.00*	—
J14	50¢ deep brown	*2,000.00*	—
	Issues of 1884, Design of J19		
J15	1¢ red brown	30.00	2.50
J16	2¢ red brown	37.50	2.50
J17	3¢ red brown	500.00	100.00
J18	5¢ red brown	250.00	12.50
J19	10¢ Figure of Value	225.00	7.00
J20	30¢ red brown	110.00	22.50
J21	50¢ red brown	1,000.00	125.00
	Issues of 1891, Design of J25		
J22	1¢ bright claret	12.50	.50
a	Imperf. pair	450.00	
J23	2¢ bright claret	15.00	.45
a	Imperf. pair	450.00	
J24	3¢ bright claret	32.50	4.00
a	Imperf. pair	450.00	
J25	5¢ Figure of Value	35.00	4.00
a	Imperf. pair	450.00	
J26	10¢ bright claret	70.00	10.00
a	Imperf. pair	450.00	
J27	30¢ bright claret	250.00	85.00
a	Imperf. pair	525.00	
J28	50¢ bright claret	275.00	85.00
a	Imperf. pair	525.00	
	Issues of 1894, Printed by the Bureau of Engraving and Printing, Design of J33, Perf. 12		
J29	1¢ vermilion	575.00	100.00
J30	2¢ vermilion	250.00	50.00

	Issues of 1894-95, Design of J33, Perf. 12, Unwmkd.	Un	U	PB	#
J31	1¢ deep claret, Aug. 14, 1894	20.00	3.00	375.00	(6)
a	Imperf. pair	225.00			
J32	2¢ deep claret, July 20, 1894	17.50	1.75	325.00	(6)
J33	3¢ Figure of Value, Apr. 27, 1895	75.00	20.00	850.00	(6)
J34	5¢ deep claret, Apr. 27, 1895	100.00	22.50	950.00	(6)
J35	10¢ deep rose, Sept. 24, 1894	100.00	17.50	950.00	(6)
J36	30¢ deep claret, Apr. 27, 1895	225.00	50.00	2,100.00	(6)
b	30¢ pale rose	210.00	45.00		
J37	50¢ deep claret, Apr. 27, 1895	500.00	150.00	5,000.00	(6)
a	50¢ pale rose	450.00	135.00		
	Issues of 1895-97, Design of J33, Wmkd. (191)				
J38	1¢ deep claret, Aug. 29, 1895	5.00	.30	190.00	(6)
J39	2¢ deep claret, Sept. 14, 1895	5.00	.20	190.00	(6)
J40	3¢ deep claret, Oct. 30, 1895	35.00	1.00	425.00	(6)
J41	5¢ deep claret, Oct. 15, 1895	37.50	1.00	450.00	(6)
J42	10¢ deep claret, Sept. 14, 1895	40.00	2.00	550.00	(6)
J43	30¢ deep claret, Aug. 21, 1897	300.00	25.00	3,750.00	(6)
J44	50¢ deep claret, Mar. 17, 1896	190.00	20.00	2,250.00	(6)
	Issues of 1910-12, Design of J33, Wmkd. (190)				
J45	1¢ deep claret, Aug. 30, 1910	20.00	2.00	400.00	(6)
a	1¢ rose carmine	17.50	1.75		
J46	2¢ deep claret, Nov. 25, 1910	20.00	.30	350.00	(6)
a	2¢ rose carmine	17.50	.30		
J47	3¢ deep claret, Aug. 31, 1910	350.00	17.50	3,850.00	(6)
J48	5¢ deep claret, Aug. 31, 1910	60.00	3.50	600.00	(6)
a	5¢ rose carmine	—	—		
J49	10¢ deep claret, Aug. 31, 1910	75.00	7.50	1,150.00	(6)
J50	50¢ deep claret, Sept. 23, 1912	600.00	75.00	7,500.00	(6)
	Issues of 1914, Design of J33, Perf. 10				
J52	1¢ carmine lake	40.00	7.50	550.00	(6)
J53	2¢ carmine lake	32.50	.20	350.00	(6)
J54	3¢ carmine lake	425.00	20.00	4,500.00	(6)
J55	5¢ carmine lake	25.00	1.50	285.00	(6)
	5¢ deep claret	—	—		
J56	10¢ carmine lake	40.00	1.00	600.00	(6)
J57	30¢ carmine lake	140.00	12.00	2,100.00	(6)
J58	50¢ carmine lake	*5,500.00*	375.00	*40,000.00*	(6)
	Issues of 1916, Design of J33, Unwmkd.				
J59	1¢ rose	1,100.00	175.00	8,750.00	(6)
	Experimental Bureau precancel, New Orleans		*125.00*		
J60	2¢ rose	85.00	10.00	800.00	(6)
	Issues of 1917, Design of J33, Perf. 11				
J61	1¢ carmine rose	1.75	.15	40.00	(6)
J62	2¢ carmine rose	1.50	.15	35.00	(6)
J63	3¢ carmine rose	8.50	.15	85.00	(6)
J64	5¢ carmine	8.50	.15	85.00	(6)
J65	10¢ carmine rose	12.50	.20	135.00	(6)
	Double transfer	—	—		
J66	30¢ carmine rose	55.00	.40	550.00	(6)
J67	50¢ carmine rose	75.00	.15	800.00	(6)

	Issues of 1925, Design of J33	Un	U	PB	#
J68	1/2¢ dull red, Apr. 13	.65	.15	11.00	(6)
	Issues of 1930-31, Design of J69				
J69	1/2¢ Figure of Value	3.00	1.00	35.00	(6)
J70	1¢ carmine	2.50	.15	27.50	(6)
J71	2¢ carmine	3.00	.15	40.00	(6)
J72	3¢ carmine	15.00	1.00	250.00	(6)
J73	5¢ carmine	14.00	1.50	225.00	(6)
J74	10¢ carmine	30.00	.50	425.00	(6)
J75	30¢ carmine	85.00	1.00	1,000.00	(6)
J76	50¢ carmine	100.00	.30	1,250.00	(6)
	Design of J78				
J77	$1 carmine	25.00	.15	275.00	(6)
a	$1 scarlet	20.00	.15		
J78	$5 "FIVE" on $	30.00	.15	375.00	(6)
a	$5 scarlet	25.00	.15		
b	As "a," wet printing	27.50	.15		
	Issues of 1931-56, Design of J69, Perf. 11 x 10 1/2				
J79	1/2¢ dull carmine	.75	.15	22.50	(4)
J80	1¢ dull carmine	.15	.15	1.50	(4)
J81	2¢ dull carmine	.15	.15	1.50	(4)
J82	3¢ dull carmine	.25	.15	2.00	(4)
b	Scarlet, wet printing	.28	.15		
J83	5¢ dull carmine	.35	.15	2.50	(4)
J84	10¢ dull carmine	1.10	.15	6.00	(4)
b	Scarlet, wet printing	1.25	.15		
J85	30¢ dull carmine	8.50	.15	35.00	(4)
J86	50¢ dull carmine	9.50	.15	50.00	(4)
	Design of J78, Perf. 10 1/2 x 11				
J87	$1 scarlet	40.00	.20	300.00	(4)
	Beginning with #J88, unused values are for never-hinged stamps.				
	Issues of 1959, June 19, Designs of J88 and J98, Perf. 11 x 10 1/2				
J88	1/2¢ Figure of Value	1.25	.85	165.00	(4)
J89	1¢ carmine rose	.15	.15	.35	(4)
a	"1 CENT" omitted	*350.00*			
	Pair, one without "1 CENT"	—			
J90	2¢ carmine rose	.15	.15	.45	(4)
J91	3¢ carmine rose	.15	.15	.50	(4)
J92	4¢ carmine rose	.15	.15	.60	(4)
J93	5¢ carmine rose	.15	.15	.65	(4)
J94	6¢ carmine rose	.15	.15	.70	(4)
	Pair, one without "6 CENTS"	*800.00*			
J95	7¢ carmine rose	.15	.15	.80	(4)
J96	8¢ carmine rose	.16	.15	.90	(4)
J97	10¢ carmine rose	.20	.15	1.00	(4)
J98	30¢ Figure of Value	.55	.15	2.75	(4)
J99	50¢ carmine rose	.90	.15	4.50	(4)
	Design of J101				
J100	$1 carmine rose	1.50	.15	7.50	(4
J101	$5 Outline Figure of Value	8.00	.15	40.00	
	Issues of 1978-85, Designs of J88 and J98				
J102	11¢ carmine rose, Jan. 2, 1978	.35	.15		
J103	13¢ carmine rose, Jan. 2, 1978	.30	.15		
J104	17¢ carmine rose, June 10, 1985	.40	.1		

Official and Penalty Mail Stamps

1873-1988

O7

O14

O18

O34

O44

O52

O57

O76

O91

O121

O127

O129A

O139

O140

O143

Official Stamps

The franking privilege having been abolished as of July 1, 1873, these stamps were provided for each of the departments of government for the prepayment on official matter. These stamps were supplanted on May 1, 1879 by penalty envelopes and on July 5, 1884 were declared obsolete.

Issues of 1873, Thin, Hard Paper, Perf. 12, Unwmkd. Department of Agriculture: Yellow

	Un	U
Franklin	90.00	40.00
...ed paper	100.00	45.00
[illegible]	70.00	15.00
[illegible]	65.00	3.50
	—	—
	75.00	12.50
	150.00	55.00
	[illegible].00	57.50
		67.50

		Un	U
O6	12¢ Clay	200.00	85.00
	12¢ golden yellow	225.00	100.00
O7	15¢ Webster	150.00	55.00
	15¢ olive yellow	160.00	65.00
O8	24¢ Scott	175.00	55.00
	24¢ golden yellow	190.00	65.00
O9	30¢ Hamilton	225.00	95.00
	30¢ olive yellow	250.00	110.00
	Executive Dept.: Carmine		
O10	1¢ Franklin	300.00	100.00
O11	2¢ Jackson	200.00	70.00
	Double transfer	—	—
O12	3¢ Washington	250.00	60.00
a	3¢ violet rose	200.00	60.00
O13	6¢ Lincoln	350.00	200.00
O14	10¢ Jefferson	325.00	160.00

1873 continued, Perf. 12		Un	U
	Dept. of the Interior: Vermilion		
O15	1¢ Franklin	20.00	3.50
	Ribbed paper	25.00	4.00
O16	2¢ Jackson	17.50	2.00
O17	3¢ Washington	27.50	2.00
O18	6¢ Lincoln	20.00	2.00
O19	10¢ Jefferson	19.00	4.00
O20	12¢ Clay	30.00	3.00
O21	15¢ Webster	50.00	6.00
	Double transfer of left side	100.00	17.50
O22	24¢ Scott	37.50	5.00
O23	30¢ Hamilton	50.00	6.00
O24	90¢ Perry	110.00	10.00
	Dept. of Justice: Purple		
O25	1¢ Franklin	60.00	20.00
O26	2¢ Jackson	95.00	20.00
O27	3¢ Washington	95.00	6.00
O28	6¢ Lincoln	90.00	8.50
O29	10¢ Jefferson	100.00	20.00
	Double transfer	—	—
O30	12¢ Clay	75.00	12.50
O31	15¢ Webster	165.00	45.00
O32	24¢ Scott	450.00	120.00
O33	30¢ Hamilton	400.00	67.50
	Double transfer at top	450.00	85.00
O34	90¢ Perry	600.00	180.00
	Navy Dept.: Ultramarine		
O35	1¢ Franklin	45.00	7.00
a	1¢ dull blue	52.50	8.50
O36	2¢ Jackson	32.50	6.00
a	2¢ dull blue	42.50	7.50
	2¢ gray blue	35.00	7.50
O37	3¢ Washington	37.50	4.00
a	3¢ dull blue	42.50	5.50
O38	6¢ Lincoln	32.50	4.00
a	6¢ dull blue	42.50	5.00
	Vertical line through "N" of "NAVY"	65.00	10.00
O39	7¢ Stanton	225.00	60.00
a	7¢ dull blue	250.00	70.00
O40	10¢ Jefferson	45.00	11.00
a	10¢ dull blue	50.00	13.00
	Cracked plate	*125.00*	—
O41	12¢ Clay	57.50	7.00
	Double transfer of left side	110.00	—
O42	15¢ Webster	95.00	18.00
O43	24¢ Scott	95.00	20.00
a	24¢ dull blue	110.00	—
O44	30¢ Hamilton	85.00	10.00
O45	90¢ Perry	400.00	57.50
a	Double impression		*2,000.00*

	Post Office Dept.: Black	Un	U
O47	1¢ Figure of Value	7.25	3.00
O48	2¢ Figure of Value	7.00	2.50
a	Double impression	300.00	
O49	3¢ Figure of Value	2.50	.55
	Cracked plate	—	—
O50	6¢ Figure of Value	8.00	1.40
	Vertical ribbed paper	—	7.50
O51	10¢ Figure of Value	40.00	14.50
O52	12¢ Figure of Value	22.50	3.50
O53	15¢ Figure of Value	25.00	5.00
a	Imperf. pair	*600.00*	
	Double transfer	—	—
O54	24¢ Figure of Value	32.50	6.00
O55	30¢ Figure of Value	32.50	5.50
O56	90¢ Figure of Value	47.50	7.50
	Dept. of State: Green		
O57	1¢ Franklin	60.00	12.50
O58	2¢ Jackson	125.00	20.00
O59	3¢ Washington	50.00	9.00
	Double paper	—	—
O60	6¢ Lincoln	47.50	9.00
O61	7¢ Stanton	90.00	15.00
	Ribbed paper	110.00	19.00
O62	10¢ Jefferson	75.00	13.50
	Short transfer	100.00	27.50
O63	12¢ Clay	110.00	30.00
O64	15¢ Webster	100.00	20.00
O65	24¢ Scott	250.00	65.00
O66	30¢ Hamilton	225.00	40.00
O67	90¢ Perry	400.00	100.00
O68	$2 Seward	550.00	225.00
O69	$5 Seward	4,250.00	1,600.00
O70	$10 Seward	3,000.00	1,000.00
O71	$20 Seward	2,250.00	800.00
	Treasury Dept.: Brown		
O72	1¢ Franklin	22.50	1.75
	Double transfer	30.00	3.50
O73	2¢ Jackson	25.00	1.75
	Double transfer	—	5.00
	Cracked plate	40.00	—
O74	3¢ Washington	16.00	.75
	Shaded circle outside right frame line	—	[illegible]
O75	6¢ Lincoln	22.50	[illegible]
	Worn plate	24.00	[illegible]
O76	7¢ Stanton	57.50	[illegible]
O77	10¢ Jefferson	57[illegible]	[illegible]
O78	12¢ Clay	[illegible]	[illegible]
O79	15¢ Webster	[illegible]	[illegible]
O80	24¢ Scott	[illegible]	[illegible]
O81	30¢ Hamilton	[illegible]	[illegible]
	Short transfer	[illegible]	[illegible]
O82	90¢ Perry	[illegible]	[illegible]

	1873 continued, Perf. 12	Un	U
	War Dept.: Rose		
O83	1¢ Franklin	82.50	3.25
O84	2¢ Jackson	75.00	4.50
	Ribbed paper	67.50	7.50
O85	3¢ Washington	72.50	1.00
O86	6¢ Lincoln	250.00	2.00
O87	7¢ Stanton	75.00	30.00
O88	10¢ Jefferson	22.50	4.00
O89	12¢ Clay	75.00	2.00
	Ribbed paper	90.00	3.50
O90	15¢ Webster	20.00	2.50
	Ribbed paper	25.00	4.50
O91	24¢ Scott	20.00	3.00
O92	30¢ Hamilton	22.50	2.50
O93	90¢ Perry	50.00	10.00
	Issues of 1879, Soft, Porous Paper, Dept. of Agriculture: Yellow		
O94	1¢ Franklin, issued without gum	1,400.00	
O95	3¢ Washington	175.00	32.50
	Dept. of the Interior: Vermilion		
O96	1¢ Franklin	125.00	70.00
O97	2¢ Jackson	2.50	1.00
O98	3¢ Washington	2.00	.60
O99	6¢ Lincoln	3.00	2.50
O100	10¢ Jefferson	32.50	20.00
O101	12¢ Clay	65.00	30.00
O102	15¢ Webster	150.00	50.00
	Double transfer	200.00	—
O103	24¢ Scott	1,200.00	
	Dept. of Justice: Bluish Purple		
O106	3¢ Washington	50.00	17.50
O107	6¢ Lincoln	110.00	70.00
	Post Office Dept.: Black		
O108	3¢ Figure of Value	7.50	1.75
	Treasury Dept.: Brown		
O109	3¢ Washington	27.50	2.50
O110	6¢ Lincoln	50.00	13.50
O111	10¢ Jefferson	65.00	15.00
O112	30¢ Hamilton	750.00	100.00
O113	90¢ Perry	775.00	100.00
	War Dept.: Rose Red		
114	1¢ Franklin	2.00	1.50
	2¢ Jackson	3.00	1.50
	3¢ Washington	3.00	.75
	mperf. pair	*800.00*	
	ble impression	500.00	
	transfer	6.00	4.00
		2.50	.70
		20.00	10.00
		15.00	3.00
		47.50	30.00

Official Postal Savings Mail

These stamps were used to prepay postage on official correspondence of the Postal Savings Division of the Post Office Department. Discontinued Sept. 23, 1914.

	Issues of 1910-11, Perf. 12, Wmkd. (191)	Un	U
O121	2¢ Postal Savings	9.00	1.10
	Double transfer	12.50	2.00
O122	50¢ dark green Postal Savings	110.00	25.00
O123	$1 ultramarine Postal Savings	100.00	7.00
	Wmkd. (190)		
O124	1¢ dark violet Postal Savings	5.50	1.00
O125	2¢ Postal Savings (O121)	30.00	3.50
	Double transfer	35.00	4.50
O126	10¢ carmine Postal Savings	10.00	1.00
	Double transfer	15.00	2.50

Penalty Mail Stamps

Stamps for use by government departments were reinstituted in 1983. Now known as Penalty Mail stamps, they help provide a better accounting of actual mail costs for official departments and agencies, etc.

Beginning with #O127, unused values are for never-hinged stamps.

	Issues of 1983-89, Perf. 11 x 10½, Unwmkd.		
O127	1¢, Jan. 12, 1983	.15	.15
O128	4¢, Jan. 12, 1983	.15	.15
O129	13¢, Jan. 12, 1983	.26	.50
O129A	14¢, May 15, 1985	.28	.50
O130	17¢, Jan. 12, 1983	.34	.40
O131, O134, O137 not assigned.			
O132	$1, Jan. 12, 1983	1.75	2.00
O133	$5, Jan. 12, 1983	9.00	5.00
O134	not assigned		
	Coil Stamps, Perf. 10 Vertically		
O135	20¢, Jan. 12, 1983	2.00	*3.00*
a	Imperf. pair	*1,500.00*	
O136	22¢, May 15, 1985	.60	*2.00*
O137	not assigned		
	Perf. 11		
O138	(14¢) D Stamp, Feb. 4, 1985	3.50	*5.00*
	Coil Stamps, Perf. 10 Vertically		
O138A	15¢, June 11, 1988	.30	.15
O138B	20¢, May 19, 1988	.40	.15
O139	(22¢) D Stamp, Feb. 4, 1985	3.50	*3.00*
O140	(25¢) E Stamp, Mar. 22, 1988	.50	*2.00*
O141	25¢, June 11, 1988	.50	.20
O142	not assigned		
O143	1¢, July 5, 1989	.15	—

Newspaper, Parcel Post and Special Handling Stamps

1865-1880

PR1 **PR2** **PR3**

Newspaper Stamps

A total of 125 Newspaper Stamps were issued between 1865 and 1897. Represented is a partial listing of those issues.

Issues of 1865, Printed by the National Bank Note Co., Thin, Hard Paper, No Gum, Perf. 12, Unwmkd., Colored Borders

		Un	
PR1	5¢ Washington	185.00	—
a	5¢ light blue	175.00	—
	5¢ blue	140.00	—
PR2	10¢ Franklin	85.00	—
a	10¢ green	85.00	—
b	pelure paper	125.00	—
PR3	25¢ Lincoln	85.00	—
a	25¢ carmine red	150.00	—
b	pelure paper	125.00	—

Yellowish Paper, White Border

		Un	U
PR4	5¢ light blue (PR1)	50.00	30.00
a	5¢ dark blue	45.00	30.00
b	pelure paper	50.00	—
	Issues of 1875, Reprints of 1865 Issue, Printed by Continental Bank Note Co., Hard, White Paper, No Gum		
PR5	5¢ dull blue (PR1), white border	70.00	
a	Printed on both sides	—	
PR6	10¢ dark bluish green (PR2), colored border	50.00	
a	Printed on both sides	*1,750.00*	
PR7	25¢ dark carmine (PR3), colored border	80.00	
	1880, Printed by the American Bank Note Co., Soft, Porous Paper, White Border		
PR8	5¢ dark blue	125.00	

PR15

PR18

PR24

PR25

PR26

PR28

PR29

PR30

PR78

PR79

	Issues of 1875, Thin, Hard Paper	Un	U
PR9	2¢ black (PR15)	12.50	11.00
PR10	3¢ black (PR15)	16.00	14.50
PR12	6¢ black (PR15)	18.00	17.00
PR14	9¢ black (PR15)	55.00	50.00
PR15	0¢ Statue of Freedom	25.00	20.00
PR1	2¢ rose (PR18)	60.00	40.00
PR18	6¢ "Commerce"	85.00	50.00
PR20	60¢ rose (PR18)	75.00	45.00
PR21	72¢ rose (PR18)	180.00	110.00
PR24	$1.92 Ceres	200.00	125.00
PR25	$3 "Victory"	275.00	135.00
PR26	$6 Clio	450.00	165.00
PR28	$12 Vesta	700.00	300.00
PR29	$24 "Peace"	700.00	325.00
PR30	$36 "Commerce"	800.00	375.00
PR32	$60 violet	1,050.00	425.00
	Special Printing, Hard, White Paper, Without Gum		
PR33	2¢ gray black (PR15)	100.00	
PR34	3¢ gray black (PR15)	105.00	
PR3	4¢ gray black (PR15)	110.00	
PR36	6¢ gray black (PR15)	150.00	
PR37	8¢ gray black (PR15)	175.00	
PR38	9¢ gray black (PR15)	200.00	
PR39	10¢ gray black (PR15)	250.00	
PR40	12¢ pale rose (PR18)	300.00	
PR41	24¢ pale rose (PR18)	425.00	
PR4	2¢ pale rose (PR18)	825.00	
PR48	$1.92 dk. brn. (PR24)	*3,500.00*	
R50	$6 ultramarine (PR26)	*8,500.00*	

All values of this issue #PR33 to PR56 exist imperforate but were not regularly issued.

	Issues of 1879, Printed by Continental Bank Note Co., Soft, Porous Paper	Un	U
PR57	2¢ black (PR15)	6.00	4.50
	Double transfer at top	.50	8.50
	Cracked plate	—	—
PR58	3¢ black (PR15)	7.50	5.00
	Double transfer at top	.00	9.00
PR59	4¢ black (PR15)	7.50	5.00
PR60	6¢ black (PR15)	15.00	11.00
	Double transfer at top	17.50	17.50
PR61	8¢ gray black (PR15)	15.00	11.00
PR62	10¢ black (PR15)	15.00	11.00
	Double transfer at top	17.50	
PR63	12¢ red (PR15)	55.00	25.00
PR64	24¢ red (PR18)	55.00	22.50
PR65	36¢ red (PR18)	170.00	95.00
PR66	48¢ red	135.00	60.00
PR67	60¢ red (PR18)	100.00	60.00
a	Imperf. pair	*600.00*	
PR68	72¢ red (PR18)	210.00	115.00
PR69	84¢ red (PR18)	165.00	85.00
PR70	96¢ red (PR18)	110.00	60.00
PR71	$1.92 pale brn. (PR24	0.00	55.00
	Cracked plate	140.00	
PR72	$3 red vermilion (PR25	0.00	55.00
PR73	$6 blue (PR26)	150.00	90.00
PR74	$9 orange Minerva	110.00	60.00
PR76	$24 dk. vio. (PR29)	200.00	110.00
PR77	$36 Indian red (PR30	250.00	135.00
PR78	$48 Hebe	325.00	165.00
PR79	$60 Indian Maiden	325.00	165.00

All values of the 1879 issue except #PR63 to PR66 and PR68 to PR70 exist imperforate but were not regularly issued.

PR116

PR118

PR119

PR120

PR121

PR122

PR123

PR124

PR125

	Issues of 1883, Special Printing	Un	U
PR80	2¢ intense blk. (PR15)	225.00	
	Issues of 1885 Printed by Continental Bank Note Co.		
PR81	¢ black (PR15)	8.50	5.00
	Double transfer at top	11.00	8.50
PR82	12¢ carmine (PR18)	27.50	12.50
PR83	24¢ carmine (PR18)	30.00	15.00
PR84	36¢ carmine (PR18)	42.50	17.50
PR8	8¢ carmine (PR18)	60.00	30.00
PR8	60¢ carmine (PR18)	85.00	40.00
PR87	2¢ carmine (PR18)	95.00	45.00
PR88	84¢ carmine (PR18)	200.00	110.00
PR89	96¢ carmine (PR18)	140.00	85.00
	All values of the 1885 issue exist imperforate but were not regularly issued.		
	Issues of 1894, Soft Wove Paper		
PR90	¢ intense blk. (PR15)	55.00	
	Double transfer at top	65.00	
PR91	2¢ intense blk. (PR15)	55.00	
	Double transfer at top	65.00	
PR92	4¢ intense blk. (PR15)	75.00	
PR93	6¢ intense blk. (PR115)	950.00	
PR94	10¢ intenso blk. (PR15)	125.00	
PR95	2¢ pink (PR18)	550.00	
PR9	24¢ pink (PR18)	575.00	
PR97	36¢ pink (PR18)	*3,500.00*	
PR98	60¢ pink (PR18)	*3,500.00*	
PR99	96¢ pink (PR)	*4,000.00*	
PR100	$3 scarlet (PR25)	*5,500.00*	
PR101	$6 pale blue (PR26)	*6,250.00*	

	Issues of 1895, Unwmkd.	Un	U
PR102	1¢ black (PR116)	25.00	7.50
PR103	2¢ black (PR116)	25.00	7.50
PR104	5¢ black (PR116)	35.00	12.50
PR105	10¢ black (PR116)	75.00	32.50
PR106	25¢ carmine (PR118)	100.00	35.00
PR107	50¢ carmine (PR118)	235.00	95.00
PR108	$2 scarlet (PR120)	275.00	65.00
PR109	$5 ultramarine (PR121)	375.00	150.00
PR110	$10 green	350.00	165.00
PR111	$20 slate	675.00	300.00
PR112	$50 dull rose (PR124)	700.00	300.00
PR113	$100 purple (PR125)	775.00	350.00
	Issues of 1895-97, Wmkd. (191), Yellowish Gum		
PR114	1¢ black (PR116)	3.50	3.00
PR115	2¢ black (PR116)	4.00	3.50
PR116	5¢ Statue of Freedom		
	on Capitol Dome	6.00	5.00
PR117	10¢ black (PR116)	4.00	3.50
PR118	25¢ "Justice"	8.00	8.00
PR119	50¢ "Justice"	10.00	12.50
PR120	$2 "Victory"	12.00	15.00
PR121	$5 Clio	20.00	25.00
a	$5 light blue	100.00	45.00
PR122	$10 Vesta	18.00	25.00
PR123	$20 "Peace"	20.00	27.50
PR124	$50 "Commerce"	25.00	30.00
PR125	$100 Indian Maiden	30.00	37.50

In 1899, the Government sold 26,989 sets of these stamps, but because the stock of the high values was not sufficient to make up the required number, the $5, $10, $20, $50 and $100 were reprinted. These are virtually indistinguishable from earlier printings.

Parcel Post Stamps
Issued for the prepayment of postage on parcel post packages only. Beginning July 1, 1913 these stamps were valid for all postal purposes.

Issues of 1913, Perf. 12, Wmkd. (190)

		Un	U	PB	#	FDC
Q1	1¢ Post Office Clerk, July 1, 1913	2.50	.85	85.00	(6)	*1,500.00*
	Double transfer	5.00	3.00			
Q2	2¢ City Carrier, July 1, 1913	3.00	.60	95.00	(6)	*1,500.00*
	2¢ lake	—				
	Double transfer	—	—			
Q3	3¢ Railway Postal Clerk, Apr. 5, 1913	5.75	4.50	185.00	(6)	*3,000.00*
	Retouched at lower right corner	15.00	12.50			
	Double transfer	15.00	12.50			
Q4	4¢ Rural Carrier, July 1, 1913	15.00	1.90	775.00	(6)	*3,000.00*
	Double transfer	—	—			
Q5	5¢ Mail Train, July 1, 1913	15.00	1.25	775.00	(6)	*3,000.00*
	Double transfer	25.00	5.00			
Q6	10¢ Steamship and Mail Tender	25.00	1.75	1,000.00	(6)	
	Double transfer	—	—			
Q7	15¢ Automobile Service, July 1, 1913	35.00	7.75	2,100.00	(6)	
Q8	20¢ Aeroplane Carrying Mail	77.50	15.00	5,750.00	(6)	
Q9	25¢ Manufacturing	35.00	4.00	2,500.00	(6)	
Q10	50¢ Dairying, Mar. 15, 1913	160.00	27.50	13,500.00	(6)	
Q11	75¢ Harvesting	45.00	22.50	3,000.00	(6)	
Q12	$1 Fruit Growing, Jan. 3, 1913	260.00	17.00	16,000.00	(6)	

Special Handling Stamps
Issued for use on parcel post packages to secure the same expeditious handling accorded First-Class mail matter.

Issues of 1925, 1928-29, 1955, Perf. 11, Unwmkd.

		Un	U	PB	#	FDC
QE1	10¢ Special Handling, 1955	1.10	.80	25.00	(6)	
a	Wet printing, June 25, 1928	2.50	.90			45.00
QE2	15¢ Special Handling, 1955	1.00	.70	35.00	(6)	
a	Wet printing, June 25, 1928	2.50	.90			45.00
QE3	20¢ Special Handling, 1955	1.75	1.00	40.00	(6)	
a	Wet printing, June 25, 1928	3.00	1.75			45.00
QE4	25¢ Special Handling, 1929	13.00	5.50	240.00	(6)	
a	25¢ deep green, Apr. 11, 1925	22.50	4.50	325.00	(6)	225.00
	"A" and "T" of "STATES" joined at top	40.00	20.00			
	"T" and "A" of "POSTAGE" joined at top	40.00	40.00			

Parcel Post Postage Due Stamps
Issued for affixing by a postal clerk to any parcel post package to denote the amount to be collected from the addressee because of insufficient prepayment of postage. Beginning July 1, 1913 these stamps were valid for use as regular postage due stamps.

Issues of 1912, Designs of JQ1 and JQ5, Perf. 12, Wmkd. (190)

		Un	U	PB	#
JQ1	1¢ Figure of Value, Nov. 27	5.00	2.75	550.00	(6)
JQ2	2¢ dark green Parcel Post Postage Due, Dec. 9	45.00	13.00	4,000.00	(6)
JQ3	5¢ dark green Parcel Post Postage Due, Nov. 27	7.00	3.50	675.00	(6)
JQ4	10¢ dark green Parcel Post Postage Due, Dec. 12	110.00	30.00	10,000.00	(6)
JQ5	25¢ Figure of Value, Dec. 16	50.00	3.25	4,500.00	(6)

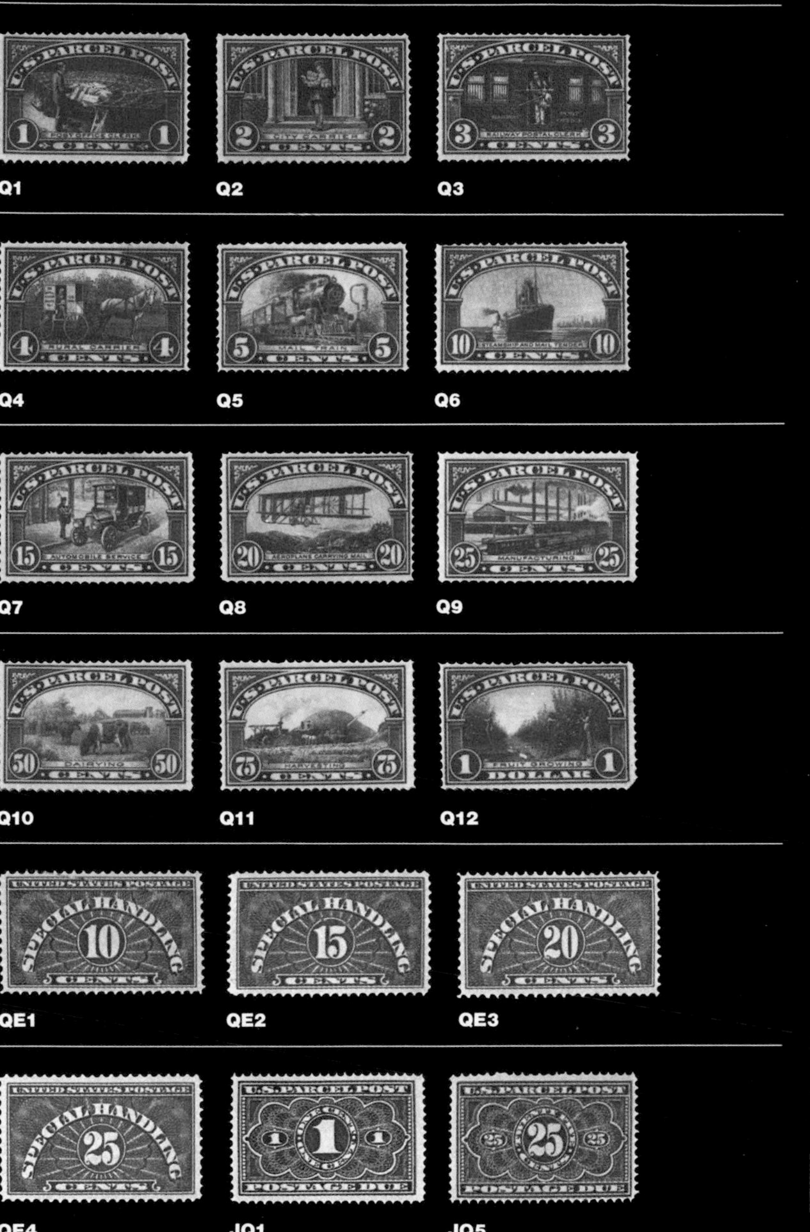

Q1 Q2 Q3

Q4 Q5 Q6

Q7 Q8 Q9

Q10 Q11 Q12

QE1 QE2 QE3

QE4 JQ1 JQ5

U172

U348

U523

U576

U609

U614

UC14

Represented below is only a partial listing of stamped envelopes. Values are for cut squares; prices for entire envelopes are higher. Color in italics is the color of the envelope paper; when no color is specified, envelope paper is white. "W" with catalog number indicates wrapper instead of envelope.

	1853-61	Un	U
U1	3¢ red Washington, die 1 (top label 13mm wide)	225.00	17.50
U4	3¢ red, die 2 (top label 15mm wide)	225.00	15.00
U8	3¢ red, die 4 (top label 20mm wide), *buff*	1,250.00	100.00
U13	6¢ green Washington	200.00	100.00
U16	10¢ grn. Washington, die 1 (label 15 1/2mm), *buff*	65.00	50.00
U19	1¢ blue Franklin, die 1 (period after "Postage"), buff	30.00	15.00
W21	1¢ blue, die 1, *manila*	42.50	42.50
U24	1¢ blue, die 3 (no period after "postage"), buff	225.00	100.00
U28	3¢ + 1¢ red and blue Washington	400.00	275.00
U34	3¢ pink Washington (outline lettering)	17.50	5.00
U39	6¢ pink Washington, *buff*	65.00	65.00
U44	24¢ Washington, *buff*	200.00	165.00
	1863-71		
U47	2¢ black Jackson, die 1 (U.S. Postage, downstroke and tail of "2" unite near point), *dark manila*	45.00	40.00
U49	2¢ black, die 1 (U.S. Postage, downstroke and tail of "2" touch but do not merge), *orange*	1,100.00	
U52	2¢ black, die 3 (U.S. Post., stamp 24-25mm wide), *orange*	12.00	8.50
U58	3¢ pink Washington (solid lettering)	6.00	1.50
U61	3¢ brn. Washington, *buff*	40.00	22.50
U65	6¢ pur. Washington, *buff*	35.00	20.00
U68	12¢ brn. Wash., *buff*	400.00	225.00
U71	24¢ bl. Washington, *buff*	90.00	85.00
U73	40¢ rose Washington, *buff*	90.00	*250.00*
U75	1¢ blue Franklin, *amber*	30.00	25.00
U78	2¢ brown Jackson	35.00	14.00
U80	2¢ brown, *orange*	8.00	5.00
U84	3¢ grn. Washington, *cream*	7.50	3.00
U89	10¢ olive blk. Jefferson	400.00	400.00
U93	12¢ plum Clay	115.00	70.00
U97	15¢ red orange Webster, *amber*	165.00	200.00
U102	30¢ black Hamilton	75.00	100.00
U105	90¢ carmine Perry	150.00	225.00

	1874-84	Un	U
U109	1¢ dk. blue Franklin, die 1 (lettering poorly executed; distinct circle in "O" of "Postage"), *amber*	120.00	75.00
U111	1¢ dark blue, *orange*	20.00	16.50
U114	1¢ lt. blue, die 2 (lower part of bust pts. to end of "E" in "Postage"), *amber*	3.75	3.00
U117	1¢ lt. blue, die 2, *blue*	5.00	4.00
W120	1¢ lt. bl., die 2, *manila*	1.25	1.00
U122	2¢ brown Jackson, die 1 (bust narrow at back; numerals thin)	90.00	40.00
W126	2¢ brown Jackson, die 1 (bust narrow at back, thin numerals), *amber*	90.00	40.00
U132	2¢ brown, die 3 (left figure "2" touches oval)	60.00	25.00
U139	2¢ brown, die 5 (bust broad; numerals short, thick)	42.50	35.00
U142	2¢ verm. Jackson, die 5 (bust broad; numerals short, thick)	5.00	2.25
U147	2¢ vermilion, die 5, *fawn*	6.00	4.00
W155	2¢ vermilion, die 7 (like die 5 but middle stroke of "N" as thin as verticals), *manila*	16.00	8.00
U159	3¢ grn. Washington, die 1 (thin lettering, long figures of value)	20.00	5.00
U163	3¢ green, die 2 (thick letters, queue not projecting below bust)	1.00	.25
U172	5¢ Taylor, die 1 (numerals have thick, curved tops)	9.00	7.00
U177	5¢ blue, die 2 (numerals have long, thin tops)	5.50	5.25
U180	5¢ blue, die 2, *fawn*	85.00	50.00
U183	6¢ red Lincoln (neck short at back), *cream*	17.50	10.00
U194	10¢ brn. Jefferson, die 2 (knot of queue stands out prominently), *amber manila*	12.00	6.00
U198	15¢ orange Webster	37.50	30.00
U204	30¢ black Hamilton	60.00	30.00
U208	30¢ black, *blue*	100.00	85.00
U212	90¢ carmine Perry (front of bust broad, sloping)	175.00	225.00
U218	3¢ red Post Rider, Train (1 line under "Postage")	60.00	25.00
U221	3¢ green (2 lines under "Postage")	60.00	17.50
U225	5¢ brown Garfield, *blue*	50.00	37.50
U228	2¢ red Washington, *amber*	4.25	1.75
U230	2¢ red (wavy lines fine, clear), *fawn*	6.00	2.50
U236	2¢ red (wavy lines thick, blurred)	5.00	3.00

	1884 continued	Un	U
U210	2¢ red (3-1/2 links over left "2")	40.00	30.00
U244	2¢ red (2 links below right "2"), *amber*	135.00	75.00
U250	4¢ grn. Jackson, die 1 (left number $2\frac{3}{4}$mm wide)	2.50	2.50
U256	4¢ green, die 2 (left number $3\frac{1}{4}$mm wide)	4.00	3.00
U259	4¢ green, die 2, *amber manila*	7.50	5.00
	1884-86		
U262	2¢ brn. Washington, *blue*	10.50	8.00
U270	2¢ brown (2 links below right "2")	75.00	40.00
U274	2¢ brown (round "O" in "Two"), *amber*	150.00	65.00
U277	2¢ brn. Washington, die 1 (extremity of bust below queue forms point)	.35	.15
U288	2¢ brn. Washington, die 2 (extremity of bust is rounded)	175.00	35.00
	1887-94		
U294	1¢ blue Franklin	.50	.20
U302	1¢ dark blue, *manila*	20.00	9.00
U307	2¢ grn. Washington, die 1 ("G" of "Postage" has no bar), *oriental buff*	65.00	30.00
U314	2¢ green, die 2 ("G" has bar, ear indicated by 1 heavy line), *blue*	.50	.20
U320	2¢ green, die 3 (as die 2 but upper head more rounded), *oriental buff*	150.00	40.00
U323	2¢ green, die 3, *amber manila*	375.00	90.00
U327	4¢ carmine Jackson, *blue*	4.00	3.50
U331	5¢ blue Grant, die 1 (space between beard and collar), *amber*	3.75	1.75
U335	5¢ blue, die 2 (collar touches beard; no button on collar), *amber*	9.00	5.00
U340	30¢ red brown Hamilton, *manila*	42.50	42.50
U348	1¢ Columbus and Liberty	2.00	1.00
U351	10¢ slate brown	40.00	30.00
	1899		
U355	1¢ green Franklin, *blue*	9.00	6.00
U358	2¢ carm. Washington, die 1, (bust points to first notch of inner oval)	2.00	.90
U362	2¢ carmine, die 2 (bust points to middle of second notch of inner oval; queue has ribbon around it)	.25	.20
U371	4¢ brown Lincoln, die 1 (bust pointed, undraped)	15.00	11.00
U374	4¢ brown, die 3 (bust broader; inner oval has no notches)	9.00	6.00

	1903	Un	U
U377	5¢ blue Grant	8.75	8.50
U379	1¢ green Franklin	.50	.15
U386	2¢ carm. Washington, *amber*	1.50	.20
U390	4¢ chocolate Grant	17.00	10.00
	1904		
U398	2¢ carm. Washington, recut die (lines at end of "Two Cents" all short), *blue*	3.00	.90
	1907-16		
U404	1¢ green Franklin, die 1 (wide "D"), *manila*	2.75	1.75
W410	2¢ brown red Washington, die 1, *manila*	40.00	30.00
U414	2¢ carmine, die 1, *blue*	.40	.15
	1916-32		
U423	1¢ grn. Franklin, die 1 (UNITED nearer inner than outer circle), *blue*	.40	.15
U429	2¢ carmine Washington, die 1 (letters broad, numerals vertical, E closer than N to inner circle)	.15	.15
U436	3¢ dk. violet Washington, die 1 (as 2¢)	.50	.15
U440	4¢ black Washington	1.00	.50
U447	2¢ on 3¢ dark violet, rose surcharge	6.00	5.50
U458	Same as U447, black surcharge, bars 2mm apart	.45	.35
U468	Same as U458, bars $1\frac{1}{2}$mm apart	.60	.35
U481	$1\frac{1}{2}$¢ brown Washington, die 1 (as U429)	.15	.15
W485	1-1/2¢ brown, *manila*	.75	.15
U490	$1\frac{1}{2}$¢ on 1¢ grn. Franklin, black surcharge	3.75	3.50
U499	$1\frac{1}{2}$¢ on 1¢, manila	11.00	7.00
U510	$1\frac{1}{2}$¢ on 1¢, outline numeral in surcharge	1.75	1.25
U523	1¢ ol. grn. Mount Vernon	1.75	1.00
U526	3¢ violet Mount Vernon	4.00	.35
U531	6¢ or. Washington, *blue*	11.00	8.00
	1950-76		
U534	3¢ dk. violet Washington, die 4 (short N in UNITED, thin crossbar in A of STATES)	.35	.15
U539	3¢ + 1¢ purple, die 1 ($4\frac{1}{2}$mm tall, thick "3")	14.00	11.50
U543	4¢ brn. Pony Express Rider	.60	.30
U547	$1\frac{1}{4}$¢ brown Liberty Bell		.15
U551	6¢ green Statue of Liberty	.70	.15
U557	8¢ ultramarine Eagle	.40	.15
U564	8¢ Aging Conference	.50	.15
U569	10¢ Tennis Centenary	.24	.15
U572	13¢ Quilt Pattern, *lt. brown*	.35	.15

	1975-90 continued	Un	U
76	13¢ Liberty Tree	.30	.15
581	15¢ red Uncle Sam	.35	.15
U587	15¢ Auto Racing	.35	.15
U591	5.9¢ Auth Nonprofit Org		.15
U594	(20¢) brown Eagle, C	.45	.15
U599	15¢ Honeybee	.35	.15
U601	20¢ Capitol Dome	.45	.15
U604	5.2¢ Auth Nonprofit Org		.15
U608	22¢ Bison	.55	.15
U609	6¢ USS Constitution		.15
U612	8.4¢ USF Constellation		.15
U614	25¢ USA, Stars (Philatelic Mail)	.50	.25
	Airmail Envelopes and Aerogrammes, 1929-89		
UC1	5¢ blue Airplane, die 1 (vertical rudder is not semicircular)	3.00	1.75
UC2	5¢ blue, die 2 (vertical rudder is semicircular)	12.50	5.00
UC4	6¢ orange Airplane, die 2b ("6" is 6mm wide)	2.50	1.25
UC6	6¢ or., die 3 (vertical rudder leans forward)	1.00	.35
UC8	6¢ on 2¢ carm. Washington (U429)	1.25	.65
UC11	5¢ on 6¢ orange (UC4)	9.00	5.00
UC12	5¢ on 6¢ orange (UC5)	.75	.50
UC14	5¢ carm. DC-4, die 1 (end of wing on right is smooth curve)	.75	.20
UC17	5¢ Postage Centenary	.40	.25
UC21	6¢ on 5¢ (UC14)	26.00	15.00
UC25	6¢ red Eagle	.75	.50
UC29	6¢ + 1¢ (UC5)	37.50	50.00
UC32	10¢ Jet Airliner, back inscription in 2 lines	6.00	5.00
UC37	8¢ red Jet Airliner	.35	.15
UC41	8¢ + 2¢ (UC37)	.65	.15

		Un	U
UC44	15¢ Birds in Flight	1.50	.90
UC47	13¢ red Bird in Flight	.28	.15
UC50	22¢ red and blue	.90	.25
UC53	30¢ blue, red, brn. Tour the United States, entire	.60	.30
UC57	30¢ Olympic Games, entire	.60	.30
UC60	36¢ Mark Twain/ Halley's Comet, entire	.72	.36
UC61	39¢ Envelope	.78	.39
UC62	39¢ Montgomery Blair	.78	.39
	Official Envelopes, 1873-79		
	Post Office Department (Numeral 9½mm high)		
UO1	2¢ black, *lemon*	11.00	6.00
	(Numeral 10½mm high)		
UO5	2¢ black, *lemon*	4.00	3.00
UO9	3¢ black, *amber*	40.00	25.00
	Postal Service		
UO16	blue, *amber*	30.00	19.00
	War Department		
UO20	3¢ dk. red Washington	55.00	35.00
UO26	12¢ dark red Clay	110.00	40.00
WO33	2¢ verm. Jackson, *manila*	200.00	
UO39	10¢ vermilion Jefferson	225.00	
UO48	2¢ red Jackson, *amber*	25.00	7.50
UO55	3¢ red Washington, *fawn*	4.00	.75
UO63	12¢ red Clay, *cream*	650.00	
	Penalty Mail Envelopes, 1983-90 (Entires)		
UO73	20¢ blue Great Seal	.60	*25.00*
UO74	22¢ blue Great Seal	.60	*3.00*
UO76	(25¢) Great Seal, E	.65	*15.00*
UO77	25¢ black, blue Great Seal (seal embossed)	.65	*1.00*
UO78	25¢ (seal typographed)	.65	*10.00*
UO80	65¢ Great Seal	1.30	—
UO82	65¢ Great Seal	1.50	—

UX14

UX27

UX56

UX83

UX94

UX131

UXC19

Represented below is only a partial listing of postal cards. Values are for entire cards. Color in italics is color of card. Cards preprinted with written address or message usually sell for much less.

		Un	U
UX1[illegible]	[illegible]¢ brown Liberty, [illegible]wmkd. (90 x 60mm)	300.00	20.00
UX3[illegible]	[illegible]¢ brown Liberty, [illegible]wmkd. (53 x 36mm)	65.00	2.25
UX5[illegible]	[illegible]¢ blk. Liberty, unwmkd.	45.00	.40
UX[illegible]	[illegible]2¢ blue Liberty, *buff*	20.00	17.50
UX8[illegible]	[illegible]¢ brown Jefferson, [illegible]arge "one-cent" wreath	35.00	1.25
c	1¢ chocolate	60.00	6.00
UX10[illegible]	[illegible]¢ black Grant	25.00	1.40
UX1[illegible]	[illegible]¢ black Jefferson, [illegible]wreath smaller than UX14	27.50	.40
UX13[illegible]	[illegible]2¢ blue Liberty, *cream*	125.00	75.00
UX14[illegible]	[illegible]¢ Jefferson	20.00	.25
UX15[illegible]	[illegible]¢ black John Adams	30.00	15.00
UX1[illegible]	[illegible]2¢ black Liberty	10.00	9.00
UX18[illegible]	[illegible]¢ black McKinley, [illegible]facing left	9.00	.30
UX19[illegible]	[illegible]¢ black McKinley, [illegible]triangles in top corners	27.50	.50
UX21[illegible]	[illegible]¢ blue McKinley, [illegible]shaded background	90.00	6.50
UX22[illegible]	[illegible]¢ blue McKinley, [illegible]white background	12.50	.25
UX23[illegible]	[illegible]¢ red Lincoln, [illegible]solid background	6.00	5.50
UX24[illegible]	[illegible]¢ red McKinley	7.50	.25

		Un	U
UX25	2¢ red Grant	1.25	8.50
UX26	1¢ green Lincoln, solid background	7.50	6.00
UX27	1¢ Jefferson, *buff*	.25	.10
a	1¢ green, *cream*	3.50	.60
UX27C	1¢ green Jefferson, *gray*, die I	*1,750.00*	
UX29	2¢ red Jefferson, *buff*	35.00	1.50
c	2¢ vermilion, *buff*	275.00	60.00
UX30	2¢ red Jefferson, *cream*	19.00	1.50
	Surcharged in two lines by canceling machine.		
UX32	1¢ on 2¢ red Jefferson, *buff*	40.00	10.00
UX33	1¢ on 2¢ red Jefferson, *cream*	6.50	1.40
	Surcharged in two lines by press printing.		
UX35	1¢ on 2¢ red Jefferson, *cream*	200.00	30.00
UX37	3¢ red McKinley, *buff*	3.00	*9.00*
UX38	2¢ carmine rose Franklin	.30	.25
	Surcharged by canceling machine in light green.		
UX39	2¢ on 1¢ green Jefferson, *buff*	.50	.25
	Surcharged typographically in dark green.		
UX41	2¢ on 1¢ green Jefferson, *buff*	3.50	1.50
UX43	2¢ carmine Lincoln	.25	*1.00*
UX44	2¢ FIPEX	.25	*1.00*
UX46	3¢ Statue of Liberty	.40	.20

Please detach at perforation.

UNITED STATES POSTAL SERVICE
KANSAS CITY MO 64144-9997

OFFICIAL BUSINESS

Penalty for private use to avoid payment of postage: $300

UNITED STATES POSTAL SERVICE
PHILATELIC SALES DIVISION
BOX 449997
KANSAS CITY MO 64144-9997

Item #8891
Price $5.95

Additional Information on Stamp Collecting Products

You can expand your stamp collection and keep it updated with philatelic products from the USPS. Check the box next to the products you'd like to learn more about.

- ☐ *American Commemorative Panels*
- ☐ *Commemorative Mint Sets*
- ☐ *Commemorative Stamp Club*
- ☐ *Souvenir Pages Program*
- ☐ *Standing Order Service*
- ☐ *Topical Mint Sets*

. . . And a FREE Offer!

Let us know if you're interested in receiving:

☐ *A copy of the* **Philatelic Catalog**, *which contains details and mail–order information on all stamps and stamp products currently available from the Postal Service.*

Neatly print your name and address below, and drop this card in the mail—no postage necessary. (Information that you provide is protected and only disclosed in accordance with the Privacy Act of 1974.)

Mr./Mrs./Ms. ______________________________

Street Address ______________________________

(Include P.O. Box, Apt. No., R.D. Route, etc. where appropriate)

City __________ State __________ ZIP Code __________

Please detach at perforation.

		Un	U
UX47	2¢ + 1¢ carmine rose Franklin	160.00	250.00
UX48	4¢ red violet Lincoln	.25	.20
UX49	7¢ World Vacationland	1.75	*30.00*
UX50	4¢ U.S. Customs	.40	*1.00*
UX51	4¢ Social Security	.40	*1.00*
UX53	4¢ Bureau of the Census	.35	*1.00*
UX55	5¢ emerald Lincoln	.25	*.50*
UX56	5¢ Women Marines	.35	*1.00*
UX57	5¢ Weather Services	.30	*1.00*
UX58	6¢ brown Paul Revere	.25	*1.00*
UX60	6¢ America's Hospitals	.25	*1.00*
UX61	6¢ USF Constellation	.30	*3.00*
UX63	6¢ Gloucester, MA	.30	*3.00*
UX65	6¢ magenta Liberty	.25	*1.00*
UX66	8¢ orange Samuel Adams	.25	*1.00*
UX67	12¢ Visit USA/ Ship's Figurehead	.35	*20.00*
UX68	7¢ Charles Thomson	.25	*5.00*
UX69	9¢ John Witherspoon	.25	*1.00*
UX71	9¢ Federal Court House	.25	*1.00*
UX73	10¢ Music Hall	.25	*1.00*
UX75	10¢ John Hancock	.25	*.15*
UX76	14¢ Coast Guard Eagle	.35	*15.00*
UX77	10¢ Molly Pitcher	.25	*1.00*
UX78	10¢ George Rogers Clark	.25	*1.00*
UX80	10¢ Olympic Games	.50	*1.00*
UX81	10¢ Iolani Palace	.25	*1.00*
UX82	14¢ Olympic Games	.50	*10.00*
UX83	10¢ Salt Lake Temple	.22	*1.00*
UX86	19¢ Drake's Golden Hinde	.60	*10.00*
UX87	10¢ Battle of Cowpens	.22	*2.50*
UX88	(12¢) violet Eagle, nondenominated	.28	*.50*
UX89	12¢ Isaiah Thomas	.28	*.50*
UX90	12¢ Nathanael Greene	.28	*1.00*
UX91	12¢ Lewis and Clark	.28	*3.00*
UX93	13¢ buff Robert Morris	.30	*.50*
UX94	13¢ "Swamp Fox" Francis Marion	.28	*.75*
UX95	13¢ La Salle Claims Louisiana	.30	*.75*
UX97	13¢ Old Post Office, St. Louis, Missouri	.30	*.75*
UX101	13¢ Ark and Dove	.30	*.75*
UX102	13¢ Olympic Games, Runner Carrying Torch	.30	*.75*
UX105	(14¢) Charles Carroll, nondenominated	.28	*.50*
UX107	25¢ Clipper Flying Cloud	.70	*5.00*
UX109	14¢ Settlement of Connecticut	.28	*.75*
UX110	14¢ Stamp Collecting	.28	*.75*

		Un	U
UX111	14¢ Francis Vigo	.28	*.75*
UX114	14¢ National Guard	.28	*.75*
UX116	14¢ Constitutional Convention	.28	*.50*
UX117	14¢ Stars and Stripes	.28	*.50*
UX119	14¢ Timberline Lodge	.28	*.50*
UX121	15¢ Blair House	.30	.15
UX122	28¢ Yorkshire	.60	*1.00*
UX123	15¢ Iowa Territory	.30	.15
UX125	15¢ Hearst Castle	.30	.15
UX126	15¢ The Federalist Papers	.30	.15
UX130	15¢ Settling of Oklahoma	.30	.15
UX131	21¢ Geese and Mountains	.42	*1.00*
UX132	15¢ Seagull and Seashore	.30	.15
UX134	15¢ Hull House, Chicago	.30	.15
UX136	Inner Harbor, Baltimore	.30	.15
UX140	The White House	1.00	.50
UX148	Isaac Royall House	.30	.15
	Paid Reply Postal Cards (Prices are: Un=unsevered, U=severed card.)		
UY1	1¢ + 1¢ black Grant	35.00	7.50
UY6	1¢ + 1¢ green G. and M. Washington, double frame line around instructions	140.00	22.50
UY7	1¢ + 1¢ green G. and M. Washington, single frame line	1.00	.50
UY12	3¢ + 3¢ red McKinley	9.00	*25.00*
UY18	4¢ + 4¢ Lincoln	2.00	*2.50*
UY23	6¢ + 6¢ John Adams	.75	*2.00*
UY31	(12¢ + 12¢) Eagle, nondenominated	.75	*2.00*
UY39	15¢ + 15¢ Bison and Prairie	.75	*1.00*
	Airmail Postal Cards		
UXC1	4¢ orange Eagle	.40	*.75*
UXC2	4¢ blue Eagle (C48)	1.50	.75
UXC5	11¢ Visit The USA	.50	*12.50*
UXC7	6¢ Boy Scout World Jamboree	.40	*6.00*
UXC11	15¢ Commerce Department Travel Service	1.50	*12.50*
UXC14	11¢ Stylized Eagle	.70	*2.00*
UXC17	21¢ Curtiss Jenny	.75	*6.00*
UXC19	28¢ First Transpacific Flight	.85	*4.00*
UXC22	33¢ China Clipper	.90	*1.00*
UXC24	36¢ DC-3	.72	*2.00*
	Official Mail Postal Cards		
UZ1	1¢ black Numeral	325.00	150.00
UZ2	13¢ blue Great Seal	.40	*35.00*
UZ3	14¢ blue Great Seal	.45	*30.00*
UZ4	15¢ blue Great Seal	.30	*3.00*

First Day Issues Straight to Your Door

- Features every stamp issued each year
- Complete with First Day cancellation and informative text
- A convenient, affordable way to collect

The U.S. Postal Service's Souvenir Pages Subscription Program is your ticket to all the year's stamp issues. It's a great way to collect and learn about the stamps and stamp subjects honored during the year.

Inexpensive and Complete
A Souvenir Page is issued for every stamp–all definitives and commemoratives, as well as airmails, coil stamps and booklet panes. Each Souvenir Page includes the featured stamp(s), postmarked with a First Day of Issue cancellation, mounted on an 8" x 10 ½" page. Information on relevant philatelic specifications and a lively narrative about the history of the stamp's subject are included.

Affordable Collectibles
Souvenir Pages are printed in a limited quantity each year. And the cost of a Souvenir Page is just $1.25 per page. (In the rare event that the face value of the stamp[s] affixed exceeds $1.25, the price will be the face value.)

Money-back Guarantee
If you are ever dissatisfied, return your Souvenir Pages within 30 days of receipt for a *full* refund. For more information and an order form, fill out the postage-paid request card in this book or write to:

USPS GUIDE
SOUVENIR PAGES PROGRAM
PHILATELIC SALES DIVISION
UNITED STATES POSTAL SERVICE
BOX 449980
KANSAS CITY MO 64144-9980

Souvenir Pages

With First Day Cancellations

The Postal Service offers Souvenir Pages for new stamps. The series began with a page for the Yellowstone Park Centennial stamp issued March 1, 1972. The pages feature one or more stamps tied by the first day cancel, along with technical data and information on the subject of the issue. More than just collectors' items, Souvenir Pages make wonderful show and conversation pieces. Souvenir Pages are issued in limited editions. Number in parentheses ( ) indicates number of stamps on Page if there are more than one.

1972

72-0	Family Planning	750.00
72-1	Yellowstone Park	110.00
72-1a	Yellowstone Park with DC cancel	500.00
72-2	2¢ Cape Hatteras	100.00
72-3	14¢ Fiorello LaGuardia	110.00
72-4	11¢ City of Refuge Park	100.00
72-5	6¢ Wolf Trap Farm Park	40.00
72-6	Colonial Craftsmen (4)	20.00
72-7	11¢ Mount McKinley	30.00
72-8	6¢-11¢ Olympic Games (4)	10.00
72-8E	Olympic Games with broken red circle on 6¢ stamp	1,000.00
72-9	PTA	7.50
72-10	Wildlife Conservation (4)	10.00
72-11	Mail Order	7.50
72-12	Osteopathic Medicine	7.50
72-13	Tom Sawyer	7.50
72-14	7¢ Benjamin Franklin	7.50
72-15	Christmas (2)	10.00
72-16	Pharmacy	7.50
72-17	Stamp Collecting	7.50

1973

73-1	$1 Eugene O'Neill	15.00
73-1E	$1 Eugene O'Neill picture perforation error	750.00
73-2	Love	10.00
73-3	Pamphleteer	6.00
73-4	George Gershwin	7.00
73-5	Broadside	20.00
73-6	Copernicus	6.00
73-7	Postal Employees	8.00
73-8	Harry S. Truman	6.00
73-9	Post Rider	6.00
73-10	21¢ Amadeo Gianninni	6.00
73-11	Boston Tea Party (4)	8.00
73-12	6¢-15¢ Electronics (4)	8.00
73-13	Robinson Jeffers	5.00
73-14	Lyndon B. Johnson	5.00
73-15	Henry O. Tanner	6.00
73-16	Willa Cather	5.00
73-17	Colonial Drummer	5.00
73-18	Angus Cattle	5.00
73-19	Christmas (2)	7.00
73-20	13¢ Winged Envelope airmail	4.00
73-21	10¢ Crossed Flags	4.00
73-22	10¢ Jefferson Memorial	4.00
73-23	13¢ Winged Envelope airmail coil (2)	4.00

1974

74-1	26¢ Mount Rushmore airmail	6.00
74-2	ZIP Code	5.00
74-2E	ZIP Code with date error 4/4/74	500.00
74-3	18¢ Statue of Liberty airmail	7.50
74-4	18¢ Elizabeth Blackwell	3.00
74-5	VFW	3.00
74-6	Robert Frost	3.00
74-7	EXPO '74	3.00
74-8	Horse Racing	3.50
74-9	Skylab	7.50
74-10	UPU (8)	6.00
74-11	Mineral Heritage (4)	7.50
74-12	Fort Harrod	3.00
74-13	Continental Congress (4)	5.00
74-14	Chautauqua	3.00
74-15	Kansas Wheat	3.00
74-16	Energy Conservation	3.00
74-17	6.3¢ Liberty Bell coil (2)	5.00
74-18	Sleepy Hollow	4.00
74-19	Retarded Children	3.00
74-20	Christmas (3)	6.00

1975

75-1	Benjamin West	3.00
75-2	Pioneer/Jupiter	7.00
75-3	Collective Bargaining	3.00
75-4	8¢ Sybil Ludington	4.00
75-5	Salem Poor	5.00
75-6	Haym Salomon	4.00
75-7	18¢ Peter Francisco	4.00
75-8	Mariner 10	6.00
75-9	Lexington & Concord	3.00
75-10	Paul Dunbar	5.00
75-11	D.W. Griffith	4.00
75-12	Bunker Hill	3.00
75-13	Military Uniforms (4)	7.00
75-14	Apollo Soyuz (2)	7.00
75-15	International Women's Year	3.00
75-16	Postal Service Bicentennial (4)	5.00
75-17	World Peace Through Law	3.00
75-18	Banking & Commerce (2)	3.00
75-19	Christmas (2)	5.00
75-20	3¢ Francis Parkman	4.00
75-21	11¢ Freedom of the Press	3.00
75-22	24¢ Old North Church	3.00
75-23	Flag over Independence Hall (2)	3.00
75-24	9¢ Freedom to Assemble (2)	3.00
75-25	Liberty Bell coil (2)	3.00
75-26	Eagle & Shield	3.00

1976

76-1	Spirit of '76 (3)	5.00
76-1E	Spirit of '76 with cancellation error Jan. 2, 1976 (3)	1,000.00
76-2	25¢ and 31¢ Plane and Globes airmails (2)	4.00
76-3	Interphil '76	4.00
76-4	State Flags, DE to VA (10)	10.00
76-5	State Flags, NY to MS (10)	10.00
76-6	State Flags, IL to WI (10)	10.00
76-7	State Flags, CA to SD (10)	10.00
76-8	State Flags, MT to HI (10)	10.00
76-9	9¢ Freedom to Assemble coil (2)	3.00
76-10	Telephone Centennial	3.00
76-11	Commercial Aviation	3.00
76-12	Chemistry	3.00
76-13	7.9¢ Drum coil (2)	3.00
76-14	Benjamin Franklin	3.00
76-15	Bicentennial souvenir sheet	10.00
76-15E	Bicentennial souvenir sheet with perforation and numerical errors	1,000.00
76-16	18¢ Bicentennial souvenir sheet	10.00
76-17	24¢ Bicentennial souvenir sheet	10.00
76-18	31¢ Bicentennial souvenir sheet	10.00
76-19	Declaration of Independence (4)	5.00
76-20	Olympics (4)	5.00
76-21	Clara Maass	3.00
76-22	Adolph S. Ochs	3.00
76-23	Christmas (3)	4.00
76-24	7.7¢ Saxhorns coil (2)	3.00

1977

77-1	Washington at Princeton	3.00
77-2	Flag over Capitol booklet pane (9¢ and 13¢) Perf. 10 (8)	20.00
77-3	Sound Recording	3.00
77-4	Pueblo Pottery (4)	4.00
77-5	Lindbergh Flight	4.00
77-6	Colorado Centennial	3.00

77-7 Butterflies (4) 4.00
77-8 Lafayette 3.00
77-9 Skilled Hands (4) 4.00
77-10 Peace Bridge 3.00
77-11 Battle of Oriskany 3.00
77-12 Alta, CA, First Civil Settlement 3.00
77-13 Articles of Confederation 3.00
77-14 Talking Pictures 3.00
77-15 Surrender at Saratoga 3.00
77-16 Energy (2) 3.00
77-17 Christmas, Mailbox and Christmas, Valley Forge (2) 3.00
77-18 10¢ Petition for Redress coil (2) 3.00
77-19 10¢ Petition for Redress sheet (2) 3.00
77-20 1¢-4¢ Americana (5) 3.00

1978

78-1 Carl Sandburg 3.00
78-2 Indian Head Penny 3.00
78-3 Captain Cook, Anchorage cancel (2) 4.00
78-4 Captain Cook, Honolulu cancel (2) 4.00
78-5 Harriet Tubman 5.00
78-6 American Quilts (4) 4.00
78-7 16¢ Statue of Liberty sheet and coil (2) 3.00
78-8 29¢ Sandy Hook Lighthouse 3.00
78-9 American Dance (4) 4.00
78-10 French Alliance 3.00
78-11 Early Cancer Detection 3.00
78-12 "A" (15¢) sheet and coil (2) 6.00
78-13 Jimmie Rodgers 5.00
78-14 CAPEX '78 (8) 10.00
78-15 Oliver Wendell Holmes coil 3.00
78-16 Photography 3.00
78-17 Fort McHenry Flag sheet and coil (2) 4.00
78-18 George M. Cohan 3.00
78-19 Rose booklet single 3.00
78-20 8.4¢ Piano coil (2) 4.00
78-21 Viking Missions 6.00
78-22 28¢ Remote Outpost 3.00
78-23 American Owls (4) 4.00
78-24 31¢ Wright Brothers airmails (2) 4.00
78-25 American Trees (4) 4.00
78-26 Christmas, Madonna 3.00
78-27 Christmas, Hobby Horse 3.00
78-28 $2 Kerosene Lamp 7.50

1979

79-1 Robert F. Kennedy 3.00
79-2 Martin Luther King, Jr. 5.00
79-3 International Year of the Child 3.00
79-4 John Steinbeck 3.00
79-5 Albert Einstein 3.00
79-6 21¢ Octave Chanute airmails (2) 4.00
79-7 Pennsylvania Toleware (4) 4.00
79-8 American Architecture (4) 4.00
79-9 Endangered Flora (4) 4.00
79-10 Seeing Eye Dogs 3.00
79-11 $1 Lamp & Candle 6.00
79-12 Special Olympics 3.00
79-13 $5 Lantern 15.00
79-14 30¢ Schoolhouse 4.00
79-15 10¢ Summer Olympics (2) 4.00
79-16 50¢ Whale Oil Lamp 5.00
79-17 John Paul Jones 4.00
79-18 Summer Olympics (4) 5.00
79-19 Christmas, Madonna 4.00
79-20 Christmas, Santa Claus 4.00
79-21 3.1¢ Guitar coil (2) 10.00
79-22 31¢ Summer Olympics airmail 6.00
79-23 Will Rogers 3.00
79-24 Vietnam Veterans 3.00
79-25 25¢ Wiley Post airmails (2) 5.00

1980

80-1 W.C. Fields 3.00
80-2 Winter Olympics (4) 6.00
80-3 Windmills booklet pane (10) 6.00
80-4 Benjamin Banneker 5.00
80-5 Letter Writing (6) 3.00
80-6 1¢ Ability to Write (2) 3.00
80-7 Frances Perkins 3.00
80-8 Dolley Madison 3.00
80-9 Emily Bissell 3.00
80-10 3.5¢ Violins coil (2) 4.00
80-11 Helen Keller/ Anne Sullivan 3.00
80-12 Veterans Administration 3.00
80-13 General Bernardo de Galvez 3.00
80-14 Coral Reefs (4) 4.00
80-15 Organized Labor 5.00
80-16 Edith Wharton 5.00
80-17 Education 5.00
80-18 Indian Masks (4) 4.00
80-19 American Architecture (4) 4.00
80-20 40¢ Philip Mazzei airmail 4.00
80-21 Christmas, Madonna 4.00
80-22 Christmas, Antique Toys 4.00
80-23 Sequoyah 3.00
80-24 28¢ Blanche Scott airmail 3.00
80-25 35¢ Glenn Curtiss airmail 3.00

1981

81-1 Everett Dirksen 3.00
81-2 Whitney M. Young 5.00
81-3 "B" (18¢) sheet and coil (3) 4.00
81-4 "B" (18¢) booklet pane (8) 3.00
81-5 12¢ Freedom of Conscience sheet and coil (3) 4.00
81-6 Flowers block (4) 4.00
81-7 Flag and Anthem sheet and coil (3) 4.00
81-8 Flag and Anthem booklet pane (8 - 6¢ and 18¢) 4.00
81-9 American Red Cross 3.00
81-10 George Mason 3.00
81-11 Savings & Loans 3.00
81-12 Wildlife booklet pane (10) 5.00
81-13 Surrey coil (2) 5.00
81-14 Space Achievement (8) 10.00
81-15 17¢ Rachel Carson (2) 3.00
81-16 35¢ Charles Drew, MD 4.00
81-17 Professional Management 3.00
81-18 17¢ Electric Auto coil (2) 5.00
81-19 Wildlife Habitat (4) 4.00
81-20 International Year of the Disabled 3.00
81-21 Edna St. Vincent Millay 5.00
81-22 Alcoholism 4.00
81-23 American Architecture (4) 4.00
81-24 Babe Zaharias 4.00
81-25 Bobby Jones 4.00
81-26 Frederic Remington 3.00
81-27 "C" (20¢) sheet and coil (3) 5.00
81-28 "C" (18¢) booklet pane (10) 4.00
81-29 18¢ and 20¢ Hoban (2) 3.00
81-30 Yorktown/ Virginia Capes (2) 3.00
81-31 Christmas, Madonna 4.00
81-32 Christmas, Bear on Sleigh 5.00
81-33 John Hanson 3.00
81-34 Fire Pumper coil (2) 7.00
81-35 Desert Plants (4) 4.00
81-36 9.3¢ Mail Wagon coil (3) 6.00
81-37 Flag over Supreme Court sheet and coil (3) 6.00
81-38 Flag over Supreme Court booklet pane (6) 5.00

1982

82-1 Sheep booklet pane (10) 4.00
82-2 Ralph Bunche 7.00
82-3 13¢ Crazy Horse (2) 3.00
82-4 37¢ Robert Millikan 3.00
82-5 Franklin D. Roosevelt 3.00
82-6 Love 3.00
82-7 5.9¢ Bicycle coil (4) 7.00
82-8 George Washington 8.00
82-9 10.9¢ Hansom Cab coil (2) 6.00
82-10 Birds & Flowers, AL-GE (10) 15.00
82-11 Birds & Flowers, HI-MD (10) 15.00
82-12 Birds & Flowers, MA-NJ (10) 15.00
82-13 Birds & Flowers, NM-SC (10) 15.00
82-14 Birds & Flowers, SD-WY (10) 15.00
82-15 USA/Netherlands 3.00
82-16 Library of Congress 3.00
82-17 Consumer Education coil (2) 4.00
82-18 Knoxville World's Fair (4) 3.00
82-19 Horatio Alger 3.00
82-20 2¢ Locomotive coil (2) 4.00
82-21 Aging Together 3.00
82-22 The Barrymores 3.00
82-23 Mary Walker 3.00
82-24 Peace Garden 3.00
82-25 America's Libraries 3.00
82-26 Jackie Robinson 15.00
82-27 4¢ Stagecoach coil (3) 5.00
82-28 Touro Synagogue 3.00
82-29 Wolf Trap Farm Park 3.00

No.	Issue	Price
82-30	American Architecture (4)	3.00
82-31	Francis of Assisi	3.00
82-32	Ponce de Leon	3.00
82-33	13¢ Kitten & Puppy (2)	4.00
82-34	Christmas, Madonna	4.00
82-35	Christmas, Seasons Greetings (4)	4.00
82-36	2¢ Igor Stravinsky (2)	3.00
	1983	
83-1	1¢, 4¢, 13¢ Penalty Mail (5)	3.00
83-2	1¢ and 17¢ Penalty Mail (4)	3.00
83-3	Penalty Mail coil (2)	4.00
83-4	1$ Penalty Mail	5.00
83-5	$5 Penalty Mail	10.00
83-6	Science & Industry	3.00
83-7	5.2¢ Antique Sleigh coil (4)	6.00
83-8	Sweden/USA Treaty	3.00
83-9	3¢ Handcar coil (3)	5.00
83-10	Balloons (4)	3.00
83-11	Civilian Conservation Corps	3.00
83-12	40¢ Olympics airmails (4)	4.00
83-13	Joseph Priestley	3.00
83-14	Volunteerism	3.00
83-15	Concord/German Immigration	3.00
83-16	Physical Fitness	3.00
83-17	Brooklyn Bridge	3.00
83-18	TVA	3.00
83-19	4¢ Carl Schurz (5)	3.00
83-20	Medal of Honor	3.00
83-21	Scott Joplin	5.00
83-22	Thomas H. Gallaudet	3.00
83-23	28¢ Olympics (4)	5.00
83-24	5¢ Pearl S. Buck (4)	3.00
83-25	Babe Ruth	10.00
83-26	Nathaniel Hawthorne	3.00
83-27	3¢ Henry Clay (7)	3.00
83-28	13¢ Olympics (4)	5.00
83-29	$9.35 Eagle booklet single	125.00
83-30	$9.35 Eagle booklet pane (3)	200.00
83-31	1¢ Omnibus coil (3)	5.00
83-32	Treaty of Paris	3.00
83-33	Civil Service	3.00
83-34	Metropolitan Opera	3.00
83-35	Inventors (4)	4.00
83-36	1¢ Dorothea Dix (3)	3.00
83-37	Streetcars (4)	4.00
83-38	5¢ Motorcycle coil (4)	5.00
83-39	Christmas,Madonna	3.00
83-40	Christmas, Santa Claus	3.00
83-41	35¢ Olympics airmails (4)	5.00
83-42	Martin Luther	4.00
83-43	Flag over Supreme Court booklet pane (10)	4.00
	1984	
84-1	Alaska Statehood	3.00
84-2	Winter Olympics (4)	5.00
84-3	FDIC	3.00
84-4	Harry S. Truman	3.00
84-5	Love	3.00
84-6	Carter G. Woodson	5.00
84-7	11¢ RR Caboose coil (2)	5.00
84-8	Soil & Water Conservation	3.00
84-9	Credit Union Act	3.00
84-10	40¢ Lillian M. Gilbreth	3.00
84-11	Orchids (4)	4.00
84-12	Hawaii Statehood	3.00
84-13	7.4¢ Baby Buggy coil (3)	5.00
84-14	National Archives	3.00
84-15	20¢ Summer Olympics (4)	5.00
84-16	New Orleans World's Fair	3.00
84-17	Health Research	3.00
84-18	Douglas Fairbanks	3.00
84-19	Jim Thorpe	10.00
84-20	10¢ Richard Russell (2)	10.00
84-21	John McCormack	3.00
84-22	St. Lawrence Seaway	3.00
84-23	Migratory Bird Hunting and Conservation Stamp Act	6.00
84-24	Roanoke Voyages	3.00
84-25	Herman Melville	3.00
84-26	Horace Moses	3.00
84-27	Smokey Bear	8.00
84-28	Roberto Clemente	10.00
84-29	30¢ Frank C. Laubach	3.00
84-30	Dogs (4)	5.00
84-31	Crime Prevention	3.00
84-32	Family Unity	3.00
84-33	Eleanor Roosevelt	3.00
84-34	Nation of Readers	3.00
84-35	Christmas, Madonna	4.00
84-36	Christmas, Santa Claus	4.00
84-37	Hispanic Americans	3.00
84-38	Vietnam Veterans Memorial	4.00
	1985	
85-1	Jerome Kern	5.00
85-2	7¢ Abraham Baldwin (3)	5.00
85-3	"D" (22¢) sheet and coil (3)	3.00
85-4	"D" (22¢) booklet pane (10)	5.00
85-5	"D" (22¢) Penalty Mail sheet and coil (3)	4.00
85-6	11¢ Alden Partridge (2)	3.00
85-7	33¢ Alfred Verville airmail	3.00
85-8	39¢ Lawrence & Elmer Sperry airmail	3.00
85-9	44¢ Transpacific airmail	3.00
85-10	50¢ Chester Nimitz	3.00
85-11	Mary McLeod Bethune	4.00
85-12	39¢ Grenville Clark	3.00
85-13	14¢ Sinclair Lewis (2)	3.00
85-14	Duck Decoys (4)	4.00
85-15	14¢ Iceboat coil (2)	5.00
85-16	Winter Special Olympics	3.00
85-17	Flag over Capitol sheet and coil (3)	4.00
85-18	Flag over Capitol booklet pane (5)	4.00
85-19	12¢ Stanley Steamer coil (2)	5.00
85-20	Seashells booklet pane (10)	5.00
85-21	Love	4.00
85-22	10.1¢ Oil Wagon coil (3)	5.00
85-23	12.5¢ Pushcart coil (2)	5.00
85-24	John J. Audubon	3.00
85-25	$10.75 Eagle booklet single	40.00
85-26	$10.75 Eagle booklet pane (3)	90.00
85-27	6¢ Tricycle coil (4)	5.00
85-28	Rural Electrification Administration	3.00
85-29	14¢ and 22¢ Penalty Mail sheet and coil (4)	5.00
85-30	AMERIPEX '86	3.00
85-31	9¢ Sylvanus Thayer (3)	3.00
85-32	3.4¢ School Bus coil (7)	6.00
85-33	11¢ Stutz Bearcat coil (2)	5.00
85-34	Abigail Adams	3.00
85-35	4.9¢ Buckboard coil (5)	6.00
85-36	8.3¢ Ambulance coil (3)	6.00
85-37	Frederic Bartholdi	3.00
85-38	8¢ Henry Knox (3)	3.00
85-39	Korean War Veterans	4.00
85-40	Social Security Act	3.00
85-41	44¢ Father Junipero Serra airmail	3.00
85-42	World War I Veterans	3.00
85-43	6¢ Walter Lippman (4)	3.00
85-44	Horses (4)	5.00
85-45	Public Education	3.00
85-46	International Youth Year (4)	3.00
85-47	Help End Hunger	3.00
85-48	21.1¢ Letters coil (2)	4.00
85-49	Christmas,Madonna	3.00
85-50	Christmas, Poinsettas	3.00
85-51	18¢ Washington/ Washington Monument coil (2)	4.00
	1986	
86-1	Arkansas Statehood	3.00
86-2	25¢ Jack London	2.50
86-3	Stamp Collecting booklet pane (4)	6.00
86-4	Love	3.00
86-5	Sojourner Truth	4.00
86-6	5¢ Hugo L. Black (5)	2.50

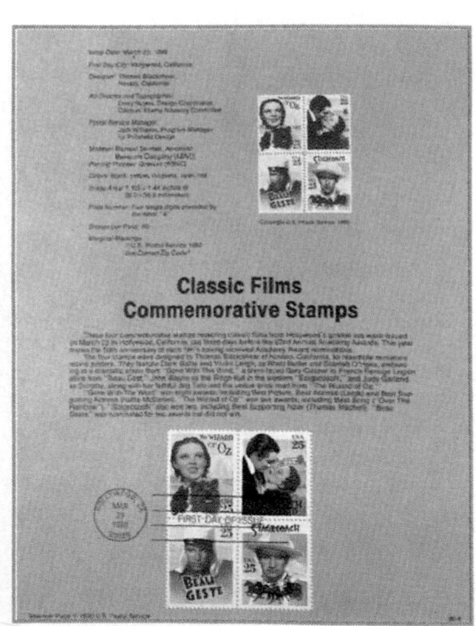

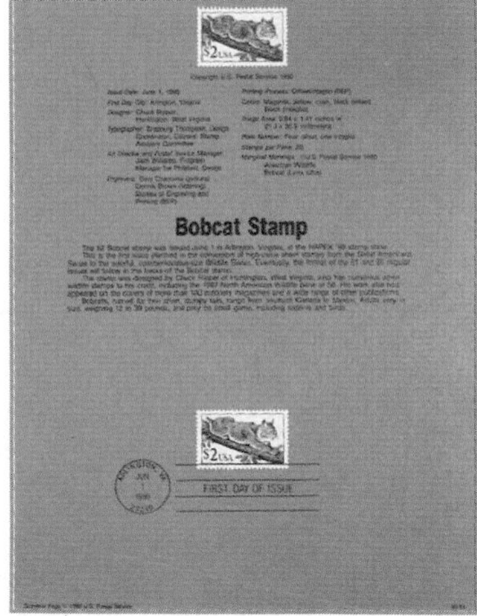

86-7 Republic of Texas (2) 2.50
86-8 $2 William Jennings Bryan 5.00
86-9 Fish booklet pane (5) 5.00
86-10 Public Hospitals 2.50
86-11 Duke Ellington 5.00
86-12 Presidents, Washington-Harrison (9) 6.00
86-13 Presidents, Tyler-Grant (9) 6.00
86-14 Presidents, Hayes-Wilson (9) 6.00
86-15 Presidents, Harding-Johnson (9) 6.00
86-16 Polar Explorers (4) 5.00
86-17 17¢ Belva Ann Lockwood (2) 3.50
86-18 1¢ Margaret Mitchell (3) 2.50
86-19 Statue of Liberty 3.00
86-20 4¢ Father Flanagan (3) 2.50
86-21 17¢ Dog Sled coil (2) 4.00
86-22 56¢ John Harvard 2.50
86-23 Navajo Blankets (4) 4.00
86-24 3¢ Paul Dudley White, MD (8) 2.50
86-25 $1 Bernard Revel 3.00
86-26 T.S. Eliot 2.50
86-27 Wood-Carved Figurines (4) 3.50
86-28 Christmas, Madonna 2.50
86-29 Christmas,Village Scene 2.50
86-30 5.5¢ Star Route Truck coil (4) 5.00
86-31 25¢ Bread Wagon coil 5.00

1987

87-1 8.5¢ Tow Truck coil (5) 4.00
87-2 Michigan Statehood 4.00
87-3 Pan American Games 4.00
87-4 Love 6.00
87-5 7.1¢ Tractor coil (5) 5.00
87-6 14¢ Julia Ward Howe (2) 3.00
87-7 Jean Baptiste Pointe Du Sable 10.00
87-8 Enrico Caruso 3.00
87-9 2¢ Mary Lyon (3) 2.50
87-10 Reengraved 2¢ Locomotive coil (6) 4.00
87-11 Girl Scouts 5.00
87-12 10¢ Canal Boat coil (5) 4.00
87-13 Special Occasions booklet pane (10) 6.00
87-14 United Way 2.50
87-15 Flag with Fireworks 2.50
87-16 Flag over Capitol coil, prephosphored paper (2) 4.00
87-17 Wildlife, Swallow-Squirrel (10) 6.00
87-18 Wildlife, Armadillo-Rabbit (10) 6.00
87-19 Wildlife, Tanager-Ladybug (10) 6.00
87-20 Wildlife, Beaver-Prairie Dog (10) 6.00
87-21 Wildlife, Turtle-Fox (10) 6.00
87-22 Delaware Statehood 3.00
87-23 U.S./Morocco Friendship 2.50
87-24 William Faulkner 2.50
87-25 Lacemaking (4) 4.00
87-26 10¢ Red Cloud (3) 2.50
87-27 $5 Bret Harte 12.00
87-28 Pennsylvania Statehood 3.00
87-29 Drafting of the Constitution booklet pane (5) 5.00
87-30 New Jersey Statehood 3.00
87-31 Signing of Constitution 3.00
87-32 Certified Public Accountants 3.00
87-33 5¢ Milk Wagon and 17.5¢ Racing Car coils (4) 4.00
87-34 Locomotives booklet pane (5) 10.00
87-35 Christmas, Madonna 2.50
87-36 Christmas, Ornaments 2.50
87-37 Flag with Fireworks booklet-pair 3.00

1988

88-1 Georgia Statehood 3.00
88-2 Connecticut Statehood 3.00
88-3 Winter Olympics 3.00
88-4 Australia Bicentennial 2.50
88-5 James Weldon Johnson 5.00
88-6 Cats (4) 5.00
88-7 Massachusetts Statehood 4.00
88-8 Maryland Statehood 4.00
88-9 3¢ Conestoga Wagon coil (8) 4.00
88-10 Knute Rockne 4.00
88-11 "E" (25¢) Earth sheet and coil (3) 5.00
88-12 "E" (25¢) Earth booklet pane (10) 6.00
88-13 "E" (25¢) Penalty Mail coil (2) 3.50
88-14 44¢ New Sweden airmail 3.00
88-15 Pheasant booklet pane (10) 6.00
88-16 Jack London booklet pane (6) 4.50
88-17 Jack London booklet pane (10) 6.00
88-18 Flag with Clouds 2.50
88-19 45¢ Samuel Langley airmail 3.00
88-19A 20¢ Penalty Mail coil (2) 3.00
88-20 Flag over Yosemite coil (2) 3.50
88-21 South Carolina Statehood 3.00
88-22 Owl & Grosbeak booklet pane (10) 6.00
88-23 15¢ Buffalo Bill Cody (2) 3.00
88-24 15¢ and 25¢ Penalty Mail coils (4) 4.00
88-25 Francis Ouimet 3.00
88-26 45¢ Harvey Cushing, MD 2.50
88-27 New Hampshire Statehood 3.00
88-28 36¢ Igor Sikorsky airmail 3.00
88-29 Virginia Statehood 3.00
88-30 10.1¢ Oil Wagon coil, precancel (3) 4.00
88-31 Love 3.00
88-32 Flag with Clouds booklet pane (6) 5.00
88-33 16.7¢ Popcorn Wagon coil (2) 4.00
88-34 15¢ Tugboat coil (2) 4.00
88-35 13.2¢ Coal Car coil (2) 4.00
88-36 New York Statehood 3.00
88-37 45¢ Love 3.00
88-38 8.4¢ Wheelchair coil (3) 4.00
88-39 21¢ Railroad Mail Car coil (2) 4.00
88-40 Summer Olympics 3.00
88-41 Classic Cars booklet pane (5) 8.00
88-42 7.6¢ Carreta coil (4) 4.00
88-43 Honeybee coil (2) 4.00
88-44 Antarctic Explorers (4) 4.00
88-45 5.3¢ Elevator coil (5) 4.00
88-46 20.5¢ Fire Engine coil (2) 4.00
88-47 Carousel Animals (4) 3.50
88-48 $8.75 Eagle 25.00
88-49 Christmas, Madonna 2.50
88-50 Christmas, Snow Scene 2.50
88-51 21¢ Chester Carlson 2.50
88-52 Special Occasions booklet pane (6), Love You 10.00
88-53 Special Occasions booklet pane (6), Thinking of You 10.00
88-54 24.1¢ Tandem Bicycle coil (2) 5.00
88-55 20¢ Cable Car coil (2) 5.00
88-56 13¢ Patrol Wagon coil (2) 5.00
88-57 23¢ Mary Cassatt 3.00
88-58 65¢ H.H. 'Hap' Arnold 3.00

1989

89-1 Montana Statehood 2.50
89-2 A. Philip Randolph 4.00
89-3 Flag over Yosemite coil, prephosphored paper (2) 3.00
89-4 North Dakota Statehood 3.00
89-5 Washington Statehood 3.00
89-6 Steamboats booklet pane (5) 6.00
89-7 WORLD STAMP EXPO '89 2.50
89-8 Arturo Toscanini 2.50

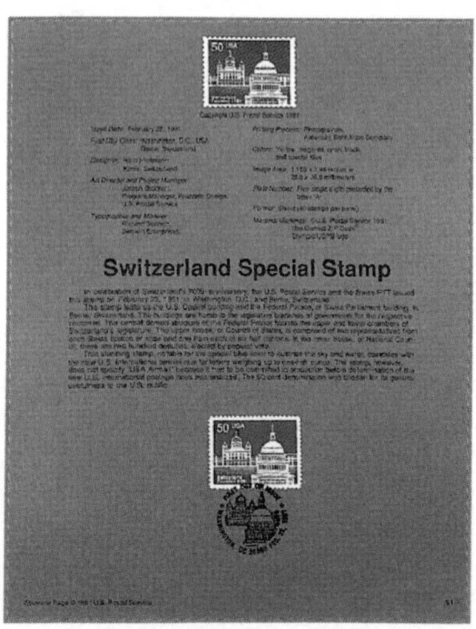

89-9	U.S. House of Representatives	3.00
89-10	U.S. Senate	3.00
89-11	Executive Branch	3.00
89-12	South Dakota Statehood	3.00
89-13	7.1¢ Tractor coil, precancel (4)	4.00
89-14	$1 Johns Hopkins	3.50
89-15	Lou Gehrig	5.00
89-16	1¢ Penalty Mail	3.00
89-17	45¢ French Revolution airmail	3.00
89-18	Ernest Hemingway	2.50
89-19	$2.40 Moon Landing	12.50
89-20	North Carolina Statehood	3.00
89-21	Letter Carriers	2.50
89-22	28¢ Sitting Bull	2.50
89-23	Drafting of the Bill of Rights	3.00
89-24	Prehistoric Animals (4)	6.00
89-25	25¢ and 45¢ PUAS-America (2)	3.00
89-26	Christmas, Madonna	6.00
89-27	Christmas, Antique Sleigh	6.00
89-28	Eagle and Shield, self-adhesive	4.00
89-29	$3.60 WORLD STAMP EXPO '89 souvenir sheet	10.00
89-30	Classic Mail Transportation (4)	3.50
89-31	$1.80 Future Mail Transportation souvenir sheet	6.00
89-32	45¢ Future Mail Transportation airmails (4)	6.00
89-33	$1 Classic Mail Transportation souvenir sheet	6.00
	1990	
90-1	Idaho Statehood	3.00
90-2	Love sheet and booklet pane (11)	6.00
90-3	Ida B. Wells	4.00
90-4	U.S. Supreme Court	3.00
90-5	15¢ Beach Umbrella booklet pane (10)	5.00
90-6	5¢ Luis Munoz Marin (5)	2.50
90-7	Wyoming Statehood	3.00
90-8	Classic Films (4)	5.00
90-9	Marianne Moore	2.50
90-10	$1 Seaplane coil (2)	5.00
90-11	Lighthouses booklet pane (5)	6.00
90-12	Plastic Flag stamp	3.00
90-13	Rhode Island Statehood	3.00
90-14	$2 Bobcat	5.00
90-15	Olympians (5)	7.00
90-16	Indian Headdresses booklet pane (10)	9.00
90-17	5¢ Circus Wagon coil (5)	3.00
90-18	40¢ Claire Lee Chennault	4.00
90-19	Federated States of Micronesia/ Marshall Islands (2)	3.00
90-20	Creatures of the Sea (4)	5.00
90-21	25¢ and 45¢ PUAS-America (2)	4.00
90-22	Dwight D. Eisenhower	2.50
90-23	Christmas, Madonna, sheet and booklet pane (11)	7.00
90-24	Christmas,Yule Tree, sheet and booklet pane (11)	7.00

1991*

"F" (29¢) ATM booklet single	2.50
4¢ Makeup	2.50
"F" (29¢) Penalty Mail coil (2)	3.00
"F" (29¢) Flower booklet panes (20)	12.50
"F" (29¢) Flower sheet and coil (3)	3.00
4¢ Steam Carriage coil (7)	2.50
50¢ Switzerland	3.00
Vermont Statehood	2.50
19¢ Fawn (2)	3.00
Flag over Mount Rushmore coil (2)	2.50
35¢ Dennis Chavez	2.50
Flower sheet and booklet pane (11)	7.50
Flower coils (4)	3.00
4¢ Penalty Mail (8)	3.00
Wood Duck booklet panes (20)	12.50
Flag with Olympic Rings booklet pane (10)	7.50
50¢ Harriet Quimby	3.00
Savings Bond	2.50
Love sheet and booklet pane, 52¢ Love (12)	7.50
19¢ Balloon booklet pane, 40¢ William Piper airmail (11)	6.00
William Saroyan	2.50
Fishing Flies booklet pane (5)	5.00
Penalty Mail coil and 19¢ sheet (3)	3.00
5¢ Canoe and 10¢ Tractor-Trailer coils (4)	3.00
Flags on Parade	2.50
52¢ Hubert H. Humphrey	3.00
Cole Porter	3.50
$9.95 Eagle with Olympic Rings	25.00
50¢ Antarctic Treaty airmail	3.00
1¢ Kestral, 3¢ Bluebird and 30¢ Cardinal (3)	3.00
Torch ATM booklet single	2.50
Desert Storm/ Desert Shield sheet and booklet pane (11)	7.50
$2.90 Eagle with Olympic Rings	7 .50
Summer Olympics (5)	5.00
Numismatics	3.00
Basketball	5.00
World War II miniature sheet (10)	7.50
District of Columbia	3.00
Comedians booklet pane (10)	7.50
Jan Matzeliger	3.00
$1 USPS/ Olympic Logo	4.00
Space Exploration booklet pane (10)	7.50
50¢ PUAS/America airmail	3.00
Christmas, Madonna sheet and booklet pane (11)	7.50
Christmas, Santa Claus sheet and booklet pane (11)	7.50

*NOTE: Numbers and prices may be changed without not ice, due to additional USPS stamp issues and/or different information that may become available on older issues.

Prices are courtesy of the American Society for Philatelic Pages and Panels, an organization specializing in Souvenir Pages.

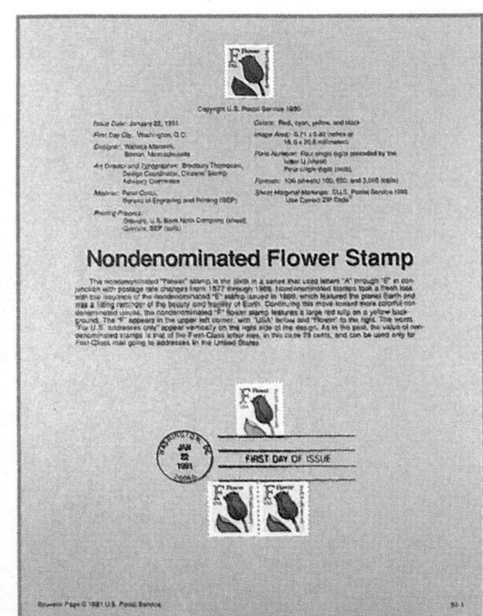

Copyright U.S. Postal Service 1990

Nondenominated Flower Stamp

FIRST DAY OF ISSUE

Vermont Statehood Commemorative Stamp

FIRST DAY OF ISSUE

History in the Making

- Includes block of four or more mint-condition commemorative stamps mounted on $8^1/_2$" x $11^1/_4$" high-quality paper

Keepsakes of Value and Elegance
Since the American Commemorative Panel series began in 1972, collectors have recognized these keepsakes as significant milestones in philatelic history. Priced at $4.95 each, these limited-edition panels are available on an advance subscription basis.

Accompanying the acetate-mounted block of four or more mint stamps are intaglio-printed reproductions of historical steel line engravings and informative articles on the stamp subject.

For Subscription Information
For more information, use the postage-paid request card in this book or write to:

USPS GUIDE
COMMEMORATIVE PANEL PROGRAM
PHILATELIC SALES DIVISION
UNITED STATES POSTAL SERVICE
BOX 449980
KANSAS CITY MO 64144-9980

American Commemorative Panels

The Postal Service offers American Commemorative Panels for each new commemorative stamp and special Christmas and Love stamp issued. The series began in 1972 with the Wildlife Commemorative Panel and will total 377 panels by the end of 1991. The panels feature mint stamps complemented by fine reproductions of steel line engravings and the stories behind the commemorated subjects.

No.	Panel	Price
	1972	
1	Wildlife	9.00
2	Mail Order	8.00
3	Osteopathic Medicine	9.00
4	Tom Sawyer	8.00
5	Pharmacy	9.00
6	Christmas, Angels	11.00
7	Christmas, Santa Claus	11.00
7E	Same with error date (1882)	750.00
8	Stamp Collecting	8.00
	1973	
9	Love	12.00
10	Pamphleteers	10.00
11	George Gershwin	11.00
12	Posting of the Broadside	10.00
13	Copernicus	10.00
14	Postal People	9.00
15	Harry S. Truman	11.00
16	Post Rider	11.00
17	Boston Tea Party	32.00
18	Electronics	9.00
19	Robinson Jeffers	9.00
20	Lyndon B. Johnson	11.00
21	Henry O. Tanner	9.00
22	Willa Cather	9.00
23	Drummer	13.00
24	Angus Cattle	9.00
25	Christmas, Madonna	13.00
26	Christmas, Needlepoint Tree	13.00
	1974	
27	VFW	9.00
28	Robert Frost	9.00
29	EXPO '74	11.00
30	Horse Racing	11.00
31	Skylab	13.00
32	Universal Postal Union	9.00
33	Mineral Heritage	11.00
34	First Kentucky Settlement	9.00
35	Continental Congress	11.00
35A	Same with corrected logo	150.00
36	Chautauqua	9.00
37	Kansas Wheat	9.00
38	Energy Conservation	9.00
39	Sleepy Hollow	9.00
40	Retarded Children	9.00
41	Christmas, Currier & Ives	13.00
42	Christmas, Angel Altarpiece	13.00
	1975	
43	Benjamin West	9.00
44	Pioneer	13.00
45	Collective Bargaining	9.00
46	Contributors to the Cause	9.00
47	Mariner 10	13.00
48	Lexington & Concord	10.00
49	Paul Laurence Dunbar	9.00
50	D.W. Griffith	9.00
51	Bunker Hill	10.00
52	Military Uniforms	10.00
53	Apollo Soyuz	13.00
54	World Peace Through Law	9.00
54A	Same with August 15, 1975 date	150.00
55	Women's Year	9.00
56	Postal Service Bicentennial	11.00
57	Banking and Commerce	10.00
58	Christmas, Prang Card	13.00
59	Christmas, Madonna	13.00
	1976	
60	Spirit of '76	16.00
61	Interphil 76	15.00
62	State Flags	35.00
63	Telephone	12.00
64	Commercial Aviation	16.00
65	Chemistry	13.00
66	Benjamin Franklin	13.00
67	Declaration of Independence	13.00
68	Olympics	17.00
69	Clara Maass	13.00
70	Adolph Ochs	13.00
70A	Same with charter logo	18.00
71	Christmas, Winter Pastime	21.00
71A	Same with charter logo	21.00
72	Christmas, Nativity	17.00
72A	Same with charter logo	21.00
	1977	
73	Washington at Princeton	23.00
73A	Same with charter logo	18.00
74	Sound Recording	41.00
74A	Same with charter logo	33.00
75	Pueblo Pottery	110.00
75A	Same with charter logo	110.00
76	Solo Transatlantic Flight	120.00
77	Colorado Statehood	22.00
78	Butterflies	25.00
79	Lafayette	22.00
80	Skilled Hands	22.00
81	Peace Bridge	22.00
82	Battle of Oriskany	22.00
83	Alta, CA, Civil Settlement	22.00
84	Articles of Confederation	22.00
85	Talking Pictures	32.00
86	Surrender at Saratoga	22.00
87	Energy	27.00
88	Christmas, Valley Forge	27.00
89	Christmas, Mailbox	46.00
	1978	
90	Carl Sandburg	14.00
91	Captain Cook	23.00
92	Harriet Tubman	14.00
93	Quilts	25.00
94	Dance	18.00
95	French Alliance	18.00
96	Early Cancer Detection	14.00

No.	Title	Price
97	Jimmie Rodgers	20.00
98	Photography	14.00
99	George M. Cohan	25.00
100	Viking Missions	44.00
101	Owls	44.00
102	Trees	44.00
103	Christmas, Madonna	20.00
104	Christmas, Hobby Horse	20.00
	1979	
105	Robert F. Kennedy	13.00
106	Martin Luther King, Jr.	12.00
107	International Year of the Child	12.00
108	John Steinbeck	12.00
109	Albert Einstein	13.00
110	Pennsylvania Toleware	12.00
111	Architecture	12.00
112	Endangered Flora	13.00
113	Seeing Eye Dogs	13.00
114	Special Olympics	17.00
115	John Paul Jones	12.00
116	15¢ Olympics	18.00
117	Christmas, Madonna	17.00
118	Christmas, Santa Claus	17.00
119	Will Rogers	16.00
120	Vietnam Veterans	17.00
121	10¢, 31¢ Olympics	18.00
	1980	
122	W.C. Fields	11.00
123	Winter Olympics	18.00
124	Benjamin Banneker	13.00
125	Frances Perkins	12.00
126	Emily Bissell	12.00
127	Helen Keller/ Anne Sullivan	12.00
128	Veterans Administration	12.00
129	General Bernardo de Galvez	12.00
130	Coral Reefs	14.00
131	Organized Labor	11.00
132	Edith Wharton	11.00
133	Education	11.00
134	Indian Masks	14.00
135	Architecture	11.00
136	Christmas, Epiphany Window	17.00
137	Christmas, Toys	17.00
	1981	
138	Everett Dirksen	12.00
139	Whitney Moore Young	12.00
140	Flowers	14.00
141	Red Cross	13.00
142	Savings & Loans	12.00
143	Space Achievement	16.00
144	Professional Management	12.00
145	Wildlife Habitats	17.00
146	Int'l. Year of Disabled Persons	10.00
147	Edna St. Vincent Millay	10.00
148	Architecture	11.00
149	Babe Zaharias/ Bobby Jones	13.00
150	James Hoban	11.00
151	Frederic Remington	11.00
152	Battle of Yorktown/ Virginia Capes	11.00
153	Christmas, Bear and Sleigh	16.00
154	Christmas, Madonna	16.00
155	John Hanson	10.00
156	U.S. Desert Plants	14.00
	1982	
157	Roosevelt	13.00
158	Love	16.00
159	George Washington	13.00
160	State Birds & Flowers	34.00
161	U.S./Netherlands	15.00
162	Library of Congress	16.00
163	Knoxville World's Fair	16.00
164	Horatio Alger	13.00
165	Aging Together	18.00
166	The Barrymores	20.00
167	Dr. Mary Walker	16.00
168	Peace Garden	18.00
169	America's Libraries	19.00
170	Jackie Robinson	34.00
171	Touro Synagogue	18.00
172	Architecture	18.00
173	Wolf Trap Farm Park	20.00
174	Francis of Assisi	20.00
175	Ponce de Leon	20.00
176	Christmas, Madonna	29.00
177	Christmas, Season's Greetings	29.00
178	Kitten & Puppy	29.00
	1983	
179	Science and Industry	9.00
180	Sweden/ USA Treaty	9.00
181	Balloons	12.00
182	Civilian Conservation Corps	9.00
183	40¢ Olympics	11.00
184	Joseph Priestley	9.00
185	Volunteerism	8.00
186	Concord/German Immigration	9.00
187	Physical Fitness	8.00
188	Brooklyn Bridge	10.00
189	TVA	9.00
190	Medal of Honor	12.00
191	Scott Joplin	14.00
192	28¢ Olympics	12.00
193	Babe Ruth	20.00
194	Nathaniel Hawthorne	9.00
195	13¢ Olympics	16.00
196	Treaty of Paris	11.00
197	Civil Service	11.00
198	Metropolitan Opera	11.00
199	Inventors	11.00
200	Streetcars	13.00
201	Christmas, Madonna	15.00

202 Christmas, Santa Claus 15.00
203 35¢ Olympics 16.00
204 Martin Luther 13.00

1984

205 Alaska Statehood 8.00
206 Winter Olympics 11.00
207 FDIC 8.00
208 Love 9.00
209 Carter G. Woodson 11.00
210 Soil and Water Conservation 8.00
211 Credit Union Act 8.00
212 Orchids 11.00
213 Hawaii Statehood 10.00
214 National Archives 8.00
215 20¢ Olympics 11.00
216 Louisiana World Exposition 10.00
217 Health Research 8.00
218 Douglas Fairbanks 8.00
219 Jim Thorpe 14.00
220 John McCormack 8.00
221 St. Lawrence Seaway 10.00
222 Preserving Wetlands 13.00
223 Roanoke Voyages 8.00
224 Herman Melville 8.00
225 Horace Moses 8.00
226 Smokey Bear 11.00
227 Roberto Clemente 16.00
228 Dogs 11.00
229 Crime Prevention 8.00
230 Family Unity 8.00
231 Christmas, Madonna 11.00
232 Christmas, Santa Claus 11.00
233 Eleanor Roosevelt 9.00
234 Nation of Readers 9.00
235 Hispanic Americans 9.00
236 Vietnam Veterans Memorial 12.00

1985

237 Jerome Kern 9.00
238 Mary McLeod Bethune 9.00
239 Duck Decoys 11.00
240 Winter Special Olympics 9.00
241 Love 9.00
242 Rural Electrification Administration 8.00
243 AMERIPEX '86 11.00
244 Abigail Adams 7.00
245 Frederic Auguste Bartholdi 13.00
246 Korean War Veterans 9.00
247 Social Security Act 8.00
248 World War I Veterans 8.00
249 Horses 11.00
250 Public Education 8.00
251 Youth 9.00
252 Help End Hunger 8.00
253 Christmas, Poinsettias 13.00
254 Christmas, Madonna 13.00

1986

255 Arkansas Statehood 7.00
256 Stamp Collecting Booklet 9.00
257 Love 9.00
258 Sojourner Truth 9.00
259 Republic of Texas 9.00
260 Fish Booklet 9.00
261 Public Hospitals 7.00
262 Duke Ellington 9.00
263 U.S. Presidents' Sheet #1 9.00
264 U.S. Presidents' Sheet #2 9.00
265 U.S. Presidents' Sheet #3 9.00
266 U.S. Presidents' Sheet #4 9.00
267 Polar Explorers 9.00
268 Statue of Liberty 10.00
269 Navajo Blankets 9.00
270 T.S. Eliot 7.00
271 Wood-Carved Figurines 9.00
272 Christmas, Madonna 9.00
273 Christmas, Village Scene 9.00

1987

274 Michigan Statehood 7.00
275 Pan American Games 7.00
276 Love 8.00
277 Jean Baptiste Pointe Du Sable 8.00
278 Enrico Caruso 8.00
279 Girl Scouts 9.00
280 Special Occasions Booklet 7.00
281 United Way 7.00
282 #1 American Wildlife 10.00
283 #2 American Wildlife 10.00
284 #3 American Wildlife 10.00
285 #4 American Wildlife 10.00
286 #5 American Wildlife 10.00
287 Delaware Statehood 7.00
288 Morocco/U.S. Diplomatic Relations 7.00
289 William Faulkner 7.00
290 Lacemaking 7.00
291 Pennsylvania Statehood 7.00
292 Constitution Booklet 7.00
293 New Jersey Statehood 7.00
294 Signing of the Constitution 7.00
295 Certified Public Accountants 9.00
296 Locomotives Booklet 9.00
297 Christmas, Madonna 9.00
298 Christmas, Ornaments 9.00

1988

299 Georgia Statehood 7.00
300 Connecticut Statehood 7.00
301 Winter Olympics 9.00

No.	Issue	Price
302	Australia	7.00
303	James Weldon Johnson	7.00
304	Cats	9.00
305	Massachusetts Statehood	7.00
306	Maryland Statehood	7.00
307	Knute Rockne	9.00
308	New Sweden	7.00
309	South Carolina Statehood	7.00
310	Francis Ouimet	7.00
311	New Hampshire Statehood	7.00
312	Virginia Statehood	7.00
313	Love	7.00
314	New York Statehood	7.00
315	Classic Cars Booklet	9.00
316	Summer Olympics	9.00
317	Antarctic Explorers	7.00
318	Carousel Animals	7.00
319	Christmas, Madonna	9.00
320	Christmas, Village Scene	7.00

1989

No.	Issue	Price
321	Montana Statehood	10.00
322	A. Philip Randolph	10.00
323	North Dakota Statehood	10.00
324	Washington Statehood	10.00
325	Steamboats Booklet	12.50
326	WORLD STAMP EXPO '89	10.00
327	Arturo Toscanini	10.00
328	U.S. House of Representatives	10.00
329	U.S. Senate	10.00
330	Executive Branch	10.00
331	South Dakota Statehood	10.00
332	Lou Gehrig	12.50
333	French Revolution	10.00
334	Ernest Hemingway	10.00
335	North Carolina Statehood	10.00
336	Letter Carriers	10.00
337	Drafting of the Bill of Rights	10.00
338	Prehistoric Animals	12.50
339	25¢ and 45¢ America/PUAS	10.00
340	Christmas, Traditional and Contemporary	12.50
341	Classic Mail Transportation	10.00
342	Future Mail Transportation	10.00

1990

No.	Issue	Price
343	Idaho Statehood	10.00
344	Love	10.00
345	Ida B. Wells	12.50
346	U.S. Supreme Court	10.00
347	Wyoming Statehood	10.00
348	Classic Films	12.50
349	Marianne Moore	10.00
350	Lighthouses Booklet	12.50
351	Rhode Island Statehood	10.00
352	Olympians	12.50
353	Indian Headdresses Booklet	12.50
354	Micronesia/ Marshall Islands	12.50
355	Creatures of the Sea	15.00
356	25c and 45c America/PUAS	12.50
357	Dwight D. Eisenhower	10.00
358	Christmas, Traditional and Contemporary	12.50

1991*

Issue	Price
Switzerland	10.00
Vermont Statehood	10.00
Savings Bonds	10.00
29¢ and 52¢ Love	12.50
Saroyan	10.00
Fishing Flies Booklet	12.50
Cole Porter	12.50
Desert Shield/ Desert Storm	10.00
Summer Olympics	12.50
Numismatics	12.50
World War II Miniature Sheet	15.00
Basketball	12.50
District of Columbia	10.00
Comedians Booklet	12.50
Jan Matzeliger	10.00
Space Exploration Booklet	15.00
America/PUAS	12.50
World Columbian Stamp Expo '92	10.00
Christmas, Traditional and Contemporary	12.50

*1991 issues subject to change.

Prices are courtesy of the American Society for Philatelic Pages and Panels, an organization specializing in Commemorative Panels.

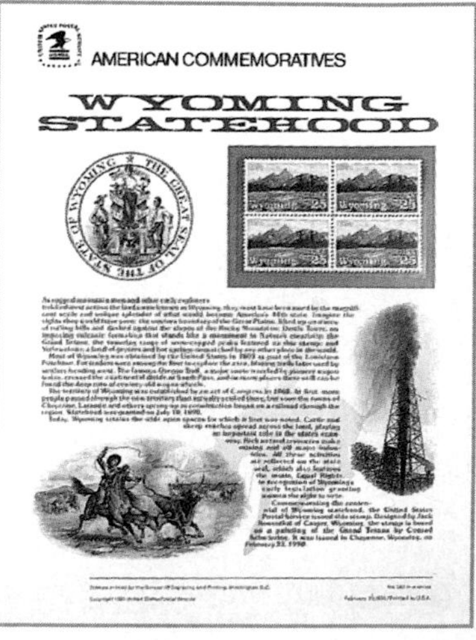

Subject Index

IMPORTANT NOTE: This Index covers all issues from the 1893 Columbian Exposition issues (#230-245) through 1991. Listings in italic typeface refer to Definitive or Regular issues. The numbers listed next to the stamp description are the Scott numbers, and the numbers in parentheses are the numbers of the pages on which the stamps are illustrated.